Other Books and Series by Jeff Bowen

Applications for Enrollment of Choctaw Newborn Act of 1905 Volumes I thru XX

Choctaw By Blood Enrollment Cards 1898-1914 Volumes I thru XX

Oglala Sioux Indians Pine Ridge Reservation 1932 Census Book I

Oglala Sioux Indians Pine Ridge Reservation Birth and Death Rolls 1924-1932 Book II

Compilation of History of the Cherokee Indians and Early History of the Cherokees by Emmet Starr with Combined Full Name Index

Visit our website at **www.nativestudy.com** to learn more about these and other books and series by Jeff Bowen

Other Books and Series by Jeff Bowen

1901-1907 Native American Census Seneca, Eastern Shawnee, Miami, Modoc, Ottawa, Peoria, Quapaw, and Wyandotte Indians (Under Seneca School, Indian Territory)

1932 Census of The Standing Rock Sioux Reservation with Births And Deaths 1924-1932

Census of The Blackfeet, Montana, 1897- 1901 Expanded Edition

Eastern Cherokee by Blood, 1906-1910, Volumes I thru XIII

Choctaw of Mississippi Indian Census 1929-1932 with Births and Deaths 1924-1931 Volume I
Choctaw of Mississippi Indian Census 1933, 1934 & 1937, Supplemental Rolls to 1934 & 1935 with Births and Deaths 1932-1938, and Marriages 1936-1938 Volume II

Eastern Cherokee Census Cherokee, North Carolina 1930-1939 Census 1930-1931 with Births And Deaths 1924-1931 Taken By Agent L. W. Page Volume I
Eastern Cherokee Census Cherokee, North Carolina 1930-1939 Census 1932-1933 with Births And Deaths 1930-1932 Taken By Agent R. L. Spalsbury Volume II
Eastern Cherokee Census Cherokee, North Carolina 1930-1939 Census 1934-1937 with Births and Deaths 1925-1938 and Marriages 1936 & 1938 Taken by Agents R. L. Spalsbury And Harold W. Foght Volume III

Seminole of Florida Indian Census, 1930-1940 with Birth and Death Records, 1930-1938

Texas Cherokees 1820-1839 A Document For Litigation 1921

Starr Roll 1894 (Cherokee Payment Rolls) Districts: Canadian, Cooweescoowee, and Delaware Volume One
Starr Roll 1894 (Cherokee Payment Rolls) Districts: Flint, Going Snake, and Illinois Volume Two
Starr Roll 1894 (Cherokee Payment Rolls) Districts: Saline, Sequoyah, and Tahlequah; Including Orphan Roll Volume Three

Cherokee Intruder Cases Dockets of Hearings 1901-1909 Volumes I & II

Indian Wills, 1911-1921 Records of the Bureau of Indian Affairs Books One thru Seven
Native American Wills & Probate Records 1911-1921

Turtle Mountain Reservation Chippewa Indians 1932 Census with Births & Deaths, 1924-1932

Other Books and Series by Jeff Bowen

Chickasaw By Blood Enrollment Cards 1898-1914 Volume I thru V

Cherokee Descendants East An Index to the Guion Miller Applications Volume I
Cherokee Descendants West An Index to the Guion Miller Applications Volume II (A-M)
Cherokee Descendants West An Index to the Guion Miller Applications Volume III (N-Z)

Applications for Enrollment of Seminole Newborn Freedmen, Act of 1905

Eastern Cherokee Census, Cherokee, North Carolina, 1915-1922, Taken by Agent James E. Henderson Volume I (1915-1916)
                                    Volume II (1917-1918)
                                    Volume III (1919-1920)
                                    Volume IV (1921-1922)

Complete Delaware Roll of 1898

Eastern Cherokee Census, Cherokee, North Carolina, 1923-1929, Taken by Agent James E. Henderson Volume I (1923-1924)
                                    Volume II (1925-1926)
                                    Volume III (1927-1929)

Applications for Enrollment of Seminole Newborn Act of 1905 Volumes I & II

North Carolina Eastern Cherokee Indian Census 1898-1899, 1904, 1906, 1909-1912, 1914 Revised and Expanded Edition

1932 Hopi and Navajo Native American Census with Birth & Death Rolls (1925-1931) Volume 1 - Hopi
1932 Hopi and Navajo Native American Census with Birth & Death Rolls (1930-1932) Volume 2 - Navajo

Western Navajo Reservation Navajo, Hopi and Paiute 1933 Census with Birth & Death Rolls 1925-1933

Cherokee Citizenship Commission Dockets 1880-1884 and 1887-1889 Volumes I thru V

Applications for Enrollment of Chickasaw Newborn Act of 1905 Volumes I thru VII

Cherokee Intermarried White 1906 Volume I thru X

Applications for Enrollment of Creek Newborn Act of 1905 Volumes I thru XIV

NATIVE AMERICAN WILLS & PROBATE RECORDS

RECORDS OF THE BUREAU OF INDIAN AFFAIRS

1911 - 1921

INCLUDING 76 NEVER BEFORE PUBLISHED WILLS

TRANSCRIBED BY

JEFF BOWEN

NATIVE STUDY
Gallipolis, Ohio
USA

Copyright © 2009
by Jeff Bowen

ALL RIGHTS RESERVED
No part of this publication may be reproduced
or used in any form or manner whatsoever
without previous written permission from the
copyright holder or publisher.

Originally published:
Baltimore, Maryland
2008

Reprinted by:

Native Study LLC
Gallipolis, OH
www.nativestudy.com

Library of Congress Control Number: 2020915163

ISBN: 978-1-64968-033-4

Book cover photograph taken by Jeff Bowen, October, 1998, titled *Early Morning at Fort Toulouse*, where the Coosa and Tallapoosa Rivers meet, Wetumpka, Alabama.

Made in the United States of America.

INTRODUCTION

These documents were found in the *Guide to Records in the National Archives of the United States Relating to AMERICAN INDIANS* on page 98, "eight volumes of copies of Indian wills, 1911-21, that, pursuant to the act of 1910 and an act of February 13, 1913 (37 Stat. 678), were referred to the Bureau and the Office of the Secretary of the Interior for Approval."

The Native American wills and probate records were listed under, "RECORDS OF THE LAW AND PROBATE DIVISIONS." The Law and Probate Divisions evolved from the Land Division that handled legal matters until a separate law office was established in 1907. By 1911, this office was mostly called the Law Division. An act of June 25, 1910 (36 Stat. 855), authorized by the Secretary of the Interior, was to determine the heirs of deceased Indian trust allottees; both the Land Division and the Law Division handled work resulting from this legislation. In 1913, an Heirship Section was established in the land Division that later was mostly concerned with probate work. By 1917, the Division was usually called the Probate Division.

The wills themselves were never filmed until they were discovered by the author and filmed in 1996. The wills and probate records consisted of 2568 pages.

The wills are not numbered in any certain order; there are 181 pages of wills without index in this volume, consisting of approximately 101 different wills. The majority of the wills are of western origin and a few eastern ones that will be reproduced as more volumes are completed.

In *Book Two* there is one will that was actually taken to the highest office in the land, the President of the United States. Also one woman bequeathed to her husband her fishing location and two canoes.

Some of the tribes included among the wills are Sioux, Arickara, Apache, Comanche, Chippewa, Ukie and Wylackie, Omaha, Blackfoot, Squaxin band, Yuma, Cheyenne-Arapahoe, Siletz, Sac and Fox, Quinaielt, Crow, Iowa, Otoe and Missouria, Umatilla, Piegan, Klamath, and many more.

Jeff Bowen
Gallipolis, Ohio
NativeStudy.com

NATIVE AMERICAN WILLS and PROBATE RECORDS, 1911 - 1921

LAST WILL AND TESTAMENT

I, **JENNIE STAR**, in the County of Marshall, and State of South Dakota, being of sound mind and memory, and considering the uncertainty of this frail and transitory life, do therefore make, ordain, publish and declare this to be my LAST WILL AND TESTAMENT.

FIRST. I order and direct that the executor, hereinafter named, pay all my just debts and funeral expenses as soon after my decease as conveniently may be.

SECOND. After the payment of such funeral expenses and debts, I give, devise and bequeath: To my son, Louis Star and to my mother, Tunkaahewin, all of my undivided interests in and to estates to which I am or will be a lawful heir, and to Charles Paul, with whom I am living, one white horse, branded ID, age about 10 years and weight about 900 lb. and worth about $75.00. The horse is not in possession of Charles Paul.

LASTLY. I make, constitute and appoint W. E. Dunn, Supt. & Sp'l. Disb. Agent, or his successor in office, to be Executor of my Last Will and Testament, hereby revoking all former Wills by me made.

In witness whereof, I have hereunto subscribed my name and affixed my seal the 19th day of June, 1917.

Jennie Star   Her Mark. (Thumb print.)

This instrument was on the day of the date thereof signed, published and declared by the said testator, Jennie Star, to be her LAST WILL AND TESTAMENT in our presence, who after request have subscribed our names thereto as witnesses in her presence and in the presence of each other.

Albert M. Fodder
Carroll R. Poffenberger

(NOTE: The last page was not dark enough to read, however, signatures and stamped dates could slightly be read. This page is signed by E. B. Meritt, Assistant Commissioner of Department of the Interior - Office of Indian Affairs, dated July 6, 1921; and F. M. Goodwin, Assistant Secretary of Department of the Interior - Office of the Secretary, dated July 13, 1921).

<<<<<<<<>>>>>>>>

LAST WILL AND TESTAMENT

OFFICE OF INDIAN AFFAIRS
RECEIVED
SEP 12, 192?
73786

IN THE NAME OF GOD, AMEN:

I, **IYATOYIK**, of Umatilla Indian Reservation, Oregon, being of sound mind, memory and understanding, do hereby make and publish this my last will and testament, hereby revoking and annulling all wills by me heretofore made, in manner and form following, that is to say:

NATIVE AMERICAN WILLS and PROBATE RECORDS, 1911 - 1921

FIRST: I direct that all my just debts and funeral expenses, and expenses of my last illness, shall be paid by my executor, hereinafter named, as soon after my decease as shall be convenient.

SECOND: I give, devise and bequeath to my daughter, Mary Agnes Crawford, my undivided interest in ½ the allotment of Hopsin, deceased Cayuse allottee 250, described as the SE/4 of SE/4 of Sec. 1; and the NE/4 of the NE/4 of Sec. 12, T2N, R33, on the Umatilla Reservation, Umatilla County, Oregon.

IN TESTIMONY WHEREOF, I have set my hand and seal to this, my last will and testament, at Umatilla Indian Agency, this 9th day of December, in the year of our Lord, 1914.

IYATOYIK Her Mark (Thumb print)

Signed, sealed, published and declared by the said Iyatoyik in our presence, as and for her last will and testament, and at her request and in our presence, and in the presence of each other, we have hereunto subscribed our names as attesting witnesses thereto.

Lee Lampson
Amy M. Hazen
Alvin Barbour

(NOTE: The last page was not dark enough to read, however, signatures and stamped dates could slightly be read. This page is signed by E. B. Meritt, Assistant Commissioner of Department of the Interior - Office of Indian Affairs, and Bo Sweeney, Assistant Secretary of Department of the Interior - Office of the Secretary, dated Feb. 6, 1915).

IN THE NAME OF GOD, Amen

I, **RICHARD STARR**, of Requa, County of Humboldt, State of California, of the age of 53 years, and being of sound and disposing mind and memory, and not acting under duress, menace, fraud, or under the influence of any person whatever, do make, publish and declare this my last WILL AND TESTAMENT in the manner following, that is to say:

FIRST: I give and bequeath to my wife, Ellen Starr, the NE ¼ of the NW ¼ of Sec. 12, and to my son, Red Starr, the SE ¼ of the NW ¼ of Sec. 12, and to my son, Harry Starr, the NE ¼ of the SW ¼ of Sec. 12, T11N, R2E, H. M.

SECONDLY: I give and bequeath to my wife, Ellen Starr, any inherited land and all of my personal property that I may die possessed of.

THIRDLY: I hereby nominate and appoint . (blank).. the executor of this, my last WILL AND TESTAMENT, ... and hereby revoke all former wills by me made.

In Witness Thereof, I have hereunto set my hand this 2nd day of August, 1915.

Richard Starr   His thumb mark

NATIVE AMERICAN WILLS and PROBATE RECORDS, 1911 - 1921

The foregoing instrument consisting of one page besides this, was at the date hereof by the said Richard Starr. Signed and published as, and declared to be his last Will and Testament, in the presence of us who at his request, and in his presence, and in the presence of each other, have subscribed our names as witnesses thereto and to his thumb mark.

RECEIVED
OCT 13, 1915
110149

Jesse B. Mortsolf, Supt. Hoopa Valley Indian Agency
Residing at Hoopa, California
Albert Obie U.S. Indian
N.T. Indian Police Private
Residing at Hoopa, CA

DEPARTMENT OF THE INTERIOR Office of Indian Affairs   Jan. 8, 1918
It is recommended that the within will be approved under the Act of June 25, 1910, (35 Stat. L, 855-856) as amended by the Act of February 14, 1913, (37 Stat. L, 678)

Respectfully,
E.B. Meritt
Assistant Commissioner

DEPARTMENT OF THE INTERIOR, Office of the Secretary   Jan. 10, 1916
The within will is hereby approved in accordance with the Act of June 25, 1910, (36 Stat. L, 855, 856) as amended by the Act of February 14, 1913, (37 Stat. L, 678).

Bo Sweeney
Assistant Secretary

LAST WILL AND TESTAMENT OF
MOSES ONE FEATHER.

I, **MOSES ONE FEATHER**, also known as **MOSES CROW FEATHER**, Cheyenne River allottee No. 295, do hereby, make, publish and declare this instrument as and for my last Will and Testament, and hereby revoke any and all other Wills Codicils by me heretofore made.

I hereby give, grant, devise and bequeath unto my son Joseph One Feather the following land: North half of Sec. 30, T15, R29, containing 320 acres, said land being the allotment of my deceased daughter Ida One Feather, deceased Cheyenne River Sioux allottee No. 312, to which I was determined the sole heir by the Department under date of October 2, 1911 (Indian Office file: Land-Sales 75644-11, 12911-12).

I hereby give, grant, devise and bequeath unto my wife, Elizabeth One Feather or Elizabeth Her Blanket Comes Out (Tasinahinapewin), my son, James One Feather, my son, Joseph One Feather, and my grandson, David Larrabee, in equal shares, all the balance of the real estate of which I may die possessed, which, to the best of my knowledge, is described as follows: my own allotment

NATIVE AMERICAN WILLS and PROBATE RECORDS, 1911 - 1921

#295 on the Cheyenne River Reservation: West half of Sec. 16, T14, R29; North half of NW qtr., SE qtr. of NW qtr., and E half of SW qtr. of NW qtr. of Sec. 21, T14, R29; SW qtr. of Sec. 9, T14, R29; and North half of NE qtr. of NW qtr. of Sec. 19, T16, R29, containing 640 acres; and the allotment of my deceased son Alfred One Feather, deceased Cheyenne River allottee #311, viz: S half of Sec. 19, T15, R29, containing 320 acres; to which I was determined by the Department to be the sole heir under date of October 6, 1914 (Indian Office file: Law-Heirship, 97146-14).

The rest and residue of the estate possessed and owned by me at the time of my death I hereby give, bequeath and devise to my wife, Elizabeth One Feather, my son James One Feather, my son Joseph One Feather, and my grandson David Larrabee, in equal shares.

IN TESTIMONY WHEREOF, I do hereby and hereunto subscribe my name and place my thumb mark in the presence of the attesting witnesses and do hereby declare and acknowledge that the foregoing instrument is my last Will and Testament and I further declare that the two subscribing witnesses attest my signature at my request and in my presence, my name being written in at my request by *Thomas Saul*. Dated at Cheyenne Agency, Dewey Co, SD, this 14th day of March, A.D, 1916.

                        Moses Crowfeather or   His thumb
                        Moses Onefeather   mark

The above instrument was, at the date thereof, subscribed by the said Moses One Feather or Moses Crow Feather, in the presence of us and each of us and he, at the time of making such subscription, acknowledged that he executed the same and declared said instrument so subscribed by him to be his last Will and Testament, whereupon we then and there at his request and in his presence and in the presence of each other, subscribed our names in witness thereof.

                        Thomas Saul Cheyenne Agency, SD
                        Penn Garfield Cheyenne Agency, SD

Probate A C W

DEPARTMENT OF THE INTERIOR, Office Of Indian Affairs   Sept. 12, 1921

It is hereby recommended that the within will of Moses One Feather or Moses Crow Feather, deceased Cheyenne River allottee, No. 295, be approved in accordance with the provisions of the Act of June 25, 1910 (36 Stat. L, 855-56), as amended by the Act of February 14, 1913 (37 Stat. L, 678).

                        Respectfully,
                        E.B. Meritt
                        Assistant Commissioner.

DEPARTMENT OF THE INTERIOR, Office of the Secretary   Sept. 13, 1921

The within will of Moses One Feather or Moses Crow Feather, deceased Cheyenne River allottee, No. 295, be approved in accordance with the provisions

NATIVE AMERICAN WILLS and PROBATE RECORDS, 1911 - 1921

of the Act of June 25, 1910 (36 Stat. L, 855-56), as amended by the Act of February 14, 1913 (37 Stat. L, 678).

F.M. Goodwin
Assistant Secretary

<<<<<<<>>>>>>>

WILL OF BROKEN KNIFE, CHEYENNE RIVER ALLOTTEE No. 287, GRANTING AND DEVISING HER ALLOTMENT OF LAND ON THE CHEYENNE RIVER RESERVATION AND HER TRUST PROPERTY.

I, **BROKEN KNIFE**, Cheyenne River Allottee No. 287, being of sound mind and disposing memory, do hereby make, publish and declare this instrument as and for my last Will and Testament, hereby revoking and declaring null and void any and all former Wills.

I hereby give, grant, devise and bequeath unto my grand nephew, by blood, and my adopted son, adopted by Indian custom, Abraham Buckley, a Standing Rock Sioux Indian, all of my allotment of land on the Cheyenne River Indian Reservation in the State of South Dakota, being Allotment No. 287 for the South ½ of Sec. 11 in T16, North of R23, East of the Black Hills Meridian, and any monies held in trust for me.

I also give, devise and bequeath unto said Abraham Buckley my two issue mares and their increase, both of said mares being branded 3 ID on left shoulder.

IN TESTIMONY WHEREOF, I Broken Knife, do hereby subscribe my name and place my thumb mark in the presence of the attesting witnesses and do hereby acknowledge and declare that the foregoing instrument is my last Will and Testament, and I further declare that the two attesting and subscribing witnesses attest my signature at my request and in my presence and in the presence of each other.

Dated Whitehorse, SD, on this 21 day of Oct, 1916.

Broken Knife   her (thumb) mark

OFFICE OF INDIAN AFFAIRS
RECEIVED
JUN 29, 1918
Probate A C W   **1668**

DEPARTMENT OF THE INTERIOR, Office of Indian Affairs   Sept. 12, 1921

It is hereby recommended that the within will of Broken Knife, deceased Cheyenne River allottee, No. 287, be approved in accordance with the provisions of the Act of June 25, 1910 (36 Stat. L, 855-56).

Respectfully,
E.B. Meritt
Assistant Commissioner

DEPARTMENT OF THE INTERIOR, Office of the Secretary   Sept. 13, 1921

The within will of Broken Knife, deceased Cheyenne River allottee, No. 287, is hereby approved in accordance with the provisions of the Act of June 25,

NATIVE AMERICAN WILLS and PROBATE RECORDS, 1911 - 1921

1910 (36 Stat. L, 855-56), as amended by the Act of February 14, 1913 (37 Stat. L, 678).

F.M. Goodwin
Asst. Secretary

The foregoing instrument was, at the date thereof, subscribed by the said Broken Knife in the presence of us and each of us and she, at the time of making such subscription, acknowledged that she executed the same and declared said instrument, so subscribed by her, to be her last Will and Testament, whereupon we then and there at her request and in her presence and in the presence of each other, subscribed our names in witness thereof.

George Thwing, Timber Lake, SD
William Swan, Timber Lake, SD

Whitehorse, South Dakota, Oct. 21, 1916

I, *William Swan*, do hereby certify that I acted as Interpreter at the time of the execution of the foregoing Will of Broken Knife; that said Will was carefully and fully interpreted to said Broken Knife by me and the purport thereof was full explained to her.

William Swan

DEPARTMENT OF THE INTERIOR
Office of Indian Affairs
In the Matter of the Will of Broken Knife,
Cheyenne River Allottee, No. 287.

State of South Dakota,)
) ss
County of Dewey   )

    Broken Knife being first duly sworn upon oath deposes and says: that she is a full blood Sioux Indian, about eighty four years of age, and a member of the Cheyenne River Tribe of Sioux Indians.
    That she is unmarried and has never had any children.
    That her only heirs at law ~~are a half sister, Mrs. Mary Black Pine, who is aged about eighty years of age and resides upon the Cheyenne River Reservation, and~~ is a niece, Nellie Larrabee, about forty four years of age, wife of George Larrabee, who ~~are~~ is a ~~members~~ of said tribe of Cheyenne River Sioux and who resides on said Reservation.
    That she herewith forwards to the Honorable Secretary of the Interior for approval her Will, disposing of her allotment of land on the Cheyenne River Reservation, and also two mares, being all of her ID property, issued to her by the Indian Department, said mares being branded 3 ID on left shoulder and said Allotment of land being Allotment numbered 287 for the S½ of Sec. 11 of T16, R of R23, E.B.H.M, SD.
    That she makes this Will for the following reasons: She is an old woman, infirm with Rheumatism and has no one dependent upon her for support. ~~That~~

NATIVE AMERICAN WILLS and PROBATE RECORDS, 1911 - 1921

~~her nearest relative, the said Mrs. Mary Black Pine is also an old woman and does not need any part of affiant's property.~~ That Nellie Larrabee, affiant's niece, is able, with her husband's help, to take care of herself. ~~That neither of said relatives have helped or aided affiant.~~

That Abraham Buckley, who is also known as Abraham Takes the Bow, the devisee under affiant's Will, is a grand nephew of affiant. That she took him when he was about six months old and had the full care and control of him until he was about sixteen years of age and has always considered him as her child. That the said Abraham Buckley is now about thirty two years of age and for a good many years last past has helped care for affiant and aided in her support, and affiant still considers him as her son.

That affiant has always intended that said Buckley should have her Allotment when she died and makes said Will for the purpose of carrying out such intention.

That affiant is so sick and infirm that she cannot go to the Cheyenne River Agency to have a personal talk with the Superintendent of said Cheyenne River Reservation, relative to said Will.

Witnesses to Mark: Broken Knife   her (thumb print) mark
George Thwing
William Swan

Subscribed and sworn to before me this 21 day of Oct, 1916.
                    George Thwing, Notary Public, SD
Whitehorse, SD, Oct. 21, 1916.   My Commission expires May 3, 1917.

I, *William Swan*, do hereby certify that the foregoing affidavit, by Broken Knife subscribed, was carefully and fully interpreted to her by me and the purport thereof was fully explained to her.
                    William Swan
                    Interpreter

<<<<<<<<>>>>>>>

LAST WILL AND TESTAMENT

IN THE NAME OF GOD, Amen

OFFICE OF INDIAN AFFAIRS
RECEIVED
FEB 23, 1921
15313

I, **FRANCIS BONGA**, of Onigum, MN, being of sound mind and memory, but mindful of the uncertainty of this frail and transitory life, do hereby make, ordain, publish and declare this to be my last will and testament, hereby revoking all former Wills or Codicils by me at any time made.

First   I direct that my Executor hereinafter named pay all my just debts and funeral expenses as soon after my demise as conveniently may be done.

NATIVE AMERICAN WILLS and PROBATE RECORDS, 1911 - 1921

Second   I give, devise, and bequeath unto John C. Schneider all of my property real, personal and mixed of whatever kind or wherever situated and especially all the real estate which has been inherited by as from my father's estate, viz: John [or Jack] Bonga, a mix blood Chippewa Indian, who died intestate on or about Nov. 20, 1898, and also all and singular of such other lands or interest in lands as are inherited from Pete Bonga [otherwise known as Pete Wright] and from Josette Cimamino.

Third   I hereby nominate and appoint J. S. Scribner of Walker, MN, to be my sole Executor of this my last will and testament.

In Testimony whereof I have hereunto set my hand and affixed my seal this 7th day of August, 1920.

Francis Bonga [SEAL]

This instrument consisting of one page, was on the day and date thereof, signed, published and declared by said Testator to be his Last Will and Testament in our presence, who, at his request, have subscribed our names thereto as witnesses in his presence and in the presence of each other.

J. H. Reed
Residing at Walker, MN

O. A. Reed
Residing at Walker, MN

PROBATE   15315-1921 / 73316-1921 L L
DEPARTMENT OF THE INTERIOR,
Office of Indian affairs, Washington, D.C.   Sept. 16, 1921

It is recommended that the within will be approved pursuant to the provisions of the Act of June 25, 1910 (36 Stats. L; 855, 856), as amended by the Act of February 14, 1913 (37 State. L, 678).

Respectfully,
E. B. Meritt
Assistant Commissioner.

DEPARTMENT OF THE INTERIOR, Office of the Secretary   Sept. 16, 1921

The within will is hereby approved pursuant to the provisions of the Act of June 25, 1910 (36 Stats. L, 855, 856), as amended by the Act of February 14, 1913 (37 Stats. L, 678).

F. M. Goodwin
Assistant Secretary

OFFICE OF INDIAN AFFAIRS
RECEIVED
AUG 20, 1920
69745

<<<<<<<>>>>>>>

LAST WILL AND TESTAMENT OF ONE TOOTH,
EUGENE PARKHURST, CROW CREEK ALLOTTEE No. 731

NATIVE AMERICAN WILLS and PROBATE RECORDS, 1911 - 1921

IN THE NAME OF GOD, Amen:

I, **ONE TOOTH**, also known as **EUGENE PARKHURST**, 42 years of age, an Indian of the Crow Creek Reservation in the state of South Dakota, being of sound mind, memory, and understanding, do hereby make and publish this my last will and testament, hereby revoking and annulling all others by me heretofore made, that is to say:

FIRST: I direct that all my just debts and funeral expenses and expenses of my last illness shall be paid as soon after my decease as shall be convenient.

SECOND: I am possessed of an allotment of land within the Crow Creek Reservation, in the state of South Dakota, which is described as the W½ and SE¼ of the NE¼ Sec. 19, T107N; R71W of the 5th P.M, South Dakota, containing 230 acres, allotted to me under the Act of March 2, 1889, (25 Stat. L, 888) trust patent to the same being issued on the 4th day of Oct, 1909. I give, devise and bequeath my said allotment of land to the following named persons, to wit:

To my wife, Josephine Parkhurst, also known as Josephine Lodge, 41 years of age, the NW¼ of the NE¼, Sec. 19, T107N, R71W of the 5th P.M, South Dakota, containing 40 acres, together with all stock and farming implements of which I am now possessed or may be possessed of at the time of my decease.

To my son, Joseph Purcell Parkhurst, 7 years of age, the SE¼ of the NE¼, Sec. 19, T107N, R71W of the 5th P.M, South Dakota, containing 40 acres.

To my son, Samuel Emerson Parkhurst, age 7 months, the SW¼ of the NE¼, Sec. 19, T107N, R71W, 5th P.M, South Dakota, containing 40 acres.

To Wallace Ashley, my cousin, 47 years of age, all my share and interest in the estate of my deceased father Has A Tail, said estate being described as the SE¼-19-107-71 W, 5th P.M, South Dakota, and the W½ and NE¼-NE¼-16-107-71 W, 5th P.M, South Dakota.

To my brother, Sam Boy, 56 years of age, all my share and interests in the estates of Bowed Head and Lone First Born, deceased Crow Creek allottees, Nos. 37 and 169.

All the rest of my property both real and personal of which I may at this time, or may hereafter be possessed of, I give, devise, and bequeath to my wife Josephine Parkhurst and my sons Joseph Purcell and Samuel Emerson Parkhurst, to be divided equally among them.

LASTLY: I am satisfied that the officers of the Department of the Interior of the United states will make proper provision for carrying into affect of this my last Will and Testament, and therefore, I have not appointed an executor to administer my estate.

IN TESTIMONY WHEREOF, I have set my hand and seal to this my last Will and Testament at the Agency office located on the Crow Creek Reservation at Fort Thompson, South Dakota, on this 9th day of October, 1919.

One Tooth   Eugene Parkhurst

NATIVE AMERICAN WILLS and PROBATE RECORDS, 1911 - 1921

Signed, sealed, published and declared by the said One Tooth, [Eugene Parkhurst] in our presence, as and for his last Will and Testament, and at his request and in his presence and in the presence of each other we have hereto subscribed our names as attesting witnesses thereto.

Charles McBride
Joe Irving
Peter W. Lightfoot
All of Ft. Thompson, SD

Probate 69745-20 / 43970-21   J M P
DEPARTMENT OF THE INTERIOR, Office of Indian Affairs

The within will of One Tooth, or Eugene Parkhurst, deceased Crow Creek allottee No. 731, is hereby recommended for approval in accordance with the provisions of the Act of June 25, 1910, (36 Stat. L, 855-6) as amended by the Act of February 14, 1913 (37 Stat. L, 678).

Respectfully,
E.B. Meritt
Assistant Commissioner.

DEPARTMENT OF THE INTERIOR, Office of the Secretary   Sept. 2, 1921
The within will of One Tooth, or Eugene Parkhurst, deceased Crow Creek allottee No. 731, is hereby approved in accordance with the provisions of the Act of June 25, 1910 (36 Stat. L, 855-6) as amended by the Act of February 14, 1913 (37 Stat. L, 678).

F. M. Goodwin
Assistant Secretary

WILL

I, **JACK RED CLOUD** of Pine Ridge Agency, South Dakota, Allottee No. 1266, do hereby make and declare this to be my last will and testament, in accordance with Section 2 of the Act of June 25, 1910 (36 stat. 855-858), and Act of February 13, 1913, (Public No. 381), hereby revoking all former wills make by us:

1. I hereby direct that, as soon as possible after my decease, that all my debts, funeral and testamentary expenses be paid out of my personal estate.
2. I give and devise my allotment on the Pine Ridge Reservation, South Dakota, described as follows:

All of Sec. 3, T39, R41.
~~Also that part of the Red Cloud allotment inherited by me and described as the NW/4 of NE/4 of SW/4, and N/2 of NW/4 of SW/4 of Sec. 12,~~

NATIVE AMERICAN WILLS and PROBATE RECORDS, 1911 - 1921

~~and N/2 of NE/4 of SE/4, and S/e of SE/4 of NE/4 of Sec. 11, T35, R45. 60 acres. (NOTE: The above paragraph was marked through.) in the following manner:~~

NE/4 of Sec. 3, T39, R41, to my sons Joseph Red Cloud and James Red Cloud, Jr.

NE/4 of Sec. 3, T39, R41, to my sons Charles Red Cloud and James Red Cloud, Sr, and to my wife, Nancy Red Cloud.

NE/4 of Sec. 3, T39, R41, to my sons Alfred Red Cloud and John Red Cloud.

SW/4 of Sec. 3, T39, R41, to my daughters Susie Chief Eagle and Lucy Afraid of Horses.

My interest in the allotment of Red Cloud to my wife, Nancy Red Cloud.

3. I give and bequeath all of my personal property of whatsoever nature and wheresoever situated unto One ID mare to my son, James Red Cloud, Jr.

4. All the rest of my property, real or personal, now possessed or hereafter acquired, of whatsoever nature and wheresoever situated, I hereby give, devise and bequeath unto my wife, Nancy Red Cloud. Property now consists of 2 cows, 9 horses, 1 house, 1 wagon, 1 mower, and farming implements.

In witness whereof I have hereunto set my hand this <u>31st</u> day of <u>January, 1917</u>.

                Jack Red Cloud   his (thumb print) mark

PROBATE 40215-1921   V L D
DEPARTMENT OF THE INTERIOR, Office of Indian Affairs   Jun 23, 1921

The within will of Jack Red Cloud is hereby recommended for approval in accordance with the Act of June 25, 1910 (36 Stats. L, 855-6), as amended by the Act of February 14, 1913 (37 Stats. L, 678).

                Respectfully,
                E.B. Meritt
                Assistant Commissioner

DEPARTMENT OF THE INTERIOR, Office of the Secretary   Jun 28, 1921

The within will is hereby approved in accordance with the Act of June 25, 1910 (36 Stats. L, 855-6), and the Act of February 14, 1913 (37 Stats. L, 678).

                F.M. Goodwin
                Assistant Secretary

The above statement was this 31st day of January, 1917 signed and published by Jack Red Cloud as his last will and testament, in the joint presence of the undersigned, the said Jack Red Cloud then being of sound and vigorous mind and free from any constraint or compulsion: whereupon we, being without any interest in the matter other than friendship, and being well acquainted with

NATIVE AMERICAN WILLS and PROBATE RECORDS, 1911 - 1921

him, but not members of his family, immediately subscribed our names hereto in the presence of each other and of the said testator, for the purpose of attesting the said will, as (blank) requested us to do. And that I, H. E. Wright at the testatrix's request have written his name in ink, and that I affixed his thumb-marks.

          Post Office Address.
         (No name) Pine Ridge, SD
         (No name) Pine Ridge, SD

           Pine Ridge, SD
           May 6, 1921

  I hereby certify that I have fully inquired into the mental competency of the Indian signing the above will; the circumstances attending the execution of the will; the influence that may have induced its execution, and the names of those entitled to share in the estate under the law of descent in South Dakota; reasons for the disposition of the property proposed by the will, differing from disposition has the property descended by operation of law.
  I respectfully forward this will with the recommendation that it be approved.
           H.M. Tidwell
          Supt. & Spl. Dist. Agent

(NOTE: The following will was handwritten on a small piece of paper)

          March 13, 1918

  I am writing a statement to say I am not lawfull[sic] *married to someone in which I want no one to heir my land but my father and mother because I want to will it to them and no one else.*
          I am Lizzie Roy

DEPARTMENT OF THE INTERIOR, Office of Indian Affairs. Jul 9, 1921
  It is hereby recommended that the within will of Lizzie Roy [DeLodge Stabler] be approved under the Act of June 24, 1910 (36 Stat. L, 855-6) as amended by the Act of February 14, 1913 (37 Stat. 678).
         Respectfully,
         E.B. Meritt
         Assistant Commissioner

DEPARTMENT OF THE INTERIOR, Office of the Secretary Jul 16, 1921
  The within will of Lizzie Roy [DeLodge Stabler] is hereby approved in accordance with the Act of June 25, 1910 (36 Stat. L, 855-6) as amended by the Act of February 14, 1913 (37 Stat. L, 678)
         F.M. Goodwin
         Assistant Secretary

NATIVE AMERICAN WILLS and PROBATE RECORDS, 1911 - 1921

LAST WILL AND (TESTAMENT) OF DOROTHY FLEURY
I MAKE THIS--------------MY LAST WILL

(1)   I give devise and bequeath to my mother, Louise Dougherty, the Quarter Section of land in Hughes County, that I own in fee and all my furniture and personal effects.

(11)   I give and bequeath to my brother Albert Dougherty all horses and cattle which I own.

(111)   And the rest residue and remainder of my estate I give devise and bequeath to my mother above named and I hereby nominate her executrix of this my last Will and Testament hereby revoking any Will by me heretofore made.

In witness whereof I have hereunto set my hand this 24th day of September, 1920, at Hughes Co, South Dakota.

Dorothy Fleury
Testratrix

On this 24th day of September, 1920, the foregoing instrument consisting of one pen written page was signed by Dorothy Fleury in our presence and in the presence of each of us and by her then and there declared and published as her last Will and Testament and at her request and in her presence and in the presence of each of us we have severally signed our names thereto as witnesses.

Chas. Lantz, residing at Pierre, SD
DeWitt Hare, residing at 3628 4th Ave. S, Minneapolis, MN

FILED
Oct. 26, 1921
and entered in County Court Record
Book No. 24, Page <u>19</u>
Fannie S. Spurling
Clerk of Courts, Hughes Co, SD

Probate A C W   6-3-21
DEPARTMENT OF THE INTERIOR, Office of Indian Affairs   Jul 9, 1921

The within will of Dorothy Fleury, deceased allottee #1350 of the Crow Creek Sioux Tribe, is respectfully recommended for approval, pursuant to the provisions of June 25th, 1910 (36 Stats. 855) as amended by the Act of February 14, 1913, (37 Stats, 678), as far as it affects her property held in trust. The designation of an executor is not recognized as to such property.

Respectfully,
E.B. Meritt
Assistant Commissioner

NATIVE AMERICAN WILLS and PROBATE RECORDS, 1911 - 1921

DEPARTMENT OF THE INTERIOR, Office of the Secretary   Jul. 14, 1921

The within will of Dorothy Fleury, deceased allottee #1350 of the Crow Creek Sioux Tribe, is hereby approved pursuant to the provisions of the Act of June 24th, 1910 (36 Stats, 855) as amended by the Act of February 14th, 1913 (37 Stat. 678) as far as it affects her property held in trust. The designation of an executor is not recognized as to such property.

F.M. Goodwin
Assistant Secretary

STATE OF SOUTH DAKOTA,)
)ss
County of Hughes,   )

I, G. H. Pinckney, Clerk of Court of said County of Hughes, do hereby certify, that I have compared the foregoing attached copies with the original Last Will of Dorothy Fleury now remaining on file and of record in my office and that the same is a correct transcript therefrom, and of the whole of such original.

WITNESS my hand and official seal the 4th day of April, 1921

H. Pinckney
Clerk of Courts

OFFICE OF INDIAN AFFAIRS
RECEIVED
JUL 11, 1921
56965

<<<<<<<<>>>>>>>>

LAST WILL AND TESTAMENT OF WRAPPEDHAIR

IN THE NAME OF GOD, Amen.

I, **WRAPPEDHAIR,** of Lamedeer, Montana, being of sound mind, memory and understanding, do hereby make and publish this, my last will and testament, hereby revoking and annulling all wills by me heretofore made, in manner and form following, that is to say:

First, I direct that all my just debts and funeral expenses and expenses of my last illness shall be paid by my executor hereinafter named as soon after my decease as convenient;

Second, I give, devise and bequeath to my wife one-half of my money at agency office and one-half of all my cattle;

William Yellowfox, my team, wagon, harness, one-sixth my money at office, one-half my cattle and my homestead;

My son, Hubert Hollowbreast, one-sixth my money at office at time of my death, but no cattle.

Walter Ant, my riding plow, only.

Third, all the rest and residue of my estate, both real and personal and mixed I give, devise and bequeath to my lawful heirs as determined after my decease.

NATIVE AMERICAN WILLS and PROBATE RECORDS, 1911 - 1921

And lastly, I do hereby nominate, constitute and appoint the superintendent executor of this my last will and testament at Lamedeer, Montana, this 21st day of December in the year, 1921.

Wrappedhair His (thumb print) mark

Signed, sealed, published and declared by Wrappedhair in our presence as and for his last will and testament and at his request and in our presence, and in the presence of each other we have hereunto subscribed our names as attesting witnesses thereto.

O.M. Boggess   of Lamedeer, MT
John Standsintimber of Lamedeer, MT

Probate 29209-21 M H W
DEPARTMENT OF THE INTERIOR, Office of Indian Affairs   Jul 16, 1921
The within will of Thomas Wrappedhair, deceased unallotted Northern Cheyenne Indian of the Tongue River Reservation, Montana, is hereby recommended for approval under the Act of June 25. 1910 (36 Stats. 855-6) as amended by the Act of February 14, 1913 (37 Stats. L, 678).

Respectfully,
E.B. Meritt
Assistant Commissioner

DEPARTMENT OF THE INTERIOR, Office of the Secretary   Jul 19, 1921
The within will of Thomas Wrapped hair, deceased unallotted Northern Cheyenne Indian of the Tongue River Reservation, Montana, is hereby approved under the Act of June 25, 1910 (36 Stats. 855-6) as amended by the Act of February 14, 1913 (37 Stats. 678).

F.M. Goodwin
Assistant Secretary

LAST WILL AND TESTAMENT

IN THE NAME OF GOD, Amen:

I, **KOPLOTSILPILP,** of Umatilla Indian Reservation, Oregon, being of sound mind, memory and understanding, do hereby make and publish this my last will and testament, hereby revoking and annulling all wills by me heretofore made, in manner and form following, that is to say:
   FIRST: I direct that all my just debts and funeral expenses, and expenses of my last illness, shall be paid as soon after my decease as shall be convenient.
   SECOND: I give, devise and bequeath to my daughter, Elizabeth Wak Wak and to my niece, Big Susie, or Susie Warner or Wawenotway, the sum of $100 each from my estate, and all the rest of my estate I give to my daughter, Susie

NATIVE AMERICAN WILLS and PROBATE RECORDS, 1911 - 1921

Koplots, who has taken care of me for many years. My estate held in trust by the government consists of my 160 acre allotment and other inherited land on Umatilla Reservation.

IN TESTIMONY WHEREOF, I have set my hand and seal to this, my last will and testament, at my home Umatilla Reservation, Oregon, this 24th day of February, in the year of our Lord, 1921.

Koplotsilpilp   His (thumb print) mark

Signed, sealed, published and declared by the said Koplotsilpilp in our presence, as and for <u>his</u> last will and testament, and at his request and in our presence, and in the presence of each other, we have hereunto subscribed our names as attesting witnesses thereto.

Paul Jones
Harry Wahsise
Lucy Panaso
Umatilla Indian Reservation, Oregon

Probate 17694-21 J W H   6-28 AD 1921
DEPARTMENT OF THE INTERIOR, Office of Indian Affairs   Jul 1, 1921

The within will of Koplotsilpilp, deceased Umatilla allottee #149, is hereby recommended for approval under the Act of June 24, 1910 (36 Stats. 855) as amended by the Act of February 14, 1913, (37 Stats. 678) and the regulations of the Department.

Respectfully,
E.B. Meritt
Assistant Commissioner

DEPARTMENT OF THE INTERIOR, Office of the Secretary   Jul 8, 1921

The within will of Koplotsilpilp, deceased Umatilla allottee is hereby approved under the Act of June 25, 1910 (36 Stats. 855) as amended by the Act of February 14, 1913 (37 Stats. 678) and the regulations of the Department.

F.M. Goodwin
Assistant Secretary

<<<<<<<>>>>>

OFFICE OF INDIAN AFFAIRS
RECEIVED
JUN 20, 1921
50750

IN THE NAME OF GOD, Amen

I, **OLD MARY**, of Cresent City. County of Del Norte, State of California of the age of about 80 years, and being of sound and disposing mind and memory, and not acting under duress, menace, fraud, or under the influence of any person whatever, do make, publish and declare this my last WILL AND TESTAMENT in the manner following, that is to say:

First, I give and bequeath to Jennie Scott, my granddaughter, all of my Indian things and other personal property, that I may own at the time of my death.

NATIVE AMERICAN WILLS and PROBATE RECORDS, 1911 - 1921

Secondly, I give and bequeath to Jennie Scott, my granddaughter, all the inherited land that I own, or may own at the time of my death. I have no allottment and no land, except inherited land.

I give my property to Jennie Scott because she is my nearest relative and the only one that does and will take care of me during my life time.

My inherited land consists in a half interest in the allottment[sic] of John Woodbury, deceased, and described as follows:

S ½ of the SW ¼ and NE ¼ of SW ½ of S 28, T18N, R1N. Containing 120 acres,

Also, one-quarter interest in the allottment[sic] of Orrie Woodbury, deceased, described as follows:

SW ¼ of S 33, T18N, R1E, containing 160 acres.

Thirdly, I hereby nominate and appoint Phineas D. Holcomb the executor of this my last Will and Testament, and hereby revoke all former wills by me made.

In Witness Whereof, I have hereunto set my hand this 22nd day of Feb, 1915.

Old Mary
Her thumb mark

The foregoing instrument consisting of 2 page(s) besides this, was at the date hereof, by the said (blank). Signed and Published as, and declared to be her last Will and Testament, in the presence of us who at her request, and in her presence, and in the presence of each other, have subscribed our names as witnesses thereto.

P.D. Holcomb
Residing at Requa, CA
E.J. Holden
Residing at Hoopa, CA

DEPARTMENT OF THE INTERIOR, Office of Indian Affairs   Jan 31, 1916

The within will is hereby recommended for approval in accordance with the Act of June 25, 1910 (36 Stats. L, 855-856) as amended by the Act of February 14, 1913 (37 Stats. L, 678) in so far as it embraces property held in trust by the Government of the United States.

Respectfully,
E.B. Meritt
Assistant Commissioner

DEPARTMENT OF THE INTERIOR, Office of the Secretary   Jan 31, 1916

The within will is hereby approved in accordance with the Act of June 25, 1910 (36 Stats. L, 855-856) as amended by the Act of February 14, 1913 (37 Stats. L 678) in so far as it embraces property held in trust by the Government of the United States.

Bo Sweeney
Assistant Secretary

NATIVE AMERICAN WILLS and PROBATE RECORDS, 1911 - 1921

<<<<<<<<>>>>>>>

Know all men by these presents that I, **ANGELINE SETTER**, of Reserve, Sawyer County, being of sound mind and memory, do make, publish and declare this my last will and testament on manner following, to wit:

After the payment of my just debts and funeral expenses, I give, devise and bequeath to my son, Frank Setter, and my daughter, Mamie Setter, in equal shares all my estate, both real and personal and wheresoever situate, share and share alike.

I hereby appoint my said son, Frank Setter, and my daughter, Mamie Setter, joint executors of this my last will without bond.

Dated this 15th day of September, 1919.

              her
           Angeline Setter   (x)
              mark

Sawyer County) ss

We the undersigned on this 15th day of September, 1919, at the request of the above named Angeline Setter, in her presence and in the presence of each other have signed our names as witnesses to the foregoing instrument which was signed by the said Angeline Setter in our presence and which was declared by her to be her will.

OFFICE OF INDIAN AFFAIRS
RECEIVED
MAY 13, 1921
39351

Jasper Cross
Joe LaRonge
Reserve, WI

DEPARTMENT OF THE INTERIOR, Office of Indian Affairs   Jul 11, 1921

It is respectfully recommended that the within certified copy of the will of Angeline Setter, a Chippewa Indian allottee, be laid before the President for approval of the will.

           Orulf Burber
           Commissioner

DEPARTMENT OF THE INTERIOR, Office of the Secretary   Jul 19, 1921

It is respectfully recommended that the within will of Angeline Setter be approved.

           E.B. Finney
           Acting Secretary

The White House   July 20, 1921
The within will of Angeline Setter is approved.
           (Signature illegible)

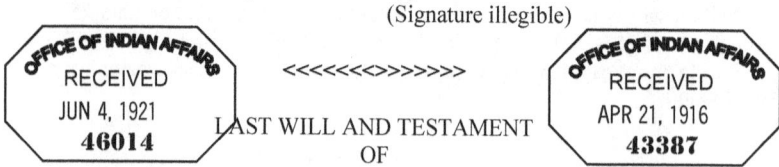

OFFICE OF INDIAN AFFAIRS
RECEIVED
JUN 4, 1921
46014

<<<<<<<<>>>>>>>

LAST WILL AND TESTAMENT
OF

OFFICE OF INDIAN AFFAIRS
RECEIVED
APR 21, 1916
43387

NATIVE AMERICAN WILLS and PROBATE RECORDS, 1911 - 1921

SUSAN DAVIS

I, the undersigned, **SUSAN DAVIS**, being of sound mind and disposing memory, but realizing the uncertainties of life, do hereby make, declare, and publish this MY LAST WILL AND TESTAMENT, as follows:

1st I desire all my debts that are right and just including my burial and funeral expenses to be paid out of any funds accruing to my estate.

2nd To my husband, Bruce Blackdeer (allotted Connokaw Blackdeer) that part of my land beginning at the Northwest corner of Sec. 36, T26N of R7E of the Sixth Principal Meridian, Nebraska, thence east 10 rods, thence south 16 rods, thence west 10 rods, thence north 16 rods to the point of beginning, containing one acre, on which certain improvements are built, the same to be his forever. This is a part of the allotment of said Bruce or Connokaw Blackdeer which he deeded to me several years ago.

3rd To my daughter, Nellie Davis, sometimes called Nellie Grayhair, I give, devise and bequeath that portion of my land described as the S ½ of the NE qtr of Sec. 25, T26N of R6E of the 6th Principal Meridian, Thurston Co, NE, and to her heirs forever.

Susan Davis
Grover Mallory

The said testator signed her name at this time to the above and foregoing instrument in the presence of the undersigned and at the same time declared it to be her last will and testament, and we at her request and in her presence and in the presence of each other do hereby sign our names hereto as attesting witnesses.

Anna G. Berkeupas Winnebago Agency, NE, Mission
Daniel Gueer

DEPARTMENT OF THE INTERIOR, Office of Indian Affairs   Oct. 13, 1916
   The within will is hereby recommended for approval in accordance with the provisions of the Act of June 24, 1910 (36 Stat. L, 855-56), as amended by the Act of February 14, 1913 (37 Stat. L, 678)

E.B. Meritt
Assistant Commissioner

DEPARTMENT OF THE INTERIOR, Office of the Secretary   Oct. 13, 1916
   The within will is hereby approved in accordance with the provisions of the Act of June 25, 1910 (36 Stat. L, 855-56), as amended by the Act of February 14, 1913 (37 Stat. L, 678)

Bo Sweeney
Assistant Secretary

<<<<<<<<>>>>>>>

NATIVE AMERICAN WILLS and PROBATE RECORDS, 1911 - 1921

OFFICE OF INDIAN AFFAIRS
RECEIVED
MAR 23, 1920
25074

LAST WILL AND TESTAMENT

I, **TINE-GOO AH (SUSIE CAT)**, Kiowa allottee (#)614, of Apache, OK, County of Caddo, being now in good health and strength of body and mind but sensible of the uncertainty of life and desiring to make disposition of my property and affairs while in health of body and strength of mind, do hereby make, publish and declare the following to be my last will and testament, hereby revoking and canceling all other or former wills by me at any time made.

1. I direct the payment of all my just debts and funeral expenses.
2. I direct that my trust allotment consisting of the NE qtr of Sec 12, T5N, R13W of the Indian Meridian, be partitioned and disposed of as follows:
3. I give and devise to my beloved husband, O-ye-bi, (Albert Cat), Kiowa allottee 613, the west half of the NE qtr of Sec. 12, T5N, R13W, comprising the west half of my own allotment.
4. I give and devise the east half of the NE qtr of Sec. 12, T5N, R13W of the Indian Meridian, in equal shares and to hold the same in proportionate undivided interests to my beloved children, as named below:
5. Thomas O-ye-bi, Kiowa allottee 616; Freeman O-ye-bi, Kiowa allottee 615; Lizzie Cat, Kiowa allottee 2271; Winston Cat, born 1908, Kiowa allottee 3310; and Fred Cat, born 1910, Kiowa allottee (unallotted.)
6. My reason for directing my trust allotment to be partitioned, and disposed of as set out above is that my resident is located on the east half of my own allotment and it is my desire that the five children receive the use and benefit of the same. My husband now has a substantial dwelling upon his own allotment and it is my intention that my children be provided a home in the event I should unexpectedly pass away while they are as yet of young and tender age.
7. I give and bequeath one black mare, 9 years old, to my beloved husband, O-ye-bi, Kiowa allottee 613.
8. All the rest, residue and remainder of my property, both real and personal, I give and devise in equal shares to my beloved children, Freeman O-ye-bi, Kiowa allottee 615; Thomas O-ye-bi, Kiowa allottee 616, Lizzie Cat, Kiowa allottee 2771; Winston Cat, born 1908, Kiowa allottee 3310; and Fred Cat, born 1910, Kiowa allottee (unallotted.).

This Will is made subject to the approval of the Secretary of the Interior.

In witness whereof, I Tine-goo-ah (Susie Cat), Kiowa allottee 614 have to this my last Will and Testament, consisting of two sheets of paper, subscribed my name this the 17th day of January, 1920.

Tine-goo-ah   her (thumb print) mark

Witnesses:
   Chas. B. Ellard
P.O. Anadarko, OK

   Susin[sic] *C. Peters*

NATIVE AMERICAN WILLS and PROBATE RECORDS, 1911 - 1921

P.O. Anadarko, OK

Subscribed by Tine-goo-ah (Susie Cat), Kiowa allottee 614, in the presence of each of us the undersigned, and at the same time declared by her to be her last will and testament, and we thereupon, at the request of Tine-goo-ah, in her presence and in the presence of each other, sign our names hereto as Witnesses, this the 17th day of January, 1920.

Chas. B. Ellard
P.O. Anadarko, OK
Susin C. Peters
P.O. Anadarko, OK

DEPARTMENT OF THE INTERIOR, Office of Indian Affairs   Jul 20, 1921

It is hereby recommended that the within will of Tine-goo-ah, deceased Kiowa allottee, #614, be approved in accordance with the provisions of the Act of June 15, 1910, (36 Stat. L, 855-6) as amended by the Act of February 14, 1913, (37 Stat. L, 678).

Respectfully,
E.B. Meritt
Assistant Commissioner

DEPARTMENT OF THE INTERIOR, Office of the Secretary   Jul 20, 1921

The within will of Tine-goo-ah, decease Kiowa allottee, #614, is hereby approved in accordance with the provisions of the Act of June 25, 1910, (36 Stat. L, 855-6) as amended by the Act of February 14, 1913, (37 Stat. L, 678).

F.M. Goodwin
Assistant Secretary

INTERPRETER'S CERTIFICATE

I, *Edward Poolaw,* hereby certify that I acted as interpreter during the execution of the foregoing last Will and Testament by Tine-goo-ah, (Susie Cat), Kiowa allottee 614, and that I interpreted fully and correctly all the terms and contents of said Will to her before she executed the same and that the devises therein contained meet with her full approval. I further certify that I have no interest in the matter whatsoever and that she is not related to me so far as I know and I personally know that said Will was drawn strictly in accordance with her desires and directions.

I further certify that I speak both the Kiowa Indian as well as the English languages.
Signed this 17th day of Jan, 1920.

Edward Poolaw
Interpreter

NATIVE AMERICAN WILLS and PROBATE RECORDS, 1911 - 1921

(NOTE: The following will was very difficult to read, the print was not dark enough. The legible print is given below.)
Triplicate

OFFICE OF INDIAN AFFAIRS
RECEIVED
MAR 25. 1916

THOMAS KILLS IN WINTER, aged 60 years, Oglala Sioux allottee 1458.
N ½ of Sec. ? & N ½ of Sec. 9 in T39N of R40W of the 6th Principal Meridian, South Dakota, containing 640 acres. Also all of the allotment of Benjamin Kills In Winter, deceased, to which I am the sole heir, described as E ½ of ? and E ½ of SW ¼ of Sec. ?, ?, ?. Heirship 132611-13 EAU". . . NW ¼ of Sec. 8 to my daughter Nancy Black Bear, aged 18 years. The NE ¼ of Sec. 8 to my daughter Lizzie Walks Fast, aged 28, and the N ½ of Sec. 9 to go to my wife Iron-cedar during her life and at her death to be divided equally between my daughters Nancy and Lizzie and my niece Lizzie Thompson. . . to be divided equally between my daughters Nancy Black Bear and Lizzie Walks Fast, which at this time consists of the allotment of Benjamin Kills In Winter. *Thomas Kills In Winter* his (thumb print) mark

Judson Shook
P.O. Address: Kyle, SD
Occupation: Farmer
Jacob White Eyes
P.O. Address: Kyle, SD
Occupation: Asst. Farmer

Pine Ridge, South Dakota
6-20-1921

    I hereby certify that I have fully inquired into the mental competency of the Indian the circumstances attending the execution of the will, the influence that may have induced the execution, and the names of the entitled to share in the estate under the law of decent in South Dakota; reasons for the disposition of the (____) proposed by the will, differing from by operation of law.
    I respectfully forward this will with the recommendation that it be approved.

H.M. Tidwell
Supt. & Spl. Disb. Agent

Probate 52009-21 V L D
DEPARTMENT OF THE INTERIOR, Office of Indian Affairs   Jul 26, 1921
    It is hereby recommended that the within will of Thomas Kills In Winter, deceased Oglala Sioux allottee #1458, be approved in accordance with the provisions of the Act of June 25, 1910, (36 Stat, Km 855-6) as amended by the Act of February 14, 1913 (37 Stat. 678).

Respectfully,
E.B. Meritt

NATIVE AMERICAN WILLS and PROBATE RECORDS, 1911 - 1921

Assistant Secretary

DEPARTMENT OF THE INTERIOR, Office of the Secretary Jul 26, 1921
The within will of Thomas Kills In Winter, deceased Oglala Sioux allottee #1458, is hereby approved in accordance with the provisions of the Act of June 25, 1910, (36 Stat. L, 855-6) as amended by the Act of February 14, 1913 (37 Stat. L, 678).

F.M. Goodwin
Assistant Secretary

LAST WILL AND TESTAMENT
of
Little Killer or Ciquwicakte

IN THE NAME OF GOD, Amen.

I, **LITTLE KILLER** or **CIQUWICAKTE** of Wakpala, SD, being of sound mind, memory and understanding, do hereby make and publish this my last will and testament, hereby revoking and annulling all wills by me heretofore made, in manner and form following, that is to say:

First: I direct that all my just debts and funeral expenses and expenses of my last illness shall be paid by my executor hereinafter named as soon after my decease as convenient.

Second: I give, devise and bequeath to:

Mrs. Wm Skinner, SW ¼ 34-29-28m cream color gelding, black gelding, white legs, brindle cow

Gus Rawhide, SW ¼ 3-19-28, cream color gelding, buckskin gelding, roan gelding, bay white faced gelding, bob sled, spring buggy, one roan cow, red-white face cow, yearling steer

Kate Looking Back, NW ¼ 3-19-28 and buildings, sorrel mare with colt and yearling, gray mare, sorrel gelding, white face heifer cow

Leo Bird Horse, 2 sorrel geldings, dark bay mare, smaller roan cow, new wagon, new set harness

Mrs. Louisa Fox, one gray gelding, one bay mare, one oregan color gelding, black cow and calf

Willie Bird Horse, bay gelding and white face yearling steer

Sophie Red Hawk, buckskin mare, white faced steer

Cecelia Skinner, gray mare and 2 year brindle cow

Genevieve Skinner, buckskin gelding with black mane, yearling steer

Robert Bird Horse, ? year old steer

NE ¼ 28-19-28 to be sold and proceeds divided equally with above heirs
$1700 to be divided equally (after expenses are paid) between heirs

Third: All the rest and residue of my estate, both real and personal and mixed, I give, devise and bequeath to my lawful heirs as determined after my decease.

NATIVE AMERICAN WILLS and PROBATE RECORDS, 1911 - 1921

And, I do hereby nominate, constitute and appoint Jas. B. Ketch, supr, executor of this my last will and testament.

In Testimony Whereof, I have set my hand and seal to this, my last will and testament, at Wakpala, SD, this 11th day of March, in the year of our Lord, 1921

And lastly, I hereby request S. W. Sevenson to sign my name to this my last will and testament and witness the same.

Little Killer or Ciquwicakte his (thumb print) mark
[Testator or Testratrix]

Signed, sealed, published and declared by said Little Killer or Ciquwicakte in our presence as and for his last will and testament, and at his request and in our presence, and in the presence of each other, we have hereunto subscribed our names as attesting witnesses thereto.

George Gabe of *Wakpala, SD*
Harry Loves War of *Wakpala, SD*
S.W. Sevenson of *Wakpala, SD*

Probate 52315-21 V L D
DEPARTMENT OF THE INTERIOR, Office of Indian Affairs Jul 27, 1921

It is hereby recommended that the within will of Little Killer or Hobart Bird Horse, deceased, Standing Rock allottee #264, be approved in accordance with the provisions of the Act of June 25, 1912, (36 Stat. L, 855-6) as amended by the Act of February 14, 1913, (37 Stat. L, 678).

Respectfully,
E.B. Meritt
Assistant Commissioner

DEPARTMENT OF THE INTERIOR, Office of the Secretary Jul 28, 1921

The within will of Little Killer or Hobart Bird Horse, deceased, Standing Rock allottee #264, is hereby approved in accordance with the provisions of the act of June 25, 1910, (36 Stat. L, 855-6) as amended by the Act of February 14, 1913, (37 Stat. L, 678).

F.M. Goodwin
Assistant Secretary

OFFICE OF INDIAN AFFAIRS
RECEIVED
FEB 12, 1921
12260

IN THE NAME OF GOD, Amen

I, **THOMAS EAGLE** of Alto Township in the County of Roberts and State of South Dakota, being of sound mind and memory, and considering the uncertainty of this frail and transitory life, do therefore make, ordain, publish and declare this to be my last Will and Testament.

First, I order and direct that my executor hereinafter named, pay all my just debts and funeral expenses as soon after my decease as conveniently may be.

NATIVE AMERICAN WILLS and PROBATE RECORDS, 1911 - 1921

Second, After the payment of said funeral expenses and debts, I give, devise, and bequeath to my daughter, Eunice Eagle, the SW ¼ of the NE ¼ of Sec. 29, T124N, R51W of the 5th Principal Meridian, containing 40 acres, also 1/3 interest in my house located on the above described land and 1/3 interest in all of my inherited land.

To my daughter, Sarah White, all of my individual bank account or any money that may be due at the Sisseton Indian Agency, also 1/3 interest in my house located on the above described land and 1/3 interest in all of my inherited land, also one horse (brown gelding).

To my daughter, Cecelia Bluedog, I bequeath 1/3 interest in the house above described and located on the above described land, also one single seated buggy, one set of single harness and also 1/3 interest in all of my inherited lands.

Lastly, I make, constitute and appoint (blank) to be Execut(or) of this my Last Will and Testament, hereby revoking all former wills by me made.

IN TESTIMONY WHEREOF, I have hereunto subscribed my name and affixed my seal, the (blank) day of (blank) in the year of our Lord, 19??.

(His mark) (thumb print)

THIS INSTRUMENT was, on the day of the date thereof, signed, published and declared by the said Testat (blank) to be h(is) Last Will and Testament in our presence who, at h(is) request, have subscribed our names thereto as witnesses in h(is) presence and in the presence of each other.

J.H. Tourtillott   residing at (blank)
Charles F. Ensign, M.D.   residing at (blank)

DEPARTMENT OF THE INTERIOR, Office of Indian Affairs   Jul 20, 1921

It is hereby recommended that the within will of Thomas Eagle, deceased Sisseton allottee #252, be approved in accordance with the provisions of the Act of June 25, 1910, (36 Stat. L, 855-60) as amended by the Act of February 14, 1913, (37 Stat. L, 678) and the Regulations of the Department.

Respectfully,
E.B. Meritt
Assistant Commissioner

DEPARTMENT OF THE INTERIOR, Office of the Secretary   Jul 26, 1921

The within will of Thomas Eagle, deceased Sisseton allottee #252, is hereby approved in accordance with the provisions of the Act of June 25, 1910 (36 Stat. L, 855-6) as amended by the Act of February 14, 1913 (37 Stat. L, 678) and the Regulations of the Department.

F.M. Goodwin
Assistant Secretary

<<<<<<<>>>>>>>

LAST WILL AND TESTAMENT OF SHEH-TAHS

NATIVE AMERICAN WILLS and PROBATE RECORDS, 1911 - 1921

I, SHEH-TAHS, of Jackson County, Kansas, and a member of the Prairie Band of Indians of the Pottawatomi Tribe, being of sound and disposing mind and memory, and realizing the uncertainty of life and the certainty of death, do hereby make, publish and declare this to be my last will and testament, hereby revoking any and all former wills by me at any time made.

Item I. It is my wish that all of my just debts be paid, as soon as convenient after my death, out of any personal property which I may have on hand at the time of my death, and if I have no personal property on hand or at the Indian Office which belongs to me, then I direct that such debts be paid by my children who are then living, in equal shares, and the same be made a lien upon the real estate hereinafter devised to them.

Item II: It is my wish and will that my son, Harry Witch-e-wah, shall have the SW ¼ of the SW ¼ of Sec. 13 all in T8, R14 in Jackson Co, Kansas.

Item III: It is my wish and will that my daughter, Gertie Mag-quat, or Num-kum-go-quah, shall have the S ½ of the NE ¼ of Sec. 15, T8, R14, in Jackson Co, Kansas.

Item IV: It is my wish that my daughter, Lucy Daugherty, shall have the S ½ of the SE ¼, R14, in Jackson Co, Kansas.

Item V: In case of the death of my son Harry prior to my death, then and in that event it is my wish and will that the land above devised to him shall pass to and be the property of his daughter, Mary Witch-e-wah.

Item VI: In case of the death of my daughter, Gertie, prior to my death, then and in that event, it is my wish and will that the land above devised to her shall pass to and be the property of the then living children of my said daughter, Gertie.

Item VII: In case of the death of my daughter, Lucy, prior to my death then and in that event it is my wish and will that the land above devised to her shall pass to and be the property of the then living children of my said daughter, Lucy.

IN WITNESS WHEREOF, I have hereunto set my hand in the presence of the attesting witnesses hereto who at my request are to sign this will as attesting witnesses.

Sheh-tahs her [+] mark
E.D. Woodburn Witness to her mark

We the undersigned, hereby certify that we were present at the office of E.D. Woodburn, on the 25th day of January, 1917, and saw Sheh-tahs sign the foregoing instrument of writing and heard her declare the same to be her last will and testament and we, at her request, in her presence, and in the presence of each other sign our names hereto as attesting witnesses thereto.
Witness our hands this 25th day of January, A.D. 1917.

Lillian Woodburn
S.F. Black

OFFICE OF INDIAN AFFAIRS
RECEIVED
MAR 24, 1921
23752

DEPARTMENT OF THE INTERIOR, Office of Indian Affairs   Jul 18, 1921

NATIVE AMERICAN WILLS and PROBATE RECORDS, 1911 - 1921

It is recommended that departmental approval of the will of Sheh-tahs or Maggie Witch-e-wah, deceased Potawatomi allottee #246, approved January 20, 1915, (L.H: 116417-14) be vacated and the instrument dated January 27, 1917, herein be approved as the last will and testament of this allottee.

            E.B. Meritt
            Assistant Commissioner

DEPARTMENT OF THE INTERIOR, Office of the Secretary Jul 26, 1921

 The departmental approval dated January 20, 1915, of the will of Sheh-tahs or Maggie Witch-e-wah, deceased Potawatomi allottee #246, is hereby vacated and the instrument dated January 27, 1917, purporting to be the last will of the decedent, is approved in accordance with the Act of February 14, 1913, (37 Stat. L, 678), and the regulations of the Department.

            F.M. Goodwin
            Assistant Secretary

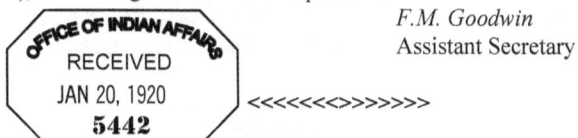

BE IT REMEMBERED THAT I, **CHARLES MOCCASIN**, Cheyenne River Sioux allottee #830, aged 61 years, being of sound and disposing mind and memory, do hereby publish, make and declare this as and for my last Will and Testament, hereby revoking all other Wills or Codicil heretofore by me made.

 FIRST: I hereby give, devise and bequeath to my wife, Mrs. Nellie Moccasin, all of the personal property of which I may be possessed at the time of my death.

 SECOND: I hereby give, devise and bequeath to my said wife, Mrs. Nellie Moccasin, all my estate described as follows:

  My own allotment, #830, described as the E ½ of Sec. 15, W 320 acres of Lot 2, Sec. 14, T14N, R31E of the Black Hills Meridian, containing 655.25 acres.

  Allotment #831, allotted to Eugene Moccasin, described as the NW ¼ of Sec. 15, T14N, R31E of the Black Hills Meridian, containing 160 acres.

  To this estate I was determined to be the sole heir by the Secretary of the Interior under date of October 14, 1914, (L.H. 97204-14)

  An undivided ½ interest in allotment #832, originally allotted to Isaac Moccasin, described as the SW ¼ of Sec. 15, T14N, R31E of the Black Hills Meridian, containing 160 acres.

  To ½ of this estate I was determined an heir under date of April 10, 1917. (L.H. 21638-17)

 IN WITNESS WHEREOF, I have hereunto put my thumb mark and seal this 5th day of May, 1919, at Cheyenne Agency, South Dakota, in the presence of two attesting witnesses.

Witnesses:
 Harry F.C. Woods   *Charles Moccasin* His (thumb print) mark
 W. C. Randolph

NATIVE AMERICAN WILLS and PROBATE RECORDS, 1911 - 1921

Probate M H W 5-31 AD 1921
DEPARTMENT OF THE INTERIOR, Office of Indian Affairs Jul 26, 1921
It is hereby recommended that the within will of Charles Moccasin, Cheyenne River Sioux allottee #830, be approved according to the Act of June 25, 1910, (36 Stats. L, 855-6), as amended by the Act of February 14, 1913, (37 Stats. L, 678).

Respectfully,
E.B. Meritt
Assistant Commissioner

DEPARTMENT OF THE INTERIOR, Office of the Secretary Jul 26, 1921
The within will of Charles Moccasin, Cheyenne River Sioux allottee #830, is hereby approved according to the Act of June 25, 1910, (36 Stats. L, 855-6), as amended by the Act of February 14, 1913, (37 Stats. L, 678), and the Regulations of the Department.

F.M. Goodwin
Assistant Secretary

SIGNED, SEALED, PUBLISHED AND DECLARED AS AND for his last Will and Testament by the said Charles Moccasin, and at his request and in his presence, and in the presence of each other we have hereunto subscribed our names as attesting witnesses this day and year first above mentioned. The testator's name was subscribed by Harry F.C. Woods who has signed as a witness to the thumb mark signature and also as an attesting witness.

Harry F. C. Woods	W. C. Randolph
Cheyenne Agency, SD	Cheyenne Agency, SD

LAST WILL AND TESTAMENT OF REBECCA PHILBRICK (BLUESTONE) UNALLOTTED LOWER YANKTONAI SIOUX INDIAN.

------ 0 ------

IN THE NAME OF GOD, Amen:

I, **REBECCA PHILBRICK**, 65 years of age, an unallotted Lower Yanktonai Sioux woman, residing on the Crow Creek Reservation, in the state of South Dakota, being of sound mind, memory and understanding, hereby make and publish this my last Will and Testament, hereby revoking and annulling all Will by me heretofore made, that is to say:

FIRST: I direct that all my just debts and funeral expenses and the expenses of my last illness shall be paid as soon after my decease as shall be convenient.

SECOND: I have no allotment or other lands to which I am heir on this reservation, but I have personal property in the form of money on deposit to my

NATIVE AMERICAN WILLS and PROBATE RECORDS, 1911 - 1921

credit in the office of the Superintendent of the Crow Creek Reservation amounting to $1771.82, and an interest in the sale of the allotment of my deceased son Charley Philbrick, Allottee #28, said sale having as yet not been approved by the Department, amounting to $567.00, of these amounts, I give, devise and bequeath to the following named persons, to wit:

To my three grandchildren, Elvirah, Adah Irene and Robert G. Philbrick, 14, 10 and 8 years of age, respectively, I give, devise and bequeath $100.00 each, said money to be deposited to their credit by the Superintendent of the Crow Creek agency and to be paid to them by him for their benefit.

To Rebecca Philbrick, my granddaughter, and daughter of my son Ernest Philbrick, 7 years of age, I give, devise and bequeath the sum of $600.00, said amount to be expended for her benefit in the erection of a house on her allotment as she has no home and it is my desire that she has a home when she grows up, also $100.00 to be deposited by the Superintendent of the Crow Creek agency for her use to her credit and under his supervision.

To my granddaughter, Edith Philbrick, daughter if my son Ernest Philbrick, 4 years of age, I give, devise and bequeath the sum of $100.00, said amount to be deposited to her credit by the Superintendent of the Crow Creek agency, and expended by him for her benefit.

To my granddaughter, Annie Philbrick, daughter of my son Ernest Philbrick, 2 years of age, I give, devise and bequeath the sum of $100.00, said amount to be deposited to her credit by the Superintendent of the Crow Creek agency, and expended by him for her benefit.

The balance of the money which I now have on deposit and of which I may be possessed of after my decease, I give, devise and bequeath to my daughters Mrs. James Rencountre, of the Lower Brule Reservation and Mrs. Mary Like Him of this reservation, said money to be divided between them in equal shares.

To my son Ernest Philbrick, I give, devise and bequeath my entire subscription in Liberty Bonds, amounting to $200.00, also my three head of horses, wagon and harness.

All of my other property, both real and personal and not mentioned herein, which I now or may hereafter be possessed of, I desire to be distributed equally between my two above named daughters and my only living son Ernest Philbrick.

AND LASTLY: I am satisfied that the officers of the Department of the Interior of the United States will make proper provision for carrying into affect of this my last will and testament, and therefore, I have not appointed an executor to administer my estate.

IN WITNESS WHEREOF: I have set my hand and seal to this my last Will and Testament at the Crow Creek agency hospital located on the Crow Creek Reservation in the state of South Dakota, this 17th day of December, 1919.

REBECCA PHILBRICK   Her (thumb print) Mark

Witness to Mark.

Dinah Rencountre   Clerk, Crow Creek, SD
Robert E. Philbrick   Crow Creek, SD

NATIVE AMERICAN WILLS and PROBATE RECORDS, 1911 - 1921

Signed, sealed, published and declared by the said Rebecca Philbrick, in our presence, as and for her last Will and Testament, and at her request and in her presence and in the presence of each other, we have hereunto subscribed our names as attesting witnesses thereto.

Charles M. Baid
Peter W. Lightfoot
All of Ft. Thompson, S. Dak.

Probate 108174-19 41747-21   J M P
DEPARTMENT OF THE INTERIOR, Office of Indian Affairs   Jul 12, 1921
The within will of Rebecca Philbrick or Mrs. Adam Bluestone, deceased unallotted Indian or the Crow Creek Tribe is hereby recommended for approval under the Act of June 25, 1910 (36 Stat. L, 855-6) as amended by the Act of February 14, 1913 (37 Stat. L, 678).

Respectfully,
E.B. Meritt
Assistant Commissioner

DEPARTMENT OF THE INTERIOR, Office of the Secretary   Jul 18, 1921
The within will of Rebecca Philbrick or Mrs. Adam Bluestone, deceased unallotted Indian of the Crow Creek Tribe is hereby approved under the Act of June 25. 1910, (36 Stat. L, 855-6) as amended by the Act of February 14, 1913 (37 Stat. L, 678)

F.M. Goodwin
Assistant Secretary

<<<<<<<<>>>>>>>
Arapahoe, Wyoming
March 22, ~~1919~~ 1920

I, **EAGLE HEAD**, aged 73 years, being a member of the Northern Arapahoe tribe, living at Arapahoe, Shoshone Agency, Fremont County, Wyoming, do hereby give, devise and bequeath unto my lawful son, John Head, aged 46 years the following property:
1. One half of SE ¼, NE ¼ and NE ¼, SE ¼ Sec. 10, T1S, R2E. W.R.M. WY, being 80 acres of the allotment of Belva Head, deceased, my lawful wife.
2. One log house on the allotment of my own, being
3. All of my remaining allotment held under trust, it being as follows: NW ¼, SE ¼, Sec. 10, T1S, R2E, W.R.M. WY, containing 40 acres.
I am aware that my lawful wife, Winnie I. Head, according to the laws of the state of Wyoming is entitled to one-half of my property but whereas said Winnie I. Head has deserted me for the last three years and has refused to live with me and whereas my lawful son, John Head, has supported me and taken care of me for one whole year. Now therefore do I give, devise and bequeath all of my property to my son, John Head, as I described and stated above.

NATIVE AMERICAN WILLS and PROBATE RECORDS, 1911 - 1921

Arapahoe. Wyoming   signed: *Eagle Head* His (thumb print) mark
March 22, 1920
Witnesses: A.J. Keel
           W.C. Hopkins
           Moses L. Friday
               Interpreter

Probate 52276-21 V L D
DEPARTMENT OF THE INTERIOR, Office of Indian Affairs   Aug. 2, 1921
     The within will of Eagle Head is hereby recommended for approval in accordance with the Act of June 25, 1910, (36 Stat. L, 855-6), and the Act of Feb. 14, 1913 (37 Stat. L, 678).

                               Respectfully,
                               E. B. Meritt
                               Assistant Commissioners

DEPARTMENT OF THE INTERIOR, Office of the Secretary   Aug. 2, 1921
     The within will is hereby approved in accordance with the Act of June 25, 1910 (36 Stat L, 855-6), and the Act of Feb. 14, 1913 (37 Stat. L, 678).

                               F.M. Goodwin
                               Assistant Secretary

<<<<<<<>>>>>>

LAST WILL AND TESTAMENT OF
Mrs. Carlo French or Wehunkaw Wilkinson

     I, **MRS. CARLO FRENCH** or **WEHUNKAW WILKINSON**, being of sound mind but very weak in body, and knowing that I may not live very long, do hereby make, declare, and publish this my last will and testament.
     1st. I desire all of my just debts to be paid, including my burial and funeral expenses, out of any funds accruing to my estate.
     2nd. I own land as follows: a 1/3 interest in the SE ¼ of Sec. 32, T27N, R7E of the 6th Principal Meridian, Nebraska, the allotment of my father, David Wilkinson, subject to the dower of my mother.
     3rd. To my daughter, Mary W. French, I give, bequeath, and devise ½ of my undivided 1/3 share of the above described property.
     4th. To my daughters, Frances Little Ox and Mary Little Ox, I give, devise and bequeath the remaining ½ interest that I own in the David Wilkinson allotment as described above, the said Mary Little Ox and Frances Little Ox, to share equally.
     5th. Any other property that I may die possessed of, I wish, divided in the same proportion as above named.
     6th. I desire at my death that my mother, Mrs. David Wilkinson or Mrs. Joseph Longtail to have possession of my children.

NATIVE AMERICAN WILLS and PROBATE RECORDS, 1911 - 1921

Interpreter: Mrs. Carlo French or Her (thumb print) mark
   John Polkey   Wehunkaw Wilkinson

The testator at this time signed her name to the above and foregoing instrument in the presence of the undersigned and at the same time declared it to be her last will and testament, and we at her request and in her presence and in the presence of each other do hereby sign our names hereto as attesting witnesses.

Winnebago, Nebraska   *Narguerite L. Johnson*
October 31, 1919   *Joseph Longtail*

Probate 50792-21 J W H
DEPARTMENT OF THE INTERIOR, Office of Indian Affairs
                                   Aug 1, 1921

    The within will of Mrs. Carlo French or Wehunkaw Wilkinson, deceased unallotted Indian of the Winnebago tribe, is hereby approved pursuant to the provisions of the Act of June 25, 1910, (36 Stat. 855), as amended by the Act of Feb. 14, 1913 (37 Stat. 678).

                                F. M. Goodwin
                                Assistant Secretary

OFFICE OF INDIAN AFFAIRS
RECEIVED
OCT 9, 1917
93949

<<<<<<<<>>>>>>>>

WILL

    IN THE NAME OF GOD, Amen: I, **JAMES MATT**, age 81, an Indian of the Nez Perce Indian Reservation, Idaho, now residing at Sweetwater, Idaho, being of sound mind and disposing memory, and not acting under duress, menace, fraud, or undue influence, of any person whatsoever, do hereby make, publish and declare this my LAST WILL AND TESTAMENT, in the manner following, that is to say:

    First.   I direct that my body be decently buried with proper regard to my station in life, and the circumstances of my estate.

    Second.   I direct that my funeral expenses and expenses of my last illness be paid from any funds belonging to my estate, or in the custody of the Superintendent of the Nez Perce Indian Reservation, Lapwai, Idaho.

    Third.   I will and bequeath to Jeanette Peterson, my granddaughter the allotment of Towti which I inherited under Law-Heirship 80655-15, described as follows: Lots 22, 23, 24, Sec. 35, Lots 17, 18, Sec. 34, T35, R4W, containing 100 acres.

    My own allotment and the balance of my inherited land, I wish to descend to my natural heirs, as determined by the Secretary of the Interior.

    In witness whereof, I have hereunto put my hand and seal this 20th day of Aug, 1917.

OFFICE OF INDIAN AFFAIRS
RECEIVED
JUN 28, 1921
53544

Witnesses: *Corbett B. Sawyer*   *James Matt* his (thumb print) mark
          F. G. Hunter, Clerk

NATIVE AMERICAN WILLS and PROBATE RECORDS, 1911 - 1921

both of Lapwai, ID

The foregoing instrument was on the date hereof signed, sealed, published and declared by said James Matt to be his LAST WILL AND TESTAMENT, in the presence of us, and at h(is) request and in h(is) presence, and in the presence of each other, we have subscribed our names as witnesses on this 20th day of August, 1917

               Corbett B. Sawyer

F.G. Hunter, Clerk
Probate 93949-17 J W H
DEPARTMENT OF THE INTERIOR, Office of Indian Affairs Aug. 1, 1921
  The within will of James Matt, deceased allottee #389, of the Nez Perce tribe, is respectfully recommended for approval, pursuant to the provisions of the Act of June 25, 1910, (36 Stat. 855) as amended by the Act of Feb. 14, 1913, (37 Stat. 678).

            Respectfully,
            E.B. Meritt
            Assistant Commissioner

DEPARTMENT OF THE INTERIOR, Office of the Secretary Aug. 2, 1921
  The within will of James Matt, deceased allottee #389 of the Nez Perce tribe, is hereby approved, pursuant to the provisions of the Act of June 25, 1910, (36 Stat. 855), as amended by the Act of Feb. 14, 1913 (37 Stat. 678).

            F.M. Goodwin
            Assistant Secretary

<<<<<<<>>>>>>

Last Will and Testament)
)
In the Name of God, Amen.)

  I, **WARPEZEWIN,** of Sisseton, in the State of South Dakota and the County of Roberts, being of sound mind, and memory, considering the uncertainties of life, hereby make, ordain, publish and declare this to be my last Will and Testament, hereby revoking any and all wills made by me at any time heretofore.

  First. It is my will and I do order and direct that all my just debts and funeral expenses be paid as soon after my decease as conveniently maybe.

  Second. After payment of such funeral expenses and debts by my legal executor, I give, devise and bequeath to my son, Charles Leaf or Canwapa also known as Itopaktena, the balance of my allotment yet remaining under trust patent, consisting of the 80 acre tract on which I make my home and 40 more located in the hills to the west of it, known as part of allotment #750, the house in which I live, my 2 horses, wagon, binder graindrill and sled, I also give and bequeath to him. I further give, devise and bequeath to my son Charles Leaf all

NATIVE AMERICAN WILLS and PROBATE RECORDS, 1911 - 1921

the rest and residue of my estate both personal and real, which I now possess or which I hereafter may acquire.

In testimony whereto I have hereunto subscribed my name and affixed my seal this 25th day of February, in the year of our Lord, 1919.

Witness to mark: Warpezewin   Her (thumb print) mark
Alan L. Owens
William Seabay

This instrument was on the day of the date thereof, signed, published and declared by the said testator, Warpezewin, to be her Last Will and Testament, in our presence, who at her request, have subscribed our names thereto as witnesses in her presence and in the presence of each other.

      William Seabay   Residing at Sisseton Agency, SD
      Alan L. Owens   Residing at Sisseton Agency, SD

Probate 36663-21 V L D
DEPARTMENT OF THE INTERIOR, Office of Indian Affairs   Aug. 4, 1921

It is hereby recommended that the within will of Warpezewin, deceased Sisseton-Wahpeton allottee #750, be approved in accordance with the provisions of the Act of June 25, 1910 (36 Stat. L, 855-6) as amended by the Act of February 14, 1913, (37 Stat. L, 678).

      Respectfully,
      E.B. Meritt
      Assistant Commissioner

DEPARTMENT OF THE INTERIOR, Office of the Secretary   Aug. 5, 1921

The within will of Warpezewin, deceased Sisseton-Wahpeton allottee #750, is hereby approved in accordance with the provisions of the Act of June 25, 1910 (36 Stat. L, 855-6) as amended by the Act of February 14, 1913 (37 Stat. L, 678).

      F.M. Goodwin
      Assistant Secretary

<<<<<<<>>>>>>

W I L L
IN THE NAME OF GOD, Amen:

OFFICE OF INDIAN AFFAIRS
RECEIVED
(Illegible)
38361

I, **WHITEFEATHER**, Fort Peck allottee #1028, on this 2nd day of March, 1916, being old and infirm of body but of sound mind, realizing the uncertainty of live, and not acting under fraud, menace, duress, or undue influence, do hereby make, publish and declare this to be my last will and testament, hereby revoking all former wills that may have been made by me:
FIRST:

I give, devise and bequeath my grazing land to the following persons in equal shares of 1/5 each: My sons Joshua and George, my daughter Lucy, my

NATIVE AMERICAN WILLS and PROBATE RECORDS, 1911 - 1921

wife Red White feather, and Birdie Benedict who is now Mrs. William Lester. My grazing land is described as the NE/4 & E/2 NW/4 & Lots 1 and 2 in Sec. 19, T28N, R53E, containing 312.10 acres more or less.
Second:
    I give, devise and bequeath unto my three children, viz: Joshua, George and Lucy White feather, my irrigable[sic] and timber allotments described as follows: Irrigable[sic] land, SW/4 of NW/4 of Sec. 5, T29N, R54E, containing 40 acres, more or less. Timber land, W/2 of NE/4 of SW/4 of Sec. 16, T27N, R52E, containing 20 acres, more or less. Said timber and irrigable[sic] land to descend in equal shares of 1/3 each to the above mentions[sic] sons and daughter.
Third:
    I give, devise and bequeath unto my daughter Lucy, my wagon and harness.
Fourth:
    All other property, both real and personal, of which I may die possessed, I give, devise and bequeath unto my wife and children and Mrs. William Lester (Birdie Benedict) in equal shares.
Fifth:
    My reason for bequeathing a portion of my estate to Birdie Benedict who is now Mrs. William Lester, is that both she and her husband have been kind to me and helped me for many years, my wife being a cripple, and it is my wish that she be reimbursed out of my estate.
Sixth:
    I hereby direct that one horse be sold for the purpose of paying my funeral expenses.
Witness:

Burton F. Roth	Poplar, MT	Whitefeather His thumb
Lucy Rattling Thunder	Poplar, MT	

    Lucy Rattling Thunder, Interpreter, Poplar, MT

    We, the undersigned, hereby certify that we were present and witnessed the execution of the foregoing will in two pages and that the said will was signed by the testator in our presence and in the presence of each of us and at the testator's request. Furthermore, we believe the testator was mentally competent to make a will and that the will expresses the testator's desires as to the disposition of his estate. Furthermore, we believe the testator was not acting under fraud, duress, menace of undue influence but that the will is made at his own instance and request. Furthermore, neither of us are in any way related to the testator nor are we interested in any way in his estate or the disposition of the same.

                                                     Burton F. Roth
                                                     Poplar, MT
                                                     Lucy Rattling Thunder
                                                     Poplar, MT

March 2nd, 1916.
DEPARTMENT OF THE INTERIOR
UNITED STATES INDIAN SERVICE

NATIVE AMERICAN WILLS and PROBATE RECORDS, 1911 - 1921

Codicil

I direct that this codicil be made a part of my will as made on the 2nd day of March, 1916.

My wife having died K direct that Circling Eagle, Fort Peck allottee #246 take and five a home to my daughter Lucy, on account of the love & kindness sh[sic] show[sic] and that he be made a beneficiary under this will for 1/5 of my grazing land described as NE/4 & E/2 NW/4 & Lots 1 & 2, Sec. 19, T28N, R53E, containing 312.10 acres more or less.

I further diclose[sic] and publish that Mrs. William Lester give a home to my sons Joshua & George.

I also request that a casket be purchased for my burial and that it be paid for and that my store bills be paid from money derived from the sale of my grazing land.

I further direct that my dead wifes body be removed from where it now lies to the side of where mine is to be placed, ie that is on the same grave and that this be done with the money aforsad[sic] to above

This with my store bill and funeral expenses is to be paid before any division is made.

Burton F. Roth   Poplar, MT   Whitefeather   His (thumb print) mark
Richard Redstone   Poplar, MT

We, the undersigned hereby certify that we were present and witnesses the execution of the foregoing codicil in two pages and that the said codicil was signed by the testator in our presence and in the presence of each of us and at the testator request.

Furthermore, we believe the testator was mentally competent to make this codicil and that the codicil expresses the testator's desires as to the disposition of his estate.

Furthermore, we believe the testator was not acting under fraud, duress, menace or under influence but that the codicil is made at his own instance and request.

Furthermore, neither of us is related to the testator nor are we interested in any way in his estate or the disposition of the same.

June 18, 1917   *Burton F. Roth*   Poplar, MT
                                    Richard Redstone   Poplar, MT
Probate 282-21   J M P
DEPARTMENT OF THE INTERIOR, Office of Indian Affairs   Jul 23, 1921

The within will and codicil of Whitefeather, deceased allottee #1028 of the Yankton Sioux Tribe is hereby recommended for approval under the provisions of the Act of June 25, 1910 (36 Stat. 856) as amended by the Act of February 14, 1913 (37 Stat. L, 678).

Respectfully,
E.B. Meritt
Assistant Commissioner

NATIVE AMERICAN WILLS and PROBATE RECORDS, 1911 - 1921

DEPARTMENT OF THE INTERIOR, Office of the Secretary   Jul 30, 1921
  The within will and codicil of Whitefeather, deceased allottee #1028 of the Yankton Sioux Tribe is hereby approved according to the Act of June 25, 1910 (36 Stat. L, 856) as amended by the Act of February 14, 1913 (37 Stat. L, 678).
F.M. Goodwin
Assistant Secretary

Last Will and Testament of
Charley Brown

  I, **CHARLEY BROWN**, Klamath allottee #11 of the Klamath Indian Reservation, in the County of Klamath, State of Oregon, being of sound mind and memory, and mindful of the uncertainty of life, do hereby make, publish and declare this my last will and testament.
  First: I desire and direct that all my just debts and all expenses incident to my last illness and funeral be paid.
  Second: I give, devise and bequeath to my wife, Kate Brown, all of my allotment described as the SW ¼ of Sec. 19, T31S, R8E, Wm, on the Klamath Indian Reservation, Oregon, and any interest in any real estate of which I may die possessed together with any and all personal property which may belong to me or in which I may have an interest at the time of my death to have and to hold the same to my said wife, Kate Brown, and her heirs forever.
  Third: I hereby revoke all former wills by me made.
  In witness whereof I have hereunto set my hand this 24th day of May, 1918, at my home on the Klamath Reservation, OR
Charley Brown   his (thumb print) mark

  The foregoing instrument consisting of 2 pages was on the date hereof signed, sealed and published as and declared by the testator, Charley Brown, to be his last will and testament, in the presence of us, who at his request and in his presence, and in the presence of each other, have subscribed our names as witnesses hereto.
Emma Wilson
Hennan V. Magmusson

DEPARTMENT OF THE INTERIOR, Office of Indian Affairs   Aug. 4, 1921
  The will of Charley Brown, deceased Klamath allottee #11, is recommended for approval in accordance with the Act of June 25, 1910, (36 Stat. L, 855), as amended by the Act of February 14, 1913 (37 Stat. L, 678), and the regulations of the Department.
Respectfully,
E.B. Meritt
Assistant Commissioner

NATIVE AMERICAN WILLS and PROBATE RECORDS, 1911 - 1921

DEPARTMENT OF THE INTERIOR, Office of the Secretary   Aug 16, 1921

The will of Charley Brown, deceased Klamath allottee #11, is hereby approved in accordance with the Act of June 25, 1913 (36 Stat L, 855) as amended by the Act of February 14, 1913 (37 Stat. L, 678), and the Regulations of the Department.

F.M. Goodwin
Assistant Secretary

WILL

I, **LONG CAT**, aged 68 yrs of Pine Ridge Agency, South Dakota, Oglala Sioux allottee #20, do hereby make and declare this to be my last will and testament, in accordance with Section 2 of the Act of June 25, 1910 (36 Stat 855-858) and Act of February 14, 1913 (Public #381) hereby revoking all former wills made by us.

1. I hereby direct that as soon as possible after my decease, that all my debts, funeral and testamentary expenses be paid out of my personal estate.

2. I give and devise my allotment on the Pine Ridge Reservation, SD, described as follows: Lots 1, 2, 3 & 4 of Sec. 6, T36N, R43W, and N ½ of SE ¼ and N ½ of SW ¼ of Sec. 36, T37N, R43W, of the 6th P.M. in SD, containing 316.22 acres in the following manner: To Elsie Long Cat, my grand-daughter, aged 12 years, Lot 4 of Sec. 6, T36N, R43W, containing 37.45 acres; to Lizzie Womans Dress, my daughter, aged 31 years, the NW ¼ of SW ¼ of Sec. 36, T37N, R43W, containing 40 acres; to Bessie Fast Horse, my daughter, aged 30 years, the NE ¼ of SW ¼ and NW ¼ of SE ¼ of Sec. 36, T37N, R43W, containing 80 acres; and to Ellen Long Cat, my wife, aged 62 years, the NE ¼ of SE ¼ of Sec. 36, T37N, R43W, containing 40 acres.

3. I give and bequeath all of my personal property of whatsoever nature and wheresoever situated unto my wife, Ellen Long Cat, if any property there be.

4. All the rest of my property, real or personal, now possessed or hereafter acquired of whatsoever nature and wheresoever situated, I hereby give and bequeath unto if any property thereby, to my wife, Ellen long Cat.

In witness whereof I have hereunto set my hand
this 26th day of April, 1916.
Long Cat

The above statement was, this 26th day of April, 1916, signed and published by Long Cat as his last will and testament, in the joint presence of the undersigned, the said Long Cat then being of sound and vigorous mind and free from any constraint or compulsion: whereupon we, being without any interest in the matter other than friendship, and being well acquainted with him, but not

NATIVE AMERICAN WILLS and PROBATE RECORDS, 1911 - 1921

members of his family, immediately subscribed our names hereto in the presence of each other and of the said testator, for the purpose of attesting the said will, as he requested us to do. And that I, Long Cat at the testator's request, have written his name in ink, and that he affixed his thumb marks.

                                        Post Office Address.
        Robert H. Stelzner   Pine Ridge, SD
        Wm White Bear   Pine Ridge, SD

Pine Ridge, South Dakota   May 31, 1921

    I hereby certify that I have fully inquired into the mental competency of the Indian signing the above will, the circumstances attending the execution of the will; the influence that may have induced its execution, and the names of those entitled to share in the estate under the law of descent in South Dakota; reasons for the disposition of the property proposed by the will differing from disposition had the property descended by operation of law.

    I respectfully forward this will with the recommendation that it be disapproved for the reasons set forth in the write-up of Examiner E.S. Stewart.

                                              H.M. Tidwell
                                        Supt. & Spl. Disb. Agent

Probate 45995-21 V L D
DEPARTMENT OF THE INTERIOR, Office of Indian Affairs Aug 12, 1921

    The within will of Long Cat is hereby recommended for approval in accordance with the Act of June 25, 1910, (36 Stat. L, 855-6), and the Act of February 14, 1913 (37 Stat. L, 678).

                                              E.B. Meritt
                                        Assistant Commissioner

DEPARTMENT OF THE INTERIOR, Office of the Secretary Aug 13, 1921

    The within will is hereby approved in accordance with the Act of June 25, 1910, (36 Stat. L, 855-6), and the Act of February 14, 1913 (37 Stat. L, 678).

                                              F.M. Goodwin
                                        Assistant Secretary

```
   OFFICE OF INDIAN AFFAIRS
        RECEIVED
        ? 23, 19221
         68530
```
                                <<<<<<<>>>>>>

    I, BILL SOCE, Indian of Lawrence Township, County of Whatcom and State of Washington, being of sound mind and memory, do make, publish and declare this to be my last Will and Testament, to wit:

    First; All my just debts and funeral expenses shall be first duly paid.

    Second; I give and bequeath my farm homestead, certificate #3921, application #7017, for lots numbered 1, 3, and 4, and the E ½ of the NW ¼ of Sec. 17, T39N, R4E, of Willamette Meridian, in Washington, containing 152 75/100 acres, according to the official Plat of the Survey of the said land returned to the General Land Office by the Surveyors General; ½ of the described land to Amy Bill and ½ to Samuel George; and to Mary Antone, one dollar.

NATIVE AMERICAN WILLS and PROBATE RECORDS, 1911 - 1921

Third; I nominate and appoint Allen L. Holstein to be the Executor of this my last Will and Testament; hereby revoking all former wills by me made.
In Witness Whereof I have hereunto set my mark and
seal this 20th day of October, 1916
Bill (X=his mark) Soce

Witnesses: A.L. Holstein
S.G. Mather

Signed, sealed, published and declared as and for his last Will and Testament by the above named testator, in our presence, who have at his request and in his presence and in the presence of each other signed our names as witnesses thereto.

A.L. Holstein,   S.G. Mather
Witnesses

Endorsed filed Mar 7, 1918
Alithea Adams, Clerk   By G.P. Kincaid, Deputy Clerk
Recorded 6 - 223

Probate 41612-19 S H E
DEPARTMENT OF THE INTERIOR, Office of Indian Affairs   Aug. 26, 1921
It is hereby recommended that the within will of Bill Soce, deceased Indian homesteader of the Nooksack Tribe under the jurisdiction of the Tulalip Agency, Washington, be approved according to the provisions of the Act of June 25, 1910, (36 Stat. L, 855), as amended by the Act of February 14, 1913, (37 Stat. L, 678).
Respectfully,
E.B. Meritt
Assistant Commissioner

DEPARTMENT OF THE INTERIOR, Office of the Secretary   Aug. 29, 1921
The within will of Bill Soce, deceased Indian homesteader of the Nooksack Tribe under the jurisdiction of the Tulalip Agency, Washington, is hereby approved according to the Act of June 25, 1910 (36 Stat. L, 855), as amended by the Act of February 14, 1913 (37 Stat. L. 678), and the Regulations of the Department.
F.M. Goodwin
Assistant Secretary

8-AME-17

STATE OF WASHINGTON, COUNTY OF WHATCOM
OFFICE OF THE COUNTY CLERK

I, Geo. M. Cook, County Clerk and Clerk of the Superior Court of the State of Washington, for the County of Whatcom, holding terms at Bellingham, do

NATIVE AMERICAN WILLS and PROBATE RECORDS, 1911 - 1921

hereby certify that I have compared the foregoing with the original Will of Bill Soce.
Cause No. 3515 in the matter of the estate of Bill Soce, an Indian as the same appears of file and of record in my office, and that the same is a true and correct transcript of the said original and of the whole thereof.
Witness my hand and the seal of the said Superior Court affixed this (illegible) day of May, 1919.
        Geo. M. Cook
        County Clerk and Clerk of the Superior Court

<<<<<<<O>>>>>>>

Statement of **RATTLING HOUSE WOMAN**
  Pine Ridge Reservation
  Wanblee, SD
  Feb. 11, 1919

OFFICE OF INDIAN AFFAIRS
RECEIVED
MAY 27, 1920

To whom it may concern,
 I am old and sick all time now most any day I would be gone. Therefore, last word I would say and that I have 320 acres of land and this allotment 160 acres go to my son, Howard Long Beat and other 160 acres go to Oliver Wellard Standing Bear, my grandson, also I gave him two young mares, two head and one head horses, these mares keeping for increase and benefit to the Oliver until his age, and above allotment I mention, government will divided[sic] for only two heirs I mention for it and I have no others nearer[sic] relation.
Witnesses to mark: Rattling House Woman Her (thumb print) mark
 Robert Two Elk
 Samuel Broken Pipe   Pine Ridge Agency, SD
           June 17, 1921

 I hereby certify that I have fully inquired into the mental competency of the Indian signing the above will; the circumstances attending the execution of the will, the influence that may have induced its execution, and the names of those entitled to share in the estate under the law of descent in South Dakota; reasons for the disposition of the property proposed by the will differing from disposition had the property descended by operation of law.
 I respectfully forward this will with the recommendation that it be approved.
         H.M. Tidwell
         Supt. & Spl. Disb. Agent
Exhibit A 746 *Edward S. Stewart*
Probate 52020-21
DEPARTMENT OF THE INTERIOR, Office of Indian Affairs Sep 2, 1921
 The within will of Rattling House Woman is hereby recommended for approval in accordance with the Act of June 25, 1910 (36 Stat. L, 855-6), and the Act of February 14, 1913 (37 Stat. L, 678).
        Respectfully,

NATIVE AMERICAN WILLS and PROBATE RECORDS, 1911 - 1921

E.B. Meritt
Assistant Commissioner
DEPARTMENT OF THE INTERIOR, Office of the Secretary Sep. (?), 1921
The within will is hereby approved in accordance with the Act of June 25, 1910 (36 Stat. L, 855-6), and the Act of February 14, 1913 (37 Stat. L, 678).

F.M. Goodwin
Assistant Secretary

<<<<<<<<>>>>>>>

69144-21

Will.

I, **CREIGHTON YANKTON** of Pine Ridge Agency, South Dakota, Allottee #125, do hereby make and declare this to be my last will and testament in accordance with Section 2 of the Act of June 25, 1910 (36 Stat. 855-858) and Act of February 14, 1913 (Public #381), hereby revoking all former wills made by me.

1: I hereby direct that as soon as possible after my decease that all my debts, funeral and testamentary expenses, be paid out of my personal estate.

2: I give and devise my allotment on the Pine Ridge Reservation, South Dakota, described as follows: all of Sec. 8, T36N, R43W of 6th Principal Meridian, South Dakota, containing 640 acres, in the following manner: NE ¼ to my wife, Jennie, N ½ of NW ¼ to my daughter Helen, the S ½ of NW ¼ to my daughter Grace, the N ½ of SW ¼ to my son Raymond, the S ½ of SW ¼ to my son Albert, the S ½ of SE ¼ to my son Noah and the N ½ of SE ¼ to my daughter Vina.

3: I give and bequeath all of my personal property of whatsoever nature and wheresoever situated unto my wife, to receive all of my personal property after my funeral expenses have been paid out of it.

4: All the rest of my property, real or personal, now possessed or hereafter acquired, of whatsoever nature and wheresoever situated, I hereby give, devise and bequeath unto to my wife, Jennie.

In witness whereof I have hereunto set my hand this 29th day of January, 1918.

Creighton Yankton

The above statement was, this 29th day of January, 1918, signed and published by Creighton Yankton as his last will and testament, in the joint presence of the undersigned, the said Creighton Yankton then being of sound and vigorous mind and free from any constraint or compulsion; whereupon we, being without any interest in the matter other than friendship, and being well acquainted with him, but not members of his family, immediately subscribed our names hereto in the presence of each other and of the said testator, for the purpose of attesting the said will as requested us to do.

Post Office Address

NATIVE AMERICAN WILLS and PROBATE RECORDS, 1911 - 1921

(Signature Illegible)   Manderson, SD
Sam Ladiany   Manderson, SD
Pine Ridge, South Dakota
August 18, 1921

 I hereby certify that I have fully inquired into the mental competency of the Indian signing the above will, the circumstances attending the execution of the will, the influence that may have induced its execution, and the names of those entitled to share in the estate under the law of descent in South Dakota, reasons for the disposition of the property proposed by the will differing from disposition had the property descended by operation of law.
 I respectfully forward this will with the recommendation that it be approved.

H.M. Tidwell
Supt. & Spl. Disb. Agent
OFFICE OF THE INTERIOR, Office of Indian Affairs Sep 2, 1921

E.B. Meritt
Assistant Commissioner

OFFICE OF THE INTERIOR, Office of the Secretary Sep 3, 1921

F.M. Goodwin
Assistant Secretary

LAST WILL AND TESTAMENT

IN THE NAME OF GOD, Amen: I, **CHARLES STEAD**, of (blank) in the County of Todd and State of South Dakota, being of sound mind and memory, and considering the uncertainty of this frail and transitory life, do therefore make, ordain, publish and declare this to be my Last Will and Testament.
 First: I order and direct that my executor hereinafter named, pay all my just debts and funeral expenses as soon after my decease as conveniently may be.
 Second: After the payment of such funeral expenses and debts, I give, devise and bequeath unto Rosa Brave Bird, one span of D gray mares, my little red wagon and one set of harness, & two hundred $200.00 easy.
 Third: I give, devise and bequeath unto Edward Brave Bird, 2 saddle horses, one a buckskin and one bay, both D, and one new man's saddle.
 Fourth: I give, devise and bequeath unto James Stead, my brother, one brown D horse.
 Fifth: I give, devise and bequeath unto Joe Harney, one buckskin D horse.
 Sixth: I give, devise and bequeath unto Russel Running Horse, one mowing machine.
 Seventh: I give, devise and bequeath unto James Claymore, $155.00, due me from George Stills.

NATIVE AMERICAN WILLS and PROBATE RECORDS, 1911 - 1921

Eight: I give, devise and bequeath unto Ines Henry Claymore, which is due me from William Eagle Prunty(?) and wife. (NOTE: No property is mentioned.)

Ninth: The balance of my estate is to be equally divided among my five grand children; Lucy, Douglas, Stephen, Morris and Cherry Walker or Jannis.

Lastly, I make, constitute and appoint the Superintendent of the Rosebud Indian Agency, Executor of this, My Last Will and Testament, hereby revoking all former Wills by me made.

IN TESTIMONY WHEREOF, I have hereunto subscribed my name and affixed my seal, the 17th day of February, in the year of Our Lord, 1921.

Charles Stead   (His thumb print)

THIS INSTRUMENT was, on the day of the date thereof, signed, published and declared by the said testator, Charles Stead, to be his Last Will and Testament, in our presence, who, at his request, have subscribed our names thereto as witnesses, in his presence and in the presence of each other.

W.L. Gardner residing at Wasaso, SD
Glora[sic] A. Gardner residing at Wasaso, SD

OFFICE OF THE INTERIOR, Office of Indian Affairs   Sep. 1, 1921

The within will is recommended for approval under the Act of June 25, 1910 (36 Stat. L, 855) as amended by the Act of February 14, 1913 (37 Stat. L, 678).

Respectfully,
E.B. Meritt
Assistant Commissioner

DEPARTMENT OF THE INTERIOR, Office of the Secretary   Sep. 3, 1921

The within will is hereby approved in accordance with the Act of June 25, 1910 (36 Stat. L, 855-6), and the Act of February 14, 1913 (37 Stat. L, 678).

F.M. Goodwin
Assistant Secretary

<<<<<<<◇>>>>>>>

OFFICE OF INDIAN AFFAIRS
RECEIVED
SEP 11, 1921

Lac Court Oreilles, Wis.   Nov. 1, 1886

I, **WA-JASHK, Sr**, an Indian of the Lac Court[sic] Orielles Reservation, being of sound and disposing mind do hereby make and publish this my last will and testament.

Item First.   I give and bequeath to each of the following of my children, viz: Way-Shay-Wash-ko-gi-jig, O-cuay gun, Kay-kat, Kit-chi-kwe, She-bi-as-i-no-kwe, Min-da-min, one dollar each, to be paid out of my estate.

Item 2nd: I give and bequeath to my son, Saint Baptiste, all the rest and residue of my property of whatsoever, consisting and more especially the E ½ SW ¼ Sec. 21, T39, R8W, containing 80 acres to have and to hold and to be his

NATIVE AMERICAN WILLS and PROBATE RECORDS, 1911 - 1921

own in fee simple. The said property being located on said Reservation in the County of Sawyer and State of Wisconsin.

        John J. Allen)   Wa-Jashk, Sr. Her[sic] X mark.
        Wm. Rusler) Witnesses
        S.G. Wright)

DEPARTMENT OF THE INTERIOR, Office of Indian Affairs   Sep 1, 1921

    It is respectfully recommended that the within certified copy of the will of Wajashk[sic], Sr, Chippewa Indian allottee #114, be laid before the President for approval of the will.

                                          E.B. Meritt
                                          Assist. Commissioner

DEPARTMENT OF THE INTERIOR, Office of the Secretary   Sep 7, 1921

    It is respectfully recommended that the within will of Wajashk, Sr, be approved.

                                          E.B. Finney
                                          Acting Secretary

The White House
September 9, 1921
The within will of Wajashk, Sr, is approved.
                                        Monroe G. Hamine

    DEPT. OF THE INTERIOR
    ☆ Rec'd. SEP 10, 1921 ☆
          To Indian Office

STATE OF WISCONSIN.   )
Sawyer County   )

    BE IT REMEMBERED, That on the 10th day of August, A.D, 1921, at the city of Hayward, in said county pursuant to notice duly given, as acquired by law at a Special Term of the County Court of said County, Sophie Hall testified that the subscribing witnesses to the last will and testament of Wa Jashk, Sr, late of Reserve in said county, deceased, hereunto and have all left the state of Wisconsin and their residence is unknown, but that she knows of her own knowledge, having been present at the time said will was signed, that said will was executed in all respects as it purports to be.

    And the proofs having been heard before said County and the Court having thereupon found that said instrument was in all things duly executed as her[sic] last will and testament by the said, Wa Jashk, Sr,

    Thereupon said instrument was by the order and decree of said Court, duly allowed and admitted to probate, as and for the last will and testament of Wa Jashk, Sr, deceased.

NATIVE AMERICAN WILLS and PROBATE RECORDS, 1911 - 1921

        In Testimony Whereof, I have hereunto set my hand and affixed the seal of the County Court of said County, at the court house in the city of Hayward this 10th day of August
    (Seal)   A.D, 1921

                                    John K. Swenson   County Judge

<<<<<<<<>>>>>>>

Will

Concho, Okla. May 4, 1921

    I, **HARRY HOWLING ELK** (or) **BIG HAWK**, 28 yrs of age, of Cantonment, Okla, Blaine Co, a full blood Cheyenne Indian, being of sound mind, but realizing the uncertainty of life do hereby make, publish and declare this my last will and testament.

1st I request that my daughter, Luella Big Hawk, now 7 years old, live with my mother's sister, Mary Preston, who has no children of her own, and whatever share this daughter of mine gets, I want Mrs. Preston to receive an allowance for the care of my daughter. My other 2 children may live with their mother if they wish.

    I want my land to be divided according to law to my wife and children.

    I owe Sam V. Deer, my cousin, $100.00, which I wish the agent to pay from my tribal funds or my estate after my funeral expenses have been paid.

    In witness whereof I hereunto subscribe my name this 4th day of May, 1921.

                                                    Big Hawk

    The foregoing instrument was subscribed, published and declared by Big Hawk as his last will and testament in our presence and in the presence of each of us and we at the same time and in his presence hereunto subscribe our names as witnesses, this 4th day of May, 1921.

                              Emma Meegan
                              Edith Roe
                              Albert (Illegible last name)
                              J.S. Bommin
                              Concho, OK

Probate 70835-21 J W H
DEPARTMENT OF THE INTERIOR, Office of Indian Affairs   Sep. 13, 1921
    The within will of Harry Howling Elk or Big Hawk, deceased, unallotted Cheyenne Indian, is respectfully recommended for approval, pursuant to the provisions of the Act of June 25, 1910, (36 Stat. 855), as amended by the Act of February 14, 1913, (37 Stat. 678).

                                          Respectfully,
                                          E.B. Meritt
                                          Assistant Commissioner

DEPARTMENT OF THE INTERIOR. Office of the Secretary   Sep 13, 1921

NATIVE AMERICAN WILLS and PROBATE RECORDS, 1911 - 1921

The within will of Harry Howling Elk or Big Hawk is hereby approved, pursuant to the provisions of the Act of June 26, 1910, (36 Stat, 855, as amended by the Act of February 14, 1913, (37 Stat. 678).

F.M. Goodwin
Assistant Secretary

LAST WILL AND TESTAMENT OF GRACE MEAN BEAR SMITH

I, **GRACE MEAN BEAR SMITH**, a member of the Ponca Tribe of Indians, of the County of Kay, State of Oklahoma, being now in poor health but of sufficient strength of body and mind and sensible of the uncertainty of life, and desiring to make disposition of my property and affairs while in sufficient health and strength, do hereby make, publish, and declare the following to be my last will and testament, hereby revoking and cancelling all other or former wills by me at any time made.

(1) I direct the payment of all my just debts and funeral expenses.
(2) I give and devise to my daughter, Irene Smith, all of my title and interest in and to the following described property, to-wit: The W ½ of the SE ¼ of Sec 19, T25, R2E, in Kay County, and Lot #3 in Sec 18, T24N, R4E, in Noble County, OK.
(3) I give and devise to my husband, George Smith, the sum of One Dollar ($1.00).
(4) I hereby appoint and designate Charles E. Norton, sole executor without bond, of this, my last will and testament.

In witness whereof, I, Grace Mean Bear Smith, have to this my last will and testament consisting of one sheet of paper, subscribed my name this 25th day of January, 1919.

Grace M B Smith

Subscribed by Grace Mean Bear Smith in the presence of each of us, the undersigned, and at the same time declared by her to us to be her last will and testament, and we, thereupon at the request of Grace Mean Bear Smith in her presence and in the presence of each other, sign our names hereto as witnesses this 25th day of January, 1919, at residence of Louis Delodge.
WITNESSES:
John C. Newton
Geo. L. Miller

I, George Smith, hereby waive all rights, which I may have under and by the virtues of the statutes of Oklahoma in and to the estate of Grace Mean Bear Smith and consent that the provisions of the will herein above made may stand as therein provided.
WITNESSES: *George Smith*

NATIVE AMERICAN WILLS and PROBATE RECORDS, 1911 - 1921

John C. Newton
Geo L. Miller

State of Oklahoma)
   County of Kay) S.S.

   Before me, John C. Newton, a Notary Public, personally appeared Grace Mean Bear Smith or Grace M.B. Smith, (one and the same person) and George Smith and acknowledged to me, the signing of the within instrument and will, of their own free will and accord for the uses and purposes therein set forth.

John C. Newton

My Commission expires October 21, 1919
Notary Public

Probate 18899-21 JMP
DEPARTMENT OF THE INTERIOR, Office of Indian Affairs Jul 12, 1921
   The within will of Grace Mean Bear Smith, deceased allottee #711 of the Ponca Tribe, is hereby recommended for approval under the Act of June 25, 1910, (36 Stat. L, 856) as amended by the Act of February 14, 1913 (37 Stat. L, 678).

Respectfully,
E.B. Meritt
Assistant Commissioner

DEPARTMENT OF THE INTERIOR, Office in the Secretary Jul 15, 1921
   The within will of Grace Mean Bear Smith, deceased allottee #711 of the Ponca Tribe, is hereby approved under the Act of June 25, 1910 (36 Stat. L. 856) as amended by the Act of February 14, 1913 (37 Stat. L, 678).

F.M. Goodwin
Assistant Secretary

6-PM-28

<<<<<<<>>>>>>>

STATE OF WISCONSIN,)
   Monroe County   ) S.S.

   I, R.A. Richards, County Judge of said county, do hereby certify that the copy hereto annexed has been compared by me with the original Last Will and Testament of Sam Wind Blow now on file and of record in my office, and required by law to be kept in my custody; And that said copy is a true copy thereof.
   IN TESTIMONY WHEREOF, I have hereunto set my hand and affixed the Seal of the County Court, at the City of Sparta, in said county, this 31st day of January, A.D, 1921

R.A. Richards
County Judge

NATIVE AMERICAN WILLS and PROBATE RECORDS, 1911 - 1921

Last Will and Testament of **Wind Blow**

    I direct that my funeral expenses and all my indebtedness shall be paid from my estate. That after this is done the residue thereof shall be disposed of as follows, The real estate to my wife Anna Wind Blow To my daughter Sarah Thunder Cloud I will and bequeath the sum of $1.00) one dollar, and to my daughter Nellie Wind Blow I will and bequeath the sum of one $1.00 dollar all the residue of my estate of what ever nature I will and bequeath to my wife Annie[sic] Wind Blow without reservation.

                                               Made and signed this 13th day of Feb, 1910

Witness to this mark   his
J.F. Hackett   Sam   [thumb print] Wind Blow
Lute White Rabbit   mark

Probate 18691-21 31899-21 C E T
DEPARTMENT OF THE INTERIOR, Office of Indian Affairs May 5, 1921
    The within will (by certified copy) of Sam Windblow, deceased Wisconsin Winnebago homesteader #88, is hereby recommended for approval under the provisions of the Act of June 25, 1910 (36 Stat. L, 855-6) as amended by the Act of February 14, 1913 (36 Stat. L, 678).

                                            Respectfully,
                                           E.B. Meritt
                                           Assistant Commissioner

DEPARTMENT OF THE INTERIOR, Office of the Secretary Jun 23, 1921
    The within will (by certified copy) of Sam Windblow, deceased Wisconsin Winnebago homesteader #88, is hereby approved in accordance with the provisions of the Act of June 25, 1910 (36 Stat. L, 855-6), as amended by the Act of February 14, 1913 (36 Stat. L, 678).

                                           F.M. Goodwin
                                           Assistant Secretary

In the Name of God, Amen

    I, **CHAS. JOHNSON** of Ponsford in the County of Becker and State of MN, being of sound mind and memory and considering the uncertainty of this frail and transitory life, do therefore make, ordain, publish and declare this to be my Last Will and Testament.
    First, I order and direct that my Executors, hereinafter named, pay all my just debts and funeral expenses as soon after my decease as conveniently may be.
    Second, after the payment of such funeral expenses and debts, I will, devise and bequeath to my mother, (Illegible name) or Marie Johnson and my brother,

NATIVE AMERICAN WILLS and PROBATE RECORDS, 1911 - 1921

Jim Johnson, share and share alike in any property both personal and real that may be derived from the sale of land or otherwise. To my wife I leave $1.00. She having left me and refusing to live with me for the past 4 years.

Lastly, I make, constitute and appoint, Jim Johnson and Ke[sic] (Illegible) to be Executor of this my Last Will and Testament, hereby revoking all former wills by me made.

IN TESTIMONY WHEREOF, I have hereunto subscribed my name and affixed my seal the 16th day of March, in the year of our Lord, 19(blank).

THIS INSTRUMENT was, on the day of the date thereof, signed, published and declared by the said Testator to be his Last Will and Testament in our presence; who, at his request, have subscribed our names thereto as witnesses in his presence and in the presence of each other.

Grant A. Nunne residing at Ponsford
Mrs. Susan Burnette residing at Ponsford

Probate 59016-21 C E T
DEPARTMENT OF THE INTERIOR, Office of Indian Affairs   Aug 1, 1921

The within will of Chas. Johnson, dec'd. Leech Lake Pillager Chippewa #0-2574, is hereby recommended for approval in accordance with the provisions of the Act of June 25, 1910 (36 Stat. L, 855-6) as amended by the Act of February 14, 1913 (37 Stat. L, 678).

Respectfully,
E.B. Meritt
Assistant Commissioner

DEPARTMENT OF THE INTERIOR, Office of the Secretary   Aug 4, 1921

The within will of Chas. Johnson, dec'd. Leech Lake Pillager Chippewa allottee #0-2574, is hereby approved in accordance with the provisions of the Act of June 25, 1910 (36 Stat. L, 855-6) as amended by the Act of February 14, 1913 (37 Stat. L. 678).

F.M. Goodwin
Assistant Secretary

Will.

Town of Bayfield, Bayfield, Wis.
Feb. 16, 1916

In the name of God, Amen.

I, **ANDREW JACKSON VANDEVENTER**, of the Town of Bayfield, in the County of Bayfield, and State of Wisconsin, being weak in body, but of sound and perfect memory, blessed be Almighty God for the same, do make and publish this my last will and testament, in manner and form following that is to say:

First: I ordain the payment of all my just debts, especially doctor bills and funeral expenses from my property which will be presently described.

NATIVE AMERICAN WILLS and PROBATE RECORDS, 1911 - 1921

Second; I give and bequeath unto my lawful wife, Mary, known before our marriage as Mary Brisette, from whom I have been separated a little over 19 years, only the sum of one (1) dollar.

Third; I do also give and bequeath unto my eldest son, Edward, only the sum of one (1) dollar.

Fourth; I do also give and bequeath unto my second oldest son, Charles, only the sum of one (1) dollar.

Fifth; I do also give and bequeath unto my youngest son, George, only the sum of one (1) dollar.

Sixth; I do also give and bequeath unto my third oldest son, Joseph, all the rest of my personal and real property namely in the Town of Bayfield, the NW of NW of Sec 21, T50, R5, in all 40 acres, together with house and other buildings on said 40 acres; Then on the Bad River of Odanah Reservation I have a allottment[sic] namely: the E ½ of the SE ¼ of Sec 19, T47N, R2W, of the 4th Principal Meridian in Wisconsin, containing 80 acres, which I do also give and bequeath unto my third oldest son, Joseph.

Seventh; I hereby appoint Mr. Benjamin Vandeventer, my sole executor of this my last will and testament.

Eighth; I hereby revoke all former wills and testaments by me made.

In witness whereof, I have hereunto set my hand and seal this 18th day of February, A.D, 1916.

                        (Seal)   A.J. Vandeventer

Signed, sealed and declared by the above named Andrew Jackson Vandeventer, to be his last will and testament, in the presence of us, who at his request, and in his presence, have subscribed our names as witnesses thereto.

                        Alex Butterfield   Bayfield, Wis.
                        Mike Vandeventer Bayfield, Wis.

STATE OF WISCONSIN - COUNTY COURT FOR BAYFIELD COUNTY.
                At a special Term of the County Court within and for said
                County of Bayfield, begun and held at the Court House, in the
                City of Washburn, on the second Tuesday of July A.D, 1918.
                Present Hon. H.P. Axelberg, County Judge
)
In the Matter of the Will of :
A.J. Vandeventer, Dec'd.   :
)

State of Wisconsin,   )
                    : ss.
  Bayfield County.   )

        Mike Vandeventer, one of the subscribing witnesses, to the instrument propounded as the will of A.J. Vandeventer, dec'd, being produced, sworn and examined by J.J. Fisher, attorney, testified as follows:

NATIVE AMERICAN WILLS and PROBATE RECORDS, 1911 - 1921

I knew A.J. Vandeventer, dec'd, in his lifetime;

The instrument now shown to me, purporting to be his will, was signed by him at the town of Bayfield, in said County on the 18th day of Feb, 1916.

He at the same time, declared said instrument to be his will in my presence;

I and Alex Butterfield were present at the same time, and we severally subscribed our names to the same instrument, as witnesses, in the presence of said A.J. Vandeventer.

The said A.J. Vandeventer was, at the time of signing said instrument, above 21 years of age, and was of sound mind, as I verily believe.

Mike Vandeventer

Sworn in open court and subscribed
before me this 96h day of July, 1918.

H.P. Axelberg, County Judge.

STATE OF WISCONSIN - COUNTY COURT FOR BAYFIELD COUNTY.

At a special Term of the County Court within and for said County of Bayfield, begun and held at the Court House, in the

City of Washburn, on the second Tuesday of July A.D, 1918.

Present Hon. H.P. Axelberg, County Judge

In the Matter of the Will of)
A.J. Vandeventer, Dec'd.)

The matter of hearing the proofs of the instrument propounded by Joseph Vandeventer as the last will and testament of A.J. Vandeventer, dec'd, having come on to be heard at this Term of said Court, and it appearing that due notice of the time and place of such hearing has been duly given as required by the order of the Court herein made on the 27th day of July, A.D, 1916, and continued to this date.

And the said proponent having appeared by John J. Fisher, attorney and Mike Vandeventer subscribing witness to said instrument having been produced, sworn and examined, upon consideration thereof, the Court finds:

That said A.J. Vandeventer died at Town of Bayfield in said County of the 18th day of February, A.D, 1916;

That at the time of his death he was an inhabitant of Town of Bayfield in said County of Bayfield;

That at the time hereinafter mentioned, the said A.J. Vandeventer was of full age and of sound mind;

That on the 18th day of February, A.D, 1916, at the Town of Bayfield, in said County the said instrument was signed by said A.J. Vandeventer.

That said instrument was at the same time duly attested and subscribed by Mike Vandeventer and Alex Butterfield who were competent witnesses thereto, in the presence of said A.J. Vandeventer, who at the same time declared it to be his will;

NATIVE AMERICAN WILLS and PROBATE RECORDS, 1911 - 1921

That said instrument is the last will and testament of said A.J. Vandeventer, dec'd, in all things duly executed.

THEREFORE IT IS ORDERED AND DECREED, that said instrument be allowed and probate thereof granted, as the last will and testament of said A.J. Vandeventer, deceased.

Dated July 9, 1918

By order of the Court,

H.P. Axelberg, County Judge

[Bayfield]
[County Court]
[Seal]

STATE OF WISCONSIN,)
County of Bayfield) $^{S.S.}$

BE IT REMEMBERED, That on the 9th day of July A.D, 1918, at the City of Washburn, in said County, pursuant to notice duly given, as required by law, at a Special Term of the County Court of said County, and Mike Vandeventer, a subscribing witness to the Last Will and Testament of A.J. Vandeventer, late of Town of Bayfield in said County, deceased, hereunto annexed, being produced and duly sworn and examined.

And the proofs having been heard before said Court, and the Court having thereupon found that said instrument was in all things duly executed as the last will and testament by the said A.J. Vandeventer on the 18th day of February, A.D, 1916; that he was then of full age and of sound mind, and that said instrument was duly attested and subscribed in the presence of the testator by the witnesses thereto. Thereupon said instrument was by the order and decree of said Court duly allowed and admitted to probate, as and for the last will and testament of the said A.J. Vandeventer, dec'd.

IN TESTIMONY WHEREOF, I have hereunto set my hand and affixed the seal [Bayfield] of the County Court of said County, at the City of Washburn, this 9th day of July
[County Court] A.D, 1918.
[Seal] H.P. Axelberg, County Judge

Probate 14134-18 C E T
DEPARTMENT OF THE INTERIOR, Office of Indian Affairs Jul 27, 1921
I have the honor to recommend that the certified copy of the will of A.J. Vandeventer, dec'd. allottee #365 of the Chippewa Tribe, be laid before the President for his signature.

Chuck Burber
Commissioner

DEPARTMENT OF THE INTERIOR, Office of the Secretary Jul 30, 1921
I have the honor to recommend that the certified copy of the will of A.J. Vandeventer, dec'd. allottee #365 of the Chippewa Tribe, be approved.

NATIVE AMERICAN WILLS and PROBATE RECORDS, 1911 - 1921

E.B. Finney
Acting Secretary

The White House
  August 9, 1921
Approved:
    Warren G. Harding
Probate Court Bayfield County
H.P. Axelberg, Judge
Washburn, Wisconsin

OFFICE OF INDIAN AFFAIRS
RECEIVED
NOV 26, 1918
94145

STATE OF WISCONSIN,)
  County of Bayfield.) ss   County Court for said County.

      I, H.P. Axelberg, County Judge of said County, DO HEREBY CERTIFY that the copy hereunto annexed has been compared by me with the Original Will, Proof of Will not Contested, Decree Allowing Will, and Certificate of Proof of Will, in the Matter of the Will of A.J. Vandeventer, dec'd, now on file and of record in my office, and required by law to be in my custody; and that said copy is a true copy thereof.
      IN TESTIMONY WHEREOF, I have hereunto set my hand and affixed the seal of the County Court of Bayfield County, at the City of Washburn, in said County this 20th day of September, A.D. 1918.

                                      H.P. Axelberg
                                      County Judge

STATE OF WISCONSIN
COUNTY OF SAWYER

      I, John K. Swenson, County Judge for Sawyer County, Wisconsin, the same being a court of record, do hereby certify, that I have carefully compared the annexed and foregoing will and certificate of probate with the original now on file in my office, and that it is a correct and true copy thereof.
      In witness whereof, I have hereunto set my hand, and affixed the seal of said court this 10th day of Jan, 1919.

OFFICE OF INDIAN AFFAIRS
RECEIVED
MAY 10, 1919
40457

                                      John K. Swenson
                                      County Judge

Feb. 3, 1906
D.E. Jacobs
  Gov't farmer.

NATIVE AMERICAN WILLS and PROBATE RECORDS, 1911 - 1921

I, **VINCENT SHEFF**, Do hereby make will to my brother, John Sheff, to 1/3 of my 80 being the SE ¼ of the SW ¼ of Sec 5, and the NE ¼ of the NW ¼ Sec 8, T39N, R7.

Wm Carufel)   Vincent Sheff
Annie Livingston) Witnesses,
                                 Reserve, Wis. Feb. 3, 1906
D.E. Jacobs, Gov't. farmer

I, **VINCENT SHEFF**, Do hereby make will to my sister, Mrs. Lizzie Sheff Dennis, to 1/3 of my eighty being the SE ¼ of the SW ¼ of Sec 5 and NE ¼ of the NW ¼ of Sec 8, T39N, R7.

Wm. Carufel)   Vincent Sheff
Annie Livingston) Witnesses
                                 Reserve, Wis. Feb. 3, 1906
D.E. Jacobs
   Gov't. farmer.

I, **VINCENT SHEFF**, Do hereby make will to my sister, Mrs. Mary Sheff-Gokey, to 1/3 of my 80, being the SE ¼ of the SW ¼ of Sec 5, and the NE ¼ of the NW ¼ of Sec 8, T39N, R7.

Wm. Carufel)   Vincent Sheff
Annie Livingston) Witnesses

                                 Reserve, Wis.
D.E. Jacobs
   Feb. 3, 1906
   Gov't. farmer.

I, **VINCENT SHEFF**, Do hereby make will to my brother, John Sheff, to 1/3 of my 80 being the SE ¼ of the SW ¼ of Sec 5, and the NE ¼ of the NW ¼ (of) Sec 8, T39N, R7.

Wm Carufel)   Vincent Sheff
Annie Livingston) Witnesses

Certificate of Proof of Will

    STATE OF WISCONSIN) SS
    SAWYER COUNTY)

BE IT REMEMBERED, That on the 26 day of November A.D, 1918, at the Court house in the City of Hayward in said County, pursuant to notice duly given, as required by law, at a special Term of the County Court of said County, Annie Livingston one of the subscribing witnesses to the last will and testament of Vincent Sheff, late, of Reserve, in said County, dec'd, hereunto annexed, produced and duly sworn and examined, stated that at the Town of Reserve,

NATIVE AMERICAN WILLS and PROBATE RECORDS, 1911 - 1921

Sawyer County, Wisconsin, Vincent Sheff signed the annexed will in her presence and in the presence of Wm Carufel, who also signed the will as witness in the presence of the deceased and in the presence of each other. That Vincent Sheff was of sound mind and memory and was over the age of 21 years.

And the proofs having been heard before said Court, and the Court having thereupon found that said instrument was in all things duly executed as his last will and testament by the said Vincent Sheff.

Thereupon said instrument was by the order and decree of said Court duly allowed and admitted to probate, as and for the last will and testament of Vincent Sheff, dec'd.

IN TESTIMONY WHEREOF, I have hereunto set my hand and affixed the seal of the County Court of said County, at Hayward, Wis, this 26 day of Nov, A.D, 1918.

Sgd. John K. Swenson, County Judge

OFFICE OF INDIAN AFFAIRS
RECEIVED
JUN 4, 1921
45994

WILL

I, **MARY COLHOFF**, of Pine Ridge Agency, South Dakota, Allottee #285, do hereby make and declare this to be my last will and testament, in accordance with Section 2 of the Act of June 25, 1910, (36 Stat. 855-858), and Act of February 14, 1913, (Public #381), hereby revoking all former wills made by me:

1. I hereby direct that, as soon as possible after my decease, that all my debts, funeral and testamentary expenses be paid out of my personal estate.
2. I give and devise my allotment on the Pine Ridge Reservation, South Dakota, described as follows:

The Lot 4 of Sec 1; and the Lots 1, 2, 3 and 4 of Sec 2; and the Lot 1 of Sec 3; in T35N or R45W; and the SE/4 of Sec 34 and S/2 of SW/4 of Sec 36, T36N of R45W, 6th P.M, South Dakota, containing 480.59 acres; in the following manner:

To Elizabeth M. Morrison, my daughter, the Lot 4 of Sec 1 and Lot 2 of Sec 2, T35N, R45W, containing 79.48 acres.

To Frederick Colhoff, my son, the Lots 2 and 3 of Sec 2, T35N, R45W, 6th P.M, SD, containing 80.21 acres.

To Louis Colhoff, my son, the Lot 4 of Sec 2 and Lot 1 of Sec 3, T35N, R45W, 6th P.M, SD, containing 80.90 acres.

To William Colhoff, my son, the S/2 of SE/4 of Sec 34, T36N, R45W, 6th P.M, SD, containing 80 acres.

To John R. Colhoff, my son, the N/1 of SE/4 of Sec 34, T36N, R45W, 6th P.M, SD, containing 80 acres.

To George Colhoff, Jr, my son, the S/2 of SW/4 of Sec 36, T36N, R45W, 6th P.M, SD, containing 80 acres.

NATIVE AMERICAN WILLS and PROBATE RECORDS, 1911 - 1921

3. I give and bequeath all of my personal property of whatsoever nature and wheresoever situated unto my natural heirs.

4. All the rest of my property, real or personal, now possessed or hereafter acquired of whatsoever nature and wheresoever situated, I hereby give, devise and bequeath unto my natural heirs.

In witness whereof I have hereunto set my hand this 3rd day of February, 1917.

Mary Colhoff her (thumb print) mark

The above statement was, this 3rd day of February, 1917, signed and published by Mary Colhoff as her last will and testament, in the joint presence of the undersigned, the said Mary Colhoff then being of sound and vigorous mind and free from any constraint or compulsion; whereupon we, being without any interest in the matter other than friendship, and being well acquainted with her but not members of her family, immediately subscribed our names hereto in the presence of each other and of the said testator, for the purpose of attesting the said will, as she requested us to do. And that I, O. C. Ross, at the testatrix's request, have written her name in ink, and that she affixed her thumb-marks.

Post Office Address
O,C. Ross   Pine Ridge, SD
Robert H. Stelzner   Pine Ridge, SD
Pine Ridge, South Dakota

May 31, 1921

I hereby certify that I have fully inquired into the mental competency of the Indian signing the above will, the circumstances attending the execution of the will, the influence that may have induced its execution, and the names of those entitled to share in the estate under the law of descent in South Dakota; reasons for the disposition of the property proposed by the will, differing from disposition had the property descended by operation of law.

I respectfully forward this will with the recommendation that it be disapproved. I concur in the write-up of examiner E.S. Stewart.

H.M. Tidwell
Supt & Spl. Disb. Agent

Probate 45994-21

DEPARTMENT OF THE INTERIOR, Office of Indian Affairs Jun 29, 1921

The within will of Mary Colhoff is hereby recommended for approval in accordance with the Act of June 25, 1910 (36 Stat. L, 855-6), as amended by the Act of February 14, 1913, (37 Stat. L, 678).

Respectfully,
E.B. Meritt
Assistant Commissioner

DEPARTMENT OF THE INTERIOR, Office of the Secretary Jun 30, 1921

NATIVE AMERICAN WILLS and PROBATE RECORDS, 1911 - 1921

The within will is hereby approved in accordance with the Act of June 25, 1910 (36 Stat. L, 855-6), as amended by the Act of Feb. 14, 1913 (37 Stat. L, 678).

F.M. Goodwin
Assistant Secretary

<<<<<<<<>>>>>>>>

I, **NELSON HENAULT**, of Family, Teton County, State of Montana, being of sound mind and memory, do make, publish and declare this my last will and testament, hereby revoking all former wills, bequests and devises by me made.
First. It is my will that all of my just debts, funeral expenses and all other charges be paid out of my personal property.
Second. I give, devise and bequeath to my wife, Mary Henault, all my real estate of every kind and nature that I may die seized of and also all my personal property that I may die seized of excepting those certain horses, cows and saddle that I hereinafter bequeath in this my last will and testament.
Third. I give, devise and bequeath to my brother, Steve Henault, of Family, Montana; one gray work horse (mare) branded (brand drawn) right hip, also one bay saddle horse, branded (brand drawn) left shoulder.
Fourth. I give, devise and bequeath to my sister, Carrie Henault, one Jersey milk cow branded (brand drawn) right hip.
Fifth. I give, devise and bequeath to my brother Mose Henault, one saddle.
Sixth. I give, devise and bequeath to Rose Hamilton, one cow, branded (brand drawn) right hip.
Seventh. I give, devise and bequeath to my friend Jesse Romsa, of Family, Montana, all buildings or improvements on my mother's ranch.
Eighth. I hereby constitute and appoint, Jesse Romsa, of Family, MT, executor of this, my last will and testament, and I do hereby empower my said executor to sell a sufficient number of my live stock to my debts and funeral expenses and divide the residue of my estate according to the above provisions by me made
IN WITNESS WHEREOF, I have hereunto set my hand and seal this 19th day of August, A.D, 1918.

Nelson Henault [Seal]

SIGNED, SEALED, PUBLISHED and DECLARED by the said Nelson Henault as and for his last Will and Testament, in the presence of us, who at his request, in his presence and in the presence of each other, have hereunto subscribed our names as attesting witnesses.

M A O Neil of Cut Bank, Montana
John W. Coburn of Cut Bank, Montana

Probate 39446-19 C E T
DEPARTMENT OF THE INTERIOR, Office of Indian Affairs   May 18, 1921

NATIVE AMERICAN WILLS and PROBATE RECORDS, 1911 - 1921

The within will of Nelson Henault, dec'd. Piegan allottee #594, is hereby recommended for approval under the provisions of the Act of June 26, 1910 (36 Stat. L, 855-6) as amended by the Act of February 14, 1913 (37 Stat. L, 678).

> Respectfully,
> *E.B. Meritt*
> Assistant Commissioner

DEPARTMENT OF THE INTERIOR, Office of the Secretary May 27, 1921

The within will of Nelson Henault, dec'd. Piegan allottee #594, is hereby approved in accordance with the provisions of the Act of June 25, 1910 (36 Stat. L, 855-6) as amended by the Act of February 14, 1913 (37 Stat. L, 678).

> *F.M. Goodwin*
> Assistant Secretary

WILL OF VINCENT OLDBEAR

I, **VINCENT OLDBEAR**, of sound mind and sensible of the uncertainty of life and the certainty of death do hereby make the following will of all of my property of every kind and character, as follows:

I give, all my cattle branded "148" on one side, I.D. on the other and all of my horses branded J and my entire improvements on my place on Rosebud, to Dick Whirlwind, age 10 years, son of Mrs. Thomas Whirlwind, and all other property of every kind which I may possess at the time of my death.

I make this gift to my great grandson in consideration of love and affection. I am excluding Thomas Whirlwind, my grandson, from this Will for the reason he has not treated me as he should.

Signed, sealed and delivered this 29th day of January, 1919.

> Vincent Oldbear   His (thumb print) mark

I certify on honor, that I can speak both English and the Cheyenne Indian language and that I have truly interpreted the foregoing Will of Vincent Oldbear.

> *John Russell*
> Interpreter.

Witnesses:

We, the undersigned, certify on honor that we heard Vincent Oldbear make his Will on this date and that we saw him sign same in our presence and in the presence of each other; that we know he fully understood what he was doing and that the foregoing is his true, free and voluntary Will.

> William Yellowrobe   His (thumb print) mark

NATIVE AMERICAN WILLS and PROBATE RECORDS, 1911 - 1921

Rufus Dives Back Wards.

Probate 21228-21 21017-21 M H W
DEPARTMENT OF THE INTERIOR, Office of Indian Affairs   Apr 11, 1921
 It is hereby recommended that the within will of Vincent Oldbear, Tongue River allottee, be approved in accordance with the provisions of the Act of June 25, 1910 (36 Stat. L, 855) as amended by the Act of February 14, 1913 (37 Stat. L. 678).

                Respectfully,
                E.B. Meritt
                Assistant Commissioner

DEPARTMENT OF THE INTERIOR, Office of the Secretary   Apr 14, 1921
 The within will of Vincent Oldbear, dec'd. Tongue River allottee, is hereby approved in accordance with the provisions of the Act of June 25, 1910 (36 Stat. L. 855) as amended by the Act of February 14, 1913 (37 Stat. L. 678).

                S.G. Hopkins
                Assistant Secretary

<<<<<<<>>>>>>>

DEPARTMENT OF THE INTERIOR
UNITED STATES INDIAN SERVICE

<u>LAST WILL AND TESTAMENT OF RED THUNDER.</u>

 Be it remembered, that I, **RED THUNDER (WAKINYANHUTE)**, of Crow Creek, South Dakota, being of sound and disposing mine, memory and understanding and considering the uncertainty of life, do therefore make, publish, and declare this to be my last will and testament in manner and form following, that is to say:
(1) I give and devise to my wife No Name the following described land: the NW/4 of Sec 21, T108N, R71W of the 5th P.M, SD. Containing 160 acres.
(2) And as to all the rest, residue and remainder of my estate, real, personal, or mixed, of whatever nature or kind, or wheresoever situate at the time of my decease, I do hereby give, devise and bequeath, unto my wife No Name. And lastly, I do make, constitute and appoint my wife No Name to be the executrix of this my last will and testament, hereby revoking all former wills and testaments by me at any time heretofore made, and declaring this to be my last will and testament.
In witness whereof, I have hereunto subscribed my name and affixed my seal the 27th day of December, A.D, 1915.
Witnesses to mark:
    O.G. Thomas   Crow Creek, SD   Red Thunder   his (thumb print) mark
    James Riley   Crow Creek, SD

NATIVE AMERICAN WILLS and PROBATE RECORDS, 1911 - 1921

Signed, sealed, published and declared by the testator above named, as and for his last will and testament, in the presence of us, who have hereunto, at his request, subscribed our names in his presence, and in the presence of each other as witness hereto.

          O.G. Thomas Crow Creek, SD
          James Riley Crow Creek, SD

Probate 17537-21 V L D
DEPARTMENT OF THE INTERIOR, Office of Indian Affairs   Apr 7, 1921

  It is hereby recommended that the within will of Red Thunder **[Wakinyanhute]**, dec'd. Crow Creek allottee #103, be approved in accordance with the provisions of the Act of June 25, 1910 (36 Stat L, 855-6) as amended by the Act of February 14, 1913 (37 Stat. L, 678).

          Respectfully,
          E.B. Meritt
          Assistant Commissioner

DEPARTMENT OF THE INTERIOR, Office of the Secretary   Apr 14, 1921

  The within will of Red Thunder **[Wakinyanhute]**, dec'd. Crow Creek allottee #103, is hereby approved in accordance with the provisions of the Act of June 25, 1910 (36 Stat. L, 855-6) as amended by the Act of February 14, 1913 (37 Stat. L, 678).

          S.G. Hopkins
          Assistant Secretary

THE LAST WILL AND TESTAMENT
OF
MRS. GREENCROW.

I, **MRS. GREENCROW**, being of sound mind, sound body and disposing memory, but realizing the uncertainties of life, do hereby make, declare and publish this MY LAST WILL AND TESTAMENT as follows:

1st. To my son, Charles Greencrow, I give, devise and bequeath that portion of my inherited land described as the SW ¼ of the SW ¼ Sec 2, T26N of R9E of the 6th P.M, Nebraska. The same to be his and his heirs forever. In case he should die before me, I desire this property to go to his children in equal shares.

  In the presence of Hugh Hunter and Walking Priest, whom I have requested to witness my signature and of my own free will and accord, I now sign this declaring it to be my last will and testament, we all three signing in the presence of each other.

        Mrs. Greencrow Her (thumb print) mark

Winnebago Agency, NE
October 14, 1916

NATIVE AMERICAN WILLS and PROBATE RECORDS, 1911 - 1921

At the request of Mrs. Greencrow, we Hugh Hunter and Walking Priest, have witnessed the signature of this will by her and certify that we have all signed in the presence of each other.

Interpreter: *Hugh Hunter*

        Hugh Hunter   *Walking Priest*

Probate 25210-21 J W N

DEPARTMENT OF THE INTERIOR, Office of Indian Affairs   Apr 12, 1921

The within will of Mrs. Greencrow, dec'd. unallotted Winnebago Indian, is respectfully recommended for approval, pursuant to the provisions of the Act of June 25, 1910 (36 Stat. 855) as amended by the Act of February 14, 1913 (37 Stat. 678).

                Respectfully,
                E.B. Meritt
                Assistant Commissioner

DEPARTMENT OF THE INTERIOR, Office of the Secretary   Apr 13, 1921

The within will of Mrs. Greencrow, dec'd. unallotted Winnebago Indian hereby approved in accordance with the provisions of the Act of June 24, 1910 (36 Stat. L. 855) as amended by the Act of February 14, 1913 (37 Stat. L, 678).

                S.G. Hopkins
                Assistant Secretary

<<<<<<<◇>>>>>>>

WILL OF BUG

I, **BUG** or (**CHA-BE-SA**), an Arapaho Indian, being of lawful age and of sound and disposing mind, but knowing the uncertainty of life, do hereby make this, my last will and testament, hereby revoking all former wills by me, at any time, made, to-wit:

1st. It is my will and request that all my just debts and obligations be paid.

2nd. I hereby devise and bequeath to my daughter, Cross Killer, and my grandson, Mathew Hail, all of my personal property and real estate, including my allotment, of every kind and nature wherever found or situated, share and share alike.

3rd. It is my will that none of my other legal heirs shall take or inherit any of my personal or real property.

In testimony where of I have hereunto set my hand at Watonga, Oklahoma, on this 28th day of April, A.D, 1920.

            Bug   her (thumb print) mark
                    Testatrix

Witness to mark of Testatrix and person who subscribed Testatrix's name by her direction and at her request:

Witness: *Henry Lincoln*

NATIVE AMERICAN WILLS and PROBATE RECORDS, 1911 - 1921

ATTESTATION

We, the undersigned witnesses to this will, do hereby certify that the said testatrix subscribed the foregoing will by mark in our presence and that at the time of subscribing the same declared to us that the same is her last will and testament and that she requested us to sign the same as witnesses, which we did in her presence and in the presence of each other at Watonga, OK, on this 28th day of April, A.D, 1920

        Henry Lincoln
        Residence: Carlton, OK
        Leslie First
        Residence: Carlton, OK

Probate 25885-21 M H W Cheyenne & Arapaho, OK Approval of will (of) Bug or Cha-be-sa
DEPARTMENT OF THE INTERIOR, Office of Indian Affairs Apr 11, 1921
  It is hereby recommended that the within will of Bug, or Cha-be-sa, dec'd. Arapaho allottee #1064, be approved in accordance with the Act of June 25, 1910 (36 Stat. L. 855-6) as amended by the Act of February 14, 1913 (37 Stat. L, 678).
        Respectfully,
        E.B. Meritt
        Assistant Commissioner

DEPARTMENT OF THE INTERIOR, Office of the Secretary Apr 12, 1921
  The within will of Bug or Cha-be-sa, dec'd. Arapaho allottee #1064, is hereby approved according to the Act of June 25, 1910 (36 Stat. L, 855-6) as amended by the Act of February 14, 1913 (37 Stat. L, 678) and the regulations of the Department.
        S.G. Hopkins
        Assistant Secretary

Exhibit A
    LAST WILL AND TESTAMENT OF EMMA DICKENS:

  I, **EMMA DICKENS**, aged 27, a resident of the Fort Berthold Reservation in North Dakota, and a member of the Grosventres tribe, being of sound mind and disposing memory, do make, declare, and publish this as my last will and testament, hereby revoking and annulling any and all other wills heretofore made by me.
  1st. It is my will that my just debts and the expenses incurred in my last illness and funeral, be paid.
  2nd. I do hereby will, devise and bequeath unto my daughter, Mamie Dickens, aged 8, an undivided 1/3 interest in and to the following described real estate, to-wit: NE ¼ SW ¼ Sec 2, T148N, R91W, 5th P.M. in McLean County,

NATIVE AMERICAN WILLS and PROBATE RECORDS, 1911 - 1921

North Dakota, containing 40 acres more or less, held in trust by the government, and being my allotment #341; Also an undivided 1/3 interest in and to my allotment #956, being the SW ¼ NE ¼ Sec 28, T149N, R90W, 5th P.M. in McLean County, North Dakota, containing 40 acres more or less, and an undivided 1/3 interest in and to the NE ¼ of Sec 29, T150N, R90W, 5th P.N. containing 160 acres more or less, being my allotment #452-a.

3rd. I do hereby will, devise and bequeath unto my daughter May Dickens, aged 6, an undivided 1/3 interest in and to the real estate described in the 2nd provision of this will.

4th. I do hereby will, devise and bequeath unto my son, Willard Dickens, an undivided 1/3 interest in and to the real estate described in the second provision of this will.

5th. I hereby will and bequeath unto my daughters, Mamie Dickens and May Dickens, and unto my son, Willard Dickens, above mentioned, an undivided 1/3 interest in and to all other property, of whatsoever nature, both real and personal, of which I may die possessed, share and share alike, 1/3 each.

Emma Dickens

Dated at Elbowoods, ND, June 30, 1919

We, the undersigned, James Y. Eagle and Stella Eagle, hereby witness the signing of the last will and testament of Emma Dickens, at her request, she signing the will in our presence, and we witnessing the same in her presence, and in the presence of each other.

James Y. Eagle aged 47
Stella Eagle aged 34

Probate 22744-21 M H W
DEPARTMENT OF THE INTERIOR, Office of Indian Affairs   Apr 11, 1921

The within will of Emma Dickens, dec'd. Fort Berthold allottee is hereby recommended for approval under the Act of June 25, 1910 (36 Stat. L, 855-6) as amended by the Act of February 14, 1913 (37 Stat. L, 678) and the Regulations of the Department.

Respectfully,
E.B. Meritt
Assistant Commissioner

DEPARTMENT OF THE INTERIOR, Office of the Secretary   Apr 18, 1921

The within will of Emma Dickens, dec'd. Fort Berthold allottee, is hereby approved under the Act of June 25, 1910 (36 Stat. L, 855-6) as amended by the Act of February 14, 1913 (37 Stat. L, 678) and the Regulations of the Department.

S.G. Hopkins
Assistant Secretary

3-29 AD 1921

NATIVE AMERICAN WILLS and PROBATE RECORDS, 1911 - 1921

LAST WILL AND TESTAMENT

I, **MANY WOMEN**, also known as **MRS. KIDNEY**, of sound mind and disposing memory, do make, declare and publish this, my last will and testament, hereby revoking and annulling any and all other wills heretofore made by me.

1st. It is my will and desire that the expenses of my last sickness and funeral be paid.

2nd. That all my just debts be paid.

3rd. I do hereby will, bequeath and devise to William Steals Bear, or William Steele, and Squash or Mrs. Antelope Nose, my cousins, and sole surviving relatives, who are residents of the Crow Indian Agency, Crow Agency, Montana, in consideration that they keep, care and protect me during the remainder of my natural life, the following described property:

To William Steals Bear or William Steele, -
The NE ¼ of the NE ¼ of Sec 18, and the NW ¼ of the NW ¼ of Sec 17, all in T149N, R90W of the 5th Principal Meridian in North Dakota, and containing 80 acres.

To Squash, or Mrs. Antelope Nose, -
Lots 3 and 4 and the S ½ of the NW ¼ of Sec 3, T150N, R90W of the 5th Principal Meridian in North Dakota, and containing 159.22 acres.

4th. I do hereby will, bequeath and devise to William Steals Bear, or William Steele, and Squash, or Mrs. Antelope Nose, all other property, both real and personal, of which I may die possessed, each to share equal.

5th. The said devises, William Steals Bear or William Steele, and Squash, or Mrs. Antelope Nose, are my only relatives, and would probably inherit my property under the laws of descent, therefore, it is my will and desire that no other person or persons shall have any part or portion of my estate.

6th. I do hereby constitute and appoint Joseph Packineau, an Indian of the Fort Berthold Indian Reservation, ND, the executor of this my last will and testament, and do hereby request that he act as such.

In witness whereof I have hereunto published and declared the foregoing instrument to be my last will and testament, at Elbowoods, ND, on the 5th day of January, 1914, and have hereunto signed my name as evidence thereof.

Many Women   Her mark

On the 5th day of January, 1914, at Elbowoods, ND, we the undersigned, were requested to sign the foregoing instrument as witnesses to the will of Many Women, or Mrs. Kidney, by the said Many Women, or Mrs. Kidney, making such request, she at the same time declaring it to be her last will and testament and publishing it as such, she signing her name in our presence, and we subscribing thereto in her presence and in the presence of each other.

Name James Eagle
Age 42

NATIVE AMERICAN WILLS and PROBATE RECORDS, 1911 - 1921

Residence *Elbowoods, ND*

Name *D.E. Murphy*
Age *24 yrs*
Residence *Elbowoods, ND*

Note. The original of this will was returned by me to Many Women, or Mrs. Kidney, on this 9th day of April, 1916, in the presence of Joseph Packineau, Mrs. Joseph Packineau, and Samuel Newman.

(Illegible handwriting)
Superintendent

Probate 21016-21 N H W
DEPARTMENT OF THE INTERIOR, Office of Indian Affairs   Apr 7, 1921
It is hereby recommended that the within will of Many Women, or Mrs. Kidney, a Fort Berthold allottee be approved in accordance with the provisions of the Act of June 25, 1910 (36 Stat. L, 855-6) as amended by the Act of February 14, 1913 (37 Stat. L, 678) and the Regulations of the Department. The rights of an executor will not be recognized.

Respectfully,
E.B. Meritt
Assistant Commissioner

DEPARTMENT OF THE INTERIOR, Office of the Secretary   Apr 20, 1921
The within will of Many Women or Mrs. Kidney, a Fort Berthold allottee, is hereby approved in accordance with the provisions of the Act of June 25, 1910 (36 Stat. L, 855-6) as amended by the Act of February 14, 1913 (37 Stat. L, 678) and the Regulations of the Department. The rights of an executor will not be recognized.

S.G. Hopkins
Assistant Secretary

WILL

I, **KEEPS BONE**, of Pine Ridge Agency, South Dakota, Allottee #6429, do hereby make and declare this to be my last will and testament, in accordance with Section 2 of the Act of June 25, 1910 (36 Stat 855-858), and Act of February 14, 1913, (Public #381), hereby revoking all former wills made by us:
1. I hereby direct that, as soon as possible after my decease, that all my debts, funeral and testamentary expenses be paid out of my personal estate.
2. I give and devise my allotment on the Pine Ridge Reservation, South Dakota, described as follows, in the following manner: NW ¼ to my son Jonas Holy Rock and the SW ¼ to my daughter, Center Woman.

NATIVE AMERICAN WILLS and PROBATE RECORDS, 1911 - 1921

3. I give and bequeath all of my personal property of whatsoever nature and wheresoever situated unto:
    one black mare branded (blank) to my daughter Center Woman
    one black mare branded (blank) to my grand daughter Eliza Black Bear
    one roan mare and colt branded (blank) to my son Jonas Holy Rock
    one black mare branded (blank) to my grand daughter Zona Holy Rock
    one buggy to my grand daughter Victoria Holy Rock
    one stove to my daughter-in-law Polly Holy Rock

4. All the rest of my property, real or personal now possessed or hereafter acquired, of whatsoever nature and wheresoever situated, I hereby give, devise and bequeath unto

    one bed, tent & tent stove to my daughter Center Woman
    any moneys I have left to be divided equally between my son, Jonas Holy Rock and my daughter, Center Woman

In witness whereof I have hereunto set my hand this 7th day of June, 1917.

| Witness | *Judson Shook* | Manderson, SD | Keeps Bone   her mark |
| " | *Sam Ladiney* | Manderson, SD | |

The above statement was, this 7th day of July, 1917, signed and published by Keeps Bone as her last will and testament, in the joint presence of the undersigned, the said Keeps Bone then being of sound and vigorous mind and free from any constraint or compulsion: whereupon we, being without any interest in the matter other than friendship, and being well acquainted with her but not members of her family, immediately subscribed our names hereto in the presence of each other and of the said testator, for the purpose of attesting the said will, as requested us to do. And that we were witnesses at the testator's request, have written her name in ink, and that we affixed her thumb marks except that her daughter-in-law was present and we feel that her presence and talk might have influenced this woman in some way to give to her and her children.

                    Jacob Runs Against   Manderson, SD
                    Joshua Spotted Owl   Manderson, SD
                    Pine Ridge, South Dakota
                    Jul 7, 1917

OFFICE OF INDIAN AFFAIRS
RECEIVED
FEB 3, 1921
9494

                    Pine Ridge Agency
                    January 28, 1921

    I hereby certify that I have fully inquired into the mental competency of the Indian, signing the above will, the circumstances attending the execution of the will; the influence that may have induced its execution, and the names of those entitled to share in the estate under the law of descent in South Dakota, reasons for the disposition of the property proposed by the will differing from disposition had the property descended by operation of law.

NATIVE AMERICAN WILLS and PROBATE RECORDS, 1911 - 1921

  I respectfully forward this will with the recommendation that it be approved and beg to state that I agree with the write-up of Examiner E.S. Stewart.

H.M. Tidwell
Superintendent

DEPARTMENT OF THE INTERIOR, Office of Indian Affairs   Apr 11, 1921
  It is hereby recommended that the within will of Keeps Bone, deceased Oglala Sioux allottee #6429, be approved according to the Act of June 25, 1910, (36 Stat. L, 855-6) as amended by the Act of February 14, 1913 (37 Stat. 678).

Respectfully,
E.B. Meritt
Assistant Commissioner

DEPARTMENT OF THE INTERIOR, Office of the Secretary   Apr 12, 1921
  The within will of Keeps Bone, dec'd. Oglala Sioux allottee #6429, is hereby approved according to the Act of June 25, 1910, (36 Stat L, 855-6) as amended by the Act of February 14, 1913 (37 Stat. 678) and the Regulations of the Department.

S.G. Hopkins
Assistant Secretary

<<<<<<<◇>>>>>>>

THE LAST WILL AND TESTAMENT
of
THOMAS PAUL

KNOW ALL MEN BY THESE PRESENTS:

  That I, **THOMAS PAUL**, a bachelor of the age of forty-six years, do hereby make, publish and declare this my last will and testament, revoking all former wills and codicils by me made.

  It is my will that after death my Executor hereinafter named pay all my debts, and the expense of my last sickness, and funeral, as soon as the condition of my estate will permit.

  I give, devise and bequeath unto my sister, Mary Ha hai ta of Flathead Indian Reserve, Montana, the E ½ of the NW ¼ of Sec 19, T47N, R5 W.B.M.

  I give, devise and bequeath unto David Vallee the following described real estate situate in Kootenai County, Idaho, to-wit: The W ½ of the NW ¼ of Sec 19, T47N, R5 W.B.M, and to so give, devise and bequeath unto said David Vallee all other property of every nature and kind, whether personal, real or mixed, of which I may die seized.

  I nominate and appoint as the Executor of this, my last will and testament, Baptiste Vallee, and it is my will that no bond be required of said Executor of my estate and that he be permitted to administer my said estate without the intervention of any court.

NATIVE AMERICAN WILLS and PROBATE RECORDS, 1911 - 1921

IN WITNESS WHEREOF, I have hereunto subscribed my name and affixed my seal this 2nd day of August in the year of our Lord, 1911.

Thomas Paul [SEAL]

The foregoing instrument, consisting of this sheet and one other, was on this 2nd day of August, 1911, subscribed by the above named testator, Thomas Paul, in the presence of us and each of us and was at said time acknowledged by the said testator to each of us to have been made by him and was at said time declared by said testator to us that the said instrument was his will and we at said time, at the request of said testator and in his presence, and in the presence of each other, subscribed our names hereto as witnesses.

Jas Anderson
Robert W. Danson

Probate 28507-19 V L D
DEPARTMENT OF THE INTERIOR, Office of Indian Affairs   Apr 19, 1921

It is hereby recommended that the within will of Thomas Paul, Coeur d'Alene allottee #416, be approved in accordance with the provisions of the act of June 25, 1910 (36 Stat. L, 855-6) as amended by the Act of February 14, 1913, (37 Stat. L, 678).

Respectfully
E.B. Meritt
Assistant Commissioner

DEPARTMENT OF THE INTERIOR, Office of the Secretary   Apr 20, 1921

The within will of Thomas Paul, dec'd. Coeur d'Alene allottee #416, is hereby approved in accordance with the provisions of the Act of June 25, 1910 (36 Stat. L, 855-6) as amended by the Act of February 14, 1913 (37 Stat. L, 678).

S.G. Hopkins
Assistant Secretary

OFFICE OF INDIAN AFFAIRS
RECEIVED
MAR 7, 1921
18542

<<<<<<<>>>>>>>

LAST WILL AND TESTAMENT

I, **MARY SLOW EAGLE**, of the Cheyenne River Indian Reservation, in Stanley County, South Dakota, considering the uncertainty of this life, do therefore make, ordain, publish and declare this to be my Last Will and Testament.

First. I order and direct that all my just debts and funeral expenses be paid.

Second. I give, devise and bequeath all my right, title and interest in and to the SE ¼ of Sec 29, T42N, R28W of the 6th Principal Meridian in Mellette County, South Dakota, to my grandson, Arthur Bordeaux, Jr, same to be held in trust for him until he becomes twenty-one years old.

Third. I give, devise and bequeath all my right, title and interest in and to the NW ¼ of Sec. 30, T42N, R28W of the 6th Principal Meridian in Mellette County, South Dakota, to my grandson Levi Bordeaux, same to be held in trust for him until he becomes twenty-one years old.

NATIVE AMERICAN WILLS and PROBATE RECORDS, 1911 - 1921

Fourth. I order and direct the trustee of the above described quarters of land, which comprises my allotment #5802 and the trustee of which is the United States of America, to hold said land for the use and benefit of my two grandsons the above names devises until they severally become twenty-one years of age or until such time as the said trustee shall deem it advisable to grant to said devises the title in fee.

In TESTIMONY WHEREOF, I have hereunto subscribed my name this 3rd day of December, in the year of our Lord, 1912.

Mary Slow Eagle Her (thumb print) mark

This INSTRUMENT WAS, on the day of the date thereof, signed, published and declared by said testator, Mary Slow Eagle, to be her Last Will and Testament, in our presence, who, at her request, have subscribed our names hereto as witnesses, in her presence, and in the presence of each other.

Alex Bordeaux residing at White River, SD
C.E. Kell residing at White River, SD

DEPARTMENT OF THE INTERIOR, Office of Indian Affairs Apr 5, 1921

It is hereby recommended that the within will be approved, under the provisions of the Act of June 25, 1910 (36 Stat. L. 855) as amended by the Act of February 14, 1913, (37 Stat. L, 678).

E.B. Meritt
Assistant Commissioner

DEPARTMENT OF THE INTERIOR, Office of the Secretary Apr 6, 1921

The within will is hereby approved under the provisions of the Act of June 25, 1910 (36 Stat L. 855) as amended by the Act of February 14, 1913 (37 Stat L. 678).

S.G. Hopkins
Assistant Secretary

Cass Lake
Jan. 7, 1919

I hereby made[sic] a will about my children and my land. Ma Ma she means mother, I leave my two boys and the baby gril[sic] To take a charge. Also I leave my land to my children. Mother I give you right to draw my children payment money. I give you right to look after my lease land and to draw the money to be paid and use it as you please to support my children. I will talk to John Tuttle when he comes home about it.

Signed *Lizzie Headbird*

NATIVE AMERICAN WILLS and PROBATE RECORDS, 1911 - 1921

This was signed
half pass[sic] eleven   Witness Signed: John F. Defore
Jan. 7, 1919   Katie Defore

Probate 58677-17 C E T
DEPARTMENT OF THE INTERIOR, Office of Indian Affairs   Apr 7, 1921
     The within will of Lizzie Headbird, dec'd. Chippewa allottee #34, is hereby recommended for approval under the provisions of the Act of June 25, 1910 (36 Stat. 855-6) as amended by the Act of February 14, 1913 (37 Stat. L, 678).
                                                                Respectfully,
                                                                E.B. Meritt
                                                                Assistant Commissioner

DEPARTMENT OF THE INTERIOR, Office of the Secretary   Apr 14, 1921
     The within will of Lizzie Headbird, dec'd. Chippewa Allottee #34, is hereby approved under the provisions of the Act of June 25, 1910, (36 Stat. 855-6) as amended by the Act of February 14, 1913 (37 Stat. L, 678).
                                                                S.G. Hopkins
                                                                Assistant Secretary

LAST WILL AND TESTAMENT OF MA-ZAE-PA-WE MORRIS.

     I, **MA-ZAE-PA-WE MORRIS**, a resident of Thurston County, Nebraska, being of sound and disposing mind and memory, do hereby make and publish this my last will and testament in words and figures, that is to say:

FIRST.
     I give, devise and bequeath unto my husband, Jesse Morris, all my personal property of whatever kind and nature, consisting of moneys, rights, credits, deposits, household goods, conveyances and horses, and any and all other personal property which I may own, in whole or in part, at the time of my death, if he shall survive me, but is my said husband, Jesse Morris, shall not survive me, then it is my will and I do, in that event, hereby give, devise and bequeath all of my personal property of whatever kind and nature, consisting of moneys, rights, credits, deposits, household goods, conveyances and horses, and any and all other personal property which I may own, in whole or in part, at the time of my death, unto my grandson, John Morris, who is the oldest child of my deceased son, Harry Morris.
SECOND.
     I give, devise and bequeath unto my husband, Jesse Morris, if he shall survive me, the exclusive use during his natural live of all of the real estate which I may own at the time of my death, being the E ½ of the NE ¼ of Sec. 28, T25, R9E, of the 6th P.M. in Thurston County, NE, and any and all other real estate or interest therein which I may own at the time of my death, devising and

NATIVE AMERICAN WILLS and PROBATE RECORDS, 1911 - 1921

bequeathing unto him, my said husband, if he shall survive me, all of the rents, profits and proceeds thereof from the time of my death, so long as he shall live, and upon his death his interest therein shall terminate, and it is my will that the remainder interest in said premises, being the full title thereto, subject to the allotment trust restrictions, and subject to the life interest and use of my said husband, Jesse Morris, shall descend to my grandson, John Morris, above named, subject, however, to the following conditions: Provided that the remainder interest which is devised in this will unto the said John Morris shall not be subject to sale, disposition, conveyance, encumbrance or other lien of any kind and nature for a period of 20 years after my death and after the death of my said husband, Jesse Morris, is he shall survive me, and it is my will that my said devises, John Morris, shall pay all legal taxes assessed against any of said premises out of the rents and proceeds of any of the above tracts of land during the said 20 year restricted term, and it is my will that the said John Morris shall not have the right to lease any of the above described premises during the 20 year restricted period above named for a longer period than five years. I have made this devise to my said grandson, John Morris, in view of his age and limited experience.

THIRD.

This will is made and executed by virtue of the Act of Congress of June 25, 1910, and the supplemental Act of February 14, 1913, and any subsequent legislation providing for the execution of wills of allotted Indians under restricted trust patents, and I do hereby revoke and cancel any former will or wills which I may have made, and I further declare that this will is made subject to the conditions and restricted provisions of the Act of Congress under which the above described premises were allotted by the Government of the United States to the allottee thereof.

FOURTH.

I hereby nominate Harry L. Keefe the executor of this my last will and testament.

IN WITNESS WHEREOF, I have hereunto set my hand this 8th day of July, 1915.

In the Presence of   *Mazapawe Morris*   His[sic] (thumb print) mark
   Harry L. Keefe
   Marguerite La F. Diddock
   Henrietta Freemont

We, the undersigned, hereby certify that Ma-zae-pa-we Morris signed the above as her last will and testament and declared the same in our presence and in the presence of each of us to be her last will and testament, and we further certify that she understood the contents thereof and requested us to sign as witnesses, and we have signed in her presence and in the presence of each of us.

                                Harry L. Keefe
                                Marguerite La F. Diddock

NATIVE AMERICAN WILLS and PROBATE RECORDS, 1911 - 1921

Henrietta Freemont

Probate 10461-21 C E T
DEPARTMENT OF THE INTERIOR, Office of Indian Affairs   Apr 14, 1921
   The within will of Mazapawe Morris, dec'd. Omaha allottee #717-N, is respectfully submitted to the Secretary of the Interior with the recommendation that it be approved in accordance with the provisions of the Act of June 25, 1910 (36 Stat. L, 855-6) as amended by the Act of February 14, 1913 (37 Stat. L, 678-9).

Respectfully,
E.B. Meritt
Assistant Commissioner

DEPARTMENT OF THE INTERIOR, Office of the Secretary   Apr 20, 1921
   The within will of Mazapawe Morris, dec'd. Omaha allottee #717-N, is hereby approved in accordance with the Act of June 25, 1910 (36 Stat. L, 855-6) as amended by the Act of February 14, 1913 (37 Stat. L, 678-9). No rights of an executor are to be recognized under this will.

S.G. Hopkins
Assistant Secretary

WILL

   I, **JOB SCOTT**, aged about 76 years, Digger Indian, of Greenville Jurisdiction, Plumas County, California, do hereby make and declare this to be my last will and testament, in accordance with Section 2 of the Act of June 25, 1910 (36 Stat. 855-858), and Act of February 14, 1913, (Public #381), hereby revoking all former wills by me made:
1. I hereby direct that as soon as possible after my decease, that all my debts, funeral and testamentary expenses be paid out of my personal estate.
2. I give and devise my two homesteads in Plumas County, California, described as follows:

   Lot 4 and the SE/4 of the SW/4 of Sec. 31, T27N, R10E of the M D M, in California, containing
      69.32 acres,
AND
      N/2 of the NE/4 of Sec. 35, T27N, R9E of the M D M, in California, containing 80 acres.

   In the following manner:
      To my niece, Mary Tims, who is taking care of me during my old age.

NATIVE AMERICAN WILLS and PROBATE RECORDS, 1911 - 1921

3. I give and bequeath all of my personal property of whatsoever nature and wheresoever situated unto
>> my niece, Mary Tims

OFFICE OF INDIAN AFFAIRS RECEIVED MAR 22, 1921 23042

4. All the rest of my property, real or personal possessed or hereafter acquired, of whatsoever nature and wheresoever situated, I hereby give, devise and bequeath unto

>> my niece, Mary Tims

In witness whereof I have hereunto set my hand this 12th day of March, 1917.

>> *Job Scott* His (thumb print) mark

The above statement was, this 12th day of March, 1917, signed and published by Job Scott as his last will and testament, in the joint presence of the undersigned, the said Job Scott then being of sound and vigorous mind and free from any constraint or compulsion: whereupon we, being without any interest in the matter other than friendship, and being well acquainted with him, immediately subscribe our names hereto in the presence of each other and of the said testator, for the purpose of attesting the said will, as he requested us to do. And that I, *J. J. Pratt* at the testator's request, have written his name in ink, and that he affixed his thumb-mark.

>> Post Office Address

J.J. Pratt	Greenville, CA
Grover Doshinka	Greenville, CA

>> Greenville, California
>> March 12, 1917

I hereby certify that I have fully inquired into the mental competency of the Indian, signing the above will; the circumstances attending the execution of the will; the influence that may have induced its execution, and the names of those entitled to share in the estate under the law of descent in California, reasons for the disposition of the property proposed by the will, differing from disposition had the property descended by operation of law.

I respectfully forward this will with the recommendation that it be approved,

>> *Edgar H. Miller*
>> Supt. & Spl. Disb. Agent.

DEPARTMENT OF THE INTERIOR, Office of Indian Affairs

It is recommended that the within will of Job Scott be approved under the Act of June 25, 1910 (36 Stat. L. 866-856), as amended by the Act of February 14, 19134 (37 Stat. L. 678).

>> Respectfully,

NATIVE AMERICAN WILLS and PROBATE RECORDS, 1911 - 1921

E.B. Meritt
Assistant Commissioner

DEPARTMENT OF THE INTERIOR, Office of the Secretary   Apr 7, 1921
The within will of Job Scott is hereby approved under the Act of June 25, 1910 (36 Stat. L. 855-856) as amended by the Act of February 14, 1913 (37 Stat. L. 678).

S.G. Hopkins
Assistant Secretary

Last Will and Testament of
David Good Village

1st. I, **DAVID GOOD VILLAGE**, being of sound mind and disposing memory but of very poor health and knowing that I may not have much longer to live, do hereby make, declare and publish this my last will and testament.

2nd. I desire all of my debts that are right and just, including my burial and funeral expenses to be paid out of any funds accruing to my estate.

3rd. I own property as follows: Some land in Wisconsin the description to me unknown, this will be known to the Superintendent of the Wisconsin Winnebagoes[sic] and I also own some personal property on this land; I further own property in Nebraska described as follows: The NE/4 of the SE/4 of Sec. 31 and the SW/4 of the NW/4 of Sec. 32 all in T27N, R6E and the SE/4 of the SE/4 of Sec. 5, T26N, R9E of the 6th P.M, NE, allotment of Jim Jones of which I own an undivided one-twelf[sic] share; I also own an undivided one-fortieth share of the John White allotment, described as the NW/4 of the NE/4, Sec. 27, T27N, R7E, and the SW/4 of NE/4 of Sec 2, T26N, R9E of the 6th P.M. I also have a small amount of money under the supervision of the Superintendent of the Winnebago Reservation, NE.

4th. All of the above named property, I desire to go to my only son, William Good Village and to his heirs after him forever.

5th. I desire the Superintendent of the Winnebago Reservation to act in conjunction with the Superintendent of the Winnebago Reservation in Wisconsin to see that my wishes in this matter are carried out.

Signed   David Good Village   his mark

The testator at this time signed his name to the above and foregoing instrument in the presence of the undersigned and at the same time declared it to be his last will and testament, and we, at his request and in his presence and in the presence of each other do hereby sign our names hereto as attesting witnesses.

Interpreter   Lucy C. Palmer
Charles Lamue   P. Richards

NATIVE AMERICAN WILLS and PROBATE RECORDS, 1911 - 1921

Winnebago Agency, NE
August 20, 1917
Probate 46145-20 C E T
DEPARTMENT OF THE INTERIOR, Office of Indian Affairs Feb 25, 1921
    The within will of David Good Village, deceased unallotted Wisconsin Winnebago Indian, is hereby recommended for approval, in accordance with the provisions of the Act of June 25, 1910 (36 Stat. 855-6) as amended by the Act of February 14, 1913 (37 Stat. L, 678)

                      Respectfully,
                      E.B. Meritt
                      Assistant Commissioner

DEPARTMENT OF THE INTERIOR, Office of the Secretary Feb 28, 1921
    The within will of David Good Village, dec'd. unallotted Wisconsin Winnebago Indian, is hereby approved in accordance with the provisions of the Act of June 25, 1910 (36 Stat. 855-6) as amended by the Act of February 14, 1913, (37 Stat. L, 678).

                      S.G. Hopkins
                      Assistant Secretary

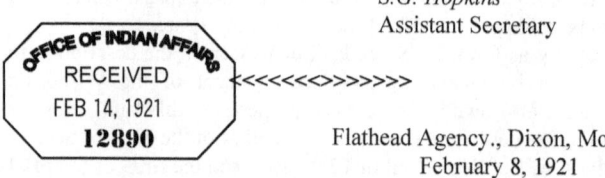

                      Flathead Agency., Dixon, Montana
                      February 8, 1921

    I hereby revoke a will executed by me under date of March 26, 1917, and approved by the Department under date of April 20, 1921, (under Probate 33147-17 CET) the beneficiaries under this will being John Clairmont and Pierre Sabine, for the following reasons:

    That when I executed this will it was with the understanding that these beneficiaries were to care and provide for me the rest of my life;

    That it is now four years since this will was executed, and that practically nothing has been contributed by these beneficiaries toward my care and support; and that I have had to care for myself and that other parties than the beneficiaries have cared for and provided for me; that one other party has cared for and provided for me since I executed the above mentioned will and for many years prior to this time;

    That because of the failure of the beneficiaries to live up to their agreement, I do not want them to share in my property which I may leave at my death.

Witness to mark: Mary Kunspee (Thumb print)
    Louis C. Cantow
        Interpreter
    Isaac Huwley
        Clerk   Both of Dixon, MT

NATIVE AMERICAN WILLS and PROBATE RECORDS, 1911 - 1921

Probate 33147-17 12890-21 C E T
DEPARTMENT OF THE INTERIOR, Office of Indian Affairs Feb 25, 1921
    The within revocation by Mary Kunspee, Flathead allottee #1733, of her will executed March 26, 1917, approved April 20, 1917, is hereby recommended for approval.
                              Respectfully,
                              E.B. Meritt
                              Assistant Commissioner

DEPARTMENT OF THE INTERIOR, Office of the Secretary Feb. 26, 1921
    The within revocation by Mary Kunspee, Flathead allottee #1733, of her will executed March 26, 1917, and approved April 20, 1917, is hereby approved.
                              S.G. Hopkins
                              Assistant Secretary

<<<<<<<>>>>>>>

STATE OF WISCONSIN,
County of Jackson
                I, Frank Johnson, County Judge in and for said County, do hereby certify that the copy hereunto annexed has been compared by me with the original Last Will and Testament of Rain Walking Woman and of Certificate of Probate, in the Matter of the Will of Rain Walking Woman, dec'd, now on file and of record in my office, and required by law to be in my custody, and that said copy is a true copy thereof.
        IN TESTIMONY WHEREOF, I have hereunto set my hand and affixed the seal of the county court of said county, at Black River Falls, in said county, this 5th day of August, A.D, 1920
                              Frank Johnson
                              County Judge

<<<<<<<>>>>>>>

WILL

    I, **RAIN WALKING WOMAN**, (Indian) of the town of Springfield, County of Jackson, and State of Wisconsin, being of sound mind and memory, do make, publish, and declare this to be my last will and testament. To wit:
First - All my just debts and funeral expenses shall be first duly paid.
Second - I give, devise and bequeath all the rest, residue and remainder of my estate, both real and personal, to my beloved daughter, Carrie Decorah. To have and to hold to her, my said daughter. I give and devise one dollar to Adam Littlebear, one dollar to Amos Littlebear, one dollar to Thomas Littlebear, and one dollar to Dan Littlebear.
Third - I nominate and appoint Mrs. James Sharp, executrix of this my last Will and testament, hereby revoking all former wills made by me.

NATIVE AMERICAN WILLS and PROBATE RECORDS, 1911 - 1921

In Witness Thereof, I have hereunto set my hand and seal this 25th day of Feb, A.D, 1913.
In presence of
    Standing Buffalo   Rain Walking Woman   her (X) mark
    Tom Thunder

Signed, sealed, published and declared as and for her last will and testament by the above named testator, in our presence, who have, at her request, and in her presence, and in the presence of each other, signed our names as witness thereto.

C.M. Vincent
Mrs. James Sharp

Probate 1411-17 67589-20 C E T
DEPARTMENT OF THE INTERIOR, Office of Indian Affairs   Feb. 19, 1921
    The within will (by certified copy of Rain Walking Woman, deceased Wisconsin Winnebago Homesteader, is hereby recommended for approval in accordance with the provisions of the Act of June 25, 1910 (36 Stat. L, 855-6) as amended by the Act of February 14, 1913 (37 Stat. L, 678).
                                          E.B. Meritt
                                      Assistant Commissioner

DEPARTMENT OF THE INTERIOR, Office of the Secretary   Feb. 24, 1921
    The within will (by certified copy) of Rain Walking Woman, dec'd. Wisconsin Winnebago Homesteader, is hereby approved, in accordance with the provisions of the Act of June 25, 1910 (36 Stat. L, 855-6) as amended by the Act of February 14, 1913, (37 Stat. L, 678).
                                          S.G. Hopkins
                                      Assistant Secretary

    Filed this 23rd day of May, A.D, 1916   Frank Johnson   County Judge [Recorded in Vol. 14, pg 297]

State of Wisconsin
    Jackson County
    BE IT REMEMBERED, That on the 20th day of June, A.D, 1916 at Black River Falls in said County, pursuant to notice duly given, as required by law, at a Special Term of the County Court of said County, Tom Thunder and C.M. Vincent, two of the subscribing witnesses (to) the last will and testament of Rain Walking Woman late of the town of Komensky, in said County, dec'd, hereunto annexed: were produced and duly sworn and examined.
    And the proofs having been heard before said Court, and the Court having thereupon found that said instrument was in all things duly executed as her last will and testament by the said, Rain Walking Woman.

NATIVE AMERICAN WILLS and PROBATE RECORDS, 1911 - 1921

Thereupon said instrument was by the order and decree of said Court duly allowed and admitted to probate, as and for the last will and testament of Rain Walking Woman, dec'd.

In Testimony Whereof, I have hereunto set my hand and affixed the seal of the County Court of said County, at Black River Falls, this 20th day of June A.D, 1916.

(County Court Seal)　　　　　　　　Frank Johnson, County Judge

Last Will and Testament of Margaret Colburn.
In the Name of God, Amen:-

I, **MARGARET DUBE**, a Chippewa Indian of the White Earth Reservation, Mahnomen County, Minnesota, now residing at Cloquet, MN, age 51 yrs, being of sound mind and memory and realizing the uncertainty of life, do hereby make this my last will and testament, revoking all former wills by me made.
-1-
I hereby direct that all my funeral expenses be first paid out of my estate as soon after my demise as expedient.
-2-
I also request that all my just debts be paid as soon as may be after my demise.
-3-
I give, devise and bequeath to my granddaughters Nancy and Lizzie Houle, daughters of Charles Colburn, one dollar each.
-4-
I give, devise and bequeath to my beloved husband, John Dube, 40 acres of land described as the

NW/4 of Lot 1, Sec 27, T49N, R17W of 4th P.M. in Minnesota, together with all buildings, furniture, implements appertaining thereto. I also bequeath to said John Dube an undivided ½ interest in 87 12/100 acres of land on the White Earth Reservation, described as Lots #4 and 12 of Sec 30, T143N, R42W of 5th P.M. in MN.
-5-
I give, devise and bequeath to my beloved daughter Julia Houle, wife of Frank Houle, Jr, age 34 yrs, and undivided ½ interest in 87 12/100 acres of land on the White Earth Reservation, MN, described as Lots #4 and 12 of Sec 30, T143N, R42W of 5th P.M. in MN.
-6-
All other property of which I may die possessed of, either real or personal I give, devise and bequeath to my husband, John Dube.
-7-

NATIVE AMERICAN WILLS and PROBATE RECORDS, 1911 - 1921

Reposing full confidence in the integrity of my said husband John Dube, I hereby appoint him sole executor of this my Last will and testament and it is my desire that he fulfill the duties of said office without being required to file any bond for the faithful performance of his said trust.

In testimony whereof I have hereunto set my hand and seal this 28th day of July, A.D, 1916.

Witnesses to mark   Margaret Dube   Her (thumb print) mark
John B. Ojibway
C.E. Dennis

I, John Ojibway, of lawful age, hereby certify that I am well acquainted with both the Chippewa and English languages, that I carefully explained the foregoing instrument to Margaret Dube, and that Margaret Dube declared the same to represent her full wishes and desires and that she was satisfied with the same.

John B. Ojibway
Interpreter

This instrument, in three pages, was on the date thereof, signed, published and declared by the said testatrix, Margaret Dube, to be her last Will and Testament, in our presence, who at her request have subscribed our names thereto as witnesses in her presence and in the presence of each other.

John B. Ojibway   Residing at Cloquet, MN
C.E. Dennis   Residing at Cloquet, MN

I, Margaret Dube, hereby declare that I am the person who executed the foregoing will and that my reason for devising my property as above is because my husband, John Dube, has been very kind to me and my daughter, Julia Houle, and my granddaughters Nancy and Lizzie have not been very kind and have done very little for my comfort in my old age and illness.

Witnesses   Margaret Dube   Her (thumb print) mark
(No names given.)

Subscribed and sworn to before me this 28th day of July, 1916, at Cloquet, MN.
G.W. Crosh
Supt. & Spl. Disb. Agt.

Probate 46755-17 C E T
DEPARTMENT OF THE INTERIOR, Office of Indian Affairs   Dec. 11, 1920
The within will of Margaret Dube (Mahgeet or Margaret Colburne), dec'd. White Earth allottee #0-2951 is hereby recommended for approval, in so far as it disposes of trust property under the supervision of the Government, in accordance

NATIVE AMERICAN WILLS and PROBATE RECORDS, 1911 - 1921

with the Act of June 25, 1910, (36 Stat. L, 855-6), as amended by the Act of February 14, 1913, (37 Stat. L, 678).

        Respectfully,
        E.B. Meritt
        Assistant Commissioner

DEPARTMENT OF THE INTERIOR, Office of the Secretary   Dec. 14, 1920

The within will of Margaret Dube (Mahgeet or Margaret Colburne), dec'd. White Earth allottee #0-2931, is hereby approved, in so far as it disposes of trust property over which the Government has jurisdiction, in accordance with the provisions of the Act of June 25, 1910, (36 Stat. L, 855-6) as amended by the Act of February 14, 1913, (37 Stat. L, 678).

        S.G. Hopkins
        Assistant Secretary

Last Will and Testament of Max Lyman

    I, **MAX LYMAN**, of Greenwood, State of South Dakota, County of Charles Mix, being of sound mind and memory, do make, publish and declare this my last will and testament, hereby revoking any and all wills made by me heretofore, particularly that executed by me on the 17th day of July, 1914.

    First. I declare it to be my will that at the time of my death, all my just debts and funeral expenses should be paid and a suitable monument erected to my grave.

    Second. It is my will that all of my property including both personal and real, that may remain after my debts and funeral expenses have been paid, shall be distributed to my legal heirs according to the laws of descent of the state of South Dakota.

    IN TESTIMONY WHEREOF, I have set my hand and seal this 19th day of October, 1918, at Greenwood, SD, in the presence of the witnesses names below.

        Max Lyman

Signed, sealed declared and published by the said Max Lyman, as and for his last will and testament, and in his personal, and in the presence of each other, we have subscribed our names as attesting witnesses thereto.

        Elmo Eddy
                Greenwood, SD
        Joseph T. Cook
                Greenwood, SD

Probate 60207-21 C E T
DEPARTMENT OF THE INTERIOR, Office of Indian Affairs   (No date given)

    It is recommended that the within will be approved pursuant to the provisions of the Act of June 25, 1910 (36 Stat. L, 855) as amended by the Act of February 14, 1913 (37 Stat. L, 678).

        Respectfully,

NATIVE AMERICAN WILLS and PROBATE RECORDS, 1911 - 1921

E.B. Meritt
Assistant Commissioner

DEPARTMENT OF THE INTERIOR, Office of the Secretary Aug. 4, 1921
The within will is hereby approved pursuant to the provisions of the Act of June 25, 1910, (36 Stat. L, 855), as amended by the Act of February 14, 1913 (37 Stat. L, 678).

F.M. Goodwin
Assistant Secretary

<<<<<<<◇>>>>>>>

COPY
LAST WILL AND TESTAMENT
In the name of God, Amen:

I, **LOTS OF STARS**, of Crow Agency, being of sound mind and memory and understanding, do hereby make and publish this my last will and testament, hereby revoking and annulling all wills ny[sic] me heretofore made, in manner and form following, that is to say:

First, I direct that all my just debts and funeral expenses and expenses of my last illness shall be paid by my executor hereinafter named as soon after my deceased as convenient;

Second, I give, devise and bequeath to Takes The Horse On The Prarie[sic], SE/4 NW/4 Sec. 25, T1S, R33E, and to Clarence Old Horn, the SE/4 NE/r Sec. 26, T1S, R33E, and I want my grazing land divided equal between Takes The Horse On The Prarie[sic], Stoops To Charge and to Clarence Old Horn, and all my personal property I give to Stoops To Charge.

Third, All the rest and residue of my estate both real and personal and mixed, I give, devise and bequeath to my legal heirs as determined after my decease.

And lastly I do hereby nominate, constitute and appoint the Supt. of the Crow Indian Agency, Montana, executor of this my last will and testament.

In testimony hereof, I have set my hand and seal to this my last will and testament at Crow Agency, Montana, this 5th day of Feb, 1919.

[Signed] Lots Of Stars   His mark

Signed, sealed and declared by said in our presence as for his last will and testament and at his request and in our presence, and in the presence of each other, we have hereunto affixed our names as attesting witnesses hereto.

[Signed] David Bad Boy   N.J. Perkins
                          Wm H. White

DEPARTMENT OF THE INTERIOR, Office of Indian Affairs July 22, 1920
It is hereby recommended that the within will of Lots Of Stars, dec'd Crow allottee #86 and 86(rest of number cut off) be approved under the provisions of the Act of June 25, 1910, (36 Stat. L 855-6) as amended by the Act of Feb. 14, 1913 (37 Stat. L, 678) and the Regulations of the Department.

NATIVE AMERICAN WILLS and PROBATE RECORDS, 1911 - 1921

Respectfully,
[Signed] E.B. Meritt
Assistant Commissioner

DEPARTMENT OF THE INTERIOR, Office of the Secretary   July 26, 1920
The within will of Lots Of Stars, dec'd. Crow allottee #86 and 8(rest of number cut off) is hereby approved under the provisions of the Act of June 25, 1910 (36 Stat. L, 855-6) and the Regulations of the Department.
[Signed] S.G. Hopkins
Assistant Secretary

<<<<<<<◇>>>>>>>

COPY

WILL

I, **JOHN M. COOK**, of lawful age and of sound mine[sic], residing at Wagner, South Dakota, do hereby make and publish this as my last will and testament and I do hereby revoke any and all former wills by me made and particularly a certain will made by me on or about the 21st day of July, 1915.

I first direct that all of my just debts and the expenses of last sickness and burial be paid.

I do then give and bequeath unto my grand-son, Peter Frederick, the sum of $300.00, cash.

I do then give, devise and bequeath unto my children, Eunice Frederick, Mary B. Hitikia, Joseph Cook, Annie Cook, Isabelle Frederick, and Sophia Frederick, share and share alike, to have and to hold in fee simple, all the rest and residue of my estate whether real or personal and wheresoever the same may be situated.

I have intentionally omitted to provide for my wife, Elmyra Cook, for the reason that she has heretofore without just reason in my opinion deserted and abondoned[sic] me and has refused to come and live with me although requested to do so by me.

Dated June 17th, 1916   Wagner, SD

[Signed] John M. Cook

Signed, published and declared by the testator, John M. Cook, as and for his last will and testament, in the presence of us who at his request and in his presence and in the presence of each other hereunto signed our names as witnesses.

Dated June 17th, 1916   [Signed] H.C. Schnieder,
Wagner, SD
[Signed] F.M. Morgan,
Wagner, SD

Probate 18024-1920 L L
DEPARTMENT OF THE INTERIOR, Office of Indian Affairs   July 22, 1920

NATIVE AMERICAN WILLS and PROBATE RECORDS, 1911 - 1921

It is recommended that the within will be approved pursuant to the provisions of the Act of June 25, 1910, (36 Stat. L, 855-6) as amended by the Act of February 14, 1913 (37 Stat. L, 678).

Respectfully,
[Signed]   E.B. Meritt
Assistant Commissioner

DEPARTMENT OF THE INTERIOR, Office of the Secretary   July 28, 1920

The within will is hereby approved pursuant to the provisions of the Act of June 25, 1910 (36 Stat. L, 855-6), as amended by the Act of February 14, 1913 (37 Stat. L, 678).

[Signed]   S.G. Hopkins
Assistant Secretary

State of South Dakota)
Charles Mix County)^{ss}

I hereby certify that I have carefully examined the within instrument and compared the same with the original now on file in this office and that it is a true and correct copy of the same and that the above dated Oct. 21, 1918.

L.L. Vandall

Clerk Co. Court in and for Chas. Mix County

Will.

IN THE NAME OF GOD, Amen. I, HANNAH JONAS, allottee #394 of the Nez Perce Tribe of Indians of Idaho, residing on the Nez Perce Reservation of Idaho, being of sound mind and disposing memory, and not acting under duress, menace, fraud or undue influence of any person whatsoever, do make, publish, and declare this my last will and testament in the following manner, that is to say;

First- I direct that my body be decently buried with proper regard for my station in life and the circumstances of my estate.

Secondly- I direct that Ka-lu-la-son-my and He-yume-wa-ke-ma-lits, beneficiaries under this will, each bear half of the expenses of my burial.

Thirdly- I give and devise to the aforesaid Ka-lu-la-son-my, her heirs and assigns, all of the following described tracts of land, to wit:

(a) Nez Perce Allotment #98 described as the SW ¼ NW ¼ of Sec. 34 and SE ¼ NE ¼ of Sec 33, in T37N, R4W of the Boise Meridian, containing in all 80 acres more or less, valued at $6000.

(b) Nez Perce Allotment #101 described as the E ½ SE ¼ Sec. 33N, R4W of the Boise Meridian, containing in all 80 acres more or less, valued at $6000.

(c) Nez Perce Allotment #102 described as Lots 3 (30.05), 2 (30.15), and 3 (30.25), Sec 4, T36N, R4W of the Boise Meridian, containing in all 90.45 acres, valued at $6750.

NATIVE AMERICAN WILLS and PROBATE RECORDS, 1911 - 1921

Fourthly - I give and devise to the aforesaid He-yume-wa-ke-ma-lits, her heirs and her assigns, all of the following described tracts of land, to wit;
(a) Nez Perce Allotment #394 described as Lots 7 (20.41), 8 (20.47), Sec 1, & N1/2 Lot 1, Lots 10 & 23 & N ½ Lot 2 (10.19) Sec 2, T34N, R4W of the Boise Meridian, Lots 29, 30 & N ½ Lot 28, Sec 35, T24N, R4W of the Boise Meridian, containing in all 111.30 acres, more or less, valued at $5550.
(b) Nez Perce Allotment #395 described as Lots 31, 32, Sec 25 & Lots 25 and 26 of Sec 36, T35N, R4W of the Boise Meridian, containing 80 acres more or less, valued at $5600.

My reasons for making the foregoing disposition of my property are that I want the devises, who are my sisters, to have my property. I have no brothers or sisters living other than the devises. They have taken care of me for several years and are taking care of me at the present time. I have no living children or issue of same. I want them to have my land because they have been good to me and will continue to take care of me. Should the devises fail to take care of me as they should I can cancel this will.

Fifthly- I had one full brother named Yah-hat-koo-tah-wal-te-moon, but he died before allotments and without issue. I had three half sisters on my father's side as follows:
(a) E-pa-lee-kit-we-yah-la-son-my who was the mother of Ah-lou-wah-tson-my, or Mrs. James Slickpoo, and who left at her death one living child whose name is Sam Slickpoo.
(b) Notes nunmy who allotment was inherited by Annie Minthorn who inherited by reason of being the wife of a deceased son.
(c) Kows-pa-ah-loo who left as her sole heir one Josphine Bronche, wife of Louie Bronche.

I had another half sister on my father's side whose mother was also my mother's sister. Her name was Naks-tsa-a-lo and when she died she left as her heir a daughter now known as Mrs. Red Elk.

With the foregoing facts I am fully familiar. I know of no one else who could possibly make claim at my death as my heir. I do not want any of the above mentioned people to inherit in my estate as they have never claimed relationship with me, cared for me in my sickness, or otherwise shown any interest in my welfare. The only parties I recognize as relatives are my sisters, Ka-lu-la-son-my and He-yume-wake-ma-lits, the devises hereinbefore mentioned, and I want them to have my land and I want it divided between them in the way I have hereinbefore directed.

In witness of the foregoing I have hereunto set my hand and seal this 24th day of July, 1916.

        Hannah Jonas Her (thumb print) mark

Witnesses
 Perry F. Brown Clerk, Lapwai, Idaho

NATIVE AMERICAN WILLS and PROBATE RECORDS, 1911 - 1921

Chett B. Sawyer   Clerk and Interpreter, Lapwai, Idaho
James Miles   Cottonwood, Idaho (Indian)

The foregoing instrument was at the date hereof by the said Hannah Jonas signed, sealed, and published and declared to be her last will and testament in the presence of us, who at her request and in the presence of each other, have subscribed our names as witnesses hereto.

                                               Perry F. Brown
                                               Chett B. Sawyer
                                               James Miles

Probate 15725-21
DEPARTMENT OF THE INTERIOR, Office of Indian Affairs   Apr 11, 1921
     The within will of Hannah Jonas is hereby recommended for approval in accordance with the provisions of the Act of June 25, 1910 (36 Stat. L, 855-6) as amended by the Act of February 14, 1913 (37 Stat. L 678).

                                               E.B. Meritt
                                               Assistant Commissioner

DEPARTMENT OF THE INTERIOR, Office of the Secretary   Apr 14, 1921
     The within will is hereby approved according to the provisions of the Act of June 25, 1910, (36 Stat. L, 855-6) as amended by the Act of February 14, 1913 (37 Stat. L, 678).

                                               S.G. Hopkins
                                               Assistant Secretary

<<<<<<<O>>>>>>>

State of Nebraska   :
                            :
County of Thurston   :

LAST WILL AND TESTAMENT OF ALBERT THOMAS

     I, **ALBERT THOMAS**, a Winnebago Indian, of Winnebago, County of Thurston, State of Nebraska, being of sound mind and memory, and considering the uncertainty of this frail and transitory life, do therefore make, ordain, publish and declare this to be my last Will and Testament, all former wills or codicils hereby being revoked:
FIRST: I order and direct that the Superintendent of the Winnebago Agency pay all orders issued against my account now on the books or will be from any source. I further direct that the Superintendent pay all my funeral expenses as soon as my decease as conveniently may be.
SECOND: After the payment of such funeral expenses and debts incurred by issuance of orders from the Winnebago Agency, I give, devise and bequeath unto Bobby Whitespirit, (blank) Dollars, and all the remainder and residue of my

NATIVE AMERICAN WILLS and PROBATE RECORDS, 1911 - 1921

property, both real and personal, including the balance of all cash remaining to my credit at the Agency, or in any or all properties in which I may be sole heir, or in part with other heirs, in which I may be, or have been declared to have all right, title, and interest, now or in the future, to Eva Lincoln.

IN WITNESS WHEREOF, I have hereunto subscribed my name and affixed my seal, this the 21st day of January, 1918.

Albert Thomas
Testator

This instrument was on the day and date thereof signed, published and declared by the testator, Albert Thomas, to be his last will and testament, in the presence of us who at his request have subscribed our names, thereto, as witnesses, in his presence and in the presence of each other, and we believe said testator at this time to be of sound and disposing mind and memory.

(blank)
Witness to signature of testator

John Ashford
Witness to signature of testator

Probate 67568-18 C E T
DEPARTMENT OF THE INTERIOR, Office of Indian Affairs   Aug. 23, 1920
    The within will of Albert Thomas, dec'd. unallotted Winnebago Indian, is recommended for disapproval in accordance with the provisions of the Act of June 25, 1910, (36 Stat. L, 855-6), as amended by the Act of February 14, 1913, (37 Stat. L, 678).

Respectfully,
E.B. Meritt
Assistant Commissioner

DEPARTMENT OF THE INTERIOR, Office of the Secretary   Aug 27, 1920
    The within will of Albert Thomas, dec'd. unallotted Winnebago Indian, is hereby disapproved under the provisions of Act of June 25, 1910 (37 Stat. L, 855-6), as amended by the Act of February 14, 1913 (37 Stat. L, 678).

S.G. Hopkins
Assistant Secretary

<<<<<<<>>>>>>>

OFFICE OF INDIAN AFFAIRS
RECEIVED
JUL 22, 1920
61609

IN THE NAME OF GOD, Amen

    I, **MAY ZHUCK GE SHIG**, of Beaulieu in the County of Mahnomen and State of Minnesota, being of sound mind and memory, and considering the uncertainty of this frail and transitory life do therefore make, ordain, publish and declare this to be my last Will and Testament.

NATIVE AMERICAN WILLS and PROBATE RECORDS, 1911 - 1921

First, I order and direct that my Execut____ hereinafter named, pay all my just debts and funeral expenses as soon after my decease as conveniently may be.

Second, After the payment of said funeral expenses and debts, I give, devise, and bequeath all of my property, real and personal, of which I died possessed to my daughter, Cornelia Madison.

Lastly, I make, constitute and appoint (blank) to be Execut____ or this my Last Will and Testament, hereby revoking all former wills by me made.

IN TESTIMONY WHEREOF, I have hereunto subscribed my name and affixed my seal the 22nd day of July, 1919

May Zhuck ge shig (Thumb print)

[Seal]

THIS INSTRUMENT was on the day of the date thereof, signed, published and declared by the said Testat____ May Zhuck ge shig to be her Last Will and Testament in our presence, who at her request have subscribed our names thereto as witnesses, in his[sic] presence and in the presence of each other.

Peter G. Trottochand residing at *Beaulieu, MN*
F.M. Archibald residing at *Mahnomen, MN*

Probate 87650-19 C E T
DEPARTMENT OF THE INTERIOR, Office of Indian Affairs Aug 13, 1920
The within will is hereby recommended for approval in accordance with the provisions of the Act of June 25, 1910 (36 Stat. L, 855-6). as amended by the Act of February 14, 1913 (37 Stat. L, 678).

Respectfully,
E.B. Meritt
Assistant Commissioner

DEPARTMENT OF THE INTERIOR, Office of the Secretary Aug. 17, 1920
The within will is hereby approved in accordance with the provisions of the Act of June 25, 1910 (36 Stat. L, 855-6), as amended by the Act of February 14, 1913 (37 Stat. L, 678).

S.G. Hopkins
Assistant Secretary

<<<<<<<<>>>>>>>>
Last Will and Testament of Christopher Wind

I, **CHRISTOPHER WIND**, of the County of Ottawa and State of Oklahoma, an allottee of the Ottawa Tribe of Indians, 70 years of age, being of sound and disposing mind and realizing my serious illness and the frailty of my body, do publish and declare this as my last Will and Testament in manner and form as follows:

First; That all my just debts and funeral expenses shall be paid.

NATIVE AMERICAN WILLS and PROBATE RECORDS, 1911 - 1921

Second; I give and bequeath to my beloved wife, Minnie Wind, the E ½ of my homestead described as Lot #2 of the NE ¼ of Sec 10, T27N, R23E of the Indian Meridian in Ottawa County and State of Oklahoma, together with all the improvements and appurtenances thereunto belonging.

I give and bequeath to my son, Thomas Wind, the West ½ of said Lot #2, in said Section 10, T27N, R23E.

I give and bequeath to my daughter, Lillian N. Wind, Elizabeth Wind, now Devens, Lizzie Wind, now French and to my son, Edgar Wind, the sum of $5 each.

In witness whereof I have hereunto set my hand and seal in the said County of Ottawa and State of Oklahoma, on this the 9th day of June in the year of our Lord, 1919.

Christopher Wind (Seal)

Signed, sealed, published and declared by Christopher Wind, the above named Testator, in the presence of us, who at his request, in his presence and in the presence of each other, have hereunto set our names as subscribing and attesting witnesses to the foregoing instrument as the Last Will and Testament of the said Christopher Wind on this the 9th day of June in the year of our Lord, 1919.

Mrs. Pink
Miami, OK RFD #1
U.A. Burton
Miami, OK RFD #1

LAST WILL AND TESTAMENT OF WAHACANKAWANJINA

I, **WAHACANKAWANJINA**, Devils Lake allottee #67, of Fort Totten, North Dakota, being of sound mind and disposing memory and understanding, and not under any compulsion or stress of circumstances, hereby make, declare and publish this my last will and testament, hereby revoking and annulling all wills heretofore made by me. It is my will and desire that my property be disposed of in the following manner, to-wit:

FIRST; I give, devise and bequeath to my wife, Kimimikoyakewin, 40 acres of my allotment described as the NE ¼ of SW ¼, Sec 31, T153N, R63W, 5th P.M.

SECOND; I give, devise and bequeath to my grand-daughter, Mary Celina Mead, the NE ¼ of SE ¼ of Sec 11, T152N, R64W, 5th P.M, containing 40 acres of my allotment.

THIRD; I give, devise and bequeath to my grand-son, Oyemazana, the SW ¼ of SE ¼, Sec 11, T152N, R64W, 5th P.M, containing 40 acres of my allotment.

NATIVE AMERICAN WILLS and PROBATE RECORDS, 1911 - 1921

FOURTH; I give, devise and bequeath jointly to my grand-son and grand-daughter, (no names given), being the children of Joseph Johns, my deceased son, the SE ¼ of SE ¼ of Sec 11, T152N, R64W, 5th P.M, containing 40 acres of my allotment.

FIFTH; I hereby appoint and constitute John Eyapaha, the executor of this my last will and testament, and direct that any funds accruing to my estate and held in the hands of the Superintendent of the Fort Totten Indian School, be applied toward my funeral expenses and other just debts, preference to be given to the payment of my funeral expenses.

IN TESTIMONY WHEREOF, I have set my hand and seal to this my last will and testament at Fort Totten, North Dakota, this 3rd day of May, in the year of our Lord, 1918, signing the same in the presence of Martin Strait, Charles Brooks, and S.A.M. Young, who as my request and in my presence have witnessed my signing hereof, we all signing in the presence of each other.

                          Wahacankawanjina   His (thumb print) mark

Signed, sealed, published and declared by the said Wahacankawanjina in our presence as and for his last will and testament; at his request and in his presence, and in the presence of each other, we have hereunto subscribed our names as attesting witnesses.

                    Chas. Brooks   *S A M Young*

Probate 12063-1920 J H H
DEPARTMENT OF THE INTERIOR, Office of Indian Affairs Aug. 13, 1920

      It is recommended that the within will be approved pursuant to the provisions of the Act of June 25, 1910 (36 Stat. L, 855-856), as amended by the Act of February 14, 1913, (37 Stat. L, 678).

                          Respectfully,
                          E.B. Meritt
                          Assistant Commissioner

DEPARTMENT OF THE INTERIOR, Office of the Secretary Aug. 24, 1920

      The within will is hereby approved pursuant to the provisions of the Act of June 25, 1910 (36 Stat. L, 855-856), as amended by the Act of February 14, 1913 (37 Stat. L, 678).

                          [Signed]   S.G. Hopkins
                          Assistant Secretary

W I L L

IN THE NAME OF GOD, Amen:

      I, **HIGH CRANE**, Fort Peck allottee #418 residing at Poplar, Montana, being of sound mind but of feeble health and realizing the uncertainty of life, and not acting under fraud, duress, menace or undue influence, do this 24th day of

NATIVE AMERICAN WILLS and PROBATE RECORDS, 1911 - 1921

Sept, 1918, make, publish and declare the following to be my last will and testament:

First;
    I give, devise and bequeath to my beloved daughter, Mrs. Otto Browning and my beloved wife, Mrs. High Crane, my grazing land described as follows: W ½ of Sec. ?-?-49(unable to read numbers, original typed over).
Second;
    I give, devise and bequeath to my beloved daughter, Mrs. Medicine Bear, the SE ¼ of the NW ¼ of Sec. 4-2u[sic]-49 being my irrigable allotment.
Third;
    I give, devise and bequeath to my beloved granddaughter, Fannie Browning, S ½ of NE ¼ of the NW ¼ of Sec. 15-27-49, being my timber allotment.
Fourth;
    I give, devise and bequeath to my beloved daughter, Mrs. Otto Browning, all my share in the estate of my deceased mother, Yellow Thunder, on at[sic] Standing Rock Reservation in North and South Dakota.

    I hereby appoint E.D. Mossman, Supt. of Fort Peck Agency or his successor in office, as executor of my estate.

                                  High Crane (thumb print)
                                  Fort Peck allottee #418

Witnesses and Interpreters.
    Joseph Culbertson
    Herman Red Elk

    We, the undersigned, hereby certify on our honor that neither of us are related in any way to the testator, that we were both present and witnessed the signature of the testator to the above instrument in one page which he read and fully understood before signing as he was apparently of sound mind and signed the same of his own free will and accord stating that his wishes were duly set forth.

                                  Joseph Culbertson
                                  Herman Red Elk

DEPARTMENT OF THE INTERIOR, Office of Indian Affairs   Aug. 20, 1920
    The within will of High Crane, deceased Yankton Sioux allottee #418, of the Fort Peck Reservation, is recommended for disapproval, in accordance with the provisions of the Act of June 25, 1910 (36 Stat. L, 855-6), as amended by the Act of February 14, 1913 (37 Stat. L, 678).

                                  Respectfully,
                                  E.B. Meritt
                                  Assistant Commissioner

DEPARTMENT OF THE INTERIOR, Office of the Secretary   Aug. 23, 1920

NATIVE AMERICAN WILLS and PROBATE RECORDS, 1911 - 1921

The within will of High Crane, deceased Yankton Sioux, allottee #418 of the Fort Peck Reservation, is hereby disapproved in accordance with the provisions of the Act of June 25, 1910, (36 Stat. L, 855-6), as amended by the Act of February 14, 1913 (37 Stat. L, 678).

S.G. Hopkins
Assistant Secretary

<<<<<<<<>>>>>>>>

WILL OF DOG LISTENS - FT. PECK, MONT

I, **DOG LISTENS**, Yankton Indian, aged 76 years, allottee #276 of Fort Peck Agency, MT, being of sound mind, make this my last Will and declare my wishes and give and bequeath my property at my death, as follows:

First; to my wife, Holy Woman Dog Listens, Yankton Indian Allottee #277, aged 58, of Fort Peck Agency, MT, I give my 120 acre allotment and described as E ½ SW ¼ and SW ¼ of SE ¼ of Sec 28, T28, R54; also I give her timber allotment of 20 acres, described #276, E ½ SW ¼ Sec. 33, T28, R54 on Fort Peck Reservation, MT.

Second; my allotment of 240 acres, described as SW ¼ and the S ½ of NW ¼ of Sec. 36, T33, R54, on Fort Peck Reservation, MT; I give and bequeath to be shared equally; one half to my grandson, James Medicine, allottee #1787, aged 6 years of Fort Peck Reservation, MT; and ½ to my niece, Good Tail Woman Dumb, aged 43, allottee #366, of Fort Peck Agency, Poplar, MT.

My nephew, Pins (?, difficult to read handwriting) Big Shield, of Standing Rock Reservation, Shields, ND. I do not wish to have any share and I intentionally leave him out of any share in my estate.

The rest of my estate is my inherited interest in the estate of my sister, Ospu, known as Mr. Lean or Watches Lodge, of Standing Rock Reservation, ND.

This my residuary estate I leave to be equally shared by the three above heirs, Holy Woman Dog Listens, James Medicine and Good Tail Woman Dumb, provided first the sum of $100 be paid to Big Foot, Fort Peck Indian, allottee #124.

Signed by my hand -my thumb- this 20th day of March, 1916, at Drew, MT, Fort Peck Reservation.

Interpreted and Witnessed by   Dog Listens   his (thumb print) thumb
Harold Red Eagle
Brockton, MT

Witnessed by:
   F.E. Farrell,   Brockton, MT
   US I.D Faruor,   Ft. Peck Resv, MT

DEPARTMENT OF THE INTERIOR, Office of Indian Affairs   Aug 20, 1920
The within will of Dog Listens, deceased Yankton Sioux allottee #276, of the Fort Peck Reservation, is recommended for approval, in accordance with

NATIVE AMERICAN WILLS and PROBATE RECORDS, 1911 - 1921

the provisions of the Act of June 25, 1910, (36 Stat L, 855-6), as amended by the Act of February 14, 1913 (37 Stat. L, 678).

Respectfully,
E.B. Meritt
Assistant Commissioner

DEPARTMENT OF THE INTERIOR, Office of the Secretary   Aug. 20, 1920
    The within will of Dog Listens, deceased Yankton Sioux allottee #276, of the Fort Peck Reservation, is hereby approved in accordance with the provisions of the Act of June 25, 1910 (36 Stat. L, 855-6), as amended by the Act of February 14, 1913 (37 Stat. L, 678).

S.G. Hopkins
Assistant Secretary

<<<<<<<>>>>>>>

OFFICE OF INDIAN AFFAIRS
RECEIVED
JUL 6, 1920
57013

Last Will and Testament of Cora E. Cockrell

Know all men by these presents: That I, **CORA E. COCKRELL**, of Wabbaseka, of the County of Jefferson, State of Arkansas, being in ill health but of sound and disposing mind and memory, do make and publish this my last will and testament, hereby revoking all former wills by me at any time heretofore made.
First;   I constitute and appoint my husband, W.G. Cockrell, of Waggaseka, Arkansas, to be sole executor of this, my last will and testament and request that he be issued letters of administration without being required to give bond.
Second;   I direct my said executor to pay all my funeral expenses and just debts as soon after my death as it shall be convenient for him to do so.
Third;   I give and bequeath to my beloved husband,   W.G. Cockrell, all of the personal estate to which I may be entitled at the time of my death except my interest in a royalty contract on some mining land in Oklahoma to have and to hold as his own property absolutely.
Fourth;   All of the rest and residue of my property, whether personal, real or mixed, including the royalty contract mentioned in the preceding paragraph, of which I may die seized and possessed, I give, bequeath and devise to my beloved husband, W.G. Cockrell, for and during his natural life, and after his death, I give bequeath and devise said property to my beloved children, Pearl Annie Cockrell, Samuel McKee Cockrell, Wheeler Gordon Cockrell and Woodrow Wilson Cockrell, to have and to hold forever in fee simple share and share alike.
Fifth;   In the event any of my said children mentioned in the preceding paragraph, shall die before my said husband, without issue living at the time of the death of my said husband, then I give, devise and bequeath the share of such deceased child or children to my children then living, but if any of my said children shall die before my said husband and shall leave issue living at the time of the death of my said husband, then I give, devise and bequeath the share of each deceased child or children to the issue of such deceased child or children.

NATIVE AMERICAN WILLS and PROBATE RECORDS, 1911 - 1921

Sixth; I request that my said husband after my death shall place my daughter, Pearl Annie Cockrell, with some refined family to be by them reared, and request my said husband to see that necessary expenses therefore are promptly met, but this is merely a request, and shall in no sense be a charge upon my estate.

In witness whereof, I have hereunto set my hand and seal this 10th day of March, 1919, in the presence of the witnesses who have signed below, in my presence and in the presence of each other and at my request.

Cora E. Cockrell   [Seal]

Signed, sealed, published and declared by the said Cora E. Cockrell as and for her last will and testament in the presence of us, who here in her presence and in the presence of each other and at her request subscribed our names hereto as witnesses.

R.J. Watkins
W.H. Townsend

March 10, 1919 Lloyd Garrett
Proof of Will.
State of Arkansas
County of Jefferson

Personally appeared before me, L.T. Sallee, Clerk of the County and Probate Courts of Jefferson County, AR, R.J. Watkins, W.H. Townsend and Lloyd Garrett, to me well known, who being duly sworn, say: That they are the subscribing witnesses to the foregoing instrument of writing purporting to be the last will and testament of Cora E. Cockrell, deceased; that said instrument was executed at the time, place, and by the person therein named; that said Cora E. Cockrell, the testatrix was at the time of signing said instrument upwards of 21 years of age, and of sound and disposing mind and memory, and that in the presence of both these affiants she declared it to be her last will and testament, and subscribed her name thereto in the presence of both these affiants; that at the request of said testatrix affiants wrote their names to her said will in her presence and in the presence of each other; that the subscriptions to the foregoing instrument of writing are genuine, and that said instrument which is hereto attached is the identical one that affiants so witnessed and saw the said Cora E. Cockrell sign.

R.J. Watkins
W.H. Townsend
Lloyd Garrett

Subscribed and sworn to before me this 8th day of April, 1919.

[Seal]   L.T. Sallee, Clerk

Endorsed: Filed April 1, 1919   L.T. Sallee, County & Probate Clerk

Examined and admitted to Probate and Record, April 14, 1919

R.H. Williams, Judge

Recorded April 14, 1919

L.T. Sallee, Clerk

NATIVE AMERICAN WILLS and PROBATE RECORDS, 1911 - 1921

A.M. Barrow, D.C.

State of Arkansas
County of Jefferson

I, L.T. Sallee, Clerk of the County and Probate Courts within and for the above named county and state, duly commissioned, qualified and acting do hereby certify that the annexed and foregoing is a true, correct and compared copy of the Last Will and Testament of Cora E. Cockrell, deceased, as the same appears of record in Will Record #3 at pages 544 and 545.
Given under my hand and seal at Pine Bluff, AR, November 3, 1919.

L.T. Sallee, County & Probate Clerk
A.M. Barrow
(County Seal) Deputy Clerk

DEPARTMENT OF THE INTERIOR, Office of Indian Affairs Aug 9, 1920
It is hereby recommended that the within will of Cora E. Cockrell, deceased allottee #136, of the Quapaw Tribe, be approved in accordance with the provisions of the Act of June 25, 1910, (36 Stat. 855-6) as amended by the Act of February 14, 1913, (37 Stat. 678), so far as relates to property under Federal control.

Respectfully,
E.B. Meritt
Assistant Commissioner

DEPARTMENT OF THE INTERIOR, Office of the Secretary (No date given)
The within will of Cora E. Cockrell, deceased Quapaw allottee #136, is hereby approved in accordance with the provisions of the Act of June 25, 1910, (36 Stat. 855-6) as amended by the Act of February 14, 1913, (37 Stat. 678) and the Regulations of the Department, so far as relates to property under Federal control.

S.G. Hopkins
Assistant Secretary

<<<<<<<>>>>>> WILL

OFFICE OF INDIAN AFFAIRS
RECEIVED
MAR 12, 1918
21682

IN THE NAME OF GOD, Amen: I, **KENTUCK TSOU-LICK**, age 82 years, allottee #1505 of the Nez Perce Indian Reservation, Idaho, now residing at Kamiah, Idaho, being of sound mind and disposing memory, and not acting under duress, menace, fraud, or undue influence, of any person whatsoever, do hereby make, publish and declare this my LAST WILL AND TESTAMENT, in the manner following, that is to say;

First; I direct that my body be decently buried with proper regard to my station in life, and the circumstances of my estate.

NATIVE AMERICAN WILLS and PROBATE RECORDS, 1911 - 1921

Second; I direct that my funeral expenses and expenses of my last illness be paid from any funds belonging to my estate or in custody of the Superintendent of the Nez Perce Indian Reservation, Lapwai, Idaho.

Third; I will and bequeath to Paul Corbett, with whom I live, and who cares for me, all the lands of which I die possessed, described as follows: My own allotment #1505, described as the W ½ of Lot 22 and E ½ & E ½ of W ½ Lot 11, S ½ of Lot 18, Sec. 7, T33N, R4E, B.M, (less 11.25 acres sold to United States for day school) and Lots 4, 5, 12 & 13, Sec. 23, T33N, R1E, B.M, Idaho.

All of allotment 1506, which I inherited from my wife Yume-yen-yekt, described as Lots 6, 7, 10, 11, Sec 23, T33N, R1E, B.M, Idaho. (L.H.124694-14)

Four-twenty fourths of allotment #1669, which I inherited from Nancy Corbett (L.H.125975-1914) described as N ½ of SW ¼ Sec. 34, N ½ of SE ½ of SE ¼ Sec. 33, & S ½ of NE ¼ of SE ¼ Sec. 33, T32N, R4E, B.M, Idaho.

One-eighth of allotment #1394 which I inherited from Meet-me-tah-ma-nin-my (Josephine) (Land Sales 50502-1911), described as S ½ of S ½ Lot 1; N ½ & W ½ of S ½ Lot 2; Lot 6, SE ¼ of SW ¼ of NE ¼ Sec. 11; SW ¼ of S ½ Lot 8; N ½ of W ½ Lot 9; Sec 12, T33N, R3E; and Lots 19 and 30, Sec 29, T21N, R2E, B.M, Idaho.

Three- thirty seconds of allotment 714 which I inherited from How-wy-how-wy in (Land Sales 50501-1911) described as Lots 30,31, 32, Sec. 33, T35N, R3W, Lot 3 (19,81a), Sec 4, T34N, R3W, B.M, Idaho.

Fourth; I will and bequeath to my half-brothers, Moses Kentuck, Pierre Corbett and Paul Corbett, Sr, the sum of one dollar each to be paid from my personal estate.

Fifth; I will and bequeath to the heirs of my half-brother, Felix Corbett, the sum of one dollar. To the heirs of my half-brother, Billy Corbett, the sum of one dollar. To the heirs of Susan Holmes Corbett, my half-sister, the sum of one dollar. To be paid from my personal estate. This paragraph is not to effect the interest of Paul Corbett, who is son of Felix Corbett, deceased, and who is to inherit all my lands, and the balance of my personal estate.

Sixth; If any other person should make claim to my estate as an heir and prove same, the sum of one dollar and no more shall be paid from personal estate.

In witness whereof, I have hereunto put my hand and seal this 17th day of November, 1917.

Kentuck Tsou lick His right thumb mark

The foregoing instrument was on the date hereof signed, sealed, published and declared by said (Kentuck Corbett) Kentuck Tsoulick to be his last will and testament, in the presence of us, and at his request and in his presence, and in the presence of each other, we have subscribed our names as witnesses on this 17th day of November, 1917.

Jacob Brent
John J. Gwyn
Henry Enos
    Interpreter

NATIVE AMERICAN WILLS and PROBATE RECORDS, 1911 - 1921

Probate 26982-20 J M P
DEPARTMENT OF THE INTERIOR, Office of Indian Affairs   Aug 19, 1920
    It is recommended that the within will be approved, pursuant to the provisions of the Act of June 25, 1910, (36 Stat. L, 855-856). as amended by the Act of February 14, 1913 (37 Stat. L, 678).
                                       Respectfully,
                                        E.B. Meritt
                                       Assistant Commissioner

DEPARTMENT OF THE INTERIOR, Office of the Secretary   Aug 19, 1920
    The within will is hereby approved pursuant to the provisions of the Act of June 25, 1910 (36 Stat. L, 855-6), as amended by the Act of February 14, 1913 (37 Stat. L, 678)
                                       S.G. Hopkins
                                       Assistant Secretary

<<<<<<<<>>>>>>>

                    Last Will and Testament
                            of
                          Pounds The Iron

IN THE NAME OF GOD, Amen,

OFFICE OF INDIAN AFFAIRS RECEIVED AUG 4, 1920 65265

    I, **POUNDS THE IRON**, of Crow Agency, Montana, being of sound mind, memory and understanding, do hereby make and publish this, my last will and testament, hereby revoking and annulling all wills by me heretofore made, in manner and form following, that is to say:
    First; I direct that all my just debts and funeral expenses, and expenses of my last illness shall be paid by my executor hereinafter named as soon after my decease as convenient.
    Second; I give, devise and bequeath to Thomas Big Lake, my only living child and son, because he and his wife, Kills the Chief, or Loretta Pretty Eagle, have been good and kind and taken care of me in my old age; all my allotment of land; inherited interests in lands of deceased relatives; all my funds, horses and other personal property. But and in case of the death of my son, Thomas, I desire that all my property conveyed to him in this will shall go to his present wife, Kills The Chief and his children.
    Third; All the rest and residue of my estate, both real and personal and mixed, I give, devise and bequeath to my lawful heirs as determined after my decease.
    And Lastly; I do hereby nominate, constitute and appoint The Superintendent of the Crow Indian Reservation executor of this, my last will and testament.

NATIVE AMERICAN WILLS and PROBATE RECORDS, 1911 - 1921

In testimony whereof, I have set my hand and seal to this, my last will and testament, at Crow Agency, Montana, this 2nd day of May, in the year of our Lord, 1918.

Pounds the Iron   her (thumb print) mark

Signed, sealed, published and declared by said Pounds the Iron in our presence, as and for her last will and testament, and at her request and in our presence, and in the presence of each other, we have hereunto subscribed our names as attesting witnesses thereto.

                     C.H. Asbury, Supt. of Crow Agency, Montana
                     S.J. Shick   of Crow Agency, Montana

DEPARTMENT OF THE INTERIOR, Office of Indian Affairs   Aug. 18, 1920

It is hereby recommended that the within will of Pounds The Iron, #76, deceased Crow allottee, be approved under the provisions of the Act of June 15, 1910 (36 Stat. L, 855-6) as amended by the Act of February 14, 1913, (37 Stat. L, 678), and the Regulations of the Department, but no right of an executor will be recognized.

                     Respectfully,
                     E.B. Meritt
                     Assistant Commissioner

DEPARTMENT OF THE INTERIOR, Office of Indian Affairs   Aug. 19, 1920

The within will of Pounds The Iron, deceased Crow allottee #76, is hereby approved under the provisions of the Act of June 25, 1910 (36 Stat. L, 855-6), as amended by the Act of Feb. 14, 1913.(37 Stat. L, 678), and the Regulations of the Department, but no rights of an executor will be recognized.

                     S.G. Hopkins
                     Assistant Secretary

<<<<<<<>>>>>>>

OFFICE OF INDIAN AFFAIRS
RECEIVED
AUG 5, 1920
65407

To Whom These Presents May Come; Greetings:

I, **JOHN DICK**, of legal age, a resident of Yakima County, Washington. Sound of mind and free from any and all mental stress or under influence, of any person or persons, do hereby make a last Will and Testament,

First; It is my desire, wish and direction, that all of my debts and funeral expenses be paid out of my estate as well as the cost of a suit, able monument to be erected at my grave;

Second; I give, devise and bequeath to my beloved wife, Elizabeth Andy, to whom I was married Indian custom and with whom I have lived as husband and wife for over twenty years, one-third of my estate, as well as all of my gentle work and saddle horses, with the promise that my son Waters Dick, may have the use from time to time, of said work horses, said Waters Dick to

NATIVE AMERICAN WILLS and PROBATE RECORDS, 1911 - 1921

promptly return said work horses to said Elizabeth Andy when through working them;

Third; I give, devise and bequeath all of my wild horses, believed to be 100 or so in number, to my son, Waters Dick;

Fourth; To the surviving heirs of my deceased son, Eddie Dick, I give, devise and bequeath the sum of one dollar ($1.00) each.

Fifth; To my surviving children, Waters Dick, Lena Dick, Frances Marpelie and Lizzie Jack, I give, devise and bequeath the remainder of my estate or property, real and personal, share and share alike.

Witnesses:

Joseph Duff Thomas   *John Dick*   his (thumb print) mark
Ransom R. Clark

Joseph Duff Thomas and Ransom R. Clark, do solemnly swear that we acted as witnesses to the will of said John Dick, at his request, that he signed the instrument in our presence, that we signed the instrument in his presence, and that all signed the instrument in the presence of each other.

Joseph Duff Thomas
Tappenish, WA
Ransom R. Clark
Tappenish, WA

This is to certify that this instrument consisting of three pages, was prepared by me at the request of said John Dick, that the contents thereof are in strict accord with his instructions and were thoroughly explained to him and the attesting witnesses before execution; that said John Dick and said witnesses executed said instrument in the presence of each other and my presence and that all are known to me to be the persons above signatures are affixed hereto.

Don Carr, Supt.

Done at his home on Tappenish Creek this 12th day of November, 1919.

DEPARTMENT OF THE INTERIOR, Office of Indian Affairs   Aug 19, 1920

It is hereby recommended that the within will of John Dick, deceased Yakima allottee #562, be approved in accordance with the provisions of the Act of June 25, 1910, (36 Stat. L, 855-6) as amended by the Act of February 14, 1913, (37 Stat. 678), and the Regulations of the Department.

Respectfully,
E.B. Meritt
Assistant Commissioner

8-MH-13

DEPARTMENT OF THE INTERIOR, Office of the Secretary   Aug 19, 1920

The within will of John Dick, deceased Yakima allottee #562, is hereby approved in accordance with the provisions of the Act of June 25, 1910 (36 Stat. L, 855-6) as amended by the Act of February 14, 1913, (37 Stat. 678), and the Regulations of the Department.

S.G. Hopkins

NATIVE AMERICAN WILLS and PROBATE RECORDS, 1911 - 1921

Assistant Secretary

WILL OF CHIEFGHOST

I, **CHIEFGHOST**, aged 70, Yankton Indian of Ft. Peck Resv, MT, allottee 169, Sheridan Co, MT, being of sound mind do hereby declare this my last Will and Testament and bequeath my estate and property and desire it distributed at my death, as follows:

First; To my wife, Bedoza Chiefghost, aged 59 years, Ft. Peck Indian allottee 170, Sheridan Co, MT, I give my personal property and my timber allotment of 20 acres described as E ½ SW ¼ SE ¼, Sec 32, T28, R54, Ft. Peck Resv, MT; also I give to her a half share on my grazing lands allotted to me the NE ¼ and N ½ SE ¼ Sec. 29, T28, R54 and S ½ NE ¼, Sec. 5, T1`, R55, being 320 acres.

Second; To my daughter, Red Dress, aged 45, Indian of Standing Rock Resv, N. Dakota. Married, I give half of my grazing allotment above described and on Ft. Peck Resv, MT.

Third; To my grandson, Joseph Whiteagle, aged 17, Ft. Peck Resv. allottee 1020, I give my 40 acre allotment, the NE ¼, NE ¼, Sec. 4, T31, R55 on Ft. Peck Resv, MT.

Fourth; To the Indians of Dist 41, Ft. Peck Resv, I give 3 acres of land on which now is built the meeting house to be used for meetings and public use.

Signed and delivered this 11th day of June, 1917 at Dow Sheridan Co, MT.

Witnesses: Chiefghost his (thumb print) mark
F.E. Farrell, farmer
Reuben Counter, Interpreter
Brockton, MT

DEPARTMENT OF THE INTERIOR, Office of Indian Affairs
The will of Chief Ghost, deceased Yankton Sioux allottee #169 of the Fort Peck Reservation, is recommended for approval in accordance with the provisions of the Act of June 25, 1910 (36 Stat. L, 855-6), as amended by the Act of February 14, 1913, (37 Stat. L, 678).

Respectfully,
E.B. Meritt
Assistant Commissioner

DEPARTMENT OF THE INTERIOR, Office of the Secretary
The will of Chief Ghost, deceased Yankton Sioux allottee #169 of the Fort Peck Reservation, is hereby approved in accordance with the provisions of

NATIVE AMERICAN WILLS and PROBATE RECORDS, 1911 - 1921

the Act of June 25, 1910 (36 Stat. L, 855-6), as amended by the Act of February 14, 1913 (37 Stat. L, 678).

S.G. Hopkins
Assistant Secretary

<<<<<<<>>>>>>>

BE IT REMEMBERED THAT I, **NANCY GARTER**, Cheyenne River Sioux allottee #573, being of sound mind, memory and understanding, do hereby make, publish and declare this as and for my last will and testament, hereby revoking all other wills or codicils heretofore by me made.

FIRST; To my adoptive father, Joseph Garter, I give, devise and bequeath my allotment on the Cheyenne River Reservation described as the SW/4 of Sec. 6, T15N, R25E, B.H.M, S.D, 160 acres. And to my adoptive father, Joseph Garter, I also give my ID cattle, and all other property real and personal, of which I may die possessed.

I hereby appoint the Superintendent or other officer in charge of the Cheyenne River Reservation, SD, as executor of this my last will and testament.

IN TESTIMONY WHEREOF, I have hereunto subscribed my name and seal this 26th day of August, 1918, at Cheyenne Agency, in the presence of two attesting witnesses.

[Seal]   *Nancy Garter*

SIGNED, SEALED, PUBLISHED AND DECLARED as and for her last will and testament by the said Nancy Garter on this day and year first above mentioned and in her presence and at her request, and in the presence of each other, we have hereunto subscribed out names as attesting witnesses.

Agnes Kingman   *Harold E. Bruce*
Clerk, Cheyenne Agency, SD   Clerk, Cheyenne Agency, SD

PROBATE 77633-1918 L L
DEPARTMENT OF THE INTERIOR, Office of Indian Affairs   Aug 18, 1920
It is recommended that the within will be approved pursuant to the provisions of the Act of June 25, 1910 (36 Stat. L, 855-856), as amended by the Act of February 14, 1913 (37 Stat. L, 678).

Respectfully,
E.B. Meritt
Assistant Commissioner

DEPARTMENT OF THE INTERIOR, Office of the Secretary   Aug. 19, 1920
The within will is hereby approved pursuant to the provisions of the Act of June 25, 1910 (36 Stat. L, 855-856), as amended by the Act of February 14, 1913 (37 Stat. L, 678).

S.G. Hopkins
Assistant Secretary

NATIVE AMERICAN WILLS and PROBATE RECORDS, 1911 - 1921

<<<<<<<>>>>>>>

LAST WILL AND TESTAMENT OF
Mahpiicasna, Allottee #1035

OFFICE OF INDIAN AFFAIRS
RECEIVED
NOV 13, 1918
90855

IN THE NAME OF GOD, Amen.

I, **MAHPIICASNA**, of Fort Totten, ND, being 85 years of age, of sound mind, memory and understanding, do hereby make and publish this my last Will and Testament, hereby revoking and annulling all wills by me heretofore made, in manner and form following, that is to say:

FIRST; I direct that all my just debts and funeral expenses and expenses of my last illness shall be paid by my executrix hereinafter named as soon after my decease as shall be convenient;

SECOND; I give, devise and bequeath to Iyosanajinwin, my stepdaughter, the daughter of my husband by a former marriage, which stepdaughter I am now living with and with who I have been making my home for the past fifteen years, all of my allotment #1035, on the Devils Lake Sioux Reservation, described as the NE ¼ of SE ¼, and SE ¼ of NE ¼ Sec. 22, and SW ¼ of NW ¼ Sec. 23, T151N, R63W, 5th P.M, North Dakota, containing 120 acres.

THIRD; As my husband is also getting old and blind, and both of us are being cared for by my said stepdaughter, and have been so cared for for the past fifteen years, I give, devise and bequeath to Iyosanajinwin, my stepdaughter, who is 45 years of age, all the rest and residue of my estate, both real and personal and mixed, including my 1/3 inherited interest in the allotment of Wancakute, deceased Devils Lake Sioux allottee #770, which allotment is described as the SE ¼ of NW ¼ and SE ¼ of NE ¼ & SE ¼ of SE ¼ Sec 19, and SW ¼ of NE ¼ Sec. 30, T152N, R64W, 5th P.M, ND, containing 160 acres,

AND LASTLY, I do hereby nominate, constitute and appoint Iyosanajinwin executrix of this my last Will and Testament.

IN TESTIMONY WHEREOF, I have set my hand and seal to this, my last Will and Testament, at Fort Totten, ND, this 5th day of July, in the year of our Lord, 1916.

Mahpiicasna her (thumb print) mark

Signed, sealed, published and declared by the said Mahpiicasna, in our presence as and for her last Will and Testament, and at her request and in our presence, and in the presence of each other, we have hereunto subscribed our names as attesting witnesses thereto.

Charles White Chas. Picard
C.E. Montgomery

Probate 90855-18 40590-20 R T B
DEPARTMENT OF THE INTERIOR, Office of Indian Affairs

NATIVE AMERICAN WILLS and PROBATE RECORDS, 1911 - 1921

It is recommended that the within will of Mahpiyaicicasnawin, Mahpiicicasna or Mahpiicasna, deceased allottee #1035 of the Devils Lake Sioux tribe, be approved under the Act of June 25, 1910, (36 Stat. L, 855-856), as amended by the Act of February 14, 1913, (37 Stat. L, 678).

> Respectfully,
> *E.B. Meritt*
> Assistant Commissioner

DEPARTMENT OF THE INTERIOR, Office of the Secretary   Aug 19, 1920

It is recommended that the within will of Mahpiyaicicasnawin, Mahpiicicasna or Mahpiicasna, deceased allottee #1035 of the Devils Lake Sioux tribe, be approved under the Act of June 25, 1910, (36 Stat. L, 855-856), as amended by the Act of February 14, 1913, (37 Stat. L, 678).

> *S.G. Hopkins*
> Assistant Secretary

<<<<<<<<>>>>>>>

LAST WILL AND TESTAMENT

OFFICE OF INDIAN AFFAIRS
RECEIVED
OCT 18, 1917
97609

Carnegie, OK
Oct. 4, 1917

I, **CHAH-YE-A-TO**, otherwise known as **ALBERT COZAD**, Kiowa allottee #282, residing near Carnegie, Caddo County, Oklahoma, being now in good health, strength of body and mind, but sensible of the uncertainty of life and desiring to make disposition of my property and affairs while in health and strength, do hereby make, publish and declare the following to be my last will and testament, hereby revoking and cancelling all other or former wills by me at any time made.

1. I direct the payment of all my just debts and funeral expenses.
2. I give and devise to my beloved wife, Tah-lah-to-ti, otherwise known as Emma Saumty, and who is Kiowa allottee #1025, all of my rights, title and interest in and to the SE/4-11-6N-11W, I.M. This is Kiowa allotment 281, and was allotted to Ke-ah-paum, deceased. In L.H.89396-14, I was declared to be an heir in said estate to the extent of 1/3 thereof.
3. I give and devise to my beloved child, Julia Cozad, born July 27, 1915, an unallotted Kiowa Indian upon the Kiowa Reservation, all of my rights, title and interest in and to the S/2 of the NE/4-11-6N-11W, I.M. being the remainder of my trust allotment of land known upon the rolls of the Interior Department as Kiowa allotment 282, remaining unsold. My reason for devising the full 80 acres of my allotment remaining unsold to my unallotted daughter is that said child has received no allotment of land upon the Kiowa Reservation, or any other Indian Reservation in the United States, and that I desire that said child receive the

benefits from an allotment and that such devise meets with the full approval of my wife.

4. I give and devise all the rest, residue and remainder of my property, real and personal, of which I may die possessed, in equal shares to my beloved son Louis Cozad, Kiowa allottee #319, and to my beloved wife Tah-lah-to-ti, otherwise known as Emma Saumty, Kiowa allottee #1025.

This will is made subject to the approval of the Secretary of the Interior.

IN WITNESS WHEREOF I, Chah-ye-a-to, Kiowa allottee #282, have to this my last will and testament, consisting of three sheets of paper, subscribed my name this 4th day of October, 1917.

Witnesses: *Chah ye a to*
Grace P. Law
John A. Law

Subscribed by Chah-ye-a-to in the presence of each of us the undersigned and at the same time declared by him to us to he his last will and testament and we thereupon at the request of Chah-ye-a-to, in his presence and in the presence of each other, sign our names this 4th day of October, 1917, at Carnegie, Oklahoma.

Grace P. Law
P.O. *Carnegie, OK*
John A. Law
P.O. *Carnegie, OK*

DEPARTMENT OF THE INTERIOR, Office of Indian Affairs

It is hereby recommended that the within will of Chah-ye-a-to, be approved under the Act of June 25, 1910, (36 Stat. L, 855-6), as amended by the Act of February 14, 1913, (37 Stat. L, 678), and the Regulations of the Department.

Respectfully
E.B. Meritt
Assistant Commissioner

DEPARTMENT OF THE INTERIOR, Office of the Secretary

The within will of Chah-ye-a-to is hereby approved under the Act of June 25, 1910, (36 Stat. L, 855-6), as amended by the Act of February 14, 1913, (37 Stat. L, 678), and the Regulations of the Department.

S.G. Hopkins
Assistant Secretary

I, **MAY-ZHUCK-E-GE-SHIG**, of Beaulieu in the County of Mahnomen and State of Minnesota, being of sound mind and memory, do make, publish and declare this to be my Last Will and Testament.

NATIVE AMERICAN WILLS and PROBATE RECORDS, 1911 - 1921

First, I order and direct that my Executors hereinafter named, pay all my just debts and funeral expenses as soon after my decease as conveniently may be.

Second, After the payment of such funeral expenses and debts, I give, devise and bequeath

(1) All my personal property to my daughter Wah-bun-un-ung-oke or Cornelia Madison.
(2) An undivided 1/3 interest in my real estate to my grand-son, William Madison,
(3) An undivided 1/3 interest in my real estate to my daughter, Wah-bun-un-ung-oke or Cornelia Madison
(4) An undivided 1/6 interest in my real estate to my grand-son, George Madison
(5) An undivided 1/6 interest in my real estate to my grand-daughter, Josephine Madison
(6) In the event that any one of the persons to whom I have willed a portion of my real estate dies before my own death, then the share of such deceased person shall be divided equally between the surviving persons to whom I have willed a share of my real estate.
(7) That no portion of my estate is willed to my step-daughter, May-maush-kow-un-ah-mo-quay or Mrs. Agnes for the reason that she is not of my blood and for the further reason that she is married to a white man who is well able to provide for her.

Lastly, I make, constitute and appoint Wah-bun-un-ung-oke or Cornelia Madison and William Madison to be Executors of this my Last Will and Testament, hereby revoking all former wills by me made.

IN TESTIMONY WHEREOF, I have hereunto subscribed my name and affixed my seal the 23rd day of July, in the year of our Lord, 1915.

May-zhucke-ge-shig   [Seal] His (thumb print) mark

THIS INSTRUMENT was, on the day of the date thereof, signed, published and declared by the said Testator to be his Last Will and Testament in our presence, who, at his request, have subscribed our names thereto as witnesses, in his presence and in the presence of each other.

Peter G. Trottochand residing at *Beaulieu, MN*
*Frank Ra*y   residing at *Beaulieu, MN*

Probate 87650-19 C E T
DEPARTMENT OF THE INTERIOR, Office of Indian Affairs   Aug 13, 1920
The within will is hereby recommended for disapproval in accordance with the provisions of the Act of June 25, 1910, (36 Stat. L, 855-6), as amended by the Act of February 14, 1913, (37 Stat. L, 678).

NATIVE AMERICAN WILLS and PROBATE RECORDS, 1911 - 1921

Respectfully,
E.B. Meritt
Assistant Commissioner

DEPARTMENT OF THE INTERIOR, Office of the Secretary
The within will is hereby disapproved in accordance with the provisions of the Act of June 25, 1910, (36 Stat. L, 855-6), as amended by the Act of February 14, 1913. (37 Stat. L, 678).

[Signed] S.G. Hopkins
Assistant Secretary

WILL OF
LOUIS STPIERRE,
Yankton Sioux Allottee #1146

DEPARTMENT OF INTERIOR) IN RE
LAST WILL AND TESTAMENT OF
) ss
LOUIS STPIERRE, YANKTON SIOUX
BUREAU OF INDIAN AFFAIRS) ALLOTTEE #1146

In THE NAME OF GOD, Amen:

I, **LOUIS StPIERRE**, of the state of South Dakota, county of Charles Mix, being of sound and disposing mind and memory, but being uncertain of life and certain of the approach of death, and desiring to dispose of all my worldly possessions while I still have the power to do so, do make and declare this to be my last will and testament hereby revoking and annulling any and all wills heretofore made by me.

1. I bequeath to such children of my daughter, Louisa Weston, as may be living at the time of my death: The NW ¼ of the SW ¼ of Sec. 17, T95N, R63W of the 5th P.M. of Charles Mix County, SD.
2. I bequeath to such children of my daughter, Sarah Wanjina, as may be living at the time of my death: The NE ¼ of the SW ¼ of Sec 17, T95N, R63W of the 5th P.M. Charles Mix County, SD.
3. I bequeath to such children of my daughter, Elizabeth Oniha as may be living at the time of my death: The SE ¼ of the SW ¼ of Sec. 17, T95N, R63W of the 5th P.M. Charles Mix County, SD.
4. I bequeath to my daughter, Nancy StPierre: The SW ¼ of the SW ¼, Sec. 17, T95N, R63W of the 5th P.M. Charles Mix County, SD.

NATIVE AMERICAN WILLS and PROBATE RECORDS, 1911 - 1921

5. I bequeath to such children of my son, Samuel StPierre, as may be living at the time of my death: The NE ¼ of the NE ¼ of Sec. 17, T95N R63W of the 5th P.M. Charles Mix County, SD.

6. I bequeath to my wife, Lydia StPierre, the SE ¼ of the NE ¼ of Sec. 17, T95N of R63W of the 5th P.M. Charles Mix County, SD.

And, also Lots 242 and 229, according to the Yankton Indian Survey, situated in Sec. 11, T94, R64, Charles Mix County, SD.

Also any personal property of which I may be possessed at the time of my death, and all moneys that may be held in trust for me by the United States at the time of my death, after all my just debts and funeral expenses have been paid.

7. It is my wish that should my daughters, Louise Weston, Sarah Wanjina and Elizabeth Oniha and my son, Samuel StPierre have no living children at the time of my death, the bequeaths made to their children shall be given to them. Each daughter and son to have that portion which I now bequeath to his or her children.

In testimony whereof, I have set my hand and seal this 28th day of August, 1917, Greenwood, Charles Mix County, South Dakota.

Louis StPierre

Witness:

Signed, sealed and published and declared this 28th day of August, 1917, by the said Louis StPierre in our presence, as and for his last will and testament, and at his request and in his presence, and in the presence of each other we have hereunto subscribed our names as attesting witnesses.

Wm F. Brazzill
J.F. Estes

Probate 99267-19 S Y T

DEPARTMENT OF THE INTERIOR, Office of Indian Affairs   Aug. 5, 1920

The within will of Louis St. Pierre is hereby recommended for approval in accordance with the Act of June 25, 1910 (36 Stat. L, 855), as amended by the Act of Feb. 14, 1913, (37 Stat. L, 678).

Respectfully,
E.B. Meritt
Assistant Commissioner

DEPARTMENT OF THE INTERIOR, Office of the Secretary   Aug 5, 1920

The within will of Louis St. Pierre is hereby approved in accordance with the Act of June 25, 1910 (36 Stat. L, 855), as amended by the Act of Feb. 14, 1913 (37 Stat. L, 678).

S.G. Hopkins
Assistant Secretary

<<<<<<<>>>>>>>

NATIVE AMERICAN WILLS and PROBATE RECORDS, 1911 - 1921

Know all men by these presents that I, **JOSEPH MONROE**, residing upon the Blackfeet Indian Reservation, being of sound mind and in my proper sense at the present time and being aware that at my age and failing condition and not having properly made and disposition of any property or chattels that I may be possessed of or that may be due me of any kind whatsoever, do now and at the present time devise and bequeath as follows; in case of my death and the only bequest that I have ever made.

    I give and bequeath to my wife, Elizabeth Ann Monroe, all that certain parcel of land or as more generally know[sic] as my allotment more particularly described in the original plat now on file in the agency office of the Blackfeet Indian Reservation to have and to hold for herself, her heirs and assigns for her own personal benefit and use and full title to same without any indebtedness whatsoever; to do as she may see fit according to her own wishes without any drawback whatsoever or question of right. And to hold the same in her own name only subject to the same laws and conditions that I now hold the aforesaid allotment under the jurisdiction of the United States Indian Department.

    Provided always that any just indebtedness that I may be responsible for individually shall finally be discharged and this with the sanction of the Indian office.

    Also, I give and bequeath to my wife, Elizabeth Ann Monroe, 5 head of horses and more said animals being at large on the range and branded (brand) and on record at the agency office of the Blackfeet Ind. Reservation. To have and to hold the said [Elizabeth Ann Monroe] to keep to and for her own proper use and benefit without any indebtedness whatsoever.

    Also, one residence situated in the Townsite of Browning, Blackfeet Indian Reservation being a frame building and being the same building purchased from Geneva Steward and more particularly known as the original "Stewart" house. This property or residence mentioned being clear of any indebtedness of any kind whatsoever, and bequeathed to my wife, Elizabeth Ann Monroe for herself, her heirs and assigns. (NOTE: Name spelled both ways.)

                           Joseph Monroe   His (thumb print) mark

Witnesses:
    Mrs. Jane Mary Pocha
    Miss Isabel Ononhal(?)

Sworn to and subscribed before me this 10th day of September, 1911.
                           James M. Amoux   Notary Public

DEPARTMENT OF THE INTERIOR, Office of Indian Affairs   Aug. 6, 1920
    It is hereby recommended that the within will of Joseph Munroe[sic], deceased Piegan allottee #1141, be approved in accordance with the provisions of the Act of June 25, 1910, (36 Stat. L, 855-6) as amended by the Act of February 14, 1913, (37 Stat. L, 678).

                           Respectfully,
                           E.B. Meritt
                           Assistant Commissioner

NATIVE AMERICAN WILLS and PROBATE RECORDS, 1911 - 1921

DEPARTMENT OF THE INTERIOR, Office of the Secretary   Aug. 6, 1920
   The within will of Joseph Munroe[sic], deceased Piegan allottee #1141, is hereby approved in accordance with the Act of June 25, 1910, (36 Stat. L, 855-6) as amended by the Act of February 14, 1913 (37 Stat. L, 678).
                                                              S.G. Hopkins
                                                              Assistant Secretary

WILL

IN THE NAME OF GOD, Amen.

   Be it remembered that I, **ANNE FINLEY**, Flathead Allottee #588, now a resident of the Flathead Reservation, in the County of Sanders, State of Montana, being of sound and disposing mind and memory, and not acting under duress, fraud, or under the influence of any person whatsoever, and being of the age of about 58 years, do hereby make, publish and declare this to be my last will and testament, that is to say:
   I hereby bequeath to my beloved husband, all of my allotment on the Flathead Reservation, Montana, being allotment #588, described as follows: SW ¼ of NE ¼; N ½ NW ½ of SE ½, & E ½ of NW ¼ of SW ¼ Sec. 27, T18N, & N20A of Lot 2, Sec. 5, T17N, all in R21W, M.M. Montana; except a tract of 7.75 A in SW ¼ NE ¼ & 1.50 A in N ½ NW ¼ SE ¼ , Sec. 27, included in R/W Nor.Pac.Ry.Co,[sic] containing after exceptions specified, 90.75 acres.
   Also, my interest in the allotment of my deceased mother on the Spokane Reservation, in Washington, the description of which I do not know.
   Also, any other inherited lands in which I may be interested in, and all personal property of which I may die possessed.
   IN WITNESS WHEREOF, I have hereunto set my hand and seal this 6th day of August, in the year of our Lord, 1919.
                                          Annie Finley   her (thumb print) mark
Witnesses to mark:
   D. Hawley   Clerk
   Lawrence Pablo   Interpreter
Both of Dixon, MT
   The foregoing instrument, consisting of this one page was, at the date thereof, by the said Anne Finley, signed, sealed and published as, and declared to be, her last will and testament, in the presence of us, who, at her request, and in her presence, and in the presence of each other, have subscribed our names as witnesses thereto.

         D. Hawley   Dixon, MT   *Lawrence Pablo*   Dixon, MT

DEPARTMENT OF THE INTERIOR, Office of Indian Affairs   Aug. 6, 1920

NATIVE AMERICAN WILLS and PROBATE RECORDS, 1911 - 1921

It is hereby recommended that the within will of Anne Finley, deceased Flathead allottee #588, be approved in accordance with the provisions of the Act of June 25, 1910, (36 Stat. L, 855-6) as amended by the Act of February 14, 1913, (37 Stat. 678).

                        Respectfully,
                        E.B. Meritt
                        Assistant Commissioner

DEPARTMENT OF THE INTERIOR, Office of the Secretary Aug. 6, 1920

The within will of Anne Finley, deceased Flathead allottee #588, is hereby approved in accordance with the provisions of the Act of June 25, 1910, (36 Stat. L, 855-6), as amended by the Act of February 14, 1913, (37 Stat. 678).

                        S.G. Hopkins
                        Assistant Secretary

OFFICE OF INDIAN AFFAIRS
RECEIVED
AUG 20, 1917
78991

<<<<<<<>>>>>>>

LAST WILL AND TESTAMENT

                        Indiahoma, OK
                        June 21, 1917

I, **WAH-WOON-AH-YETCHY**, Comanche Indian allottee #2316, 78 years of age of Indiahoma, Comanche County, OK, being now in good health, strength of body and mind, but sensible of the uncertainty of life and desiring to make disposition of my property and affairs while in health and strength do hereby make, publish and declare the following to be my last will and testament, hereby revoking and cancelling all other or former wills by me at any time made.

1; I direct the payment of all my just debts and funeral expenses.

2; I give and devise to the following Indians, who would be my sole heirs at law were I to die intestate, all of my property real and personal of which I may die possessed, including my trust allotment of land comprising the NE/4-11-2N-15,W, of the I.M. in Comanche County, OK, known upon the rolls of the Interior Department as Comanche Indian allottee #2316. The said beneficiaries to share alike, that is each beneficiary to take one-third [1/3] interest in and to real and personal property. The beneficiaries are:

                    a; To-pay, Comanche Indian allottee #2256, my only living daughter

                    b; Elsie To-wis-chy, Comanche Indian allottee #2265, my granddaughter

                    c; Kelsey To-pay, (Parker), Comanche Indian allottee #2257, my grandson

In the event that I should die my property should pass in equal share to my daughter, To-pay and to my granddaughter Elsie To-wis-chy; Kelsey To-pay is the son of To-pay. This will is made subject to the approval of the Secretary of the Interior.

NATIVE AMERICAN WILLS and PROBATE RECORDS, 1911 - 1921

In witness whereof I, Wah-woon-ah-yetchy, have to this my last will and testament, consisting of (3) sheets of paper, subscribed my name this 21st day of June, 1917.

Witnesses:
Magdalena Becker   Indiahoma, OK
A.J. Becker   Indiahoma, OK

Wah-woon-ah-yetchy
Her right thumb mark

Subscribed by Wah-woon-ah-yetchy, in the presence of each of us the undersigned and at the same time declared by her to be her last will and testament and we thereupon at the request of Wah-woon-ah-yetchy, in her presence and in the presence of each other, sign our names hereto as witnesses this 21st day of June, 1917, near Indiahoma, Comanche County, OK

A.J. Becker
P.O. Indiahoma, OK
M. Becker
P.O. Indiahoma, OK

INTERPRETER'S CERTIFICATE

I, *Magdalena Becker,* hereby certify on honor that I acted as interpreter during the execution of the foregoing last will and testament by Wah-woon-ah-yetchy; that I interpreted clearly and correctly all the conditions thereof to the testatrix before she executed said instrument and that said will meets with her full approval as it is drawn strictly in accordance with her desires and directions.

I further certify that I speak both the Comanche Indian as well as the English languages fluently and that I have no interest in this matter whatsoever. Signed this 21st day of June, 1917.

Magdalena Becker
Interpreter

DEPARTMENT OF THE INTERIOR, Office of Indian Affairs   Aug 6, 1920

It is hereby recommended that the within will of Wah-woon-ah-yetchy, deceased Comanche allottee #2316, be approved in accordance with the Act of June 25, 1910, (36 Stat. L, 855-6), as amended by the Act of February 14, 1913, (37 Stat. 678), and the Regulations of the Department.

Respectfully,
E.B. Meritt
Assistant Commissioner

DEPARTMENT OF THE INTERIOR, Office of the Secretary   Aug. 6, 1920

The within will of Wah-woon-ah-yetchy is hereby approved in accordance with the Act of June 25, 1910, (36 Stat. L, 855-6) as amended by the Act of February 14, 1913, (37 Stat. 678) and the Regulations of the Department.

S.G. Hopkins

NATIVE AMERICAN WILLS and PROBATE RECORDS, 1911 - 1921

Assistant Secretary

Will of Antoine Rouillard

IN THE NAME OF GOD, Amen:
    I, **ANTOINE ROUILLARD**, of the state of Nebraska, County of Knox, being of sound and disposing mind and memory but being uncertain of life and certain of the approach of death, and desiring to dispose of my worldly possessions while I still have the power to do so, do make and declare this to be my last will and testament, hereby revoking and annulling any and all wills heretofore made by me.
    1. I, Antoine Rouillard, do will and bequeath - the NW/4 of the SE/5 of Sec. 10, T31, R5, to my son, Gabriel Rouillard, and the SW/5 of the SE/5 of Sec. 10m T31, T5, to my other son, Theodore Rouillard.
    In testimony whereof, I have set my hand and seal this 14th day of March, 1919, at Niobrara, Knox County, Nebraska.
                      Antoine Rouillard   His mark

    Signed, sealed and published this 14th day of March, 1919, by the said Antoine Rouillard, in our presence, as and for his last will and testament, and at his request, and in his presence, and in the presence of each other we have hereunto subscribed our names as attesting witnesses.
                      Virgil L. Marks
                      Henry Robinson

PROBATE 62591-20 S Y T
DEPARTMENT OF THE INTERIOR, United States Indian Service   Jul 30, 1920
    It is recommended that the within will of Antoine Rouillard, deceased Santee Sioux Allottee #767, be approved pursuant to the provisions of the Act of June 25, 1910 (36 Stat. L, 855-856)as amended by the Act of February 14, 1913, (37 Stat. L, 678).
                      Respectfully,
                      E.B. Meritt
                      Assistant Commissioner
DEPARTMENT OF THE INTERIOR, Office of the Interior[sic]
    The within will of Antoine Rouillard, deceased Santee Sioux Allottee #767, is hereby approved pursuant to the provisions of the Act of June 25, 1910 (36 Stat. L, 855-856), as amended by the Act of February 14, 1913, (37 Stat. L. 678).   *S.G. Hopkins*
                      Assistant Secretary

NATIVE AMERICAN WILLS and PROBATE RECORDS, 1911 - 1921

Webb, Idaho Dec. 27, 1918

In the Name of God, Amen:

OFFICE OF INDIAN AFFAIRS
RECEIVED
MAR 31, 1920
27640

Know all men that I, **MAGGIE JACK** (PIT-YOU-STUNS NEY), being of sound mind, desire to make final disposition of my property and to that end make this last will and testament.

I desire to leave to my daughter, Lucy Raywoud, all my property both personal and real of which I die possessed of any kind whatsoever either heired[sic] or my own patent.

Maggie Jack   her mark
(*Pit-you-stuns ney*)

Witnesses:
Chas. C. Miles
Celia Alexander
Amy J. Webb
Probate 27640-20 J M P

DEPARTMENT OF THE INTERIOR, Office of Indian Affairs Jul 29, 1920

It is recommended that the within will be approved pursuant to the provisions of the Act of June 25, 1910 (36 Stat. L. 855-6), as amended by the Act of February 14, 1913 (37 Stat. L, 678).

Respectfully,
E.B. Meritt
Assistant Commissioner

DEPARTMENT OF THE INTERIOR, Office of the Secretary Aug. 2, 1920

The within will is hereby approved, pursuant to the provisions of the Act of June 25, 1910 (36 Stat. L, 855-6), as amended by the Act of February 14, 1913 (37 Stat. L, 678).

OFFICE OF INDIAN AFFAIRS
RECEIVED
NOV 7, 1919
95821

S.G. Hopkins
Assistant Secretary

<<<<<<<◇>>>>>>>

Last Will and Testament of James Moody

IN THE NAME OF GOD, Amen: I, **JAMES MOODY**, age 90, an Indian of the Nez Perce Indian Reservation, Idaho, now residing at Ahsahka, Idaho; being of sound mind and disposing memory, and not acting under duress, menace, fraud, or under undue influence, of any person whatsoever, do hereby make, publish this my LAST WILL AND TESTAMENT, in the manner following, that is to say:

First; I direct that my body be decently buried with proper regard to my station in life, and the circumstances of my estate;

Second; I direct that my funeral expenses and expenses of my last illness be paid from any funds belonging to my estate, or in the custody of the Superintendent of the Nez Perce Indian Reservation, Lapwai, Idaho.

NATIVE AMERICAN WILLS and PROBATE RECORDS, 1911 - 1921

Third; I will and bequeath to my wife, Lydia Moody, two small tracts of land in Sec. 33 and 34, T37N, R1E, B.M. together with buildings there on, with my personal effects, and also one-half of the residue, from the sale of Allotment #1870, described as the W ½ of the NW ¼ of Sec. 28, T37N, R1E, B.M.

Fourth; To Susie Moody Corbett, my daughter, an undivided ½ interest in Allotment #1814, described as the S ½ of the SW ¼ of Sec. 14, T37N, R1W, B.M.

Fifth; To my son, Charles Moody, all of Allotment #1868, described as the NW ¼ of the NE ¼ and NE ¼ of the NW ¼ and the N ½ of the SE ¼ of the NW ¼ of Sec. 28 and the S ½ of the S ½ of the S ½ of the SW ¼ of the SE ¼ of Sec. 21, T37N, R1E, B.M; also ½ of the residue from the sale of Allotment #1870, and three head of horses, which I now own.

In witness whereof I have hereunto put my hand and seal this the 26th day of May, 1919.

James Moody   His (thumb print) mark

The foregoing instrument was on the date hereof signed, sealed, published and declared by said James Moody to be his LAST WILL AND TESTAMENT, in the presence of us, and at his request and in his presence, and in the presence of each other, we have subscribed our names as witnesses, on this the 26th day of May, 1919.

John H. Rodgers
Orofino, Idaho
Amos H. Powaukee
Ahsahka, Idaho
Louie A. Powaukee
Ahsahka, Idaho

Probate 27631-20 J M P
DEPARTMENT OF THE INTERIOR, Office of Indian Affairs   Jul 29, 1920

It is recommended that the within will be approved pursuant to the provisions of the Act of June 25, 1910 (36 Stat. L, 855-856), as amended by the Act of February 14, 1913 (37 Stat.. 678).

Respectfully,
E.B. Meritt
Assistant Commissioner

DEPARTMENT OF THE INTERIOR, Office of the Secretary   Aug. 2, 1920

The within will is hereby approved pursuant to the provisions of the Act of June 25, 1910 (36 Stat. L. 855-856), as amended by the Act of February 14, 1913 (37 Stat. L, 678).

S.G. Hopkins
Assistant Secretary

NATIVE AMERICAN WILLS and PROBATE RECORDS, 1911 - 1921

STATE OF WISCONSIN,)
Jackson County   )

I, Frank Johnson, County Judge in and for said county do hereby certify that the copy hereunto, annexed has been compared by me with the original Will of Mrs. Jane Black Cloud, deceased, in the Matter of the Last Will and Testament of Mrs. Jane Black Cloud, deceased, now on file and of record in my office, and required by law to be in my custody, and that said copy is a true copy thereof.
      IN TESTIMONY WHEREOF, I have hereunto set my hand and affixed the seal of the county court of said county, at Black River Falls, in said County, this 10th day of July, A.D, 1918.

Frank Johnson
County Judge

      I, **MRS. JANE BLACK CLOUD**, of the Town of Komensky, Jackson County, State of Wisconsin, being of sound mind and memory, do make, publish and declare this, my last will and testament.
      First; It is my will that all my just debts, funeral expenses and all other charges be fully paid.
      Second; I give and bequeath and devise all of my property, both personal and real to Grace D. Brown Eagle, hereby meaning and intending to give to the said Grace D. Brown Eagle all of my real estate in Nebraska and all moneys which are from the United Stated Government providing Grace D. Brown Eagle takes good care of me until I die.
      In Witness Whereof, I have hereunto set my hand and seal this 20th day of April, 1917.

          her
Mrs. Jane   thumb   Black Cloud
          mark

Signed, sealed, published and declared by the said Mrs. Jane Black Cloud, of and for her last will and testament, in the presence of us, who, at her request, in her presence, and in (the) presence of each other, have hereunto subscribed our names as attesting witnesses.

                    Jacob Stucki   Black River Falls, WI
                    David Decorah Black River Falls, WI

Probate 35869-19   J W H
DEPARTMENT OF THE INTERIOR, Office of Indian Affairs   May 3, 1920
      The within will of Jane Blackcloud, a deceased unallotted Indian of the Winnebago tribe, is respectfully recommended for approval, pursuant to the provisions of the Act of June 25, 1910 (36 Stat. 855) as amended by Act of February 14, 1913 (37 Stat. 678).

E.B. Meritt
Assistant Commissioner

NATIVE AMERICAN WILLS and PROBATE RECORDS, 1911 - 1921

DEPARTMENT OF THE INTERIOR, Office of the Secretary   Jun 28, 1920
      The within will of Jane Blackcloud, a deceased unallotted Indian of the Winnebago tribe, is hereby approved pursuant to the provisions of the Act of June 25, 1910, (36 Stat. 855), as amended by Act of February 14, 1913, (37 Stat. 678).

                      S.G. Hopkins
                      Assistant Secretary

<<<<<<<>>>>>>>

OFFICE OF INDIAN AFFAIRS
RECEIVED
OCT 9, 1917
94055

IN THE NAME OF GOD, Amen:

      I, **RATTLING LEAF SHOOTS TIGER**, an Assiniboin female Indian of Wolf Point, Montana, born in the year 1846, A.D, allottee #1651, being of sound mind, but of infirm body, do hereby and by these presents make, declare, and publish this to be my last Will and Testament.

1st: I hereby direct that a decent burial be given me.

2nd: I hereby give, devise and bequeath unto Shoots Tiger, a male Indian of Wolf Point, Montana, of the Fort Peck tribe, my husband, allottee #1650, born in the year 1872, A.D; and to Thomas Duck, a male Indian of Wolf Point, Montana of the Fort Peck Tribe, allottee #1291, born in the year 1861, A.D, my brother; and unto Minnie Day, a female Indian of Wolf Point, Montana, of the Fort Peck Tribe, allottee #1282, born in the year 1892, A.D, my daughter; my land described as follows:

      NW/2 of Sec. 16, T27N, R46E, 160 acres grazing land, and the NE/4 of SW/4 of Sec. 33, T27N, R46E, 40 acres irrigable land, each to share and share alike, for and in consideration of the many kindness' shown me in my declining years.

3rd: I hereby direct that all other property of which I may die possessed be distributed to my natural heirs in accordance with the laws of the state of Montana.

      IN WITNESS WHEREOF: I have hereunto set my hand this the 8th day of September, in the year 1917.

                      Rattling Leaf Shoots Tiger   Her Mark

      We, the undersigned hereby certify that we were present at, and witnessed the signing by Rattling Leaf Shoots Tiger, of the above Will, and that she signed the same in the presence of each of us, and that it was her voluntary act, and that we have signed the Will as witnesses in the presence of each other, and in the presence of the testator, on the day and year above written.

                      Interpreter   *Minnie Sibbits Thomson*
                      Witnesses   *Victor E. Brown Turtle*

NATIVE AMERICAN WILLS and PROBATE RECORDS, 1911 - 1921

DEPARTMENT OF THE INTERIOR, Office of the Indian Affairs   Jul 28, 1920
    The within will of Rattling Leaf Shoots Tiger, deceased Assiniboin allottee #1651, of the Fort Peck Reservation, is recommended for approval in accordance with the provisions of the Act of June 25, 1910 (36 Stat. L, 855-856), as amended by the Act of February 14, 1913 (37 Stat. L, 678).
                                 Respectfully,
                                 E.B. Meritt
                                 Assistant Commissioner

DEPARTMENT OF THE INTERIOR, Office of the Secretary   Jul 29, 1920
    The within will of Rattling Leaf Shoots Tiger, deceased Assiniboin allottee #1651, of the Fort Peck Reservation, is hereby approved in accordance with the provisions of the Act of June 25, 1910 (36 Stat. L, 855-856), as amended by the Act of February 14, 1913 (37 Stat. L, 678).

                                 S.G. Hopkins
                                 Assistant Secretary

<<<<<<<<>>>>>>>

LAST WILL AND TESTAMENT

In the Name of God, Amen. I, **BEN LANGLOIS**, of Geddes in the County of Charles Mix and State of South Dakota, being of sound mind and memory, and considering the uncertainty of this frail and transitory life, do therefore make, ordain, publish and declare this to be my Last Will and Testament.
    First, I order and direct that my Executor hereinafter named, pay all my just debts and funeral expenses as soon after my decease as conveniently may be.
    Second, After the payment of such funeral expenses and debts, I give, devise and bequeath unto L.A. Steckley, all of my property of every kind and character including monies and credits.
    Lastly, I make, constitute and appoint L.A. Steckley to be Executor of this, my Last Will and Testament without bond hereby revoking all former Wills by me made.
    IN TESTIMONY WHEREOF, I have hereunto subscribed my name and affixed my seal the 31st day of July in the year of our Lord, 1918.
                                 Ben Langlois   [SEAL]

    THIS INSTRUMENT was, on the day of the date thereof, signed, published and declared by said testator Ben Langlois to be his Last Will and Testament, in our presence, who, at his request, have subscribed our names hereto as witnesses, in his presence, and in the presence of each other.

                (Illegible signature)   residing at Geddes, South Dakota
                        Burt Burton   residing at Geddes, South Dakota

NATIVE AMERICAN WILLS and PROBATE RECORDS, 1911 - 1921

PROBATE 97759-1919 S Y T
DEPARTMENT OF THE INTERIOR, Office of Indian Affairs   Jul 22, 1920
   It is recommended that the within will be approved pursuant to the provisions of the Act of June 25, 1910 (36 Stat. L, 855-856), as amended by the Act of February 14, 1913 (37 Stat. L, 678).

>Respectfully,
>*E.B. Meritt*
>Assistant Commissioner

DEPARTMENT OF THE INTERIOR, Office of the Secretary   Jul 29, 1920
   The within will is hereby approved pursuant to the provisions of the Act of June 25, 1910 (36 Stat. L, 855-856), as amended by the Act of February 14, 1913, (37 Stat. L, 678).

>*S.G. Hopkins*
>Assistant Secretary

>WILL of Robert Obeshaw

IN THE NAME OF GOD, Amen

   I, **ROBERT OBESHAW**, of the county of Charles Mix, State of South Dakota, being of sound mind and memory, but being uncertain of life, and feeling the approach of death, do make and declare this to be my last Will and Testament, hereby revoking and annulling any and all Wills heretofore made by me:
1. I give and devise unto my daughter, Anna Obeshaw, 73.40 acres of my original allotment, said land being situated in the county of Charles Mix, state of South Dakota, and being fully described as follows: NW/4 of the NE/4 (Lot 2), and NE/4 of the NW/4 (Lot 1219), in Sec. 28-95-62, containing 73.89 acres.
2. I give and bequeath unto my wife, Julia Obeshaw, all the rest and residue of my property, both real and personal, after the expenses of my last sickness, and funeral expenses have been paid.

   IN TESTIMONY WHEREOF, I have set my hand and seal this 29th day of March, 1915, at Greenwood, South Dakota.

>*Robert Obeshaw*

Signed, sealed, published and declared this 29th day of March, 1915, by the said Robert Obeshaw, in our presence as being that of his last will and testament and at his request and in his presence and in the presence of each other, we have herein assigned our names as attesting witnesses to this the last will and testament of the said Robert Obeshaw.

>*Homer ReabigSkinny?*
>*David Ree*

NATIVE AMERICAN WILLS and PROBATE RECORDS, 1911 - 1921

PROBATE 2786-1920 L L
DEPARTMENT OF THE INTERIOR, Office of Indian Affairs   Jul 22, 1920
    It is recommended that the within will be approved pursuant to the provisions of the Act of June 25, 1910, (36 Stat. L, 855-856), as amended by the Act of February 14, 1913, (37 Stat. L, 678).

                            Respectfully,
                            E.B. Meritt
                            Assistant Commissioner

DEPARTMENT OF THE INTERIOR, Office of the Secretary   Jul 28, 1920
    The within will is hereby approved pursuant to the provisions of the Act of June 25, 1910, (36 Stat. L, 855-856), as amended by the Act of February 14, 1913, (37 Stat. L, 678).

                            S.G. Hopkins
                            Assistant Secretary

State of South Dakota   )
) SS
County of Charles Mix   )

OFFICE OF INDIAN AFFAIRS
RECEIVED
Illegible
38325

    My reason for making this will at this time is that I am growing old, and it has always been my belief that a person should make their will when they are well and strong and in possession of their good health, and not wait until they are sick and in bed, before doing so.
    I have already given my son, Frank Obeshaw, 148.41 acres of land, the same being a portion of my original allotment and situated lying and being in the County of Charles Mix. He has a trust patent already issued to him for this property, hence I have not mentioned him in the will I have this day made believing that this gift already made is sufficient for him.
    I have not given my daughter, Eliza Obeshaw, now Mrs. Eliza Louder, any of my property for the fact that she has an allotment of her own, and is married and is well provided for.
    It is my desire to sell 40 acres of my allotment, and after the sale I wish the money to be placed on deposit with the superintendent of the Yankton Reservation, to be used by me in any manner I see fit from now until the time of my death, after which all this property shall go in accordance with my will this day made. The property that I wish to sell contains 40 acres and is described as follows: SE/4 Lot 1236, NW/4 of Sec. 28-95-62, containing 40 acres.
                            Robert Obeshaw

Subscribed and sworn to before me this 29th day of March, 1915.
                            Al Church
                            Superintendent

NATIVE AMERICAN WILLS and PROBATE RECORDS, 1911 - 1921

<<<<<<<◇>>>>>>>

LAST WILL and TESTAMENT
of
MARY ANN JACK

OFFICE OF INDIAN AFFAIRS
RECEIVED
SEP 9, 1919
77090

IN THE NAME OF GOD, Amen.

I, **MARY ANN JACK**, an Indian of the Muckleshoot Tribe residing on the Muckleshoot Reservation, County of King, State of Washington, of the age of about 80 years, being of sound and disposing mind and memory, and not acting under duress, menace, fraud or undue influence of any person whatever, do make, publish and declare this my LAST WILL AND TESTAMENT, in manner following, that is to say:

First: I hereby direct that all my just debts and funeral expenses be first paid.

Second: I hereby give and bequeath to my son, Alex Jack, age 60 years, the sum of ten dollars, ($10).

Third: I hereby give, devise and bequeath to my daughter, Annie Lobehan, age 47, all of my personal property, also all of my share in the estate of my deceased husband, Stuck Jack, Muckle-shoot Allottee #22, the same being a 1/3 interest in the SE ¼ of the NE ¼ of Sec. 2, T20N, R5E,
W.M, Muckleshoot Reservation.

IN WITNESS WHEREOF, I have hereunto set my hand and seal at Muckleshoot Reservation, Washington, on this 1st day of May, in the year of our Lord, 1918, A.D.

Witnesses to mark.   Her thumb mark
   Chas. A. Reynolds   *Mary Ann Jack*   [Seal]
   Alex Morris

The foregoing instrument was, at the date thereof, to-wit: on May 1, 1918, by the said Mary Ann Jack, signed, sealed, published as and declared to be her Last Will and Testament, in (the) presence of us, who at her request and in her presence and in the presence of each other, have subscribed our names as witnesses thereto.

                        Chas. A. Reynolds
                        Residing at Muckleshoot Reservation
                        Auburn, P.O. Kind County, WA

                        Alex Morris
                        Residing at Muckleshoot Reservation
                        Auburn, P.O. King County, WA

NATIVE AMERICAN WILLS and PROBATE RECORDS, 1911 - 1921

DEPARTMENT OF THE INTERIOR, Office of Indian Affairs   Jul 28, 1920
 It is hereby recommended that the within will of Mary Ann Jack, deceased unallotted Indian under the Cushman Agency jurisdiction, be approved in accordance with the Act of June 25, 1910, (36 Stat. L, 855), as amended by the Act of February 14, 1913, (37 Stat. 678).

      Respectfully,
      E.B. Meritt
      Assistant Commissioner

DEPARTMENT OF THE INTERIOR, Office of the Secretary   Jul 29, 1920
 The within will of Mary Ann Jack, deceased unallotted Indian, under the jurisdiction of the Cushman Agency, Washington, is hereby approved in accordance with the Act of June 25, 1910, (36 Stat. L, 855), as amended by the Act of February 14, 1913, (37 Stat. 678).

      S.G. Hopkins
      Assistant Secretary

OFFICE OF INDIAN AFFAIRS
RECEIVED
JUL 10, 1917
1432

<<<<<<<>>>>>>>

 In the name of God, I, **CHARLES JACKSON**, cause to be published my last will and testament on this 7 day of July, 1917.
 I am 31 years old and I have no wife or children living, the child that bears my name and lives at John Dawson, is not my child but I was to claim this child by Col. Downs.
I. I will and bequeth[sic] all of my real estate, (of which the title is held in trust by the Government to Barnard Standing and Patty Standing, each one shall shear[sic] equal in this land. The above named paties[sic] are to pay all of my indebetness[sic] and funeral expenses.
II. I appoint the Officer in charge of the Fort Peck Agency as adminstator[sic] of this my last will and testament, praying the Indian Office to hear and give respect to these my last wishes, Amen.

      Charles Jackson

Will was wrote[sic] by John F. Hargrave, Government Farmer, and I believe that it Charles Jackson is of sound mind and made the disposal of this property of his own free will.

      John F. Hargrave
      Gov't. Farmer

Witnesses:
 Robert White
 Edward Bearskin

DEPARTMENT OF THE INTERIOR, Office of Indian Affairs   Jul 22, 1920
 The within will of Charles Jackson, deceased Assiniboin allottee #1432, is hereby recommended for approval in accordance with the provisions of the Act of

NATIVE AMERICAN WILLS and PROBATE RECORDS, 1911 - 1921

June 25, 1910 (36 Stat. L, 855-856), as amended by the Act of February 14, 1913, (37 Stat. L, 678), and the Regulations of the Department.

                                              E.B. Meritt
                                        Assistant Commissioner

DEPARTMENT OF THE INTERIOR, Office of the Secretary   Jul 23, 1920

The within will of Charles Jackson, deceased Assiniboin allottee #1432, of the Fort Peck Reservation, is hereby approved in accordance with the provisions of the Act of June 25, 1910, (36 Stat. L, 855-6), as amended by the Act of February 14, 1913, (37 Stat. L, 678).

                                              S.G. Hopkins
                                          Assistant Secretary

<<<<<<<◇>>>>>>   " " WILL " "

IN THE NAME OF GOD, Amen: I, **PILLOW SHOOTER**, of Wolf Point, Montana, an Assiniboin female Indian, born in the year 1855, A.D, and allottee #1648, being of sound mind, but of infirm body, do hereby and by these presents make, declare, and publish this to be my last Will and testament.

1st,   I hereby direct that a decent burial be given me.

2nd,   I hereby give, devise and bequeath unto, Two Woman, of Lodge Pole, Montana, my daughter of the Fort Belknap Reservation, 160 acres of my grazing allotment, described as the SW/4 of Sec. 34, T28N, R48E, in consideration that she is my daughter and of the many kindness' she has shown me.

3rd,   I hereby direct that all other property of which I may die possessed be distributed to my natural heirs in accordance with the laws of the state of Montana.

IN WITNESS WHEREOF, I have hereunto set my hand this the 23rd day of July, in the year, 1917.

                                Pillow Shooter   Her (thumb print) mark

We, the undersigned hereby certify that we were present at and witnessed the signing by Pillow Shooter, of the above Will, and that she signed the same in the presence of each of us, and that it was her voluntary act, and that we have signed the Will, as witnesses in the presence of each other, and in the presence of the testator, on the day and year above written.

                                      Victor E Brown
                                      Charles Ross

DEPARTMENT OF THE INTERIOR, Office of Indian Affairs   Jul 29, 1920

The within will of Pillow Shooter, deceased Assiniboin allottee #1648, of the Fort Peck Reservation, is recommended for approval in accordance with the

NATIVE AMERICAN WILLS and PROBATE RECORDS, 1911 - 1921

provisions of the Act of June 24, 1910, (36 Stat. L, 655-6), as amended by the Act of February 14, 1913 (37 Stat. L, 678).

          Respectfully,
          E.B. Meritt
          Assistant Commissioner

DEPARTMENT OF THE INTERIOR, Office of the Secretary Jul 29, 1920

  The within will of Pillow Shooter, deceased Assiniboin allottee #1648, of the Fort Peck Reservation, is hereby approved in accordance with the provisions of the Act of June 25, 1910, (36 Stat L, 855-6), as amended by the Act of February 14, 1913, (37 Stat. L, 678).

          S.G. Hopkins,
          Assistant Secretary

OFFICE OF INDIAN AFFAIRS
RECEIVED
MAY 27, 1918
44617

<<<<<<<>>>>>>>
LAST WILL AND TESTAMENT
Anadarko, OK
May 20, 1918

  I, **TO-WA-KO-NIE (JIM)**, Wichita allottee #157, about 72 years of age, of Anadarko, Caddo County, OK, being now in good health, strength of body and mind, but sensible of the uncertainty of life, and desiring to make disposition of my property and affairs while in health and strength, do hereby make, publish and declare the following to be my last will and testament, hereby revoking and cancelling all other or former wills by me at any time made.

  FIRST: I direct the payment of all of my just debts and funeral expenses.

  SECOND: I give and devise to my beloved wife, Hoo-iye-day-as-sun-a-sis-sus, Wichita Indian allottee #158, all of my rights, title and interest in and to Lots 1 and 2 and the S ½ of the NE ¼ of Sec. 5, T8N, R10W, of the Indian Meridian, which is my trust allotment of land, and is known upon the rolls of the Interior Department as Wichita Indian allotment #157.

  THIRD: I give and devise to my beloved grand nephew, Frank Swift, an unallotted Wichita Indian upon the Kiowa Reservation, all or my right, title and interest in and to Lots 1 and 2 of Sec. 6, T8N, R10W, and the S ½ of the SE ¼ of Sec. 31, T9N, R10W of the Indian Meridian, being Wichita Indian allotment #278, originally allotted to Nan-da-kis. The allottee died on or about February 2, 1909, and the Department, in L H 27602-15 E G T declared that I was entitled to the entire estate.

  FOURTH I give and devise all of my rights, title and interest in and to the SW ¼, Sec. 32, T9N, R10W of the Indian Meridian, Wichita allotment #277, in equal shares to Leo Carruth, Wichita allottee #138, he being my great-great niece[sic], and to John Wolf, Jr, Wichita allottee #140, who is my great-great nephew. The above lands were originally allotted to Sun-tose, Wichita allottee #277, who died, and the Department in L H 27603-15 E G T declared that I was entitled to ½ of the estate of the deceased.

NATIVE AMERICAN WILLS and PROBATE RECORDS, 1911 - 1921

I give and bequeath all of the rest, residue and remainder of my property, real and personal, or which I might die possessed in equal shares to the four foregoing beneficiaries.

This will is made subject to the approval of the Secretary of the Interior.

In Witness Whereof, To-wa-ko-nie (Jim), have to this my last will and testament, consisting of three sheets of paper, subscribe my name this 20th day of May, 1918.

                        To-wa-ko-nie (Jim)   his (thumb print) mark

Witnesses:
    Warner L. Wilneeth
    Anadarko, OK
    H.E. Bretschneider

Subscribed by To-wa-ko-nie (Jim) in the presence of each of us, the undersigned, and at the same time declared by him to us to be his last will and testament, and we, thereupon, at the request of To-wa-ko-nie (Jim) in his presence and in the presence of each other, sign our names hereto as witnesses this 20th day of May, 1918, at Kiowa Indian Agency, Anadarko, OK.

                    Warner L. Wilneeth
                    Anadarko, OK P.O.
                    H.E. Bretschneider
                    Anadarko, OK P.O.

PROBATE 44617-1918 L L
DEPARTMENT OF THE INTERIOR, Office of Indian Affairs Jul 29, 1920

It is recommended that the within will be approved pursuant to the provisions of the Act of June 25, 1910 (36 Stat. L, 855-856), as amended by the Act of February 14, 1913 (37 Stat. L, 678).

                    Respectfully,
                    E.B. Meritt
                    Assistant Commissioner

DEPARTMENT OF THE INTERIOR, Office of the Secretary Jul 29, 1920

The within will is hereby approved pursuant to the provisions of the Act of June 25, 1910 (36 Stat. L, 855-856), as amended by the Act of February 14, 1913, (37 Stat. L, 678).

                    S.G. Hopkins
                    Assistant Secretary

<<<<<<<>>>>>>

LAST WILL AND TESTAMENT OF KATE FARRENSBY

IN THE NAME OF GOD, Amen

NATIVE AMERICAN WILLS and PROBATE RECORDS, 1911 - 1921

I, **KATE FARRENSBY**, wife of John Farrensby and mother of Charles A. Wilbur, by a husband now dead, now living with John Farrensby, on the Swinomish Reservation, in Skagit County, Washington, and being over the age of 21 years, and being of sound and disposing mind and memory, do hereby make, publish and declare this to be my last will and testament, in the manner following, that is to say:-

    First:-   I hereby revoke all former wills and codicils by me made.
    Second:-   I desire that after my death my body be given a decent burial, by my executor herein after named.
    Third:-   I desire that after my death my executor hereinafter named pay all my just debts and funeral expenses from the first money coming into his hands from my estate.
    Fourth:-   I hereby give, devise and bequeath to my son, Charles A. Wilbur, now living on the Swinomish Reservation, in Skagit County, Washington, all of my property and estate, wheresoever found, both real and personal, SUBJECT however to a life estate in all that I may possess, which I hereby give to my husband, John Farrensby, it being my intention that all of my property, both real and personal shall become the separate property of my said son, Charles A. Wilbur, after the said John Farrensby has used the same so long as he shall live.
    Fifth:-   I hereby give to my son, Dave Wilbur, now living at Wapata, Washington, the sum of one dollar.
    Sixth:-   I hereby nominate and appoint my said son, Charles A. Wilbur, sole executor of this my last will and testament and hereby request that he be not required to give bond nor to take out letters testamentary, but that after the manner of non-intervention wills this will shall be probated and after the laws of the state of Washington have been complied with so far as non-intervention wills are concerned then my said son and executor shall have the right to do as he may see fit and without the aid or intervention of any court whatsoever.

    IN TESTIMONY WHEREOF, I have hereunto set my hand and seal this 25th day of August, A.D, 1915.

                                  her
                           Kate   +   Farrensby [SEAL]
                                  mark

The foregoing instrument consisting of one page beside this, was on this 25th day of August, A.D, 1915, by the said testatrix named therein to-wit; Kate Farrensby, executed by the placing of her mark thereto, and by her sealed and published as, and declared by her to be her last will and testament, in the presence of Mrs. H.E. Loop, R.J. Cassel and myself, who at her request and in her presence and in the presence of each other, subscribed our names as witnesses thereto; and I further certify and declare that under the direction of the said testatrix and at her request, and in her presence, and in the presence of the subscribing witnesses thereto, I did sign the name of the said testatrix to said last will and testament.

                                  Dave Hammack

NATIVE AMERICAN WILLS and PROBATE RECORDS, 1911 - 1921

Residing at Mount Vernon, WA

We, the undersigned, hereby certify that we were present on the 25th day of August, A.D, 1915, and saw one Kate Farrensby make her mark to the foregoing instrument, consisting on one page beside this and we did also hear her request one Dave Hammack, to sign her name for her, and that the said Hammack did so sign her name in our presence, in her presence and we the undersigned did each sign in the presence of the said testatrix and in the presence of each other, and that the said testatrix in said manner and at said time did then and there declare the same to be her last will and testament.

Mrs. H.E. Loop
Residing at Mount Vernon, WA

R.J. Cassel
Residing at Mount Vernon, WA

DEPARTMENT OF THE INTERIOR, Office of Indian Affairs Jul 28, 1920
It is hereby recommended that the within will of Kate Farrensby, deceased unallotted Indian of the Swinomish Tribe, be approved according to the provisions of the Act of June 25, 1910 (36 Stat. 855-6), as amended by the Act of February 14, 1913, (37 Stat. 678), and the Regulations of the Department.

Respectfully,
E.B. Meritt
Assistant Commissioner

DEPARTMENT OF THE INTERIOR, Office of the Secretary Jul 28, 1920
The within will of Kate Farrensby, deceased unallotted Indian of the Swinomish Tribe, is hereby approved according to the Act of June 25, 1910, (36 Stat. 855-6), as amended by the Act of February 14, 1913, (37 Stat. 678), and the Regulations of the Department.

S.G. Hopkins
Assistant Secretary

LAST WILL AND TESTAMENT OF CHARLIE CONHEPE

I, **CHARLIE CONHEPE**, of Chehalis Reservation, Cushman Agency, Washington, of the age of upwards of 81 years, and being of sound and disposing mind and memory, and not acting under duress, menace, fraud or undue influence of any person whatever, do make, publish, and declare this my LAST WILL AND TESTAMENT, in the manner following, that is to say:

NATIVE AMERICAN WILLS and PROBATE RECORDS, 1911 - 1921

FIRST, for and in consideration of personal care and a comfortable home during the remainder of my lifetime, I do give, devise and bequeath all of my estate, both real and personal, of whatever kind or nature owned by me at the time of my death, to Mary Sampson Johns, my step-daughter.
SECOND; I hereby revoke all former wills.

In witness whereof, I have hereunto set my hand and seal this 3rd day of August, 1915.
Witnesses to Thumb mark: Charlie Conhepe (His thumb print)
    Oscar H. Keller, Chief Clerk
       Tacoma, WA
    Joe Pete
       Oakville, WA

The above and foregoing instrument was, at the date thereof, by said Charlie Conhepe, signed and sealed and published as and declared to be his last will and testament in the presence of us, who, at his request and in his presence, and in the presence of each other have subscribed our names as witnesses thereto.

                         Oscar H. Keller
                         Joe Pete

DEPARTMENT OF THE INTERIOR, Office of Indian Affairs Jul 26, 1920
    It is hereby recommended that the within will of Charles Conhepe, deceased Indian Homesteader under the jurisdiction of the Cushman Agency, Washington, be approved under the Act of June 25, 1910, (36 Stat. L, 855), as amended by the Act of February 14, 1913, (37 Stat. L, 678).
                         Respectfully,
                         E.B. Meritt
                         Assistant Commissioner

DEPARTMENT OF THE INTERIOR, Office of the Secretary Jul 26, 1920
    The within will of Charles Conhepe, deceased Indian Homesteader under the jurisdiction of the Cushman Agency, Washington, is hereby approved under the Act of June 25, 1910, (36 Stat. L, 855), as amended by the Act of February 14, 1913, (37 Stat. L, 678).
                         S.G. Hopkins
                         Assistant Secretary

Last Will and Testament of Susan Sherman

    I, **SUSAN SHERMAN**, of Greenwood, Charles Mix County, South Dakota, being of sound mind and memory, do hereby make, declare and publish

NATIVE AMERICAN WILLS and PROBATE RECORDS, 1911 - 1921

this to be my last will and testament hereby revoking and annulling any (and) all wills heretofore made by me.

First: I bequeath to my daughter-in-law, Fannie Sherman, the small cottage belonging to me situated on the Agency Reserve, Greenwood, South Dakota.

Second: I bequeath to my grand-son, Freddie Kezena, the SE ¼ of the SE ¼, Sec. 8, T96N, R63W, Charles Mix Co, SD, the same being a portion of my original allotment #939.

Third: I bequeath to my grand-son, Henry Sherman, that portion of my allotment described as the S/2 of the SE ¼ of the NE ¼, Sec. 19, T94, R64W, Charles Mix Co, SD.

Fourth: I bequeath to my two grand-children living on the Santee Reservation, Nebraska, named, Clorina and Marcella Sherman, each to share equally that portion of the sale of the SE ¼ of the NE ¼,
Sec. 2, T94N, R64W, which I received under the terms of the will of Edgar Sherman, my deceased husband.

Fifth: I bequeath to Agnes Frederick, for caring for me during my last days the sum of $300.00 in cash form the funds deposited to my credit under the supervision of the Superintendent, Yankton Indian Agency.

Sixth: I bequeath to my grand-children, Clorina and Marcella Sherman of Santee, Nebraska; Henry Sherman, Freddie Kezena, Annie Sherman, Stella Sherman and Rosalie Sherman of Greenwood, SD; each to share alike all the remainder of my property both real and personal, inherited and otherwise, which has not been disposed of in the foregoing clauses of this will, and which shall remain after all my just debts and funeral expenses are paid and a suitable monument erected to my grave to cost not less than $200.00. In Testimony whereof I have hereunto set my hand and seal this 22nd day of November, at Greenwood, SD.

           Susan Sherman her (thumb print) mark

SIGNED, SEALED, PUBLISHED AND DECLARED this 22nd day of November, 1918, by the said Susan Sherman in our presence as and for her last will and testament, and at her request and in her presence and in the presence of each other we have hereunto set out hands as attesting witnesses.

       Daniel Yellowhair Greenwood, SD
       E.E. McNeilly Greenwood, SD

Probate 30887-20 S Y T
DEPARTMENT OF THE INTERIOR, Office of Indian Affairs Jul 26, 1920

The within will of Susan Sherman, deceased Yankton Sioux Allottee #939, executed November 22, 1918, is hereby recommended for approval pursuant to the provisions of the Act of June 25, 1910 (36 Stat. L, 855-6), as amended by the Act of February 14, 1913 (37 Stat. L, 678).

          Respectfully,

NATIVE AMERICAN WILLS and PROBATE RECORDS, 1911 - 1921

E.B. Meritt
Assistant Commissioner

DEPARTMENT OF THE INTERIOR, Office of the Secretary
The within will of Susan Sherman, deceased Yankton Sioux Allottee #939, executed November 22, 1918, is hereby approved pursuant to the provisions of the Act of June 25, 1910 (35 Stat. L, 855-6). as amended by the Act of February 14, 1913 (37 Stat. L, 678).

S.G. Hopkins
Assistant Secretary

<<<<<<<<>>>>>>>

LAST WILL AND TESTAMENT OF SUSAN MALLETTE

I, **SUSAN MALLETTE**, of Greenwood, Charles Mix Co, South Dakota, of sound mind and memory do hereby make and declare this to be my last will and testament, revoking any and all other Wills heretofore made by me.

First; I bequeath to my cousin, Moses Standingbull and his daughters, Agnes Standingbull and Emma Mayle, each to share alike my allotment #938, described as follows: The E ½ of the SE ¼ of Sec. 36, T96N, R64W, of the 5th P.M, SD, containing 80 acres and located in Charles Mix Co.

Second; I bequeath to Louisa Generation, the sum of $40.00 cash if there be that amount on deposit to my credit after all my just debts and funeral expenses are paid and a suitable monument erected to my grave to cost not to exceed $200.00.

Third; I bequeath to Julia Lowe the sum of $40.00 if there be that amount on deposit with the Supt. Yankton Indian Agency after the bequest provided for in Article 2 of my will has been complied with.

Fourth; I bequeath to my cousin who resides on the Crow Creek Reservation whose name I do not know other than that he was "He ate enough plums" the sum of $40.00 if there be that amount to my credit with the Supt. Yankton Agency after the provisions of Article 2 and 3 have been complied with.

Fifth; I direct that any residue of my property either real or personal of which I may be possessed at the time of my death and which I have not bequeathed in the foregoing provisions of this will, be distributed among my legal heirs, according to the laws of inheritance of this state.

IN TESTIMONY WHEREOF, I have set my hand and seal this 24th day of December, 1917, at Greenwood, South Dakota.

Susan Mallette Her thumb

SIGNED, SEALED, PUBLISHED AND DECLARED this 24th day of December, 1917, by the said Susan Mallette in our presence, as and for her last will and testament, and at her request and in her presence and in the presence of each other we have hereunto set our names as attesting witnesses.

NATIVE AMERICAN WILLS and PROBATE RECORDS, 1911 - 1921

                         David Simmons   Greenwood, SD
                         Gilbert St Pierre   Greenwood, SD

PROBATE 30886-20 S Y T
DEPARTMENT OF THE INTERIOR, Office of Indian Affairs   Jul 26, 1920
     The within will of Susan Mallette, deceased Yankton Sioux Allottee #938, executed December 24, 1917, is hereby recommended for approval pursuant to the provisions of the Act of June 25, 1910 (36 Stat. L, 855-6), as amended by the Act of Feb. 14, 1913 (37 Stat. L, 678).

                               Respectfully,
                               E.B. Meritt
                               Assistant Commissioner

DEPARTMENT OF THE INTERIOR, Office of the Secretary
     The within will of Susan Mallette, deceased Yankton Sioux Allottee #938, executed December 24, 1917, is hereby approved pursuant to the provisions of the Act of June 25, 1910 (36 Stat. L, 855-6). as amended by the Act of February 14. 1913 (37 Stat. L, 678).

                           S.G.
                           Assistant
                 <<<<<<<>>>>>>   JUL 22, 1920

                   Will   61577
     RECEIVED   Mountain View, OK,
     JUL 27, 1914   June 12, 1914
       81062

I, **KOOD-LAW-KOY**, Kiowa Indian allottee #1401, of Mountain View, Kiowa County, OK, being now in good health, strength of body and mind, but sensible of the uncertainty of life, and desiring to make disposition of my property and affairs while in strength and health, do hereby make, publish and declare the following to be my last will and testament, hereby revoking and canceling all other or former wills by me at any time made.
     First: I direct the payment of all of my just debts and funeral expenses.
     Second: I give and devise to my beloved wife, Aun-pau-hom, Kiowa Indian allottee #1408, to my beloved daughter Pau-ko-ya, Kiowa Indian allottee #1015, and to my beloved son, Sate-pe-ah-taw, Kiowa Indian allottee #1374, all of my property, real and personal, of which I may die possessed, my wife and two children to share alike, that is, to take 1/3 share in my property each. I do this for the reason that Aun-po-he is my only living wife, Pau-ko-ye my only living daughter and Sate-pe-ah-taw my only living son.
     (NOTE: Name spelled both ways.)
In witness whereof I, Kood-law-koy, have to this my last will and testament, consisting of one sheet of paper, subscribed my name this 12th day of June, 1914.

     Witnesses: Kood-law-koy   His thumb mark

H. Bretschneider
Oscar Queton

NATIVE AMERICAN WILLS and PROBATE RECORDS, 1911 - 1921

Subscribed by Kood-law-koy in the presence of each of us the undersigned, and at the same time declared by him to us to be his last will and testament, and we, thereupon at the request of Kood-law-koy, in his presence and in the presence of each other, sign our names as witnesses this 12th day of June, 1914, at Mountain View, OK.

H.E. Bretschneider
P.O. Anadarko, OK
Oscar Queton
P.O. Carnegie, OK

I, Jasper Saun-ke-ah, of Mountain View, OK, hereby certify that I interpreted the foregoing will to Kood-law-koy, and that he fully understands all the terms thereof, and that the will as written is as he desires the same to be made. Signed this 12th day of June, 1914. *Jasper Saunkeah*
Interpreter

DEPARTMENT OF THE INTERIOR, Office of Indian Affairs, Washington, DC Aug. 24, 1914

It is recommended that the within will be approved pursuant to the provisions of the Act of June 25, 1910, (36 Stat. L, 855), as amended by the Act of February 14, 1913, (37 Stat. L, 678).

Respectfully,
E.B. Meritt
Assistant Commissioner

DEPARTMENT OF THE INTERIOR, Office of the Secretary, Washington, DC Aug. 25, 1914

The within will is hereby approved pursuant to the provisions of the Act of June 25, 1910, (36 Stat. L, 855), as amended by the Act of February 14, 1913, (37 Stat. L, 678).

Bo Sweeney
Assistant Secretary

<<<<<<<>>>>>>>

OFFICE OF INDIAN AFFAIRS
RECEIVED
NOV 19, 1917
106334

LAST WILL AND TESTAMENT OF BEAR CHILD

I, **BEAR CHILD**, an Indian of the Fort Peck Indian Reservation, Sheridan County, Montana, and allottee #37, do hereby make, publish and declare this my last will and testament, in manner and form following:

First: I direct that all of my just debts and funeral expenses be paid as soon after my decease as possible.

Second: I nominate, constitute and appoint Mrs. G.O. West of the Fort Peck Indian Reservation, executrix of this my last will and testament and request

NATIVE AMERICAN WILLS and PROBATE RECORDS, 1911 - 1921

and direct that she be allowed to probate the same and do all things necessary thereto without the necessity of furnishing a bond as required by law.

Third: I give and devise to Mrs. G.O. West, aforesaid, her heirs and assigns, the following described real estate situate and being on the Fort Peck Indian Reservation, Montana, and which is now allotted to me and held in trust for me by the government, to wit: NE ¼ of Sec. 11, T30N, R54E, Montana Meridian, together with all the hereditaments and appurtenances thereunto belonging or in anywise appertaining.

TO HAVE AND TO HOLD the premises above described to the said Mrs. G.O. West, her heirs and assigns forever.

Fourth: I hereby revoke all former wills by me made.

IN WITNESS WHEREOF I have hereunto subscribed my name by mark and affixed my seal this 8 day of July, Oct. A.D, 1917, in the presence of *G.M. Headerich* and *Harold Red Eagle* whom I have requested to become witnesses hereto.

Bear Child   [Seal]   His X mark

The foregoing instrument, was on the 8 day of Oct, A.D, 1917, signed, sealed, published and declared by the testator Bear Child, to be his last will and testament, in the presence of each of us, the undersigned, who thereupon, at his request, and in the presence of the testator and in the presence of each other, have hereunto subscribed our names as the attesting witnesses thereof, the day and year last above written.

G.M. Headerich   *Popular, MT*
Harold Red Eagle   *Brockton, MT*

DEPARTMENT OF THE INTERIOR, Office of Indian Affairs   Jul 23, 1920

The within will of Bear Child, deceased Yankton Sioux allottee #37, of the Fort Peck Reservation, is recommended for approval, in accordance with the provisions of the Act of June 25, 1910, (36 Stat. L, 855-6), as amended by the Act of February 14, 1913, (37 Stat. L, 678).

Respectfully,
E.B. Meritt
Assistant Commissioner

DEPARTMENT OF THE INTERIOR, Office of the secretary   Jul 23, 1920

The within will of Bear Child, deceased Yankton Sioux allottee #37, of the Fort Peck Reservation, is hereby approved in accordance with the provisions of the Act of June 25, 1910, (36 Stat. L, 855-6). as amended by the Act of February 14, 1913 (37 Stat. L, 678).

S.G. Hopkins
Assistant Secretary

NATIVE AMERICAN WILLS and PROBATE RECORDS, 1911 - 1921

WILL

IN THE NAME OF GOD, Amen:

I, **JENNIE IRONDOOR WHITRIGHT**, Fort Peck allottee #442, residing at Poplar, Montana, being of sound mind but of feeble health and realizing the uncertainty of life, and not acting under fraud, duress, menace or undue influence, do this 19th day of July, 1919, make, publish and declare the following to be my last will and testament:

First:
    I give, devise and bequeath to my beloved husband, Robert Whitright, all my property be both real and personal, of which I may die possessed or which may accrue to my estate after my death because I have no children and he has taken care of me for many years, and he is now blind and deserves and needs the property and money.
    I hereby appoint E.D. Mossman, Supt. of Fort Peck Agency, or his successor in office, as executor of my estate.

                      Jennie Irondoor Whitright   Her (thumb print) mark
Witnesses: Fort Peck Allottee #(442)
    Joseph Culbertson
    David Medicine Horse
    We, the undersigned, hereby certify on our honor that neither of us are related in any way to the testatrix, that we were both present and witnessed the signature of the testatrix to the above instrument in one page which she read and fully understood before signing as she was apparently of sound mind and signed the same of her own free will and accord stating that her wishes were duly set forth.

                                    Joseph Culbertson
                                    David Medicine Horse

DEPARTMENT OF THE INTERIOR, Office of Indian Affairs   Jul 22, 1920
    The within will of Jennie Irondoor Whitright, deceased Fort Peck Yankton Sioux allottee #442, of the Fort Peck Reservation, is recommended for approval, in accordance with the provisions of the Act of June 25, 1910, (36 Stat. L, 855-6), as amended by the Act of February 14, 1913, (37 Stat. L, 678).
                                    Respectfully,
                                    E.B. Meritt
                                  Assistant Commissioner

DEPARTMENT OF THE INTERIOR, Office of the secretary   Jul 22, 1920
    The within will of Jennie Irondoor Whitright, deceased Yankton Sioux allottee #442, of the Fort Peck Reservation, is hereby approved in accordance with the provisions of the Act of June 25, 1910, (36 Stat. L, 855-6). as amended by the Act of February 14, 1913 (37 Stat. L, 678).
                                    S.G. Hopkins
                                    Assistant Secretary

NATIVE AMERICAN WILLS and PROBATE RECORDS, 1911 - 1921

WILL

IN THE NAME OF GOD, Amen:

I, **EUGENE RED BOY,** Fort Peck allottee #739, residing at Poplar, Montana, being of sound mind but of feeble health and realizing the uncertainty of life, and not acting under fraud, duress, menace or undue influence, do this 8th day of November, 1919, make, publish and declare the following to be my last will and testament.

First:

I give devise and bequeath to my beloved wife all my personal property, all of my land described as SE/4, Sec. 14, T30N, R52E, and the N/2 NE/4 NE/4, Sec. 21, T27N, R52E, and NW/4 SE/4, Sec. 4, T31N, R55E, and all inheritable interest that I may have now or in the future.

I hereby appoint E.D. Mossman, Supt. of Fort Peck Agency, or his successor in office, as executor of my estate.

Eugene Red Boy
Fort Peck allottee #739

Witnesses:
Burton F. Roth
William Lester

We, the undersigned, hereby certify on our honor that neither of us are related in any way to the testator that we were both present and witnessed the signature of the testator to the above instrument in one page which he read and fully understood before signing as he was apparently of sound mind and signed the same of his own free will and accord stating that his wishes were duly set forth.

Burton F. Roth
William Lester

DEPARTMENT OF THE INTERIOR, Office of Indian Affairs Jul 22, 1920

The within will of Eugene Red Boy, deceased Yankton Sioux allottee #739, of the Fort Peck Reservation, is recommended for approval, in accordance with the provisions of the Act of June 25, 1910, (36 Stat. L, 855-6), as amended by the Act of February 14, 1913, (37 Stat. L, 678).

Respectfully,
E.B. Meritt
Assistant Commissioner

DEPARTMENT OF THE INTERIOR, Office of the Secretary Jul 22, 1920

The within will of Eugene Red Boy, deceased Yankton Sioux allottee #739, of the Fort Peck Reservation, is hereby approved in accordance with the provisions of the Act of June 25, 1910, (36 Stat. L, 855-6). as amended by the Act of February 14, 1913 (37 Stat. L, 678).

NATIVE AMERICAN WILLS and PROBATE RECORDS, 1911 - 1921

S.G. Hopkins
Assistant Secretary

WILL

IN THE NAME OF GOD, Amen:

I, **BRIGHT WOMAN NO MOTHER**, Fort Peck allottee #689, on this 3rd day of May, 1916, being old and inform of body but of sound mind, realizing the uncertainty of life, and not acting under fraud, menace, duress, or undue influence, do hereby make, publish and declare this to be my last will and testament, hereby revoking all former wills that may have been made by me.
First:
    I give, devise and bequeath all my lands described as follows: The NW/4, Sec. 17 and the NE/4, Sec. 18, T30N, R53E, and the NW/4 of NW/4, Sec. 11, T27N, R50#, containing 360 acres. To my grand-daughter, Julia Christian.

                                            Bright Woman No Mother
Witnesses: Her (thumb print) mark
    Burton F. Roth, Poplar, MT
    Joseph Culbertson, Poplar, MT
    We, the undersigned, hereby certify we were present and witnessed the execution of the foregoing will and that the said will was signed by the testator in our presence and in the presence of each of us and at the testator's request. Furthermore, we believe the testator was mentally competent to make a will and that the will expresses the testator's desires as to the disposition of her estate. Furthermore, we believe the testator was not acting under fraud, duress, menace or undue influence but that the will is made at her own instance and request. Furthermore, neither of us are in any way related to the testator nor are we interested in any way in her estate or the disposition of the same.

                                              Burton F. Roth
                                              Poplar, MT
                                              Joseph Culbertson
                                              Poplar, MT

DEPARTMENT OF THE INTERIOR, Office of Indian Affairs   Jul. 22, 1920
    The within will of Bright Woman No Mother, deceased Yankton Sioux allottee #689, of the Fort Peck Reservation, is recommended for approval, in accordance with the provisions of the Act of June 25, 1910, (36 Stat. L, 855-6), as amended by the Act of February 14, 1913, (37 Stat. L, 678).
                                              Respectfully,
                                              E.B. Meritt
                                              Assistant Commissioner

DEPARTMENT OF THE INTERIOR, Office of the Secretary   Jul. 22, 1920

NATIVE AMERICAN WILLS and PROBATE RECORDS, 1911 - 1921

The within will of Bright Woman No Mother, deceased Yankton Sioux allottee #689, of the Fort Peck Reservation, is hereby approved in accordance with the provisions of the Act of June 25, 1910, (36 Stat. L, 855-6). as amended by the Act of February 14, 1913 (37 Stat. L, 678).

S.G. Hopkins
Assistant Secretary

<<<<<<<⚬>>>>>>>

WILL OF HAIR FACE (DAVID ITEOKAHI)

IN THE NAME OF GOD, Amen:

I, **HAIR FACE** or **(DAVID ITEOKAHI)**, of the State of South Dakota, county of Charles Mix, being of sound and disposing mind, and being uncertain of life and certain of the approach of death, and desiring to dispose of all my worldly possessions while I still have the power to do so, do make and declare this to be my last will and testament hereby revoking and annulling any and all wills heretofore made by me.

FIRST: I give and bequeath to my wife, Tasagyegyegiwin, that part of my allotment described as the N ½ of the NE ¼ of Sec. 23, T95N, R65W, of the 5th P.M. with all improvements thereon.

SECOND: I give and bequeath unto my brother, Huto, that part of my allotment described as the S ½ of the NE ¼, Sec. 23, T95N, R65W of the 5th P.M.

THIRD: I give and bequeath unto my sister, Little Woman, that part of my allotment described as the S ½ of the NW ¼ of Sec. 24, T95N, R65W of the 5th P.M.

FOURTH: I give and bequeath unto my wife, Tasagyegyegiwin, that part of my allotment described as the N ½ of the NW ¼ of Sec. 24, T95N, R65W of the 5th P.M.

FIFTH: I give and bequeath unto my sister, Little Woman, one team of ponies Gray and Roan and one set of work harness.

SIXTH: I give and bequeath unto my wife, Tasagyegyegiwin, all my personal property of whatever character and wheresoever except one cow and bull.

SEVENTH: I give and bequeath unto my brother, Huto, one white faced bull, 2 years old.

EIGHTH: I give and devise unto my grand child, Ellen Zimmerman, one cow and calf.

NINTH: All my inherited interest, all money that I may have on deposit with the Yankton Agency to be divided equal among my wife, Tasagyegyegiwin, my sister, Little Woman, and my brother, Huto, after the expense of my last sickness has been paid and a suitable monument has been erected at my grave, each to share equal and alike.

In testimony whereof, I have set my hand and seal this 10th day of October, 1918, at Lake Andes, South Dakota.

NATIVE AMERICAN WILLS and PROBATE RECORDS, 1911 - 1921

Signed, sealed, published and declared this 10th day of October, 1918, by the said Hair Face, in our presence, as and for his last will and testament, and at his request and in his presence, and in the presence of each other we have hereunto subscribed our names as attesting witnesses.

L. Skunk
Lake Andes, SD
Joseph Ookiye
Lake Andes, SD

DEPARTMENT OF THE INTERIOR, Office of Indian Affairs   Jul 22, 1920

It is hereby recommended that the within will of Hair Face [David Iteokahi], deceased Yankton Sioux allottee #1303, be approved under the provisions of the Act of June 25, 1910, (36 Stat. L, 855-6), as amended by the Act of February 14, 1913, (37 Stat. L, 678), and the Regulations of the Department.

Respectfully,
E.B. Meritt
Assistant Commissioner

DEPARTMENT OF THE INTERIOR, Office of the Secretary   Jul 23, 1920

The within will of Hair Face [David Iteokahi], deceased Yankton Sioux allottee #1303, is hereby approved in accordance with the provisions of the Act of June 25, 1910, (36 Stat. L, 855-6). as amended by the Act of February 14, 1913 (37 Stat. L, 678), and the Regulations of the Department.

S.G. Hopkins
Assistant Secretary

Last Will and Testament
of Big That

IN THE NAME OF GOD, Amen:

  I, **BIG HAT**, of Wyola, Montana, being of sound mind, memory and understanding, do hereby make and publish this my last will and testament, hereby revoking and annulling all wills by me heretofore made, in manner and form following, that is to say:
  First: I direct that all my just debts and funeral expenses, and expenses of my last illness shall be paid by my executor hereinafter named as soon after my decease as convenient;
  Second: I give, devise and bequeath to Cut Ear, my husband, my own allottment[sic] on or near Buffalo Creek; To Pretty Horse, my son, the Hat allottment[sic] near Wyola, from my mother. All horses belonging to me, to Cut Ear, except such horses as bear the Pretty Horse brand.

NATIVE AMERICAN WILLS and PROBATE RECORDS, 1911 - 1921

Third: All the rest and residue of my estate, both real and personal and mixed, I give, devise and bequeath to my lawful heirs as determined after my decease.

And lastly: I do hereby nominate, constitute and appoint, Supt. of Crow Reservation, executor of this my last will and testament.

In testimony whereof, I have set my hand and seal to this, my last will and testament, at Wyola, Montana, this 27th day of April, in the year of our Lord, 1917.

Big Hat her X mark

Signed, sealed, published and declared by said Big Hat in our presence, as and for her last will and testament, and at my[sic] request and in our presence, and in the presence of each other, we have hereunto subscribed our names as attesting witnesses thereto.
Witnesses to mark and will:

R.H. Shipman of *Wyola, MT*
Eli Blackhawk of *Wyola, MT*
Otto Bear Grand of *Wyola, MT*

Probate 64648-18 C E T
DEPARTMENT OF THE INTERIOR, Office of Indian Affairs   Jul 8, 1920
It is recommended that the within will of Big Hat, deceased Crow allottee #1614, be approved in accordance with the provisions of the Act of June 25, 1910, (36 Stat. L, 855-6), as amended by the Act of February 14, 1913, (37 Stat. L, 678), and the Regulations of the Department.

Respectfully,
E.B. Meritt
Assistant Commissioner

DEPARTMENT OF THE INTERIOR, Office of the Secretary   Jul 13, 1920
The within will of ,Big Hat, deceased Crow allottee #1614, is hereby approved under the provisions of the Act of June 25, 1910, (36 Stat. L, 855-6). as amended by the Act of February 14, 1913 (37 Stat. L, 678).

S.G. Hopkins
Assistant Secretary

Last Will and Testament
of Cut Ear
IN THE NAME OF GOD, Amen:

I, CUT EAR, of Wyola, Montana, being of sound mind, memory and understanding, do hereby make and publish this my last will and testament,

NATIVE AMERICAN WILLS and PROBATE RECORDS, 1911 - 1921

hereby revoking and annulling all wills by me heretofore made, in manner and form following, this is to say:

First: I direct that all of my just debts and funeral expenses and expenses of my last illness shall be paid by my executor hereinafter named as soon after my decease as convenient.

Second: I give, devise and bequeath to Yellow Head, my brother, one roan mare and colt and spotted horse; to Pretty Horse, my stepson, one pinto mare and brown colt. All the rest of my horses, which are branded **03** on left hip, I wish be given to Pretty Shield, my cousin. I wish my mowing machine be given to Good Goes Ahead, and my two seated spring wagon to Pretty Horse.

My land I wish be divided as follows: To my sister, Rides Behind the Other Way, 40 acres of my allotment described as NW ¼ SW ¼ of Sec. 35, T7S, R35E, MM. The balance of my allotment, I wish divided equally between my brother, Yellow Head and my cousin, Pretty Shield. My inherited interest in the estate of Big Hat, my deceased wife, I wish be given to Pretty Horse, my stepson.

Third: All the rest and residue of my estate, both real and personal and mixed, I give, devise, and bequeath to my lawful heirs as determined after my decease.

And lastly, I do nominate, constitute, and appoint the Superintendent of the Crow Reservation executor of this my last will and testament.

In testimony whereof, I have set my hand and seal to this, my last will and testament at Crow Agency, Montana, this 1st day of February, in the year of our Lord, 1918.

Cut Ear his (thumb print) mark

Signed, sealed, published and declared by said Cut Ear, in our presence, as and for his last will and testament, and at his request and in our presence and in the presence of each other, we have hereunto subscribed our names as attesting witnesses thereto.

S.J. Shick of Crow Agency, MT
Ned Old Bear of Crow Agency, MT
Chas. Wilson   his (thumb print) mark
of Crow Agency, MT

Probate 64670-18 C E T
DEPARTMENT OF THE INTERIOR, Office of Indian Affairs   Jul 8, 1920

The within will of Cut Ear, deceased Crow allottee #1613, is hereby recommended for approval in accordance with the provisions of the Act of June 25, 1910, (36 Stat. L, 855-6), as amended by the Act of February 14, 1913, (37 Stat. L, 678).

Respectfully,
E.B. Meritt
Assistant Commissioner

DEPARTMENT OF THE INTERIOR, Office of the Secretary   Jul 13, 1920

NATIVE AMERICAN WILLS and PROBATE RECORDS, 1911 - 1921

The within will of Cut Ear, deceased Crow allottee #1613, is hereby approved in accordance with the provisions of the Act of June 25, 1910, (36 Stat. L, 855-6). as amended by the Act of February 14, 1913 (37 Stat. L, 678).

S.G. Hopkins
Assistant Secretary

WILL

IN THE NAME OF GOD, Amen:

I, **FRANK SMITH**, Fort Peck allottee #874, residing at Brockton, Montana, being of sound mind but of feeble health and realizing the uncertainty of life, and not acting under fraud, duress, menace or undue influence, do this 13th day of May, 1918, make, publish and declare the following to be my last will and testament.

First:
I give, devise and bequeath to my beloved wife, Alice Blackduck Smith, Fort Peck Allottee #77, all of my personal property consisting of team, wagon, harness and other chattels. Also 1;2 of my allotment described as follows: NE/4 & E/2 NW/4 and Lots 1 & 2, Sec. 30, T30N, R49E, Lot 17, Sec. 19, T27N, R50, SE/4 of SW/4, Sec. 8, T27N, R50E.

Second:
I give, devise and bequeath to my daughter, Jennie Smith, Fort Peck allottee #2490, ¼ of the above described lands.

Third:
I give, devise and bequeath to my nephew, Hills In House, Fort Peck allottee #487, ¼ of my allotment as described above.

I hereby appoint E.D. Mossman, Supt. of Fort Peck Agency, or his successor in office, as executor of my estate.

Frank Smith His (thumb print) mark
Witness: Fort Peck allottee #874
Burton F. Roth, Farmer
Poplar, MT
Daniel Mitchell
Poplar, MT

We, the undersigned, hereby certify on our honor that neither of us are related in any way to the testator, that we were both present and witnessed the signature of the testator to the above instrument in one page which he read and fully understood before signing as he was apparently of sound mind and signed the same of his own free will and accord stating that his wishes were duly set forth.

NATIVE AMERICAN WILLS and PROBATE RECORDS, 1911 - 1921

Burton F. Roth, Farmer
Poplar, MT
Daniel Mitchell
Poplar, MT

DEPARTMENT OF THE INTERIOR, Office of Indian Affairs   Jul. 18, 1920
The within will of Frank Smith, deceased Yankton Sioux allottee #874, of the Fort Peck Reservation, is hereby recommended for approval in accordance with the provisions of the Act of June 25, 1910, (36 Stat. L, 855-6), as amended by the Act of February 14, 1913, (37 Stat. L, 678).

Respectfully,
E.B. Meritt
Assistant Commissioner

DEPARTMENT OF THE INTERIOR, Office of the Secretary
The within will of Frank Smith, deceased Yankton Sioux allottee #874, of the Fort Peck Reservation, is hereby approved in accordance with the provisions of the Act of June 25, 1910, (36 Stat. L, 855-6). as amended by the Act of February 14, 1913 (37 Stat. L, 678).

S.G. Hopkins
Assistant Secretary

<<<<<<<>>>>>>>

LAST WILL AND TESTAMENT OF WICANHPIDUTA

I, **WICANHPIDUTA**, Devils Lake allottee #566, of Fort Totten, North Dakota, being of sound mind and disposing memory and understanding, and not under any compulsion or stress of circumstances, hereby make, declare and publish this my last will and testament, hereby revoking and annulling all wills heretofore made by me. It is my will and desire that my property be disposed of in the following manner, to-wit:

FIRST: I direct that all my just debts and funeral expenses and the expense of my last illness shall be paid from money on deposit with the Superintendent of the Fort Totten School and Agency, as soon after my decease as shall be convenient, and also direct that my executrix arrange for the erection of (a) tombstone over my grave, the expense likewise to be paid from the funds on deposit with the Superintendent above mentioned;

SECOND: the balance of funds to my credit held in trust or the Government, I give and bequeath in equal shares to John Ieska Noel, my second cousin and to my grand-niece, Frances Langie. I likewise bequeath to John Ieska Noel and Frances Langie, in equal shares all of my real estate, comprising (of) my own allotment #566, described as the SW ¼ of NE ¼ and the NW ¼ of SE ¼ of Sec. 15, T151N, R64W, and the N ½ of SW ¼ of Sec. 8, T150N, R64W, 5th P.M, North Dakota, containing 160 acres; also my ¼ inherited interest in the allotment of Tunkantiyomani, #863, deceased, described as the N ½ of NE ¼ of Sec. 13, T151N, R63W, and my ¼ inherited interest in the allotment of Hake,

NATIVE AMERICAN WILLS and PROBATE RECORDS, 1911 - 1921

#864, deceased, described as the S ½ of NE ¼ of Sec. 13, T151N, R64W, 5th P.M, in North Dakota, containing 80 acres in each case;

THIRD: to my niece, Smile Fox, I give and bequeath, one dollar, $1.00, my reason for not giving her more is that she has sufficient inherited lands of her own;

FOURTH: any real estate or personal property not included in the foregoing provisions, I give and bequeath share and share alike to John Ieska Noel and Frances Langie.

AND LASTLY, I hereby nominate, constitute and appoint Frances Langie executrix of this my last will and testament.

IN TESTIMONY WHEREOF, I have set my hand and seal to this my last will and testament at Fort Totten, North Dakota, this 11th day of March, in the year of our Lord, 1918, signing the same in the presence of Martin Strait, Charles Brooks and S.A.M. Young, who at my request and in my presence have witnessed my signing hereof, we all signing in the presence of each other.

             Wicanhpiduta His Mark

Signed, sealed, published and declared by the said Wicanhpiduta in our presence as and for his last Will and Testament; at his request and in his presence, and in the presence of each other, we have hereunto subscribed our names as attesting witnesses.

  Martin Strait   Charles Brooks
  S.A.M. Young

PROBATE 12079-1920 L L
DEPARTMENT OF THE INTERIOR, Office of Indian Affairs June 29, 1920

  It is recommended that the within will be approved pursuant to the provisions of the Act of June 25, 1910, (36 Stat. L, 855-6), as amended by the Act of February 14, 1913, (37 Stat. L, 678).

                 Respectfully,
                 E.B. Meritt
                 Assistant Commissioner

DEPARTMENT OF THE INTERIOR, Office of the Secretary June 30, 1920

  The within will is hereby approved pursuant to the provisions of the Act of June 25, 1910, (36 Stat. L, 855-6). as amended by the Act of February 14, 1913 (37 Stat. L, 678).

                 S.G. Hopkins
                 Assistant Secretary

OFFICE OF INDIAN AFFAIRS RECEIVED DEC 5, 1918 96352 WILL

IN THE NAME OF GOD, Amen: I, **LUCY HORN**, age 74, an Indian of the Nez Perce Indian Reservation, Idaho, now residing at Ferdinand, Idaho Co, Idaho,

NATIVE AMERICAN WILLS and PROBATE RECORDS, 1911 - 1921

being of sound mind and disposing memory, and not acting under duress, menace, fraud, or undue influence, of any person whatsoever, do hereby make, publish and declare this my LAST WILL AND TESTAMENT, in the manner following, that is to say:

First: I direct that my body be decently buried with proper regard to my station in life, and the circumstances of my estate.

Second: I direct that my funeral expenses and expenses of my last illness be paid from any funds belonging to my estate, or in the custody of the Superintendent of the Nez Perce Indian Reservation, Lapwai, Idaho.

Third: I will and bequeath to George Moody, any land on which I reside, allotment #1102, described as follows: Lots 17, 18, 19, 20 & 21, Sec. 7, T32N, R1E, 100 acres. After all expenses are settled and adjusted, balance of money, if any, I also leave to George Moody. My reason for leaving and bequeathing the land to George Moody, I do for the care and kindness that he has done for me during my sickness.

The sewing machine, I leave to Eliza Miller, coat I leave to Matilda Bronchean. Balance of my personal property will be distributed among my friends.

In witness whereof, I have hereunto put my hand and seal this 16th day of November, 1918.

Lucy Horn   Her (thumb print) mark

The foregoing instrument was on the date hereof signed, sealed, published and declared be said Lucy Horn to be her LAST WILL AND TESTAMENT, in the presence of us, and at her request and in her presence, and in the presence of each other, we have subscribed our names as witnesses on this 16th day of November, 1918.

Post Office:	Ferdinand, Idaho	*Elias Pond, Minister*
	Ferdinand, Idaho	*Andrew Moody, Farmer*
	Residence Idaho	*Jesse Pane, Forest guard*

Probate 96352-19 J W H
DEPARTMENT OF THE INTERIOR, Office of Indian Affairs   Jun 18, 1920

The within will of Lucy Horn, deceased allottee #1102, of the Nez Perce tribe, is respectfully recommended for approval, pursuant to the provisions of the Act of June 25, 1910, (36 Stat. L, 855-6), as amended by the Act of February 14, 1913, (37 Stat. L, 678).

Respectfully,
E.B. Meritt
Assistant Commissioner

6-FBM-14
DEPARTMENT OF THE INTERIOR, Office of the Secretary   Jun 30, 1920

NATIVE AMERICAN WILLS and PROBATE RECORDS, 1911 - 1921

The within will of Lucy Horn, deceased allottee #1102 of the Nez Perce tribe, is hereby approved pursuant to the provisions of the Act of June 25, 1910, (36 Stat. L, 855-6). as amended by the Act of February 14, 1913 (37 Stat. L, 678).

S.G. Hopkins
Assistant Secretary

<<<<<<<>>>>>>>

WILL OF ADELIA PETERSON

I, **ADELIA PETERSON**, formerly **ADELIA HALE**, Yankton Indian, allottee #172, aged 22, of Fort Peck Reservation, Montana., and residing at Brockton, Sheridan Co, Montana, being of sound and disposing mind, do make and declare this my last Will and Testament and wish and bequeath my property at my death to my two children, Ethel, aged 3, and Margaret, aged 3 months. [Ethel is three years old.] Both born upon the Fort Peck Reservation, Montana, and residing now at Brockton, Montana. My estate to be equally divided between these two children named. My land to be shared is described as follows:

First; my grazing allotment of 320 acres, on the Fort Peck Reservation, Montana, described as NE ¼ of SW ¼ of Sec. 35, T28, R53, all being in Sheridan County, MT.

I wish my husband, Charles Peterson, aged 34, residing at Brockton, Montana, to be appointed guardian of my children herein named and to have the charge of them. I wish the U.S. Indian Department to have charge of their property until they become of legal age and competency.

Feeling that I am very sick and likely to die, I am hereby providing for the future welfare of my children and providing for the division of such estate as I may have at my death.

Signed and delivered this 7th day of March, 1918, at Brockton, MT, in Sheridan County and on Fort Peck Reservation by me,

Adelia Peterson

Witnesses by:
Phillip Wettlin, Brockton, MT
F.E. Farrell, Farmer, Brockton, MT

I hereby certify that I prepared this Will by direction of Adelia Peterson, formerly Adelia Hale. That the provisions herein were her own expressed desires and made of her own free will, that she was then of sound and disposing mind and that I talked with her of her illness, her children and her property, its location and extent, that she read this Will and wrote her own name thereto. I recommend that approval of this her will.

F.E. Farrell
Farmer, Fort Peck Reservation, MT
Dist. 1, Brockton, MT; March 7, 1918

NATIVE AMERICAN WILLS and PROBATE RECORDS, 1911 - 1921

DEPARTMENT OF THE INTERIOR, Office of Indian Affairs
 The within will of Adelia Hale Peterson, deceased Yankton Sioux allottee #172, or the Fort Peck Reservation is recommended for approval in accordance with the provisions of the Act of June 25, 1910, (36 Stat. L, 855-6), as amended by the Act of February 14, 1913, (37 Stat. L, 678).

Respectfully,
E.B. Meritt
Assistant Commissioner

DEPARTMENT OF THE INTERIOR, Office of the Secretary
 The within will of Adelia Hale Peterson, deceased Yankton Sioux allottee #172, of the Fort Peck Reservation is hereby approved in accordance with the provisions of the Act of June 25, 1910, (36 Stat. L, 855-6). as amended by the Act of February 14, 1913 (37 Stat. L, 678).

S.G. Hopkins
Assistant Secretary

<<<<<<<<>>>>>>>>

State of Nebraska	:	
	: SS	Last Will and Testament of
County of Thurston	:	Albert Thomas

I, **ALBERT THOMAS**, Winnebago Indian of Winnebago, county of Thurston, State of Nebraska, being of sound mind and memory, and considering the uncertainty of this frail and transitory life, do therefore make, ordain, publish and declare this to be my last WILL and TESTAMENT.

FIRST: I order and direct that the Superintendent of the Winnebago Agency, pay all orders issued against my account now on the books or will be from any source. I further direct that the Superintendent pay all my funeral expenses as soon as my decease as conveniently may (be).

SECOND: After the (payment) of such funeral expenses and debts incurred by issuance (of orders) from the Winnebago Agency, I give, devise and bequeath unto Eva Lincoln, the balance of all cash remaining to my credit at the Agency; all real and personal property in which I may be sole heir, or in part with other heirs, or in any estate, real or personal, in which I may be, or have been declared to have all right, title, and interest, now, or in the future.

IN WITNESS WHEREOF, I have hereunto subscribed my name and affixed my seal, this (date blocked out) day of January, in the year of our Lord, 1918.

Albert Thomas
Testator

This instrument was on the day and date thereof signed, published and declared by the testator, Albert Thomas, to be his last will and testament, in the presence of us who at his request have subscribed our names thereto, as witnesses, in his

NATIVE AMERICAN WILLS and PROBATE RECORDS, 1911 - 1921

presence and in the presence of each other, and we believe said testator at this time to be of sound and disposing mind and memory.

Paul Land
Garrett J. Garner

Probate 67568-18 C E T
DEPARTMENT OF THE INTERIOR, Office of Indian Affairs   Aug. 23, 1920
    The within will of Albert Thomas, deceased unallotted Winnebago Indian, is recommended for disapproval in accordance with the provisions of the Act of June 25, 1910, (36 Stat. L, 855-6), as amended by the Act of February 14, 1913, (37 Stat. L, 678).

Respectfully,
E.B. Meritt
Assistant Commissioner

DEPARTMENT OF THE INTERIOR, Office of the Secretary   Aug. 27, 1920
    The within will of Albert Thomas, deceased unallotted Winnebago Indian, is hereby disapproved under the provisions of the Act of June 25, 1910, (36 Stat. L, 855-6). as amended by the Act of February 14, 1913 (37 Stat. L, 678).

S.G. Hopkins
Assistant Secretary

<<<<<<<◇>>>>>>>

37234-20 53001-20 WOMLL
LAST WILL & TESTAMENT OF BICHEA [CHARCOAL]

TO WHOM IT MAY CONCERN:

    I, **BICHEA [CHARCOAL]**, being of lawful age and of sound and disposing mind and memory, do hereby publish and declare this to be my last will and testament in that same is made of my own volition and that as such, it supersedes and annuls any and all wills that may have been made heretofore by me.
    FIRST: I direct that all my just debts be paid and that my funeral expenses be paid from any funds on deposit to my credit and that a suitable tombstone be erected at my grave.
    SECOND: I give and bequeath to my half-brother, Jock Bull Bear, all of my interests in and title to the N ½ of the NE ¼ of Sec. 22, T10, R16W of the Indian Meridian in Washita County, same being ½ of my original allotment, he to have and to hold the same as his own.
    THIRD: I give and bequeath to my niece, Night Walker, all of my interests in and title to the N ½ of the NW ¼ of Sec. 23, T10, R16W, of the Indian Meridian in Washita County, OK, same being ½ of my original allotment, she to have and to hold the same as her own.
    FOURTH: I give and bequeath to Jock Bull Bear and Night Walker, a ½ undivided interest each in my share of the S ½ of the NE ¼ of Sec. 22, T10,

NATIVE AMERICAN WILLS and PROBATE RECORDS, 1911 - 1921

R16W, of the Indian Meridian in Washita County, OK, such land being known as the Walking Bird estate and to which I have been declared an heir by the Secretary of the Interior.

FIFTH: I give and bequeath to Jock Bull Bear and Night Walker, each a ½ undivided interest to my share in the S ½ of the NW ¼ of Sec. 23, T10, R16W of the Indian Meridian in Washita County, OK, such land being known as the Walkingbird estate, and I was declared to be an heir to such estate by the Secretary of the Interior. (NOTE: Name spelled both ways.)

SIXTH: I give and bequeath to Jock Bull Bear and Night Walker, each a 2/3 interest in any personal property of which I may be possessed at the time of my death and any realty not above described also any money that I may have on deposit to my credit at the Seger Indian Agency.

Signed and sealed in my presence and in the presence of J.L. Read and Lizzard at Colony, OK, May 15. 1918.

Bichea [Charcoal]   Her (thumb print) mark

Witnesses:
    J.L. Read
    Lizzard

<u>Interpreter's Oath</u>

I, *John Little,* Interpreter, do solemnly swear that I have made true interpretation of all matters set forth in the foregoing will to Mrs. Bichea [Charcoal] and I further swear that after having interpreted such to her that she has expressed to me that this will sets forth fully and clearly her intentions throughout.

John Little

Subscribed and sworn to before me on this 15th day of May, 1918.
Harry W. Ehy
Notary Public

My commission expires Aug. 21, 1921.

Probate 37234-20 53001-20 MHW
DEPARTMENT OF THE INTERIOR, Office of Indian Affairs   Jul 12, 1920

The within will of Bichea or Mrs. Charcoal, deceased Arapaho allottee #1726 of the Seger Indian Agency, is recommended for approval in accordance with the Act of June 25, 1910, (36 Stat. L, 855-6), as amended by the Act of February 14, 1913, (37 Stat. L, 678).

Respectfully,
E.B. Meritt
Assistant Commissioner

DEPARTMENT OF THE INTERIOR, Office of the Secretary   Jul 13, 1920

The within will of Bichea or Mrs. Charcoal, deceased Arapaho allottee #172 of the Seger Indian Agency in OK, is hereby approved pursuant to the

NATIVE AMERICAN WILLS and PROBATE RECORDS, 1911 - 1921

provisions of the Act of June 25, 1910, (36 Stat. L, 855-6). as amended by the Act of February 14, 1913 (37 Stat. L, 678).

S.G. Hopkins
Assistant Secretary

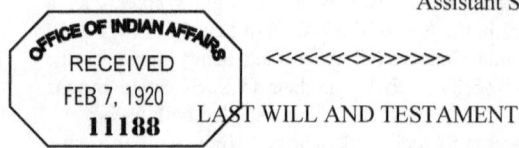

<<<<<<<>>>>>>>

LAST WILL AND TESTAMENT

In the name of God, Amen. I, **ANTOINE LeCLAIRE**, Fort Hall allottee #323, of Fort Hall, County of Bingham, State of Idaho, a member of the Shoshone Tribe of Indians, being about 36 years of age and of sound and disposing mind and memory, and sensible of the uncertainty of life, desiring to make provision for the disposition of any and all property, rights, interests and estates of which I may die seized and possessed, and not acting under duress, menace or fraud or undue influence of any person whatsoever, do hereby make, publish and declare this, my last will and testament in manner and form as follows; that is to say:

First: I direct that all my just debts and funeral expenses shall be paid out of my estate as soon after my decease as shall be found convenient.

Second: I give and devise to my minor son, Herbert LeClaire, ½ interest in my allotment on the Fort Hall Reservation, described as follows: W ½ SW ¼ SW ¼ Sec. 15, T5S, R34E, and the SW ¼ Sec. 26, T4S, R37E, Boise Meridian, in Idaho.

Fourth[sic]: I give and devise to my minor son, LeRoy LeClaire, ½ interest in my allotment on the Fort Hall Reservation, described as follows: W ½ SW ¼ SW ¼ Sec. 15, T5S, R34E, and the SW ¼, Sec. 26, T4S, R37E, Boise Meridian, in Idaho.

Fifth: I give and devise all other property, both real and personal, which I may die possessed, and not otherwise bequeath in this my last will and testament, to my two minor children, Herbert and LeRoy LeClaire, the same to be divided equally between them.

Sixth: It is my desire that Jennie Baker Jimmie be given the custody of my son Hubert LeClaire until he reaches his 21st birthday.

IN WITNESS THEREOF, I have executed the within and foregoing instrument [2 pages only] this 3rd day of November, 1919.

Antoine LeClaire

Witness:
Lee C. Hardy
Lease Clerk, Fort Hall, Idaho

The foregoing instrument of two (2) pages only was on this 3rd day of November, 1919, executed by Antoine LeClaire, by himself causing his name to be subscribed thereto in the presence of each of us, and at the time of his subscribing said instrument he declared it to be his last will and testament, and at his request and in his presence, and in the presence of each of us, we subscribe

NATIVE AMERICAN WILLS and PROBATE RECORDS, 1911 - 1921

our names as witnesses, with our respective places of residence, the day and year last above written.

Antoine LeClaire

Witnesses:
    Lee C. Hardy
        Fort Hall, Idaho
    L.S. Reay
        Fort Hall, Idaho

    Subscribed and sworn to before me this 3rd day of November, 1919.

Lee C. Hardy
Notary Public

My commission expires December 19, 1921.

State of Idaho   )
                 (SS
Bingham County)

    I, Antoine LeClaire, being first duly sworn, depose and say:
    That the will to which I have this day set my hand and seal is my last will and testament.
    That I have made my two minor children Herbert LeClaire and LeRoy LeClaire, the sole beneficiaries thereunder, in exclusion of all or any person who may claim himself or herself to be related to me in any way.
    That I made the will referred to while possessing a sound and disposing mind and memory, and that I did not act under duress, menace, fraud or undue influence of any person whatsoever.
    That further the deponent sayeth not.

Antoine LeClaire

Witnesses:
    Lee C. Hardy
        Fort Hall, Idaho
    L.S. Reay
        Fort Hall, Idaho

    The foregoing page containing the affidavit of Antoine LeClaire was subscribed to and sworn to before me at Fort Hall Indian Agency, Fort Hall, Idaho, this 3rd day of November, 1919.

Lee C. Hardy
Notary Public

My commission expires December 19, 1921.

DEPARTMENT OF THE INTERIOR, Office of Indian Affairs Jun 24, 1920
    The within will of Antoine LeClaire, deceased allottee #323 of the Shoshone tribe, , is respectfully recommended for approval pursuant to the provisions of the Act of June 25, 1910, (36 Stat. L, 855-6), as amended by the

NATIVE AMERICAN WILLS and PROBATE RECORDS, 1911 - 1921

Act of February 14, 1913, (37 Stat. L, 678), so far as it affects the trust property involved.

Respectfully,
E.B. Meritt
Assistant Commissioner

DEPARTMENT OF THE INTERIOR, Office of the Secretary   Jun 30, 1920
The within will of Antoine LeClaire, deceased allottee #323 of the Shoshone tribe, is respectfully approved pursuant to the provisions of the Act of June 25, 1910, (36 Stat. L, 855-6). as amended by the Act of February 14, 1913 (37 Stat. L, 678), so far as it affects the testator's trust property.

S.G. Hopkins
Assistant Secretary

WILL OF JANE YANNER
--o--

I, **JANE YANNER**, an Indian woman, residing on the Siletz Indian Reservation, Oregon, being of legal age, [Records show her to be 80 years of age], of sound mind and acting under no duress or undue influence, do hereby voluntarily devise and bequeath unto my daughter, Mollie Carmichael, wife of Charles Carmichael, any and all of my real and personal property of which I may possess at the time of my death. Said real and personal property being more particularly described as follows, to wit:

That part of my own allotment, #170, described as #10 and 11 in Sec. #2, T7S, R11W, of Willamatte Meridian, in Oregon, 40 acres.

The allotment of Charles Yanner which I inherited, [#535], [I.O. file # Law-Heir. 102341-15, J.C. McG], described as the NW ¼ of the NE ¼, the Lot #11 and the E ½ of the SW ¼ of the NE ¼ of Sec. 27, T9S, R10W, of Willamette Meridian in Oregon, 79.96 acres.

The allotment of Mary Yanner, which I inherited [#536]. [I.O. File #102340-15, J.C. McG], described as the NE ¼ of the NW ¼, and the Lost #7,9,14 and 16, in Sec. 27, T9S, R10W of Williamette Meridian in Oregon, 72.30 acres.

Such interest as I may have in the one story frame house on Lots 12 and 13, Block 6, in the Siletz Townsite, and my interest in 3 cows and one calf, and such other personal property as I may possess at the time of my death.

Witness my hand and seal this 19th day of November, 1917, at Siletz, Oregon.

Jane Yanner Her right thumb mark

Witnesses:
John Adams
    Siletz, Oregon
J.L. Goodell

NATIVE AMERICAN WILLS and PROBATE RECORDS, 1911 - 1921

Siletz, Oregon

I, Arthur Bensell, hereby certify that I faithfully and truthfully interpreted the contents of the above Will to Jane Yanner and I am fully satisfied that she fully understood its contents and expresses her wish and intent.

Arthur Bensell
Interpreter

Signed, sealed, published and declared by Jane Yanner as and for her last will and testament in our presence and in the presence of each of us, on this 19th day of November, 1917.

John Adams
J.L. Goodell

Probate 85957-18
DEPARTMENT OF THE INTERIOR, Office of Indian Affairs
The within will of Jane Yanner, is hereby recommended for approval in accordance with the provisions of the Act of June 25, 1910, (36 Stat. L, 855-6), as amended by the Act of February 14, 1913, (37 Stat. L, 678).

Respectfully,
E.B. Meritt
Assistant Commissioner

DEPARTMENT OF THE INTERIOR, Office of the Secretary
The within will is hereby approved in accordance with the provisions of the Act of June 25, 1910, (36 Stat. L, 855-6). as amended by the Act of February 14, 1913 (37 Stat. L, 678).

S.G. Hopkins
Assistant Secretary

LAST WILL AND TESTAMENT OF
WILLIAM DOG SKIN

STANDING ROCK ALLOTTEE No. _____
------ O ------

I, **WILLIAM DOG SKIN**, 69 years of age, an allottee of the Standing Rock Indian Reservation, in the state of North Dakota, being of sound mind, memory and understanding, do hereby make and publish this my last will and testament, hereby revoking and annulling all wills by me heretobefore made, that is to say:

FIRST: I direct that all my just debts and funeral expenses and expenses of my last illness shall be paid as soon after my decease as shall be convenient.

NATIVE AMERICAN WILLS and PROBATE RECORDS, 1911 - 1921

SECOND: I am possessed of an allotment of land within the boundaries of the Standing Rock Indian Reservation, in North Dakota, provision for the disposition of this allotment has already been filed with the Superintendent of the above named reservation, together with all stock and personal property that I now have or may be possessed of at the time of my decease.

THIRD: The allotment of my deceased son, Samuel Dog Skin, is now posted for sale at the above named reservation, and my desire is, that in case of my death, if the same be sold that my share of the sale be given to my sister One Who Flies, 70 years of age, who resides on the Crow Creek Reservation, in South Dakota, and with whom I am now staying.

AND LASTLY: I am satisfied that the Officers of the Department of the Interior of the United States, will make proper provision for carrying into effect of this my last will and testament, and therefore, I have not appointed an executor to administer my estate.

IN TESTIMONY WHEREOF, I have set my hand and seal to this my last will and testament at the home of my sister One Who Flies, located on the Crow Creek Indian Reservation, in the state of South Dakota, this 7th day of October, 1918.

WITNESSES: William Dog Skin His (thumb print) mark
    Peter W. Lightfoot
    Charles McBride
        Both of Ft. Thompson, SD

Signed, sealed, published and declared by the said William Dog Skin, in our presence, as and for his last will and testament, and at his request and in his presence and in the presence of each other we have hereunto subscribed our names as attesting witnesses thereto.

        Peter W. Lightfoot   *Charles McBride*
        Fort Thompson, SD   Fort Thompson, SD

80141-20
DEPARTMENT OF THE INTERIOR, Office of Indian Affairs, Washington
Dec. 13, 1920

It is respectfully recommended that the within will of William Dogskin, deceased Standing Rock Sioux Allottee #2571, dated October 7, 1918, be approved under the Act of June 25, 1910, (36 Stat. L, 855-6), as modified by the Act of February 14, 1913, (37 Stat. L, 678).

        Respectfully,
        E.B. Meritt
        Assistant Commissioner

DEPARTMENT OF THE INTERIOR, Office of the Secretary, Washington
Dec. 20, 1920

NATIVE AMERICAN WILLS and PROBATE RECORDS, 1911 - 1921

The accompanying will of William Dogskin, deceased Standing Rock Sioux allottee #2571, dated October 7, 1918, is hereby approved under the Act of June 25, 1910, (36 Stat. L, 855-6). as modified by the Act of February 14, 1913 (37 Stat. L, 678).

[Signed] S.G. Hopkins
Assistant Secretary

<<<<<<<<>>>>>>>

Land Allot. 2101

LAST WILL and TESTAMENT of
Gerald Gray Bear
IN THE NAME OF GOD, Amen.

I, **GERALD GRAY BEAR**, Standing Rock Sioux allottee #2101, of Cannon Ball, North Dakota, being of sound mind, memory and understanding, do hereby make and publish this my last will and testament, hereby revoking and annulling all wills by me heretofore made, in manner form following, that is to say:

First: I direct that all my just debts and funeral expenses and expenses of my last illness shall be paid by my executor hereinafter named as soon as after my decease as convenient;

Second: I give, devise and bequeath to Mrs. Eli Swift Eagle, my daughter, the NE ¼ of Sec. 29, T133N, R79W, 5th P.M, containing 160 acres, more or less; one team of my bay issue mares, both being branded 366 on Rt Thi and ID on Rt Sho. with their spring colts; one, 5-year old gray gelding being branded 366 on Rt. Thi; one 2-year old gray gelding being branded 366 on Rt Thi; one 2-year old black steer, white spots in the face being branded 366 on Rt Side, S on Rt hip; 2 head yearling steers, red, white spots in the fact, both being branded 366 on Rt side and S on Rt hip;

Third: I give, devise and bequeath to Mrs. Gerald Gray Bear, or Wasteinapewin, the S ½ of Sec. 29, T133N, R79W, 5th P.M, containing 320 acres more or less; one white gelding, 16-years old being branded 366 on Rt Thi; one bay gelding 10-years old, being branded 366 on Rt. Thi;

Fourth: I give, devise and bequeath to Mrs. John Good Bear, one work team of white geldings both being branded 81 on Rt Thi, CW on Left Thi;

Fifth: All the rest and residue of my estate, both real and personal and mixed, I give, devise and bequeath to my lawful heirs as determined after my decease.

In testament whereof, I have set my hand and seal to this my last will and testament, at Cannon Ball, SD, this 11th day of July, in the year of our Lord, 1918.

And lastly, I hereby request Asa Littlecrow to sign my name to this my last will and testament and witness the same.

Gerald Gray Bear His (thumb print) mark

NATIVE AMERICAN WILLS and PROBATE RECORDS, 1911 - 1921

Witnesses:
> *Asa Littlecrow*
> *Acting Farmer*

Signed, sealed, published, and declared by said Gerald Gray Bear, of Cannon Ball, ND, in our presence, as and for his last will and testament, and at his request and in our presence, and in the presence of each other, we have hereunto subscribed our names as attesting witnesses thereto.

> *Jerome Cottonwood*
> *Darks Fool Bear*
> *Stephen Douglas*
> (All of) P.O. Cannon Ball, ND

DEPARTMENT OF THE INTERIOR, Office of Indian Affairs, Washington Oct. 23, 1920

It is respectfully recommended that the within will of Gerald Graybear, be approved under the Act of June 25, 1910, (36 Stat. L, 855-6), as amended by the Act of February 14, 1913, (37 Stat. L, 678).

> Respectfully,
> *E.B. Meritt*
> Assistant Commissioner

DEPARTMENT OF THE INTERIOR, Office of the Secretary, Washington Dec. 11, 1920

The within will of Gerald Graybear is hereby approved under the Act of June 25, 1910, (36 Stat. L, 855-6). as amended by the Act of February 14, 1913 (37 Stat. L, 678).

> *S.G. Hopkins*
> Assistant Secretary

<<<<<<<<>>>>>>>

KNOW ALL MEN BY THESE PRESENTS that I, **ANTHONY REVARRE**, of Bement, Illinois, late of Truedale, Oklahoma, do hereby by these presents, make, declare and publish this instrument as and for my last will and testament, hereby revoking all former wills by me made.

FIRST: I direct my executrices hereinafter named to pay all my just debts and funeral expense.

SECOND: I give, devise and bequeath to my nieces by marriage, Mrs. Millie Anders and Pearl Groves, all my property, both real and personal, wherever situated to be held by them absolutely and in fee simple.

THIRD: I also give, devise and bequeath to my said nieces by marriage all benefit which may be derived or which may accrue from any litigation in which I am now engaged as a party and direct that my said executrices shall be

NATIVE AMERICAN WILLS and PROBATE RECORDS, 1911 - 1921

empowered to carry on said litigation in so far as it shall be necessary to secure a decision in regard to the merits thereof.

FOURTH: I hereby appoint Mrs. Millie Anders of Decatur, Illinois and Pearl Groves of Danville, IL, to serve as executrices of this my last Will and testament without bond.

Dated this 31st day of October, A.D, 1918.

Anthony Revarre

On this 31st day of October, 1918, personally appeared before us Anthony Revarre, who signed the above instrument in writing in our presence, at the same time declaring it to be his last will and testament, and we in his presence and in the presence of each other and at his request have signed our names as witnesses thereto and we believe him to be of sound mind and memory and acting under no restraint.

W.G. McPherson
Bement, IL

Austin Petry
Bement, IL

Endorsed: Filed Nov. 16, 1918, Harvey Fay, Clerk of the County Court
Recorded in Will Record E, page 3.

STATE OF ILLINOIS,)
) SS   In the County Court of said County
PIATT COUNTY)
                In Probate, December Term, A.D, 1918.

Personally appeared in open Court, Austin Petry and W.G. McPherson, subscribing witnesses to the annexed instrument of writing, purporting to be the Last Will and Testament of Anthony Revarre, late of said County, deceased, who being duly sworn according to law, do depose and say, each for himself, that he was present and saw the said Anthony Revarre sign said Will in his presence, and that they believed that the said testator was of sound mind and memory, of lawful age, and under no constraint when he signed said Will.

Subscribed and sworn to in open Court
this 14th day of December, A.D, 1918
    Harvey Fay, County Clerk
        By C.O. Houk, Deputy

Austin Petry

W.G. McPherson

      IN THE MATTER OF THE LAST WILL AND TESTAMENT OF
                  ANTHONY REVARRE, DECEASED

STATE OF ILLINOIS)
) SS IN THE COUNTY COURT OF SAID COUNTY,
PIATT COUNTY   )   NOVEMBER TERM, A.D, 1918

TO THE HON. THE JUDGE OF THE COUNTY COURT OF SAID COUNTY:

NATIVE AMERICAN WILLS and PROBATE RECORDS, 1911 - 1921

  The undersigned Petitioner represents to the Court that on, that is to say, the 4th day of November, A.D, 1918, Anthony Revarre departed this life at Bement, Illinois, in the County of Piatt and State of IL, leaving an instrument in writing purporting to be his Last Will and Testament which is now here produced by the Petitioner and proposed for probate, and that said decedent was a resident of Bement in the County and State aforesaid, at the time of his death.

  The Petitioner further represents to the Court that the decedent left surviving him no widow, and no heirs-at-law, known to your petitioner.

  The Petitioner further represents to the Court that the following named persons are also legatees under the said last Will and Testament, to-wit:

      Pearl Groves, residing at 135½ N. Franklin St, Danville, IL
      Mrs. Millie Anders, residing at 227 S. Main St, Decatur, IL

  The Petitioner further represents to the Court that said decedent left Personal Estate to the probable amount of value of $200.00. The petitioner further represents to the Court that Pearl Groves and Mrs. Millie Anders are nominated as executrices in said will to serve without bond.

  The Petitioner therefore prays that the said instrument in writing may be admitted to probate, and that the Court will make such other and further orders in the matter as may be necessary and lawful.

(1) And codicil thereto (if any)

            Pearl Groves

STATE OF ILLINOIS)
) SS
VERMILION COUNTY)

        Pearl Groves, the Petitioner being duly sworn, deposes and says that the facts averred in the above petition are true, according to the best of her knowledge, information and belief.

            Pearl Groves.

Subscribed and sworn to before me this 12th day of November, A.D, 1918.
            Oliver D. Mann
            Notary Public

(SEAL)

Endorsed as follows:

           PETITION
      In the Matter of the Last Will
   and Testament of Anthony Revarre, Deceased.

      Recorded in Ex. Rec. D. page 118,
     Filed this 16th day of November, A.D, 1918
        Harvey Fay, Clerk

NATIVE AMERICAN WILLS and PROBATE RECORDS, 1911 - 1921

Estate of Anthony Revarre, Deceased.
BOND OF EXECUTOR.

STATE OF ILLINOIS,)
County of Piatt,) ss   IN COUNTY COURT, December Term, 1918.

KNOW ALL MEN BY THESE PRESENTS, That we Pearl Groves and Millie Anders and Alphonse Meis, of the County of Piatt and State of Illinois, are held and firmly bound unto the People of the State of Illinois, in the penal sum of Five Hundred Dollars, current money of the United States, which payment, well and truly to be made and performed, we, and each of us, being ourselves, our heirs, executors and administrators, jointly, severally and firmly by these presents.
Witness our hands and seals, this 21st day of Dec, A.D, 1918.

THE CONDITION OF THE ABOVE OBLIGATION IS SUCH, That is the above bound Pearl Groves and Millie Anders, Execut____ of the last Will and Testament of Anthony Revarre, deceased, do make, or cause to be made a true and perfect inventory of all and singular the goods and chattels, rights and credits, lands, tenements and hereditaments, and the rents and profits issuing out of the same, of the said deceased, which have or shall come to the hands, possession or knowledge of the said Pearl Groves and Millie Anders or into the possession of any other person for them and the same so made do exhibit in the County Court for the said County of Piatt as required by law; and also make and render a fair and just account of their actings and doings as such Executrices to said Court, when thereunto lawfully required, and to well and truly fulfill the duties imposed upon them in and by the said Will; and shall, moreover, pay and deliver to the persons entitled thereto, all the legacies and bequests contained in said Will, so far as the estate of the said testator will thereunto extend, according to the value thereof, and as the law shall charge, them and shall in general do all other acts which may from time to time be required of them by law, then this obligation to be void, otherwise to remain in full force and virtue.

                                          Pearl Groves   [SEAL]
Signed, Sealed and Delivered in Presence of   Millie Anders   [SEAL]
                                          Alphonse Meis   [SEAL]

    I, Oliver D. Mann, a Notary Public, in and for said County and State, do hereby certify that Pearl Groves, Millie Anders and Alphonse Meis who are each personally known to me to be the same persons whose names are subscribed to the foregoing instrument, appeared before me this day in person and acknowledged that they signed, sealed and delivered said instrument as their free and voluntary act, for the uses and purposes therein set forth.
                      Given under my hand and notarial seal, this 21st day of December, A.D, 1918.

NATIVE AMERICAN WILLS and PROBATE RECORDS, 1911 - 1921

Oliver D. Mann
Notary Public

STATE OF ILLINOIS,)
County of Piatt   ) ss   In the matter of the Official Bond of
Pearl Groves and Millie Anders, Executrices of the Estate of Anthony Revarre, deceased, Alphonse Meis who offers himself as security upon said Bond, being duly sworn, each upon his oath says that he is the owner of Real Estate located in this State of the value over and above all his debts and liabilities of every nature and kind, not exempt by the laws of this State from levy and sale on execution, the said Alphonse Meis of the value of Twenty-five Thousand Dollars; and the said (blank) of the value of (blank) Thousand Dollars; and the said (blank) of the value of (blank) Thousand Dollars; and that he is a resident of Vermilion County and a freeholder.

Subscribed and sworn to before me, this 21st day of December, A.D. 1918.

(No name given)
Notary Public'

ESTATE OF Anthony Revarre, DECEASED
OATH OF EXECUTOR
STATE OF ILLINOIS,)
COUNTY OF PIATT   ) ss   In County Court, in Probate Dec. Term, A.D. 1918

I DO SOLEMNLY SWEAR, That this writing contains the true last will and testament of the within named Anthony Revarre, deceased, as far as I know or believe, and that I will well and truly execute the same, by paying first the debts, and then the legacies mentioned therein, so far as his goods and chattels will thereunto extend, and the law charge me; and that I will make a true and perfect inventory of all such goods and chattels, rights and credits, as may come to my hands or knowledge, belonging to the estate of said deceased, and render a fair and just account of my executorship, when thereunto required by law, to the best of my knowledge and abilities, so help me God.

Pearl Groves
Millie Anders

Sworn to and subscribed, this 21st day of December, A.D. 1918, in open court before me.

Oliver D. Mann, Notary Public

NATIVE AMERICAN WILLS and PROBATE RECORDS, 1911 - 1921

LETTERS TESTAMENTARY

STATE OF ILLINOIS) ss
Piatt County)

IN COUNTY COURT, IN PROBATE: January Term, 1919, The People of the state of Illinois, to All to Whom These Presents Shall Come---GREETING:
    KNOW YE, That whereas Anthony Revarre, late of the County of Piatt and State of Illinois, died on or about the 4th day of November, A.D, 1918, as it is said, after having duly made and published his last Will and Testament, a copy whereof is hereunto annexed, leaving, at the time of his death, property in this State, which may be lost, destroyed or diminished in value, if speedy care be not taken of the same; and inasmuch as it appears that Pearl Groves and Millie Anders, have been appointed executrices in and by the last Will and Testament, to execute the same.

    Now to the end that the said property may be preserved for those who shall appear to have a legal right or interest therein; and that the said Will may be executed according to the request of the said testator, we do hereby authorize the said Pearl Grove and Millie Anders as such executrices collect and secure all and singular the goods and chattels, rights, and credits, which were of the said Anthony Revarre at the time of his decease, in whosoever hands or possession the same may be found in this State; and well and truly to perform and fulfill all such duties as may be enjoined upon them by the said Will, so far as there shall be property, and the law charge then and in general to do and perform all other acts which now are or hereafter may be required of them by law.

    WITNESS, HARVEY FAY, Clerk of the County Court of said County of Piatt, and the seal of said Court, this 11th day of January, A.D, 1919.

                          Harvey Fay,
[SEAL]   Clerk of the County Court
                        by C. Myrtle Turley, Deputy

NATIVE AMERICAN WILLS and PROBATE RECORDS, 1911 - 1921

PUBLISHER'S CERTIFICATE

STATE OF ILLINOIS)
PIATT COUNTY) ss

PETITION TO PROBATE
WILL
State of Illinois)
Piatt County) ss

COUNTY COURT, PIATT COUNTY
November Term, 1918

In the matter of the Probate of the Last Will and Testament of Anthony Revarre, deceased,-- In Probate.
To all persons whom this may concern:- GREETING:
Notice is hereby given, that on the 16th day of November, A.D, 1918, a Petition was filed in the County Court of Piatt County, Illinois, asking that the Last Will and Testament of Anthony Revarre, deceased, be admitted to Probate. The same Petition further states that the following names persons are all the heirs-at-law and legatees:
No Heirs-at-law known to your petitioner. Pearl Groves legatee, Mrs. Millie Anders, legatee.
You are further notified that the hearing of the proof of said Will has been set by said Court for the 18th day of December, A.D, 1918, at the hour of 10 o'clock in the forenoon, at the Court House in Monticello, in said County when and where you can appear if you see fit, and show cause if any you have, why said Will should not be admitted to Probate.

                Harvey Fay
[SEAL}   County Clerk

Dated at November 16, 1918

THE PIATT COUNTY REPUBLICAN
A Weekly Public Newspaper
Printed and published in the City of Monticello, in said County for at least 6 months prior to the first publication of the annexed notice do hereby certify that the annexed printed notice has been published in said paper, and in every copy and impression thereof, three weeks successively, of the issues commencing on the 21st day of November, A.D, 1918, and ending on the 5th day of December, A.D. 1918 which are the first and last papers containing the same.

WITNESS my hand this seventh day of December, A.D, 1918.
Printer's Fee. $3.00
              J.C. Tippett
              Publisher

Endorsed as follows
Filed Dec. 3, 1918

Harvey Fay, Clerk of
the County Court.

STATE OF ILLINOIS,)
) ss
COUNTY OF PIATT)

In County Court, in Probate, December Term, A.D, 1918.
On Saturday, The Fourteenth day of December, A.D, 1918

Present:- Hon. W.A. Doss, Judge.

NATIVE AMERICAN WILLS and PROBATE RECORDS, 1911 - 1921

Attest:- Harvey Fay, Clerk

Harvey Fay, Clerk
Edward R. Gale, Sheriff
Charles W. Firke, State's Attorney

In the matter of the Petition of Pearl Groves, for the Probate of an Instrument of Writing, purporting to be the Last Will and Testament of Anthony Revarre, deceased.

And now on this day, the same being one of the regular judicial days of the present term of this court, and the day set for the hearing on the above entitled cause, comes Pearl Groves, by her attorney, Oliver D. Mann, and presents to the Court an instrument of writing, purporting to be the last will and testament of Anthony Revarre, deceased, and presents also her Petition, duly verified, praying that said instrument of writing be admitted to probate and record in this Court as and for the last will and testament of said deceased, and that Letters Testamentary be issued to Pearl Groves and Millie Anders, the Executrices named therein.

And it appearing to the Court from the files and exhibits submitted in said cause herein, that the said Anthony Revarre, late of the County of Piatt and state of Illinois, deceased, departed this life on or about the 4th day of November, 1918, leaving said instrument of writing as and for his last will and testament, and leaving him surviving no heirs at law known to the petitioner herein, but leaving Pearl Groves and Millie Anders as his legatees under said will.

And it further appearing to the Court from the certificate of the Publisher on file herein, that due notice of the time and place of the hearing and making proof of said will, has been made by publication in the Piatt County Republican, a weekly, secular public newspaper of general circulation, printed and published in said County of Piatt, in the regular issues thereof, dated, issued and published commencing on the 21st day of November and ending on the 5th day of December, 1918, and the said notice by publication having been made in due and regular form, the same is by the Court hereby approved.

And it further appearing to the Court from the testimony of Austin Petry and W.G. McPherson, the subscribing witnesses to said last will and testament who appeared in open Court and upon their separate oaths testified that they were present at the execution of said last will and testament, and saw the said Anthony Revarre sign the same in their presence and acknowledged the same to be his last will and testament, and that thereupon, they, at his request and in his presence and in the presence of each other, did then and there, subscribe their names to said last will and testament, as attesting witnesses thereto, and that they believed that the said Anthony Revarre was of sound mind and memory, of lawful age, and under the constraint, at the time of signing the same.

And now the Court having heard all the evidence produced and being fully advised in the premises, doth find that said instrument of writing bearing date of October 31st, 1918, it the true last will and testament of said Anthony Revarre, deceased, and the Court further finds that said last will and testament was duly executed and attested.

It is therefore ordered and adjudged by the Court, that said instrument of writing bearing date of October 31, 1918, be and the same is hereby admitted to

NATIVE AMERICAN WILLS and PROBATE RECORDS, 1911 - 1921

Probate and Record in this Court as and for the last will and testament of said Anthony Revarre, deceased, and it is further ordered by the Court that Letters Testamentary be issued to Pearl Groves and Millie Anders, upon their taking the oath prescribed by the Statute and entering into Bond, in the penal sum of $500.00, conditioned according to law, and with securities to be approved by the Court.

State of Illinois,) In County Court, in Probate, January Term, A.D, 1919
) ss On Saturday, The Eleventh day of January, A.D, 1919
County of Piatt) Present:-   Hon. W.A. Doss, Judge
                              Harvey Fay, Clerk
                              Edward R. Gale, Sheriff
Attest:-Harvey Fay, Clerk   Charles W. Firke, State's Attorney

In the matter of the estate of Anthony Revarre, deceased.)
    Pearl Groves and Millie Anders, Executrices.   ) ORDER APPROVING BOND

    And now on this 11th day of January, A.D, 1919, the same being one of the regular judicial days of the present term of this Court, comes Pearl Groves and Millie Anders, by their attorney, Oliver D. Mann, and file herein and present to the Court their bond ad the Executrices of the last will and testament of Anthony Revarre, deceased, in the penal sum of $500.00, conditioned according to law, and with Alphonse Mees (Meis), as surety thereon.
    And the Court having duly examined said Bond, and being satisfied of the responsibility of the surety thereon, it is therefore ordered and adjudged that said bond be and the same Is hereby approved, and it is further ordered by the Court that Letters Testamentary be issued to the said Pearl Groves and Millie Anders, as Executrices of the last will and testament of said Anthony Revarre, deceased.

STATE OF ILLINOIS,)
Piatt County   ) ss.

    I, Harvey Fay, Clerk of the County Court in and for said County, in the State aforesaid, do hereby certify the foregoing to be a true, perfect and complete copy of Last Will and Testament of Anthony Revarre, deceased. Proof of Will Petition for Probate, Bond, Oath, Letters, Publisher's Certificate and Order admitting Will to Probate.
                IN TESTIMONY WHEREOF, I have hereunto set my hand and affixed the seal of said Court, at my office in Monticello this 15th day of January, A.D, 1919
                        Harvey Fay,   Clerk
                        By *C. Myrtle Turley*,   Deputy

STATE OF ILLINOIS,)
Piatt County   ) ss.

                I, William A. Doss, Judge of the County Court, of the State of Illinois, do hereby certify that Harvey Fay whose name is

NATIVE AMERICAN WILLS and PROBATE RECORDS, 1911 - 1921

subscribed to the foregoing Certificate of Attestation, now is, and was at the time of signing and sealing the same, Clerk of the County Court of Piatt County aforesaid, and keeper of the Records and Seal thereof, duly elected and qualified to office; that full faith and credit are and of right ought to be given to all his official acts as such in all Courts of Record and elsewhere; and that his said attestation is in due form of law, and by the proper officer.
  Given under my hand and seal this 15th day of January, A.D, 1919

[SEAL]
                William A. Doss

STATE OF ILLINOIS,)
 Piatt County   ) ss.

         I, Harvey Fay, Clerk of the County Court, in and for said County in the State aforesaid, do hereby certify that William A. Doss,. whose genuine signature is appended to the foregoing certificate, was, at the time of signing the same, Judge of the County Court of Piatt County duly commissioned and qualified; that full faith and credit are and of right ought to be given to all his official acts as such, in all Court of record and elsewhere.
         IN TESTIMONY WHEREOF, I have hereunto set my hand and affixed the seal of said Court, at my office in Monticello this 15th day of January, A.D, 1919.
              Harvey Fay, Clerk
             By *C. Myrtle Turley,* Deputy

DEPARTMENT OF THE INTERIOR, Office of Indian Affairs, Dec. 8, 1920
  The within certified copy of the will of Anthony Revarre, an unallotted Miami Indian. is respectfully recommended for approval under the provisions of the Act of June 25, 1910, (36 Stat. L, 855-6), as amended by the Act of February 14, 1913, (37 Stat. L, 678), so far as it relates to trust property under the jurisdiction of the Government.
            E.B. Meritt
            Assistant Commissioner

DEPARTMENT OF THE INTERIOR, Office of the Secretary, Dec. 14, 1920
  The within certified copy of the will of Anthony Revarre, an unallotted Miami Indian, is hereby approved pursuant to the provisions of the Act of June 25, 1910, (36 Stat. L, 855-6). as amended by the Act of February 14, 1913 (37 Stat. L, 678), so far as it disposes of trust property under the jurisdiction of the Government.
            S.G. Hopkins
            Assistant Secretary
        <<<<<<<<>>>>>>>

    LAST WILL AND TESTAMENT OF MICHAEL CIJAN
Devils Lake Allottee, #197

NATIVE AMERICAN WILLS and PROBATE RECORDS, 1911 - 1921

IN THE NAME OF GOD, Amen:

I, **MICHAEL CIJAN**, of Fort Totten, North Dakota, being of sound mind, memory and understanding, and not under any stress of circumstances, do hereby make, declare and publish this my last will and testament, revoking and annulling all wills heretofore made by me, in the manner and form following, that is to say:

First; I direct that all my just debts and the expense of my last illness and burial be paid as soon as shall be convenient.

Second; I give, devise and bequeath in equal shares all my allotment and inherited lands on the Devils Lake reservation to Tatankanpa, brother; Tatankagina, brother; Nakiskinwin, niece; Bessie Leftbear, niece; and John Smith, Jr, nephew.

Third; I give, devise and bequeath all my personal property of any description to my brother, Tatankanpa.

Fourth; it is my will that my wife, Hantemazawin, shall inherit no part of my estate for the reason that she deserted me.

And lastly, I hereby nominate, constitute and appoint Tatankanpa to be executor of this my last will and testament.

In testimony whereof, I have set my hand and seal to this my last Will and Testament, at Fort Totten, North Dakota, this 18th day of May, in the year of our Lord, 1920.

                                        Michael Cijan

Signed, sealed, published and declared by Michael Cijan as his last will and testament, in our presence, we signing as witnesses at his request and in his presence, we all signing in the presence of each other.

                                        Martin Strait
                                        Frank Christy
                                        S.A.M. Young

Probate 65538-20 RTB
DEPARTMENT OF THE INTERIOR, Office of Indian Affairs, Nov. 24, 1920

    It is recommended that the within will of Michael Cijan, deceased Fort Totten allottee #197, be approved under the Act of June 25, 1910, (36 Stat. L, 855-6), as amended by the Act of February 14, 1913, (37 Stat. L, 678), and the Regulations of the Department.

                                        Respectfully,
                                        E.B. Meritt
                                        Assistant Commissioner

11-EC-12
DEPARTMENT OF THE INTERIOR, Office of the Secretary, Dec. 15, 1920

    The within will of Michael Cijan, deceased Fort Totten allottee #197, is hereby approved in accordance with the Act of June 25, 1910, (36 Stat. L, 855-6).

NATIVE AMERICAN WILLS and PROBATE RECORDS, 1911 - 1921

as amended by the Act of February 14, 1913 (37 Stat. L, 678), and the Regulations of the Department.

OFFICE OF INDIAN AFFAIRS
RECEIVED
NOV 7, 1919
95852

S.G. Hopkins
Assistant Secretary

<<<<<<<>>>>>>>

LAST WILL AND TESTAMENT OF NAPOLEON DUCHENEAUX
August 22, 1913

I, **NAPOLEON DUCHENEAUX**, of Promise, South Dakota, being now 82 years of age and knowing that life is uncertain and being of sound mind do hereby ordain that the following bequests shall constitute my last will and testament.

First. I will and bequeath to each of my grandchildren, Fred Hill and Henry Hill, the sum of $50 each.

Second. After all my lawful debts and funeral expenses have been paid, I will and bequeath to each of my living sons and daughters; Victor and Henry Ducheneaux, Angiluque Arpan, Jose LeBeau, Camille and Douglass Ducheneaux, Lille Marshall, and to the heirs of Willie Ducheneaux, namely Napoleon, Mamie, Moses, Patrick, Mabel, Baryney[sic], and Fred Ducheneaux; [these several heirs of Willie Ducheneaux, my seven grandchildren, to be considered as entitled to their father's share in my estate]. An equal share in all my property both real and personal.

I hereby appoint my son, Douglass Ducheneaux, to execute this last will and testament. My estate to remain undivided for two years after my death. After two years have elapsed, and the lawful debts and funeral expenses have been paid and after the $50.00 have been paid to my grandson, Fred Hill, and $50.00 to my grandson Henry Hill, all the balance of my property both real and personal shall be divided into eight shares of which my seven children now living whose names I have before given, shall each receive one share, and the heirs of Willie Ducheneaux, whose names I have before given shall each receive 1/7 pare of one share of my estate. In case that I should out live any of my children whose names I have mentioned, then I decree that their share shall be equally divided among their children, and in the case that I should outlive any of the heirs of Willie Ducheneaux, I further decree that the 1/8 of my estate set aside for the heirs of Willie Ducheneaux be equally divided amongst the surviving heirs of Willie Ducheneaux.

Witnesses)	Napoleon Ducheneaux
Mrs. W.H. Kessler)	State of South Dakota, County of Dewey
W.H. Kessler)	Filed in my office, December 19, 1918
	S.M. Smith, Clerk of Courts
Dated August 22, 1913	Recorded in Book I.P 16 Will Record

NATIVE AMERICAN WILLS and PROBATE RECORDS, 1911 - 1921

STATE OF SOUTH DAKOTA ⎫ CIRCUIT COURT
County of Dewey   ⎬ In County Court Judicial Circuit

OFFICE OF INDIAN AFFAIRS
RECEIVED
NOV 7, 1919
95852

I, J. Ivan Wilson, Clerk of the Circuit Court in and for said County, the same being a Court of Record, do hereby certify that I have carefully compared the foregoing copy of Last Will and Testament of Napoleon Ducheneaux as file(ed) and recorded in the Clerk Of Courts office on December 19, 1918, with the original now on file in this office, and that the same is a correct transcript therefrom and of the whole thereof.

IN TESTIMONY WHEREOF, I have hereunto set my hand and the seal of said Court, at Timber Lake, SD, this 20th day of October, in the year, 1919.

J. Ivan Wilson
Clerk

Probate 34909-19; 95852-19 MHW
DEPARTMENT OF THE INTERIOR, Office of Indian Affairs, Dec. 4, 1920

The within will of Napoleon Ducheneaux, deceased Cheyenne River allottee #2900, is hereby recommended for approval according to the Act of June 25, 1910, (36 Stat. L, 855-6), as amended by the Act of February 14, 1913, (37 Stat. L, 678), and the Regulations of the Department.

Respectfully,
E.B. Meritt
Assistant Commissioner

DEPARTMENT OF THE INTERIOR, Office of the Secretary   Dec. 6, 1920

The within will of Napoleon Ducheneaux, deceased Cheyenne River allottee #2900, is hereby approved under the Act of June 25, 1910, (36 Stat. L, 855-6), and the Regulations of the Department.

S.G. Hopkins
Assistant Secretary

LAST WILL AND TESTAMENT OF
ROW STANDING

I, **ROW STANDING**, Cheyenne Indian and being the widow of Little Coyote, my residence being Clinton, Custer County, Oklahoma, being now in good health, strength of body and mind, but sensible of the uncertainty of life and desiring to make disposition of my property and affairs while in health and strength, do hereby make, publish and declare the following to be my last will and testament, hereby revoking and cancelling all other or former wills by me at any time made.
-1-
I direct the payment of all my just debts and funeral expenses.
-2-

NATIVE AMERICAN WILLS and PROBATE RECORDS, 1911 - 1921

I give and devise to Ruth Heap-of-Birds of Clinton, OK, the E ½ of the SW ¼, Sec. 30, T12N, T16W, I.M, in Custer County, OK

-3-

I give and devise unto Medicine Bull of Birney, Montana, he being my brother, and unto my sister, Sage Woman, of Birney, Montana, share and share alike, all my interest in and to the allotment of my daughter Carrie Pendleton, deceased, said land being described as follows, to-wit: The NW ¼, Sec. 30, T12M, R16W, I.M. in Custer County, OK.

-4-

I give and devise unto Medicine Bull, my brother named in the above clauses of this will, and unto Esther Heap-of-Birds, and unto Sage Woman, my sister, the said three to share the same share and share alike, the following described land, it being the allotment of my deceased husband named Spotted Wolf, and also known as Little Coyote, and also known as Little Woman, he having gone by all three names, to-wit: the NW ¼, Sec. 21, T19N, R16W, I.M. in Dewey County, OK

-5-

All the rest and residue of my real estate wherever situated to which I may die seized, I give and devise unto Medicine Bull, Sage Woman and Alfred Heap-of-Birds, share and share alike.

-6-

All the personal property of whatever kind, including cash, of which I may die possessed, I bequeath unto Medicine Bull, Sage Woman and Alfred Heap-of-Birds, share and share alike.

-7-

I hereby appoint and designate ___(blank)___, of ___(blank)___, my sole executor of this my last will and testament.

    In Witness Whereof, I Row Standing, have to this my last will and testament consisting of two sheets of type writing paper subscribed my name this 10th day of April, 1919.

                      Row Standing her (thumb print) mark

Witness to Signature:
    J.B. Edigar
    W.W. Bryant

Subscribed by Row Standing, in the presence of each of us, the undersigned and at the same time declared by her to us to be her last will and testament, and we, whereupon at the request of Row Standing, in her presence and in the presence of each other, sign our names hereto as witnesses, this 10th day of April, 1919.

                      J.B. Edigar   Clinton, OK
                      W.W. Bryant   Clinton, OK
                      Trenton Antelope Clinton, OK

Probate 47397-20 MHW, Seger Agency, OK

NATIVE AMERICAN WILLS and PROBATE RECORDS, 1911 - 1921

DEPARTMENT OF THE INTERIOR, Office of Indian Affairs,   Dec. 3, 1920
    The within will of Row Standing, deceased Cheyenne allottee #104 of the Seger Agency, OK, is hereby recommended for approval pursuant to the Act of June 25, 1910, (36 Stat. L, 855-6), as amended by the Act of February 14, 1913, (37 Stat. L, 678), and the Regulations of the Department.

                              Respectfully,
                              E.B. Meritt
                              Assistant Commissioner

DEPARTMENT OF THE INTERIOR, Office of the Secretary   Dec. 9, 1920
    The within will of Row Standing, deceased Cheyenne allottee #104 of the Seger Agency, OK, is hereby approved according to the Act of June 25, 1910, (36 Stat. L, 855-6), as amended by the Act of February 14, 1913, (37 Stat. L, 678), and the Regulations of the Department.

                              S.G. Hopkins
                              Assistant Secretary

<<<<<<<>>>>>>>

Round Valley Indian Reservation
Covelo, California
March 27, 1920 A.D.

OFFICE OF INDIAN AFFAIRS
RECEIVED
APR 26, 1920
35725

LAST WILL AND TESTAMENT OF
Eliza Major Spencer

    I, **ELIZA MAJOR SPENCER**, an Indian woman of the Round Valley Indian Reservation, County of Mendocino, State of California, of the age of 23 years, being of sound and disposing mind and memory, do make this my last will and testament, to wit:--
    First;- I give, devise and bequeath to my beloved mother, Mary Major, also of the Round Valley Indian Reservation, any and all of my personal estate of which I may be seized at the time of my death and the following real estate located on the Round Valley Indian Reservation, County Mendocino, State of California and more particularly described as follows:
    Lot 4 & N/2, SW/4, NW/4 and the N/2, S/2, SW/4, NW/4, Sec. 2, and E/2, Lot 1, and the NE/4, SE/4, NE/4 and N/2, SE/4, SE/4, NE/4, Sec. 3, T23N, R14W, M.D.M, containing 69.58 acres. Or any other property, real or personal to which I may hereafter become an heir.

    I nominate and appoint the Superintendent of the Round Valley Indian Reservation the executor of this my last will, without bonds.
    I am the lawful wife of Annert Spencer of the Round Valley Indian Reservation, but my reason of his neglect and desertion of me during the greater part of the last two years and his non-support in any way, I do not wish that he

NATIVE AMERICAN WILLS and PROBATE RECORDS, 1911 - 1921

shall share in any of my property real or personal, or any other realty to which I may hereafter be found to be an heir.

IN WITNESS WHEREOF, I have hereunto set my hand and seal this 27th day of March, A.D, 1920.

Eliza Major Spencer   her thumb mark

WITNESSES:
W.W. McCombe
Frank Bartch

The foregoing instrument, all being on the one page upon which it is written, was at the date hereof, by the said Eliza Major Spencer, signed, sealed and published as and declared by her to be her last will and testament, in the presence of us who at her request and in her presence and in the presence of each other, subscribed our names as witnesses.

W.W. McCombe
Supt. Round Valley Agency
Residing at Covelo, CA
Frank Bartch
Residing at Covelo, CA

Probate 35735-20 R T B
DEPARTMENT OF THE INTERIOR, Office of Indian Affairs,   Dec. 4, 1920

It is hereby recommended that the within will of Eliza Major Spencer, deceased Round Valley allottee #955, be approved under (the) Act of June 25, 1910, (36 Stat. L, 855-6), as amended by the Act of February 14, 1913, (37 Stat. L, 678), and the Regulations of the Department. No executor to be recognized.

Respectfully,
E.B. Meritt
Assistant Commissioner

DEPARTMENT OF THE INTERIOR, Office of the Secretary   Dec. 8, 1920

The within will of Eliza Major Spencer, deceased Round Valley allottee #955, is hereby approved according to the Act of June 25, 1910, (36 Stat. L, 855-6), as amended by the Act of February 14, 1913, (37 Stat. L, 678), and the Regulations of the Department. No executor to be recognized.

S.G. Hopkins
Assistant Secretary

I, **ROBERT or JAMES TAKES THE SHIELD**, being of sound mind and memory, do give, devise and bequeath all my property, both real and

NATIVE AMERICAN WILLS and PROBATE RECORDS, 1911 - 1921

personal, to Joseph Takes The Shield, Sr, hereby revoking all former will(s) by me made.

    In witness whereof, I, Robert or James Takes The Shield, have to this my last will and testament, subscribed my name, this the 1st day of July, 1918, at Wakpala, SD.

Robert or James Takes The Shield

Witness(es): *Frowin Reel*
              F. Godfrey
              Thrissie Takes The Shield   her (thumb print) mark

Witness to mark: *F. Godfrey*
                  Frowin Reel

<<<<<<<>>>>>>>
WILL

OFFICE OF INDIAN AFFAIRS
RECEIVED
OCT 23, 1920
86841

    I, **CHASING HAWK**, of Pine Ridge Agency, South Dakota, allottee #1297, do hereby make and declare this to be my last will and testament, in accordance with Section 2 of the Act of June 25, 1910, (36 Stat. 855-858), hereby revoking all former wills made by me:

1. I hereby direct that, as soon as possible after my decease, that all my debts and funeral and testamentary expenses be paid out of my personal estate.

2. I give and devise my allotment on the Pine Ridge Reservation, South Dakota, described as follows: Lots 4, 5, 6, and 7 and SE 8/4[sic] of NW ¼, and E ½ of SW ¼ of Sec. 6, T38, R40W of the 6th P.M, containing 310.16 acres in the following manner: all of said land to my daughter Mrs. Mattie Last Horse of Kyle, South Dakota. None to my wife for a cause that she deserted me while I was in a helpless condition and she could be punished for this but as I am not able to take action against her and also according to her wishes I did not give her anything.

3. I give and bequeath all of my personal property of whatsoever nature and wheresoever situated unto Mrs. Mattie Last Horse of Kyle, South Dakota, including one unfinished house with twenty bundles of shingles.

4. All the rest of my property, real or personal, now possessed or hereafter acquired, or whatsoever nature and wheresoever situated, I hereby give, devise and bequeath unto Mrs. Mattie Last Horse of Kyle, South Dakota.

    In witness whereof I have hereunto set my hand this 26th day of July, 1918.

Chasing Hawk His (thumb print) mark

NATIVE AMERICAN WILLS and PROBATE RECORDS, 1911 - 1921

The above statement was, this 26th day of July, 1918, signed and published by Chasing Hawk as his last will and testament, in the joint presence of the undersigned, the said Chasing Hawk then being of sound and vigorous mind and free from any constraint or compulsion; whereupon we, being without any interest in the matter other than friendship, and being well acquainted with him but not members of his family, immediately subscribed our names hereto in the presence of each other and of the said testator, for the purpose of attesting the said will, as he requested us to do.

     Chas Little Hoop His (thumb print) mark Allen, SD
     Whirlwind Horse   Allen, SD

Witness to mark: Pine Ridge, South Dakota
 Clarence Three Starr
 Joseph Makes Good

  I hereby certify that I have fully inquired into the mental competency of the Indian, signing the above will; the circumstances attending the execution of the will; the influences that may have induced its execution, and the names of those entitled to share in the estate under the law of descent in South Dakota; reasons for the disposition of the property proposed by the will, differing from disposition had the property descended.
  I respectfully forward the will, above, with the recommendation that it be approved.

            H.M. Tidwell
           Supt. & Spl. Disb. Agent

PROBATE 86841-1920 M H W
DEPARTMENT OF THE INTERIOR, Office of Indian Affairs, Nov. 17, 1920
  It is recommended that the within will be approved pursuant to the provisions of the Act of June 25, 1910, (36 Stat. L, 855-6), as amended by the Act of February 14, 1913, (37 Stat. L, 678), and the regulations of the Department.

            Respectfully,
            E.B. Meritt
           Assistant Commissioner

DEPARTMENT OF THE INTERIOR, Office of the Secretary Nov. 29, 1920
  The within will is hereby approved pursuant to the provisions of the Act of June 25, 1910, (36 Stat. L, 855-6), as amended by the Act of February 14, 1913, (37 Stat. L, 678), and the regulations of the Department.

            S.G. Hopkins
            Assistant Secretary

NATIVE AMERICAN WILLS and PROBATE RECORDS, 1911 - 1921

WILL

IN THE NAME OF GOD, Amen:

I, **ELIZA S. PROCTOR**, Fort Peck allottee #881, residing at Poplar, Montana, being of sound mind but of feeble health and realizing the uncertainty of life, and not acting under fraud, duress, menace or undue influence, do make, publish and declare the following to be my last will and testament, this 19th day of November, 1917.

First:

I give, devise and bequeath my 160-acre grazing allotment described as the SE/4 of Sec. 25, T28N, R51E, and my irrigable allotment described as the SE/4 of NE/5 of Sec. 30, T28N, R51E, and containing 40 acres, to the following named persons, share and share alike: Cecelia Smith, Vina Smith, Julian Smith, #2, and Ethel Proctor, all being my children, Fort Peck allottees, #'s. 882, 883, 1795 and 2260, respectively.

Second:

I give, devise and bequeath my determined share in the estate of my former husband, Julian Smith, #2, deceased Fort Peck allottee #880 (L.H. 119789-1915 dated Nov. 20, 1915), to the following named persons, share and share alike: Cecelia Smith, Vina Smith and Julian Smith, #2, Fort Peck allottee #'s 882, 883 and 1795, respectively.

Third:

I give, devise and bequeath to my present husband, Peter Proctor, Fort Peck allottee #725, the sum of $5.00.

Fourth:

I give, devise and bequeath all other property, both real and personal, of which I may die possessed, including my rights which I now have or may acquire later in any estates, to the following named persons, share and share alike: Cecelia Smith, Vina Smith and Julian Smith, #2, Fort Peck allottees #'s 882, 883 and 1795, respectively.

Fifth:

I direct that Supt. E.D. Mossman or his successor in office act as executor of this will and that all funeral expenses and other just bills contracted by me and unpaid at my death be paid by him from the proceeds of my estate.

Mrs. Eliza S. Proctor
Fort Peck allottee #881

Witness(es):
Robt. H. Covington
Joseph Culbertson
both of Poplar, Montana

NATIVE AMERICAN WILLS and PROBATE RECORDS, 1911 - 1921

We, the undersigned, hereby certify on our honor that neither of us are related in any way to the testatrix, that we were both present and witnessed the signature of the testatrix to the above instrument in one page which she read and fully understood before signing as she was apparently of sound mind and signed the same of her own free will and accord stating that her wishes were duly set forth.

Robt. H. Covington
Joseph Culbertson

66363-20 M N W
DEPARTMENT OF THE INTERIOR, Office of Indian Affairs,   Nov. 29, 1920

The within will of Eliza Smith Proctor, deceased Yankton Sioux allottee #881 of the Fort Peck Reservation, is recommended for approval in accordance with the Provisions of the Act of June 25, 1910, (36 Stat. L, 855-6), as amended by the Act of February 14, 1913, (37 Stat. L, 678).

Respectfully,
E.B. Meritt
Assistant Commissioner

DEPARTMENT OF THE INTERIOR, Office of the Secretary   Dec. 1, 1920

The within will of Eliza Smith Proctor, deceased Yankton Sioux allottee #881 of the Fort Peck Reservation, is hereby approved in accordance with the provisions of the Act of June 25, 1910, (36 Stat. L, 855-6), as amended by the Act of February 14, 1913, (37 Stat. L, 678).

S.G. Hopkins
Assistant Secretary

Disapprove.

Lodge Grass, Montana
March 8, 1919

This is to certify that I, **FRANK L. LOCKE**, of Porcupine, South Dakota, made my will this 8th day of March, in the year of our Lord, 1919, and are as follows, to:

Frank Black Hair
Percy Black Hair
Sidney Black Hair
Wilbur Black Hair
Mary Black Hair

320 acres of land, to be heir to after my decease.

Percy Black Hair, Crow Agency, Montana

NATIVE AMERICAN WILLS and PROBATE RECORDS, 1911 - 1921

      Frank L. Locke is very low and a will to we boys and I like for you to come up right away.

Frank Black Hair

(Probate) 86846-20 M H W
DEPARTMENT OF THE INTERIOR, Office of Indian Affairs   Nov. 17, 1920
      It is hereby recommended that the within will of Frank Locke, deceased allottee #'s 35 and 6683 of the Oglala Sioux Tribe of Indians be disapproved in accordance with the provisions of the Act of June 25, 1910 (35 Stat. L 855-6), as amended by the Act of February 14, 1913 (37 Stat. L, 678).

> Respectfully,
> E.B. Meritt
> Assistant Commissioner

DEPARTMENT OF THE INTERIOR, Office of the Secretary   Nov. 29, 1920
      The within will of Frank Locke, deceased allottee #'s 35 and 6683 of the Oglala Sioux Tribe of Indians, is hereby disapproved in accordance with the provisions of the Act of June 25, 1910, (36 Stat. L, 855-6), as amended by the Act of February 14, 1913, (37 Stat. L, 678), and the Regulations of the Department.

> S.G. Hopkins
> Assistant Secretary

KNOW ALL MEN BY THESE PRESENTS:
      That I, **SHEH-TAHS**, a resident of Jackson County, Kansas, being of sound mind and memory, do hereby make, publish and declare this to be my last will and testament, hereby revoking all other and former wills by me at any time made.

ITEM I.   I desire and direct that the executor of this will shall as soon as convenient after my death, pay all my just debts, including my funeral expenses and the expenses of my last sickness, out of the personal property owned by me at the time of my death.

ITEM II.   I give, devise and bequeath to my daughter, Lucy M. Daugherty, all my right, title and interest in and to allotment #404, and which is described as the S ½ of the SE ¼ of Sec. 11, T8, R14E of the 6th P.M. in Jackson County, Kansas, to be hers for her use and benefit so long as she may live and, at her death, I desire that said land shall become and be the property of her lawful heirs.
      It is understood, however, that my right to dispose of said property is not absolute, but is restricted by certain laws, rules and regulations imposed

NATIVE AMERICAN WILLS and PROBATE RECORDS, 1911 - 1921

upon me by the Government of the United States, which restrictions will be removed at the end of a period of time fixed by the U.S. Government.

ITEM III.   I give, devise and bequeath to my daughter, Gertie M-joe-tah (Now-kum-ge-quah), allotment #403, which land I inherited from Witch-e-wah, my late husband, and which is described as the NW ¼ of the NW ¼ of Sec. 13, T8, R14, and the SW ¼ of the SW ¼ of Sec. 12, T8, T14, all east of the 6th P.M. in Jackson County, Kansas, to be hers for her use and benefit so long as she may live and at her death, said property I desire to be and become the property of her lawful heirs and it is understood, however, that my right to dispose of said property is not absolute, but is restricted by certain laws, rules and regulations imposed upon me by the Government of the United States, which restrictions will removed at the end of a period of time fixed by the United States Government.

ITEM IV.   I will, devise and bequeath to my son, Harry Witch-e-way, all my right, title and interest in and to allotment #637, which allotment I inherited in and to allotment #837, which allotment I inherited from Kaw-batche, a deceased child of mine, said allotment being described as the S ½ of the NE ¼ of Sec. 15, T8, R14 east of the 6th P.M, in Jackson County, Kansas, to be his for his use and benefit so long as he may live and at his death, said property is to be and become the property of his lawful heirs.

It is understood, however, that my right to dispose of said property is not absolute, but is restricted by certain laws, rules and regulations imposed upon me by the Government of the United States, which restrictions will be removed at the end of a certain period of time fixed by the United States Government.

ITEM V.   It is my desire that my son, Harry Witch-e-way, shall have the two horses and the harness which I now own, which shall be subject, however, to the payment of my debts and funeral expenses as provided for in Item I, provided there is not sufficient money on hand or in the hands of the Government of the United States or its agents to pay the said debts, funeral expenses and expenses of last sickness, and if there is sufficient funds with which to pay said debts, funeral expenses and expenses of last sickness, then I desire that the personal property above enumerated shall pass to my son, Harry, to be his absolutely.

ITEM VI.   I will and bequeath to my granddaughter, Ethel M-joe-tah, the Jersey cow which I now own.

ITEM VII.   It Is my wish and will that the parties to whom I have bequeathed the above described land, and each and every one of them, shall be restricted in this that they shall not have the right to sell, mortgage or otherwise encumber said land during their lifetime, but that same shall pass, at their death, to their legal heirs unencumbered.

IN WITNESS, WHEREOF, I have hereunto set my hand this 20th day of October, 1914.

NATIVE AMERICAN WILLS and PROBATE RECORDS, 1911 - 1921

                                    Sheh-tahs   Her (thumb print) mark

(Witness)
    A.R. Snyder
    Mayetta, KS

We, and each of us, do hereby certify that we saw Sheh-tahs sign her name to the foregoing will and heard her declare that it was her last will and testament and we, in her presence, and in the presence of each other and at her request, sign the same as witnesses thereto.

    IN WITNESS WHEREOF, we have hereunto set our hands this 20th day of October, 1914.

                    A.R. Snyder
                       P.O.   Mayetta, KS
                  Richard Rice
                       P.O.   Mayetta, KS

DEPARTMENT OF THE INTERIOR, Office of Indian Affairs, Washington, DC
    The within will is recommended for approval pursuant to the provisions of the Act of June 25, 1910, (36 Stat. L, 855-6), as amended by the Act of February 14, 1913, (37 Stat. L, 678).

                    Respectfully,
                    E.B. Meritt
                    Assistant Commissioner

DEPARTMENT OF THE INTERIOR, Office of the Secretary, Washington, DC Jan 20, 1915
    The within will is hereby approved pursuant to the provisions of the Act of June 25, 1910, (36 Stat. L, 855-6), as amended by the Act of February 14, 1913, (37 Stat. L, 678).

                    Bo Sweeney
                    Assistant Secretary

<<<<<<<<>>>>>>>

LAST WILL AND TESTAMENT

    I, **ESAU JANDRON**, Yankton Sioux allottee #156, being of sound and disposing mind and memory, do hereby make, publish and declare this to be my last will and testament, hereby revoking and annulling any and all wills heretofore made by me.

FIRST: I give and devise to my brother, Felix Jandron, that portion of my original allotment described as the NE/4 of the NW/4, Sec. 31, T97N, R61W, 5th P.M, South Dakota.

NATIVE AMERICAN WILLS and PROBATE RECORDS, 1911 - 1921

SECOND: I give and bequeath to James Bourissau, that part of my original allotment described as the W/2 of SE/4 of SE/4, Sec. 18, T93N, R62W, of the 5th P.M, South Dakota.

THIRD: I give and devise to my brother, Albert Jandron, all of my inherited interest in the estate of Frank Jandron, Sr, whose allotment is described as Lots 1488, 1489, 1496 and 1497, according to the survey of the Yankton Reservation, South Dakota.

FOURTH: It is my will and desire that the remainder of my original allotment described as the SE/4 of NW/4, Sec. 31, T97N, R61W of the 5th P.M, South Dakota; be sold and that from the proceeds of this sale all my just debts, contracted during my last sickness and burial, be paid; that a monument be erected to my grave at a cost not to exceed $100.00; that $100.00 be paid to my sister, Amelia Jandron, and $100.00 be paid to James Bourissau mentioned in paragraph two above and that any remainder from this sale or that may be on deposit for me with the Superintendent Yankton Indian Agency be given to my mother, Katie Jandron, Yankton Sioux allottee #202.

FIFTH: I give and devise to my brother Felix Jandron, any personal property that I may possess at the time of my death.

Asa Jandron

SIGNED, SEALED, PUBLISHED AND DECLARED this 5th day of Feb, 1918, by the said Esau Jandron in our presence as and for his last will and testament, and at his request and in his presence and in the presence of each other, we have hereunto set our names as attesting witnesses.

Joseph H. Cook P.O. Box Dante, SD
Louis Jandron P.O. Box Avon, SD
His (thumb print) mark

(Probate) 90267-29 W M H
DEPARTMENT OF THE INTERIOR, Office of Indian Affairs, Nov. 18, 1920
In accordance with the provisions of the Act of June 25, 1910, (36 Stat. L, 855-6), as amended by the Act of February 14, 1913, (37 Stat. L, 678), and the regulations of the Department, it is recommended that the within will of Esau or Asa Jandron, deceased Yankton Sioux allottee #156, be approved and that the name of William be substituted for that of James Bourissau, and the amount of money to be given him be changed from $100 to $200 in accordance with the wishes of the testator and for the reason that a typographical error was made in writing same.

Respectfully,
E.B. Meritt
Assistant Commissioner

NATIVE AMERICAN WILLS and PROBATE RECORDS, 1911 - 1921

DEPARTMENT OF THE INTERIOR, Office of the Secretary   Nov. 16, 1920

Pursuant to the provisions of the Act of June 25, 1910, (36 Stat. L, 855-6), as amended by the Act of February 14, 1913, (37 Stat. L, 678) and the Regulations of the Department, the within will of Esau or Asa Jandron, deceased Yankton Sioux allottee #156, is hereby approved and authority given for correction of typographical errors by the substitution of the word William for that of James Bourisseau, and the amount to be given him changed from $100 to $200.

S.G. Hopkins
Assistant Secretary

Standing Rock Indian School, Supt.
Fort Yates, North S-Dakota
Commissioner of Indian Affairs
   Washington, D.C.

Sep. 14, 1920

Sir:

I am enclosing herewith papers purporting to be the last will and testament of Mrs. Gray Spotted Horse or Mrs. Joseph Takes the Shield. Attention is invited in this case to the heirship of Shell or Pankaskewin, deceased allottee #705, submitted of even date. You will notice a similarity in these cases in the fact that these wills were made almost immediately prior to the death of these allottees.

I can see no reason for the approval of this will, as the only reason for naming Sam Red Pheasant as beneficiary to 80 acres of land was the fact that he cared for her for some time. I have no means of knowing who prepared this will, but I believe that it was as in the case of many others, advantage taken of an Indian in the proximity of death, in which these at the death-bed generally participate in whatever property an Indian leaves.

I believe that this estate should descend to the legal heirs as recommended by the Examiner of Inheritance, and that the will be disproved and disregarded and that if Sam Red Pheasant has any claim for the care of this woman, that said claim be settled between himself and the heirs after determination on a basis of proper and equitable compensation.

I, therefore, respectfully recommend that the enclosed will be disproved.

Very truly yours,
James B. Kitt
Superintendent

JBK:RS
6-22-20

NATIVE AMERICAN WILLS and PROBATE RECORDS, 1911 - 1921

Kenel, SD March 8, 1919

Last will made by Gray Spotted Horse as follows:

1st Joseph Take the Shield, my husband, will have the NE/4 of Sec. 16, T22, R28, containing about 160 acres. Also one bay mare branded 1500 ID and one wagon, one set of harnes[sic].

2nd Samuel Red Pheasant will have the following: E/2 of the NW/4 of Sec. 16, T22, R28, containing about 80 acres.

3rd Frank Jewett and his sister, Magie Jewett of Cheyenne Agency, will have as follows, also Mack Iron Horn and Sophie Iron Horn of this reservation, Standing Rock Agency, W/2 of the NW/4 of Sec. 16, T22, R28, containing about 80 acres.

4th Frank Jewett and Magie Jewett will have this two satchels - one for each.

Witness(es): Mrs. Gray Spotted Horse
Luke Two Hearts Her (thumb print) mark
Charles Marshall

DEPARTMENT OF THE INTERIOR, Office of Indian Affairs, Washington
It is respectfully recommended that the within will be approved under the Act of June 25, 1910, (36 Stat. L, 855-6), as amended by the Act of February 14, 1913, (37 Stat. L, 678).

Respectfully,
E.B. Meritt
Assistant Commissioner

DEPARTMENT OF THE INTERIOR, Office of the Secretary, Washington Nov. 19, 1920
The within will of Mrs. Gray Spotted Horse, is hereby approved under the Act of June 25, 1910, (36 Stat. L, 855-6), as amended by the Act of February 14, 1913, (37 Stat. L, 678).

S.G. Hopkins
Assistant Secretary

Testimony in will of Gray Spotted Horse by Joseph Takes The Shield.

State your name, age and residence.
  Joseph Takes The Shield, aged 52, living at Wakapala, SD
Did you know Gray Spotted Horse?
  Yes, she was my wife, she died last April.
Did you ever see this will?
  Yes. [Will is here explained to witness who understands English.]

NATIVE AMERICAN WILLS and PROBATE RECORDS, 1911 - 1921

Were you present when your wife made this will?
    Yes.
Was she in her right mind at that time?
    Yes.
Do you wish this will approved as it stands?
    Yes.
Did she ever give any reason why she admitted Sam Red Phesant[sic] in this will?
    Yes, she said he had taken care of her when she was a widow, and had helped her often, and was the son of her older sister that's why she wanted him in this will
Did she say why she did not give the Jewett and Iron Horn children their full share?
    She did not say why she did it but it was her wish.
Did the Jewett or Iron Horn children ever come to see her when she was sick?
    No.

                Joseph Takes The Shield

Subscribed and sworn to before me this 4th day of November, 1919.
                James B. Kitt
                Superintendent

Testimony in case of Gray Spotted Horse by Sam Red Pheasant.

State your name, age and residence.
    Sam Red Pheasant, aged 39, living at Kenel, SD
Did you know Gray Spotted Horse?
    Yes, she was my aunt, my mother's sister.

Do you understand this will?
    Yes, I understand it.
Do you know why she included you in this will?
    Yes, I took care of her and supported her when she was a widow between the time she lost her first husband and the time she married Takes The Shield.
Were you present when she made this will?
    Yes.
Did she ever say before this time that she was going to leave you this land?
    Yes.
Do you want this will approved?
    Yes.
How long did you take care of her?
    8 years.
Is there anything else you wish to add?
    No.
Was she in her right mind when she made this will?
    Yes.

NATIVE AMERICAN WILLS and PROBATE RECORDS, 1911 - 1921

Who suggested to her that she make this will?
    She thought of it first.
                                            Sam Red Pheasant

Subscribed and sworn to before me this 4th day of November, 1919.
                                            James B. Kitt
                                              Superintendent

STATUTORY DECLARATION
Dominion of Canada
Prov. of Manitoba

     I, **POPOPA** OR **HINKANKOYAKEWIN**, of the Oak River Reserve, Griswold Agency in the Prov. of Manitoba.

     Do solemnly declare that Mrs. John Hapa of the Oak River Reserve is my grand daughter and Geo Pahakadokiseni of the Oak, River Reserve is my sister's son.

     Mrs. John Hapa has looked after me for the last seven years and I would like to leave all the property I own, or any interests I may have at Fort Totten, to her. Her Indian name is Tawoholakonzewin. I think she should have more than the rest of my relations.

     My husband's property at Fort Totten, I hear, is to be sold in 1916 on 1917 and I would like my share of it to be sent here to me as soon as possible, as I am very old and ill.

     And I make this solemn declaration conscientiously believing it to be true, and knowing that is of the same force and effect as if made under oath, and by virtue of "The Canada Evidence Act."

                                         Hinkankoyakewin
Declared before me at Griswold   or Popopa
    in the Prov. of Manitoba   her thumb mark
    this 28th day of December, 1916   Witnesses:
                                                R. Havard
                                                M. McDonald
                                                Jas. McDonald
                                                        Indian Agent

Probate 62922-20 J M P
DEPARTMENT OF THE INTERIOR, Office of Indian Affairs   Sep. 28, 1920
     It is recommended that the within will be approved pursuant to the provisions of the Act of June 25, 1910, (36 Stat. L, 855-6), as amended by the Act of February 14, 1913, (37 Stat. L, 678).
                                            Respectfully,
                                            E.B. Meritt
                                            Assistant Commissioner

NATIVE AMERICAN WILLS and PROBATE RECORDS, 1911 - 1921

DEPARTMENT OF THE INTERIOR, Office of the Secretary   Oct. 1, 1920
    The within will is hereby approved pursuant to the provisions of the Act of June 25, 1910, (36 Stat. L, 855-6), as amended by the Act of February 14, 1913, (37 Stat. L, 678).

S.G. Hopkins
Assistant Secretary

> OFFICE OF INDIAN AFFAIRS
> RECEIVED
> JUN 24, 1920

IN THE NAME OF GOD, Amen:

    I, **BROOKIE TOM**, Fort Peck allottee #1700, residing at Frazer, Montana, being of sound mind but of feeble health and realizing the uncertainty of life, and not acting under fraud, duress, menace or undue influence, do this 22nd day of December, 1919, make, publish and declare the following to be my last will and testament:

First:

    I give, devise and bequeath to my beloved daughter, Anna Lambert, all my personal and real property, described as follows: The E/4 of Sec. 34, T27N, and the W/2 of SW/4 of NW/4, Sec. 3, T26N, all in R43E; and to my beloved nephew, Isaac Bount, the SE/4 of the NE/4, Sec. 36, T27N, R42E.

    I hereby appoint E.D. Mossman, Supt. of Fort Peck Agency, or his successor in office, as executor of my estate.

                            Brookie Tom His (thumb print) mark
Witness(es):   Fort Peck allottee #1700
    Simon (Illegible last name)
    Henry Archdale, Jr.

    We, the undersigned, hereby certify on our honor that neither of us are related in any way to the testator, that we were both present and witnessed the signature of the testator to the above instrument in one page which he read and fully understood before signing as he was apparently of sound mind and signed the same of his own free will and accord stating that his wishes were duly set forth.

                         Simon (Illegible last name)
                         Henry Archdale, Jr.

DEPARTMENT OF THE INTERIOR, Office of Indian Affairs   Jul 14, 1920
    It is recommended that the within will of Brookie Tom, deceased allottee #1700 of the Assiniboin Tribe, be approved pursuant to the provisions of the Act of June 25, 1910, (36 Stat. L, 855-6), as amended by the Act of February 14, 1913, (37 Stat. L, 678).

                         Respectfully,
                         E.B. Meritt

NATIVE AMERICAN WILLS and PROBATE RECORDS, 1911 - 1921

Assistant Commissioner

DEPARTMENT OF THE INTERIOR, Office of the Secretary   Oct. 7, 1920

The within will of Brookie Tom, deceased allottee #1700 of the Assiniboin tribe, is hereby approved pursuant to the provisions of the Act of June 25, 1910, (36 Stat. L, 855-6), as amended by the Act of February 14, 1913, (37 Stat. L, 678).

S.G. Hopkins
Assistant Secretary

Will

I, **BETSEY DOG HORN**, of Pine Ridge Agency, South Dakota, allottee #6210, do hereby certify, make and declare this to be my last will and testament, in accordance with Sec. 2 of the Act of June 25, 1910 (36 Stat. 855-858), and Act of February 14, 1913, (Public #381), hereby revoking all former wills made by me:

1. I hereby direct that, as soon as possible after my decease, that all my debts and funeral and testamentary expenses be paid out of my personal estate.
2. I give and bequeath my allotment of the Pine Ridge Reservation, South Dakota, described as follows:
   in the following manner: All to Henry Little Soldier.
3. I give and bequeath all of my personal property of whatsoever nature and wheresoever situated unto Henry Little Soldier.
4. All the rest of my property, real or personal, now possessed or hereafter acquired, of whatsoever nature and wheresoever situated, I give, devise and bequeath unto Henry Little Soldier.

In witness whereof, I have hereunto set my hand this 27th day of August, 1915.

Witnesses to signature by mark: Betsey Dog Horn   Her (thumb print) mark
  L.L. Smith   Farmer, Oglala, SD
  Paul White Magpie   Sioux, Oglala, SD

The above statement was, this 27th day of August, 1915, signed and published by Betsey Dog Horn, as her last will and testament, in the joint presence of the undersigned, the said Betsey Dog Horn then being of sound and vigorous mind and free from any constraint or compulsion; whereupon we, being without any interest in the matter other than friendship, and being well acquainted with her, but not a member of her family, immediately subscribed our names hereto in the presence of each other and of the said testator, for the purpose of

NATIVE AMERICAN WILLS and PROBATE RECORDS, 1911 - 1921

attesting the said will, as she requested us to do. And that I, Paul W. Magpie at the testatrix's request, have written her name in ink, and that I affixed her thumb mark.

L.L. Smith   Oglala, SD
Paul White Magpie   Interpreter
    Oglala, SD
Pine Ridge, SD
Feb. 8, 1919

    I hereby certify that I have fully inquired into the mental competency of the Indian signing the above will; the circumstances attending the execution of the will; the influence that may have induced its execution, and the names of those entitled to share in the estate under the law of descent in South Dakota; reasons for the disposition of the property proposed by the will, differing from disposition has the property descended by operation of law.
    I respectfully forward this will with the recommendation that it be approved.

H.M. Tidwell
Supt. & Spl. Dist. Agent

Probate 13502-19 V L D
DEPARTMENT OF THE INTERIOR, Office of Indian Affairs   Oct. 8, 1920
    The within will of Betsey Dog Horn is hereby recommended for approval in accordance with the Act of June 25, 1910, (36 Stat. L, 855-6), as amended by the Act of February 14, 1913, (37 Stat. L, 678).

Respectfully,
E.B. Meritt
Assistant Commissioner

DEPARTMENT OF THE INTERIOR, Office of the Secretary   Oct. 8, 1920
    The within will is hereby approved in accordance with the Act of June 25, 1910, (36 Stat. L, 855-6), as amended by the Act of February 14, 1913, (37 Stat. L, 678).

S.G. Hopkins
Assistant Secretary

WILL

IN THE NAME OF GOD, Amen:

    I, **MARY THOMPSON**, age 65, an Indian of the Nez Perce Indian Reservation, Idaho, now residing at Lapwai, Idaho, being of sound mind and disposing memory, and not acting under duress, menace, fraud, or undue influence, of any person whatsoever, do hereby make, publish and declare this my LAST WILL AND TESTAMENT, in the manner following, that is to say:

NATIVE AMERICAN WILLS and PROBATE RECORDS, 1911 - 1921

First: I direct that my body be decently buried with proper regard to my station in life, and the circumstances of my estate.

Second: I direct that my funeral expenses and expenses of my last illness be paid from any funds belonging to my estate, or in the custody of the Superintendent of the Nez Perce Indian Reservation, Lapwai, Idaho.

Third: I will and bequeath to Lucy Armstrong, my own allotment on the Nez Perce Reservation, #277.

Fourth: I will and bequeath all of my inherited land to my brother, Titus Thompson, which consists of allotment #276, and ½ interest in allotment #275, on the Nez Perce Reservation.

Lucy Armstrong has been taking care of me during my old age and last illness. Titus Thompson is the only near relative I have.

Any personal property or real estate of any description other than above enumerated of which I may die possessed, I will and bequeath to my brother, Titus Thompson.

In witness whereof, I have hereunto put my hand and seal this 16th day of October, 1919.

      Mary Thompson Her (thumb print) mark

The foregoing instrument was on the date hereof signed, sealed, published and declared by said Mary Thompson, to be her LAST WILL AND TESTAMENT, in the presence of us, and at her request and in her presence, and in the presence of each other, we have subscribed our names as witnesses on this 16th day of October, 1919.

      Corbett B. Lawyer
      Leta E. Brock
      William N. Seckes

Probate 64400-20 J M P
DEPARTMENT OF THE INTERIOR, Office of Indian Affairs   Sep 29, 1920

It is recommended that the within will be approved pursuant to the provisions of the Act of June 25, 1910, (36 Stat. L, 855-6), as amended by the Act of February 14, 1913, (37 Stat. L, 678).

      Respectfully,
      E.B. Meritt
      Assistant Commissioner

DEPARTMENT OF THE INTERIOR, Office of the Secretary   Oct. 8, 1920

The within will is hereby approved pursuant to the provisions of the Act of June 25, 1910, (36 Stat. L, 855-6), as amended by the Act of February 14, 1913, (37 Stat. L, 678).

      S.G. Hopkins
      Assistant Secretary

NATIVE AMERICAN WILLS and PROBATE RECORDS, 1911 - 1921

Poplar, Mont.
12/18/17

IRON WING RED, being of sound mind but weak body and realizing that like is uncertain does hereby make and declare this to be my last and only will and bequeath my property as follows:

To my beloved husband, Red, $5.00.

To my four children, George Red, Minnie Red, Dorothy Red and Daisy Red, share and share alike my allotment on the Ft. Peck Reservation, described as follows: W/2 of Sec. 10, T31, T49, and E/2 of SE/4 of SE/4, Sec. 13, T27, R49 and SE/4 of SW/4 of Sec. 7, T27, R50, all on the former Ft. Peck Reservation, Montana.

I hereby appoint Supt. E.D. Mossman or his successor in office, executor of my will.

Signed Iron Wing Red   Her (thumb print) mark

We, Henry Keller and Joseph Culbertson, do hereby certify that we were present when Iron Wing Red executed the above instrument and that she was acquainted with conditions of the same and that they were her expressed wishes and that the above instrument was signed by her in our presence.

Henry Keller
Joseph Culbertson

I, Joseph Culbertson, certify that I truthfully interpreted Iron Wing Red's wishes as expressed in above instrument.

Joseph Culbertson

DEPARTMENT OF THE INTERIOR, Office of Indian Affairs   Sep. 30, 1920
The within will of Iron Wind Red, deceased Fort Peck Yankton Sioux allottee #752 of the Fort Peck Reservation, is recommended for disapproval, in accordance with the provisions of the Act of June 25, 1910, (36 Stat. L, 855-6), as amended by the Act of February 14, 1913, (37 Stat. L, 678).

Respectfully,
E.B. Meritt
Assistant Commissioner

DEPARTMENT OF THE INTERIOR, Office of the Secretary   Oct. 8, 1920
The within will of Iron Wing Red, deceased Fort Peck Yankton Sioux allottee #752 of the Fort Peck Reservation, is hereby disapproved in accordance

NATIVE AMERICAN WILLS and PROBATE RECORDS, 1911 - 1921

with the provisions of the Act of June 25, 1910, (36 Stat. L, 855-6), as amended by the Act of February 14, 1913, (37 Stat. L, 678).

[Signed]   S.G. Hopkins
Assistant Secretary

<<<<<<<<>>>>>>>

LAST WILL AND TESTAMENT OF WAHACANKAWANJINA

I, **WAHACANKAWANJINA**, Devils Lake allottee #67, of Fort Totten, North Dakota, being of sound mind and disposing memory and understanding, and not under any compulsion or stress of circumstances, hereby make, declare and publish this my last will and testament, hereby revoking and annulling all wills heretofore made by me. It is my will and desire that my property be disposed of in the following manner, to-wit:

FIRST: I give, devise and bequeath to my wife, Kimimikoyakewin, 40 acres of my allotment described as the NE/4 of SW/4 Sec. 31, T153N, R63W, 5th P.M.

SECOND: I give, devise and bequeath to my grand daughter, Mary Celina Mean, the NE/4 of SE/4 of Sec. 11, T 152N, R64W, 5th P.M, containing 40 acres of my allotment.

THIRD: I give, devise and bequeath to my grand son, Oyemazana, the SW/4 of SE/4, Sec. 11, T152N, R64W, 5th P.M, containing 40 acres of my allotment.

FOURTH: I give, devise and bequeath, jointly, to my grand son and grand daughter, being the children of Joseph Johnson, my deceased son, the SE/4 of SE/4 of Sec. 11, T152N, R64W, 5th P.M, con taining 40 acres of my allotment.

FIFTH: I hereby appoint and constitute, John Eyapaha; the executor of this my last will and testament, and direct that any funds accruing to my estate and held in the hands of the Superintendent of the Fort Totten Indian School, be applied toward my funeral expenses and other just debts, preference to be given to the payment of my funeral expenses.

IN TESTIMONY WHEREOF, I have set my hand and seal to this my last will and testament at Fort Totten, North Dakota, this 3rd day of May, in the year of our Lord, 1918, signing the same in the presence of Martin Strait, Charles Brooks and S.A.M. Young, who at my request and in my presence have witnessed my signing hereof, we all signing in the presence of each other.

Wahacankawanjina His (thumb print) mark

Signed, Sealed, Published and Declared by the said Wahacankawanjina in our presence as and for his last will and testament; at his request and in his presence,

NATIVE AMERICAN WILLS and PROBATE RECORDS, 1911 - 1921

and in the presence of each other, we have hereunto subscribed our names as attesting witnesses.

          Chas. Brooks   S.A.M. Young

PROBATE 12063-1920 J H H
DEPARTMENT OF THE INTERIOR, Office of Indian Affairs Aug 13, 1920

  It is recommended that the within will be approved pursuant to the provisions of the Act of June 25, 1910, (36 Stat. L, 855-6), as amended by the Act of February 14, 1913, (37 Stat. L, 678).

              Respectfully,
              E.B. Meritt
              Assistant Commissioner

DEPARTMENT OF THE INTERIOR, Office of the Secretary

  The within will is hereby approved pursuant to the provisions of the Act of June 25, 1910, (36 Stat. L, 855-6), as amended by the Act of February 14, 1913, (37 Stat. L, 678).

              S.G. Hopkins
              Assistant Secretary

<<<<<<<<>>>>>>>

WILL OF LUCY JOURDAN

Confederated Siletz Allottee #232

OFFICE OF INDIAN AFFAIRS
RECEIVED
OCT 15, 1915
110811

  I, **LUCY JOURDAN**, an Indian and allottee #232, of the Siletz Reservation, Oregon, being of legal age [Records show 96], sound mind and acting under no duress or undue influence, do hereby voluntarily devise and bequeath unto Bensell Orton, my second cousin, all of my personal property, consisting of certain moneys on deposit in The Roseburg National Bank, Roseburg, Oregon, and any and all other personal property that I may die possessed of. It is further my will, that the aforesaid Bensell Orton shall have any and all real-estate that I may now own or may afterwards possess.

  All the rest and residue of my estate both real and personal that I may now own or hereafter acquire, I devise and bequeath unto the aforesaid Bensell Orton.

  I, Charles W. Holdiman, Clerk at the Siletz Agency, Oregon, hereby do attach the name and signature of Lucy Jourdan to this her last will, in her presence and at her request and in the presence of *John M. McClelland* and *Isaac Washington.*

          Lucy Jourdan
         By *Charles W. Holdiman*

  I, *John M. McClelland* and *Isaac Washington*, both of legal age and residents of the State of Oregon, do hereby sign our names and affix our signatures to this the last will of Lucy Jourdan, and that we have signed our

NATIVE AMERICAN WILLS and PROBATE RECORDS, 1911 - 1921

names at the request of the testator in her presence and in the presence of each other. Upon this 20th day of September, 1915, as attesting witnesses thereof.

John M. McClelland
Isaac Washington

DEPARTMENT OF THE INTERIOR, Office of Indian Affairs   Sep 18, 1920
 The within will of Lucy Jourdan, deceased Siletz allottee #232, bearing date of September 20, 1915, is hereby approved in accordance with the provisions of the Act of June 25, 1910, (36 Stat. L, 855-6), as amended by the Act of February 14, 1913, (37 Stat. L, 678), and the Regulations of the Department as far as it involves properties within the jurisdiction of the United States.

Respectfully,
E.B. Meritt
Assistant Commissioner

DEPARTMENT OF THE INTERIOR, Office of the Secretary   Sep 20, 1920
 The within will of Lucy Jourdan, deceased Siletz allottee #232, bearing date of September 20, 1915, is hereby approved in accordance with the provisions of the Act of June 25, 1910, (36 Stat. L, 855-6), as amended by the Act of February 14, 1913, (37 Stat. L, 678), and the Regulations of the Department as far as it involves properties within the jurisdiction of the United States.

S.G. Hopkins
Assistant Secretary

WILL

IN THE NAME OF GOD, Amen: I, **SUSIE McCONVILLE DICKSON**, age 26, an Indian of the Nez Perce Indian Reservation, Idaho, now residing at Lapwai, Idaho, being of sound mine and disposing memory, and not acting under duress, menace, fraud, or undue influence, of any person whatsoever, do hereby make, publish and declare this my LAST WILL AND TESTAMENT, in the manner following, that is to say:

First: I direct that my body be decently buried with proper regard to my station in life, and the circumstances of my estate.

Second: I direct that my funeral expenses and expenses of my last illness be paid from any funds belonging to my estate, or in the custody of the Superintendent of the Nez Perce Indian Reservation, Lapwai, Idaho.

Third: I will and bequeath to my husband, Clayton Dickson and my daughter, Freda Dickson, share and share alike, my undivided 14/18 interest in

NATIVE AMERICAN WILLS and PROBATE RECORDS, 1911 - 1921

allotment #1706; 1/8 interest in allotment #421, 2/27 interest in allotment #420; ½ interest in allotment #1967; 1/18 interest in allotment #'s 344, 245 and 347; and 1/3 in allotment #1705. To my grandmother, Mrs. John Mills the sum of $50.00. My piano to be sold and the proceeds divided equally between my husband and daughter.

In witness whereof, I have hereunto put my hand and seal this 10th day of Aug, 1919.

Susie McConville Dickson

The foregoing instrument was on the date hereof signed, sealed, published and declared by said Susie McConville Dickson to be her LAST WILL AND TESTAMENT, in the presence of us, and at her request and in her presence, and in the presence of each other, we have subscribed our names as witnesses on this 18th day of Aug, 1919.

Jacob Breed
James E. Tibbitts
Sam Tilden

Probate 28184-20 J M P
DEPARTMENT OF THE INTERIOR, Office of Indian Affairs Sep 18, 1920
It is recommended that the within will be approved pursuant to the provisions of the Act of June 25, 1910, (36 Stat. L, 855-6), as amended by the Act of February 14, 1913, (37 Stat. L, 678).

Respectfully,
E.B. Meritt
Assistant Commissioner

DEPARTMENT OF THE INTERIOR, Office of the Secretary Sep 20, 1920
The within will is hereby approved pursuant to the provisions of the Act of June 25, 1910, (36 Stat. L, 855-6), as amended by the Act of February 14, 1913, (37 Stat. L, 678).

S.G. Hopkins
Assistant Secretary

LAST WILL AND TESTAMENT OF ELLA STONECOAL, UNALLOTTED PITT RIVER
OF THE COUNTY OF LASSEN, STATE OF CALIFORNIA, UNDER THE JURISDICTION
OF THE ROSEBURG INDIAN SCHOOL, ROSEBURG, OREGON.

I, **ELLA STONECOAL**, aged 20 years, unallotted Pitt River Indian, of the County of Lassen, State of California, being of sound mind and memory, do

NATIVE AMERICAN WILLS and PROBATE RECORDS, 1911 - 1921

hereby make, publish and declare this, my last will and testament, in manner and form as follows, that is to say:

FIRST: I direct the payment of the expenses of my last illness, of my funeral, and of all my just debts which may be paid under the laws of the United States and the Regulations of the Department of the Interior, promulgated thereunder.

SECOND: I give, devise and bequeath unto my father, Sampson Stonecoal, aged 43 years, Pitt River Indian Allottee #984, of the County of Lassen, State of California; and to my grandmother, Annie Roseberry, aged 70 years, Pitt River Indian Allottee #615, of the County of Lassen, State of California, in equal shares, share and share alike, all my right, title and interest in and to the following described real property situated in the County of Lassen, State of California, to wit:

The allotment of Jack Roseberry, deceased Pitt River Indian Allottee, #584, Susanville Series under the jurisdiction of the Roseburg Indian School, Roseburg, Oregon, being the W/2 of the SW/4, Sec. 28, and the E/2 of the SE/4 of Sec. 29, T38N, R9E of the M.D.M, California, containing 160 acres.

I also give, devise and bequeath unto the said Sampson Stonecoal and Annie Roseberry heretofore mentioned, in equal shares, share and share alike, all other property both real and personal, of whatsoever kind the same may be, or wheresoever situated, of which I may die possessed or to which I may be entitled or in which I may have any right, title or interest.

THIRD: I nominate and appoint Sampson Stonecoal, my father, executor of this my last will and testament, and I hereby revoke any and all former wills by me made.

IN WITNESS WHEREOF, I have hereunto set my hand and seal this 26th day of June, 1917, at my home near Susanville, Lassen County, California.

Ella Stonecoal   Her right thumb mark

The foregoing instrument consisting of one page besides this, was at the date hereof, by the said Ella Stonecoal, signed, sealed, and published as and declared to be her last will and testament, in the presence of us, who, at her request and in her presence, and in the presence of each other have subscribed our names as witnesses hereto:

E.M. Young, Field Motion residing at Susanville, CA
F.A. Baker   residing at Fort Bidwell, CA

DEPARTMENT OF THE INTERIOR, Office of Indian Affairs   Sep 18, 1920

It is recommended that the within will of Ella Stonecoal, deceased unallotted Indian of the Pitt River tribe, be disapproved under the provisions of the Act of June 25, 1910, (36 Stat. L, 855-6), as amended by the Act of February 14, 1913, (37 Stat. L, 678).

Respectfully,
E.B. Meritt
Assistant Commissioner

NATIVE AMERICAN WILLS and PROBATE RECORDS, 1911 - 1921

DEPARTMENT OF THE INTERIOR, Office of the Secretary   Sep 20, 1920
The within will of Ella Stonecoal, deceased unallotted Indian of the Pitt River tribe, is hereby disapproved under the provisions of the Act of June 25, 1910, (36 Stat. L, 855-6), as amended by the Act of February 14, 1913, (37 Stat. L, 678).

S.G. Hopkins
Assistant Secretary

LAST WILL AND TESTAMENT

I, **WER-WICK-AH**, Comanche Indian allottee #377, about 68 years of age, of Cache, Comanche County, Oklahoma, being now in good health and strength of body and mind, but sensible of the uncertainty of life, and desiring to make disposition of my property and affairs while in health and strength, do hereby make public and declare the following to be my last will and testament; hereby revoking and cancelling all other or former wills by me at any time made.

1. I direct the payment of all my just debts, and funeral expenses.
2. I give and devise to my beloved step-child, See-ah-vah, Comanche allottee #378, all of my property of which I may die possessed, real and personal, including my trust allotment of land comprising N/2 of NW/4 of Sec. 36, and the N/2 of the NE/4 of Sec. 35, all in T2N, R14W of the Indian Meridian, known upon the rolls of the Interior Department at Comanche Indian allotment #377.

This beneficiary was raised by me from childhood, and she now cares for me in my old age, and I shall continue to live with her during the remainder of my days. I have neither husband, children nor grandchildren alive, who could take my estate, and for the reasons set out herein, I desire to invest her with all of my property.

This will is made, subject to the approval of the Secretary of the Interior.
In witness whereof, I Wer-wick-ah, Comanche Indian allottee #377, have to this, my last will and testament, consisting of one sheet of paper, subscribed my name this 1st day of October, 1917.

Witness to mark: Wer wick ah (Her thumb print mark)
Magdalena Becker
A.J. Becker

Subscribed by Wer-wick-ah, Comanche Indian allottee #377, in the presence of each of us, the undersigned, and at the same time, declared by her to us to be her last will and testament, and we, thereupon, at the request of Wer-Wick-ah, and in her presence, and in the presence of each other, sign our names hereto, as witnesses this 1st day of October, 1917, at Cache, Oklahoma.

NATIVE AMERICAN WILLS and PROBATE RECORDS, 1911 - 1921

Magdalena Becker
P.O. Indiahoma, OK
Abraham J. Becker
P.O. Indiahoma, OK

Interpreter's Certificate

I, Magdalena Becker, hereby certify on honor that I have acted as interpreter during the execution of the foregoing last will and testament, by Wer-wick-ah, and that I truly interpreted all the contents thereof to Wer-wick-ah before she executed the foregoing will. I certify that this will was drawn strictly in accordance with her desires and directions; that I speak both the Comanche Indian as well as the English language fluently, and that I have no interest in this matter whatever.

Signed this 1st day of October, 1917.

Magdalena Becker
Interpreter

DEPARTMENT OF THE INTERIOR, Office of Indian Affairs Sep 9, 1920

It is hereby recommended that the within will of Wer-wick-ah, deceased allottee #377 of the Comanche tribe of Indians, be approved under the provisions of the Act of June 25, 1910, (36 Stat. L, 855-6), as amended by the Act of February 14, 1913, (37 Stat. L, 678), and the Regulations of the Department.

Respectfully,
E.B. Meritt
Assistant Commissioner

8-MH-31

DEPARTMENT OF THE INTERIOR, Office of the Secretary Sep 10, 1920

The within will of Wer-wick-ah, deceased allottee #377 of the Comanche tribe of Indians, is hereby approved under the provisions of the Act of June 25, 1910, (36 Stat. L, 855-6), as amended by the Act of February 14, 1913, (37 Stat. L, 678), and the Regulations of the Department.

S.G. Hopkins
Assistant Secretary

<<<<<<>>>>>>

WILL OF WALKING RED #995
Fort Peck, Montana, Indian

I, **WALKING RED**, Yankton Indian, allottee #995, of Fort Peck Reservation, Montana, widow, aged 89 years, being of sound mind and wishing to dispose of my property at my death, do hereby declare this my last will and testament and wish that at my death my property shall all be given to Charles Takes Them, Yankton Indian of Fort Peck Reservation, Montana, aged 48 years and residing at Brockton, Sheridan County, Montana.

NATIVE AMERICAN WILLS and PROBATE RECORDS, 1911 - 1921

The estate and property I hereby will to him and wish given to him is as follows: My grazing allotment of 320 acres, described as E/2 of Sec. 23, T28, R53; My 40 acre tract allotment described as NW/4 of SW/4 of Sec. 25, T28, R53; My 20 acre timber allotment described as allotment #995 in Sec. 1, T27, R53.

These three described allotments being on the Fort Peck Reservation, Sheridan Co, MT.

My reason for making Charles Takes Them my sole heir to this property is that he has been as my son and cared for me for the past seven years.

I purposely do not will any share in my estate to my distat[sic] relatives, Begs His Own and Beavertail, or any other relative for the reason that Charles Takes Them has been the only one taking care of me for the past seven years and he has been as a son to me and this I have told to the relatives herein mentioned and they know this is my wish as to my property here described.

Signed by me and delivered this date, March 13, 1916, at Box Elder Station, Brockton, MT

                                        Walking Red   her thumb

Interpreted by Maurice Big Horn of Brockton, MT
Witnesses:

        Harold Red Eagle   FORT PECK AGENCY
        Brockton, MT   Poplar, Montana
        F.E. Farrell
        Brockton, MT

I hereby certify that I prepared this Will at the request of Walking Red, who signed this instrument in my presence; that it is according to her wishes; that she was of good mental capacity and strength of body and answered promptly and clearly and properly a series of questions I asked her, that she chatted and laughed in correcting herself and in converse with others, that she appeared very emphatically to dispose of her property and estate as here stated to Charles Takes Them and gave here reasons therefore and reason for excluding any other persons or relatives from participating in her estate.

                                      F.E. Farrell
Brockton, MT,   March 13, 1916   Indian Service Farmer
                                       Fort Peck Reservation, MT

DEPARTMENT OF THE INTERIOR, Office of Indian Affairs   Aug. 31, 1920

The within will of Walking Red, deceased Yankton Sioux allottee of the Fort Peck Reservation, allottee #995, is recommended for approval in accordance with the provisions of the Act of June 25, 1910, (36 Stat. L, 855-6), as amended by the Act of February 14, 1913, (37 Stat. L, 678).

                                                    Respectfully,
                                                    E.B. Meritt
                                                 Assistant Commissioner

DEPARTMENT OF THE INTERIOR, Office of the Secretary   Sep 1, 1920

NATIVE AMERICAN WILLS and PROBATE RECORDS, 1911 - 1921

The within will of Walking Red, deceased Yankton Sioux allottee #995 of the Fort Peck Reservation, is hereby approved in accordance with the provisions of the Act of June 25, 1910, (36 Stat. L, 855-6), as amended by the Act of February 14, 1913, (37 Stat. L, 678).

S.G. Hopkins
Assistant Secretary

WILL

I, **ALBERT HIGH BULL** of Pine Ridge Agency, South Dakota, Allottee nmber 253 do hereby make and declare this to be my last will and testament, in accordance with Section 2 of the Act of June 25, 1910, (36 Stat. 855-858) hereby revoking all former wills made by me:

1. I hereby direct that, as soon as possible after my decease, that all my debts and funeral and testamentary expenses be paid out of my personal estate.

2. I give and devise my allotment on the Pine Ridge Reservation, South Dakota, described as follows: SE/4 Sec. 4, and S/2 & Lots 1, 2, 3, 4, Sec. 3, T 36, R 44.

in the following manner:

    SE/4, Sec. 4, to my son, Chas. High Bull.
    SW/4, Sec. 3, to my wife, Susie High Bull.
    SE/4, Sec. 3, to my daughter, Alice White Whirlwind.
    Lots 1, 2, 3, 4, to my son, Cleveland High Bull. (Sec. 3)

3. I give and bequeath all of my personal property of whatsoever nature and wheresoever situated unto my wife, Susie High Bull.

4. All the rest of my property, real or personal, now possessed or hereafter acquired, or whatsoever nature and wheresoever situated, I hereby give, devise and bequeath unto (blank)

    In witness whereof I have hereunto set my hand this 10th day of July 1913.
                                              his
                    ALBERT HIGH BULL   thumb
                                                 mark.

The above statement was, this 10th day of July, 1913, signed and published by Albert High Bull as his last will and testament in the joint presence of the undersigned, the said Albert High Bull then being of sound and vigorous mind and free from any constraint or compulsion; whereupon we, being without any interest in the matter other than friendship, and being well acquainted with him, but not members of his family, immediately subscribed our names hereto in

NATIVE AMERICAN WILLS and PROBATE RECORDS, 1911 - 1921

the presence of each other and of the sid testator, for the purpose of attesting the said will, as he requested us to do.

J.K. KILLER   Pine Ridge, S.D.   Post Office address.
SAMUEL FEW TAILS   Kyle, S.D.

Pine Ridge, South Dakota.
April 3, 1914.

    I hereby certify that I have fully inquired into the mental competency of the Indian signing the above will; the circumstances attending the execution of the will; the influence that may have induced its execution, and the names of those entitled to share in the estate under the law of descent in South Dakota; reasons for the disposition of the property proposed by the will, differing from disposition had the property descended.

    I respectfully forward the will, above, with the recommendation that it be approved.

JOHN R. BRENNAN
Supt. & Spl. Disb. Agent

Department of The Interior,
Office of Indian Affairs,
Washington, D.C.   May 29 1914

It is recommended that the within will be approved pursuant to the Act of June 25, 1910 (36 Stats. L., 855-6) as amended by the Act of February 14, 1913 (37 Stat. L, 678).

Respectfully,
E. B. MERITT
Assistant Commissioner

Department of The Interior
Office of The Secretary
Washington, D.C.   Jun 2 1914

The within will hereby approved pursuant to the Act of June 25, 1910 (36 Stats. L., 855-6) as amended by Act of February 14, 1913 (37 Stat. L., 678).

LEWIS C. LAYLIN
Assistant Secretary

WILL

I, **RUNS ABOVE** of Pine Ridge Agency, South Dakota. Allottee number 1152 do hereby make and declare this to be my last will and testament, in accordance with Section 2 of the Act of June 25, 1910, (36 Stat. 855-858), and Act of

NATIVE AMERICAN WILLS and PROBATE RECORDS, 1911 - 1921

February 14, 1913, (Public No. 381), hereby revoking all former wills made by me.

1. I hereby direct that, as soon as possible after my decease, that all my debts and funeral and testamentary expenses be paid out of my personal estate.

2. I give and devise my allotment on the Pine Ridge Reservation, South Dakota, described as follows:

Sec. 23, T 36 N, R 47 W of 6th P.M., South Dakota.

in the following manner:

E/2 of Sec. 23, T 36 N, R 47 W of 6th P.M. to my son, Peter Runs Above.
SW/4 of Sec. 23, T 36 N, R 47 W of 6th P.M. to my wife, Day Comes Out.
NW/4 of Sec. 23, T 36 N, R 47 W of 6th P.M. to my grandson, George Runs Above.

3. I give and bequeath all of my personal property of whatsoever nature and wheresoever situated unto

4. All the rest of my property, real or personal, now possessed or hereafter acquired, of whatsoever nature and wheresoever situated, I hereby give, devise and bequeath unto
    my son, Peter Runs Above.

In witness whereof I have hereunto set my hand this 11th day of March 1914.
Wit. to signature: O.C. ROSS   his
          ROBERT H. STELZNER   RUNS ABOVE   thumb
                                                                         mark.

The above statement was, this 11th day of March 1914, signed and published by Runs Above as his last will and testament, in the joint presence of the undersigned, the said Runs Above then being of sound and vigorous mind and free from any constraint or compulsion; whereupon we, being without any interest in the matter other than friendship, and being well acquainted with him, but not members of his family, immediately subscribed our names hereto in the presence of each other and of the said testator, for the purpose of attesting the said will, as he requested us to do.

H.E. WRIGHT   Pine Ridge Agency, S.D.   Post Office address
J.K. KILLER   Pine Ridge Agency, S.D.

Pine Ridge, South Dakota.
Mar 16 1914

I hereby certify that I have fully inquired into the mental competency of the Indian signing the above will; the circumstances attending the execution of the will; the influence that may have induced its execution, and the names of those

NATIVE AMERICAN WILLS and PROBATE RECORDS, 1911 - 1921

entitled to share in the estate under the law of descent in South Dakota; reasons for the disposition of the property proposed by the will, differing from disposition had the property descended by operation of law.

    I respectfully forward this will with the recommendation that it be approved.

JOHN R. BRENNAN
Supt. & Spl. Disb. Agent

Department of The Interior,
Office of Indian Affairs,
Washington, D.C.   May 28 1914

It is recommended that the within will be approved pursuant to the provisions of the Act of June 25, 1910 (36 Stats. L., 855-6) as amended by the Act of February 14, 1913 (37 Stat. L, 678).

Respectfully,
E. B. MERITT
Assistant Commissioner

Department of The Interior
Office of The Secretary
Washington, D.C.   Jun 1 1914

The within will is hereby approved pursuant to the provisions of the Act of June 25, 1910 (36 Stats. L., 855-6) as amended by Act of February 14, 1913 (37 Stat. L., 678).

LEWIS C. LAYLIN
Assistant Secretary

WILL

I, **STEPHEN OLD HAIR** of Pine Ridge Agency, South Dakota, Allottee number 1220 do hereby make and declare this to be my last will and testament, in accordance with Section 2 of the Act of June 23, 1910 (36 Stat. 855-858), and Act of February 14, 1913, (Publis No. 381), hereby revoking all former wills made by me:

1.   I hereby direct that, as soon as possible after my decease, that all my debts and funeral and testamentary expenses be paid out of my personal estate.

2.   I give and devise my allotment on the Pine Ridge Reservation, South Dakota, described as follows:

    All of Sec. 28, T 36, R 47 W of 6th P.M., S.D., 640 acres.

NATIVE AMERICAN WILLS and PROBATE RECORDS, 1911 - 1921

in the following manner:

    NE/4 to my wife, Belle Old Hair.
    SE/4 to my daughter, Josie Old Hair.
    SW/4 to my son, Alfred Old Hair.
    NW/4 to my son, Thomas Old Hair.

3.

4. All the rest of my property, real or personal, now possessed or hereafter acquired, of whatsoever nature and wheresoever situated, I hereby give, devise and bequeath unto

    My wife, Belle Old Hair; my daughter, Josie Old Hair; my son Alfred Old Hair, and my son, Thomas Old Hair; to be divided equally among these four persons.

In witness whereof I have hereunto set my hand this 11th day of March 1914.
                                              STEPHEN OLD HAIR.

    The above statement was, this 11th day of March 1914, signed and published by Stephen Old Hair as his last will and testament, in the joint presence of the undersigned, the said Stephen Old Hair then being of sound and vigorous mind and free from any constraint or compulsion; whereupon we, being without any interest in the matter other than friendship, and being well acquainted with him, but not members of his family, immediately subscribed our names hereto in the presence of each other and of the said testator, for the purpose of attesting the said will, as he requested us to do.

H.E. WRIGHT   Farmer, Pine Ridge, S.D.   Post Office address
J.K. KILLER   Asst. Farmer, Pine Ridge, S.D.

    I hereby certify that I have fully inquired into the mental competency of the Indian signing the above will; the circumstances attending the execution of the will; the influence that may have induced its execution, and the names of those entitled to share in the estate under the law of descent in South Dakota; reasons for the disposition of the property proposed by the will, differing from disposition had the property descended by operation of law.
    I respectfully forward this will with the recommendation that it be approved.
                                              JOHN R. BRENNAN
                                             Supt. & Spl. Disb. Agent

Department of The Interior,
Office of Indian Affairs
Washington, D.C.   May 29, 1914

NATIVE AMERICAN WILLS and PROBATE RECORDS, 1911 - 1921

It is recommended that the within will be approved pursuant to the provisions of the Act of June 25, 1910 (36 Stats. L., 855-6) as amended by the Act of February 14, 1913 (37 Stat. L, 678).

Respectfully,
E. B. MERITT
Assistant Commissioner

Department of The Interior
Office of The Secretary   June 2 1914
Washington, D.C.

The within will is hereby approved pursuant to the provisions of the Act of June 25, 1910 (36 Stats. L., 855-6) as amended by Act of February 14, 1913 (37 Stat. L., 678).

LEWIS C. LAYLIN
Assistant Secretary

WILL

I, **DIRT KETTLE** of Pine Ridge Agency, South Dakota, Allottee number 1233 do hereby make and declare this to be my last will and testament, in accordance with Section 2 of the Act of June 25, 1910, (36 Stat. 855-858) hereby revoking all former wills made by me:

1. I hereby direct that, as soon as possible after my decease, that all my debts and funeral and testamentary expenses be paid out of my personal estate.

2. I give and devise my allotment on the Pine Ridge Reservation, South Dakota, described as follows:

> All of Sec. 35, T 36, R 46.

in the following manner:

> NW/4 of Sec. 35, T 36, R 46, to my step-son, Silas Shield.
> NE/4 of Sec. 35, T 36, R 46, to my step-daughter, Mary Dirt Kettle.
> SW/4 of Sec. 35, T 36, R 46, to my wife, Eagle Woman.
> SE/4 of Sec. 35, T 36, R 46, to my daughter, Julia Dirt Kettle.

4. All the rest of my property, real or personal, now possessed or hereafter acquired, of whatsoever nature and wheresoever situated, I hereby give and devise and bequeath unto
> My wife, Eagle Woman.

NATIVE AMERICAN WILLS and PROBATE RECORDS, 1911 - 1921

In witness whereof I have hereunto set my hand this day 19th of February, 1914.

                      DIRT KETTLE   his thumb mark.

The above statement was, this 19th day of February, 1914, signed and published by Dirt Kettle as his last will and testament, in the joint presence of the undersigned, the said Dirt Kettle then being of sound and vigorous mind and free from any constraint or compulsion; whereupon we, being without any interest in the matter other than friendship, and being well acquainted with him, but not members of his family, immediately subscribed our names hereto in the presence of each other and of the said testator, for the purpose of attesting the said will, as he requested us to do, and that I H.E. Wright, at the request of the testator signed his name in ink but the testator made his thumb-mark.

H.E. WRIGHT   Farmer, Pine Ridge, S.D.   Post Office address
J.K. KILLER   Asst. Farmer, Pine Ridge, S.D.

    I hereby certify that I have fully inquired into the mental competency of the Indian signing the above will; the circumstances attending the execution of the will; the influence that may have induced its execution, and the names of those entitled to share in the estate under the law of descent in South Dakota; reasons for the disposition of the property proposed by the will, differing from disposition had the property descended.

    I respectfully forward the will, above, with the recommendation that it be approved.

                      JOHN R. BRENNAN
                      Supt. & Spl. Disb. Agent

Department of The Interior,
Office of Indian Affairs
Washington, D.C.   May 28, 1914

It is recommended that the within will be approved pursuant to the provisions of the Act of June 25, 1910 (36 Stats. L., 855-6) as amended by the Act of February 14, 1913 (37 Stat. L, 678).

                Respectfully,
                E. B. MERITT
                Assistant Commissioner

Department of The Interior
Office of The Secretary   June 1 1914
Washington, D.C.

The within will is hereby approved pursuant to the provisions of the Act of June 25, 1910 (36 Stats. L., 855-6) as amended by Act of February 14, 1913 (37 Stat. L., 678).

                LEWIS C. LAYLIN
                Assistant Secretary

NATIVE AMERICAN WILLS and PROBATE RECORDS, 1911 - 1921

WILL

I, **MARY LONE WOLF** of Pine Ridge Agency, South Dakota, Allottee number 5659 do hereby make and declare this to be my last will and testament, in accordance with Section 2 of the Act of June 25, 1910, (36 Stat. 855-858) hereby revoking all former wills made by me.

1. I hereby direct that, as soon as possible after my decease, that all my debts and funeral and testamentary expenses be paid out of my personal estate.

2. I give and devise my allotment on the Pine Ridge Reservation, South Dakota, described as follows:

All of Section 31, T. 42, R. 37 W. of 6th P.M. in South Dakota, containing 646.48 acres.

in the following manner: All to my daughter Maggie M. Williams, of Ash Grove, Missouri; and in case of her death prior to mine, then in equal portion to my three grand children, Blanche Williams, Barney Williams and Cleopatra Williams;

3. I give and bequeath all of my personal property of whatsoever nature and wheresoever situated unto the persons named and in the manner described in the provision for disposition of my allotment, as above; excepting only that I give and bequeath unto my daughters, Fannie Finnegan, Ettie Bingham, and my husband, Dr. Lonewolf one dollar each.

4. All the rest of my property, real or personal, now possessed or hereafter acquired, of whatsoever nature and wheresoever situated; I hereby give, devise and bequeath unto Maggie M. Williams, my daughter, and in case of her death to my three grand children, Blanche Williams, Barney Williams and Cleopatra Williams.

In witness whereof I have hereunto set my hand this day 21st of May 1913.

MARY LONE WOLF

The above statement was, this 21st day of May, 1913, signed and published by Mary Lone Wolf as her last will and testament in the joint presence of the undersigned, the said Mary Lone Wolf then being of sound and vigorous mind and free from any constraint or compulsion; whereupon we, being without any interest in the matter other than friendship, and being well acquainted with her, but not members of her family, immediately subscribed our names hereto in the presence of eath other and of the said testator, for the purpose of attesting the said will, as she requested us to do.

NATIVE AMERICAN WILLS and PROBATE RECORDS, 1911 - 1921

ADRIAN M. LANDMAN
CHARLES M. SMITH

Post Office address.
Pine Ridge, So. Dak.

I hereby certify that I have fully inquired into the mental competency of the Indian signing the above will; the circumstances attending the execution of the will; the influence that may have induced its execution, and the names of those entitled to share in the estate under the law of descent in South Dakota; reasons for the disposition of the property proposed by the will, differing from disposition had the property descended.

I respectfully forward the will, above, with the recommendation that it be approved.

Supt. & Spl. Disb. Agent

Department of The Interior,
Office of Indian Affairs
Washington, D.C.   May 29, 1914

The within will of Mary Lone Wolf, Pine Ridge allottee No. 5659, is respectfully forwarded, recommending approval in accordance with the Act of June 25, 1910 (36 Stats. L., 855) as amended by the Act of February 14, 1913 (37 Stat. L., 678).

Respectfully,
E. B. MERITT
Assistant Commissioner

Department of The Interior
Office of The Secretary   June 1 1914
Washington, D.C.

The within will is hereby approved pursuant to the provisions of the Act of June 25, 1910 (36 Stats. L., 855-6) as amended by Act of February 14, 1913 (37 Stat. L., 678).

LEWIS C. LAYLIN
Assistant Secretary

<<<<<<<>>>>>>>

IN THE NAME OF GOD, AMEN

I, **JOSEPH THOMAS**, of Baird, County of Shasta, State of California, of the age of 85 years and being of sound and disposing mind and memory, and not acting under duress, menace, fraud, or under the influence of any person whatever, do make, publish and declare this my last WILL AND TESTAMENT in the manner following, that is to say:

FIRST: to Clara McKenzie, also known as Clara Conway. I give the allotment now held in trust for me by the United States Government, described as the North half of the Northwest quarter (N/2 NW/4) of Section Twenty (20), Township Thirty-three (33) North, Range Three (3) West M.D.M. in Shasta County, California.

NATIVE AMERICAN WILLS and PROBATE RECORDS, 1911 - 1921

SECONDLY: I hereby nominate and appoint Willie Conway, the executor of this, my last will and testament, and hereby revoke all former wills made by me.

IN WITNESS WHEREOF I have hereunto set my hand this Tenth day of February, one thousand nine hundred and thirteen.

His
Joseph thumb Thomas
mark

The foregoing instrument was at the date hereof, by the said Joseph Thomas Signed and Published as, and declared to be his last Will and Testament, in presence of us who at his request, and in his presence, and in the presence of each other, have subscribed our names as witnesses thereto.

Perrin C. Radcliff.
Residing at Baird, California.
W.C. Randolph
Residing at Redding California.

Department of The Interior,
Office of Indian Affairs
Washington, D.C.   Aug 13/13

I recommend that the within will be approved under the provisions of the Act of June 25, 1910 (36 Stats. L., 855-856), as amended by the Act of February 14, 1913 (37 Stat. L, 678).

Respectfully,
C.F. Hauke
Second Assistant Commissioner

Department of The Interior
Washington, D.C.   Aug. 14/13

The within will hereby approved pursuant to the provisions of the Act of June 25, 1910 (36 Stats. L., 855-6) as amended by Act of February 14, 1913 (37 Stat. L., 678).

Lewis C. Laylin
Assistant Secretary
WCP

WILL OF JENNIE TAVOOTS HARRIS

Uintah and White River Allottee No. 150. of the Uintah and Ouray Reservation, Utah.

Uintah and Ouray Indian Agency
Fort Duchesne, Utah.

NATIVE AMERICAN WILLS and PROBATE RECORDS, 1911 - 1921

February 24, 1914.

KNOW ALL MEN BY THESE PRESENTS that I, **JENNIE TAVOOTS HARRIS**, being of sound mind and memory do make and declare the following to be my last will and testament:

I hereby devise and bequeath to my sister, Weep Harvey, an undivided one-half interest in my allotment, which allotment consists of the Southwest quarter of the Northwest quarter of Section one, Township two South of Range one East of the Uintah Special Base and Meridian, Utah, and containing forty acres. The other half of above described allotment of land I hereby bequeath to my brother, Ben Butler or Okra. Both of the above bequests aremade subject to the trust jurisdiction of the U.S. Government.

JENNIE TAVOOTS HARRIS   Her thumb mark.

We, Jewell D. Martin and Fred Mart, both of Fort Duchesne, Utah, do hereby certify that Jennie Tavoots Harris signed the above will in our presence, and declared at that time that this was her last will and testament, that we signed this will at the request of Jennie Tavoots Harris and in her presence and in the presence of each other.

JEWELL D. MARTIN
    Supervisor in Charge, Fort Duchesne, Utah.
FRED MART
    Official Interpreter, Fort Duchesne, Utah.

Department of The Interior,
Office of Indian Affairs
Washington, D.C.   Jun. 8, 1914

It is recommended that the within will be approved pursuant to the provisions of the Act of June 25, 1910 (36 Stats. L., 855-6) as amended by the Act of February 14, 1913 (37 Stat. L, 678).

Respectfully,
(Signed) E. B. MERITT
Assistant Commissioner

Department of The Interior
Washington, D.C.   Jun. 8, 1914

The within will hereby approved pursuant to the provisions of the Act of June 25, 1910 (36 Stats. L., 855-6) as amended by Act of February 14, 1913 (37 Stat. L., 678).

(Signed) Lewis C. Laylin
Assistant Secretary

NATIVE AMERICAN WILLS and PROBATE RECORDS, 1911 - 1921

<<<<<<<<>>>>>>>
(COPY)

Ex. A.

Last Will and Testament of
Hattie Wells Grant.

I, **HATTIE WELLS GRANT**, being of sound and disposing mind and memory, do hereby and by these presents, make and publish this my last will and testament as follows, to-wit:

First

I hereby give, devise and bequeath unto my children, Pollock Wells, Eliza Wells and Peter Wells, the East half of the northeast quarter of section 20, township 25 north of range 9 E. of the 6th P.M. and the East half of the southeast quarter of section 11, township 25 north of range 7 East of the 6th P.M., Nebraska.

Second

I give, devise and bequeath unto my children, Maggie Grant, Hanika Grant and Mercy Grant, the West half of the southeast quarter of section 13, township 25 north of range 8 East and the south half of northwest quarter of section 13, township 25 north of range 7 E. 6th P.M., Nebraska.

In witness whereof I have this 28th day of March, 1913 signed and executed this my last will and tesament in the presence of the witnesses herein after named.

    George Fields   Nattie[sic] Wells Grant, her thmb mark
    Fannie Wolf
In the presence of
    George Fields
    Fannie Wolf

We, the undersigned, hereby certify that Hattie Wells Grant signed the above as her last will and testament and declared the same in our presence and in the presence of each of us to be her last will and testament and we further certify that she understood the contents thereof and requested us to sign as witnesses and we have signed in her presence and in the presence of each of us.

                                            George Fields
                                            Fannie Wolf.

Department of The Interior,
Office of Indian Affairs
Washington, D.C.   May 16, 1914

NATIVE AMERICAN WILLS and PROBATE RECORDS, 1911 - 1921

It is recommended that the within Will be approved pursuant to the provisions of the Acts of June 25, 1910 (36 Stats. L., 855-6) and February 14, 1913 (37 Stat. L, 678).

                                      Respectfully,
(Signed)   E. B. MERITT
                                  Assistant Commissioner

Department of The Interior
Washington, D.C.   May 21, 1914

The within Will is approved pursuant to the provisions of the Acts of June 25, 1910 (36 Stats. L., 855-6) and February 14, 1913 (37 Stat. L., 678).

                               (Sgd)   Lewis C. Laylin
                                         Assistant Secretary

<<<<<<<>>>>>>

                                      Winnebago Agency, Nebr.
                                               February 18, 1913.

To the Superintendent of the
    Winnebago Agency, Nebr.

Sir.
    As my dying request I wish to ask that all funds belonging to me and now held in trust by the United States Government, partifularly my share of the Tribal Funds, be paid, when available, to my beloved wife, Irene.

                                        Respectfully,
                                        DAN. RICE.

Signed in the presence of
    ALBERT H. KNEALE.
    FRANK BEAVER.
Department of The Interior,
Office of Indian Affairs
Washington, D.C.   Jun 8, 1914

It is recommended that the within will be approved pursuant to the provisions of the act of June 25, 1910 (36 Stats. L., 855-6) as amended by the act of February 14, 1913 (37 Stat. L, 678).

                                      Respectfully,
                                        E. B. MERITT
                                        Assistant Commissioner

Department of The Interior
Washington, D.C.   Jun 9, 1914

NATIVE AMERICAN WILLS and PROBATE RECORDS, 1911 - 1921

The within will is hereby approved pursuant to the provisions of the act of June 25, 1910 (36 Stats. L., 855-6) as amended by act of February 14, 1913 (37 Stat. L., 678).

LEWIS C. LAYLIN
Assistant Secretary

<<<<<<<<>>>>>>>
COPY

Cheyenne & Arapaho Agency
Darlington, Oklahoma
October 15, 1913

IN THE NAME OF GOD, AMEN:

Know all men by these presents that I, **KIOWA WOMAN**, a Cheyenne Indian of the age of sixty-three (63) years, residing at the Cheyenne & Arapaho Agency, Oklahoma, or under its jurisdiction, being, at the making of this will, of sound mind and intelligence, through an interpreter of my tribe, and knowing the uncertainty of life and the certainty of death, do make, publish and declare this to be my last WILL AND TESTAMENT as provided by law and in the presence of competent witnesses:

FIRST. I direct that the expense of my last sickness and funeral expenses shall be paid from any moneys on hand and to my credit at this Agency or otherwise.

SECOND. I direct my executor, hereinafter named, to pay all my just debts of every kind and character out of my estate.

THIRD. I give, devise, and bequeath and hereby will to my beloved children in the following order to-wit: Julia Bent (Prentiss), my daughter, George Bent, Jr., and Neal Bent, my two sons, and to Nellie Bent Burns, my daughter, to each of them share and share alike equally my allotment of land at this agency, described as the southeast quarter (SE/4) of Sec. fifteen (15) in Township fifteen (15) north of Range twelve (12), Blaine County, Oklahoma, containing 160 acres, to either be partitioned as provided, or sold through the Superintendent of this agency and the proceeds of such sale equally divided among the four children aforesaid; and also all my rights title and interest by was of heirship in the estates of my relatives when determined by the Secretary of the Interior, shall be divided as a part of my estate, equally among the four children herein named, it being my desire and last wish that these children should share equally in all property of whatever character, moneys or otherwise, thereof.

FOURTH. I give and bequeath, to my son, Neal Bent, additional, the following personal property, to wit: One harness, one iron gray mule, one lumber wagon, one bed and one stove, to him forever.

NATIVE AMERICAN WILLS and PROBATE RECORDS, 1911 - 1921

FIFTH. I give and bequeath to my loved daughter, Nellie Bent (Burns) additional, one grey mule and one bed, said personal property named in 4th and 5th paragraphs being now in my possession. I also give and bequeath to said Nellie Bent (Burns), one bay horse, in addition to the above named.

SIXTH. I give, devise and bequeath to Robert Burns, one race horse, known as "Orme Drop" and aged four years, to him and his heirs forever.

And finally, I nominate and appoint my son, George Bent, Jr., to be the executor of this, my last will, without a bond, in the distribution and care of the property, in whitness[sic] whereof I have hereunto set my hand and seal this 15th day of October, A.D. 1913.

Kiowa Woman, her thumb mark

In presence of
    A.H. Spears
    Dewitt C. Hayes

The above last will and testament was signed, sealed and declared by the above named Kiowa Woman to be her last will and testament, in the presence of each of the undersigned three witnesses and in the presence of each other, each of us are fully satisfied in our own minds that the said testator is of sound mind and fully understands the import of this will.

A.H. Spears
C.W. Ruckman
Dewitt C. Hayes

Subscribed and sworn to before me this 15th day of October, 1913.

Peidine Bonnin
Notary Public.

State of Oklahoma
County of Canadian   ss

Mrs. Anna Van Horn, being duly sowrn[sic], deposes and says: that she is a member of the Cheyenne tribe of Indians and understands well both the English and the Cheyenne languages: that she has interpreted the above and foregoing last will and testament of Kiowa Woman, to her and explained each of its provisions in the Cheyenne language, and she declares to me that Kiowa Woman fully understands the same and says that it is as she desired it to be.

Anna Van Horn
Interpreter

NATIVE AMERICAN WILLS and PROBATE RECORDS, 1911 - 1921

Subscribed and sworn to by Anna Van Horn this 15th day of October, 1913, before me.
Witness my hand and seal

                                        Peidine Bonnin
                                        Notary Public.

Department of The Interior,
Office of Indian Affairs
Washington, D.C.   Jul 9-1914

It is recommended that the within will of Kiowa Woman, Cheyenne allottee No. 643, dated October 15, 1913, be approved in accordance with the Act of June 25, 1910 (36 Stats. L., 855-6) as amended by the Act of February 14, 1913 (37 Stat. L., 678).

                                        signed. C.F. Hauke
                                        Assistant Commissioner

Department of The Interior
Washington, D.C.   Jul 17-1914

The within will is hereby approved in accordance with the Act of June 25, 1910 (36 Stats. L., 855-6) as amended by Act of February 14, 1913 (37 Stat. L., 678).

<<<<<<<>>>>>>>

COPY

********W I L L********

    I, **MRS. SPOTTED CALF**, of Calumet, Canadian County, State of Oklahoma, being of sound and disposable mind, memory and understanding, do make my last will and testament in manner and form following:

"First" It is my will that the East Eighty (80) acres of my allotment, being the Northeast quarter of Section 14 Township 13 Range 9 W. I devise to my beloved son, George Frass, of the town of Calumet, Canadian County, State of Oklahoma.

"Second" I give bequeath and devise all my personaly[sic] property, the West Eighty (80) acres of my allotment as above stated, and all my interest in the inherited allotment of Kiowa Little Bear, being the South West quarter of Sec. 4 twonship[sic] 14 Range 9 W. in Candaian[sic] County State of Oklahoma, to my beloved daughter, Mary Spotted Calf.

    "Third" I give and bequeath to my beloved daughter Emma Kingsley, One ($1) Dollar, to be paid to her by my executor, or Administrator.

    "Fourth" I give and bequeath to my beloved daughter Rosa Seneca, One ($1) dollar, to be paid to her by my executor, or Administrator.

NATIVE AMERICAN WILLS and PROBATE RECORDS, 1911 - 1921

"Fifth" It is father[sic] my will that my son George Frass pay off all my legal debts that is outstanding at my death same to be paid by him either by the sale of a part of his own personal estate, or the property left by me to him after he has the same in his hands. George Frass to pay all my indebtedness from his own recourse and the property mentioned in this will not to be disturbed to pay the indebtedness.

"Sixth" I hereby appoint George Frass Executor of this my last will and testament. In witness whereof I Mrs. Spotted Calf, the testator, have, to this my last will and testatemt, set my hand and seal this the 31st day of May A.D. 1913.

    Herbert Walker   Mrs. Spotted Calf, Her thumb mark

Signed and sealed and declared by the Above Named Mrs. Spotted Calf, as and for her last will testament in the presence of us who have hereunto subscribed our names at her present, as witnesses thereto, in the present of the said testator and of each other. We each and all of [sic] are satisfied in our own mind that the said testator is now in a sound and disposing mind.

    Herbert Walker
    Mack Haag
    Julia Prentiss
Subscribed and sworn to before me this the 31st day of May, 1913.
        Seal
                My commission expires April 3, 1915
                                            C.C. Thompson
                                                  Notary Public

        Cheyenne & Arapaho Agency, filed in this office July 3, 1913
                Dewitt C. Hayes   Land and Est. Clerk.

Department of The Interior,
Office of Indian Affairs
Washington, D.C.   Jun 8, 1914
It is recommended that the within will be approved pursuant to the provisions of the act of June 25, 1910 (36 Stats. L., 855-6) as amended by the act of February 14, 1913 (37 Stat. L, 678).
                                    Respectfully,
                                    signed E. B. Meritt
                                  Assistant Commissioner
Department of The Interior
Washington, D.C.   Jun 9, 1914

The within will is hereby approved pursuant to the provisions of the act of June 25, 1910 (36 Stats. L., 855-6) as amended by act of February 14, 1913 (37 Stat. L., 678).

NATIVE AMERICAN WILLS and PROBATE RECORDS, 1911 - 1921

Signed Bo Sweeney
Assistant Secretary

<<<<<<<<>>>>>>>

- LAST WILL AND TESTAMENT -
of
Antoine Enno of Belcourt N Dak

IN THE NAME OF GOD, AMEN.

    I, **ANTOINE ENNO SR.** of Belcourt N Dak being of lawful age, sound mind, memory and understanding, do hereby make and publish this my last Will and Testament, hereby revoking and annulling all wills by me heretofore made, in the manner and form following, that is to say:

FIRST. I direct that all my just debts and funeral expenses, and expenses of my last illness shall be paid by my execut hereinafter named as soon after my decease as shall be convenient:

SECOND. I give, devise, and bequeath to Louis Enno my son son sleigh and all my farm Tools and give to Sarah Enno one Cow and give to my wife Catherine Enno one horse one mare one heifer two year old one heifer one years old and leave my wife Catherine Enno In care to Louis Enno my som and I give Antoine Louis Enno my grand son one wagon one set of harnes[sic] complette[sic]

THIRD. All the rest and residue of my estate, both real, personal and mixed, I give, devise, and bequeath to Louis Enno my son my own allotment Containing 160 acres of land on the southwest quarter of Section 32 Township 162 N. R. 71 W 5th P.M. Providing or Provided That Louis Enno my son is to take care of his mother.

AND LASTLY. I do hereby nominate, constitute and appoint Louis Enno, my son, without bond, executor of this my last Will and Testament.

    IN TESTIMONY WHEREOF, I have set my hand and seal to this, my last Will and Testament, at Belcourt, North Dakota, this 1st day of November 1 first in the year of our Lord one thousand and nine hundred thirteen.

                                                     His
                                                     Thumb
Antoine Enno Sr . . . . .(Seal) Mark

SIGNED, SEALED PUBLISHED, AND DECLARED

    By the said Antoine Enno Sr in our presence, as and for his last Will and Testament, and at his request and in his presence, and in the presence of each other, we have hereunto subscribed our names as attesting witnesses thereto.

                                          Eustache Reaussin
                    Residence: Belcourt N Dak

NATIVE AMERICAN WILLS and PROBATE RECORDS, 1911 - 1921

                                                          Louis Parisien
                            Residence: Belcourt N Dak
                                                          Alex Enno
                            Residence: Belcourt N Dak

Department of The Interior,
Office of Indian Affairs
Washington, D.C.   Jun 1 1914

It is recommended that the within will be approved pursuant to the provisions of the act of June 25, 1910 (36 Stats. L., 855-6) as amended by the act of February 14, 1913 (37 Stat. L, 678).

                                                        Respectfully,
                                                        E. B. Meritt
                                                        Assistant Commissioner

Department of The Interior
Washington, D.C.   Jun -2 1914

The within will is hereby approved pursuant to the provisions of the act of June 25, 1910 (36 Stats. L., 855-6) as amended by act of February 14, 1913 (37 Stat. L., 678).

                                                        Lewis C. Laylin
                                                        Assistant Secretary

<<<<<<<>>>>>>>

LAST WILL AND TESTAMENT
of
PRETTY FACE, OR NANCY TOBACCO SACK, CHEYENNE RIVER ALLOTTEE NO. 1318

----o----

IN THE NAME OF GOD, AMEN.

    I, **PRETTY FACE**, or **NANCY TOBACCO SACK**, Cheyenne River allottee No. 1318, of the Cheyenne River Reservation, South Dakota, being of sound mind, memory and understanding, do herebt make and publish this my last Will and Testament, hereby revoking and annulling all wills by me heretofore made, in manner and form following, that is to say:

    FIRST: I direct that all my just debts and funeral expenses, and expenses of my last illness shall be paid by my executor hereinafter names as soon after my decease as shall be convenient:

    SECOND: I give, devise and bequeath to my beloved niece, Jones, or Agnes Tobacco Sack, Cheyenne River allottee No. 1319, my allotment described as follows: The SW/4 of section 36, township 15 north; S/2 of N/2 and lots 1, 2, 3 and 4 of section, township 14 north, range 29; SE/4 of NE/4, NE/4 of SE/4 and E/2 of NW/4 of SE/4 of section 18, and NW/4 of SW/4 and lot 8 of section 17,

NATIVE AMERICAN WILLS and PROBATE RECORDS, 1911 - 1921

township 9 north, range 26 east of B.H.M., South Dakota, containing 639.91 acres.

THIRD: All the rest and residue of my estate, both real, personal and mixed and held in trust by the United States, I give, devise and bequeath to my beloved niece, the said Jones, or Agnes Tobacco Sack, Cheyenne River allottee No. 1319.

AND LASTLY: I do hereby nominate, constitute and appoint John Garreau, Cheyenne River allottee No. 598, of the Cheyenne River Reservation, South Dakota, executor of this my last Will and Testament.

IN TESTIMONY WHEREOF, I have set my hand and seal to this, my last Will and Testament, at Cheyenne River Agency, Cheyenne Agency, South Dakota, this twenty-eighth day of April in the year of our Lord one thousand nine hundred and thirteen.

Witnesses to Mark:

Penn Garfield
William Warnock

Her
Pretty Face or Nancy Tobacco Sack   Thumb
Mark.

SIGNED, SEALED, PUBLISHED AND DECLARED

By the said Pretty Face, or Nancy Tobacco Sack, Cheyenne River allottee No. 1318, in our presence, as and for her last Will and Testament, and at her request and in her presence, and in the presence of each other, we have hereunto subscribed our names as attesting witnesses thereto.

C A Shultis
Cheyenne River Agency, S.D.
R. C. Craige
Cheyenne River Agency, S.D.
Louis Egna
Cheyenne River Agency, S.D.

Department of The Interior,
Office of Indian Affairs
Washington, D.C.

It is recommended that the within will be approved pursuant to the provisions of the act of June 25, 1910 (36 Stats. L., 855-6) as amended by the Act of February 14, 1913 Public 381.

F H ABBOTT
Acting Commissioner

Department of The Interior
Washington, D.C.   May -9 1913

NATIVE AMERICAN WILLS and PROBATE RECORDS, 1911 - 1921

The within will approved pursuant to the provisions of the act of June 25, 1910 (36 Stats. L., 855-6) as amended by the Act of February 14, 1913 Public 381.

Lewis C. Laylin
Assistant Secretary

C O P Y

LAST WILL AND TESTAMENT
OF
AFRAID OF THE LODGE, or MARY CHADRON
Cheyenne River Allottee No. 156.

IN THE NAME OF GOD, AMEN:

I, **AFRAID OF THE LODGE**, or **MARY CHADRON**, of the Cheyenne River Reservation near Promise, South Dakota, being of sound mind, memory and understanding, do hereby make and publish this my last will and testament, hereby revoking and annulling all wills by me heretofore made, in manner and form following, that is to say:

First. I direct that all my just debts and funeral expenses, and the expenses of my last illness shall be paid by my exector, hereinafter named, as soon after my decease as shall be convenient.

Second. I give, devise and bequeath my allotment of land on the Cheyenne River Reservation, South Dakota, known as Allotment No. 156. The W/2 of Section 13, Township 17 north, range 29 east of the B.H.M., South Dakota, containing 321 acres, as follows:

To my beloved grand-son, Felix LeBeau, I give, devise and bequeath the NW1/4 of Sec. 13, township 17 north, range 29 east of B.H.M., South Dakota containing 160 acres;

To my beloved grand son, Jesse Hodgkiss, I give, devise and bequeath, the SW/4 of Sec. 13, township 17 north, range 29 east, of B.H.M. South Dakota, containing 160 acres;

And lastly, I do hereby nominate, constitute and appoint, Alex LeBeau, of the Cheyenne River Reservation, near Promise, South Dakota, executor of this my last will and testament.

In testimony whereof, I have set my hand and seal to this, my last will and testament, at Cheyenne Agency, South Dakota, this Fifth (5) day of August in the year of our Lord one thousand nine hundred and twelve.

Afraid of the Lodge, or Mary Chadron, Her thumb mark.

NATIVE AMERICAN WILLS and PROBATE RECORDS, 1911 - 1921

Witnesses to mark:
    Penn Garfield,
    Wm. Warnock

SIGNED, SEALED, PUBLISHED AND DECLARED

By said Afraid of the Lodge, or Mary Chadron, in our presence, as and for her last will and testament, and at her request and in her presence, and in the presence of each other, we have hereunto subscribed our names as attesting witnesses thereto.

                      Henry LeBeau, Promise, S.Dak.
                      John B. Lebeau, LeBeau, S.D.
                      Allen Fielder, Cheyenne Agency, S.D.

Department of The Interior,
Office of Indian Affairs
Washington, D.C.   JUN 17-1913

It is recommended that the within will be approved pursuant to the provisions of the Act of June 25, 1910 (36 Stats. L., 855-6) as amended by the Act of February 14, 1913 (Public 381).

                      signed C. F. Hauke
                      Acting Commissioner

Department of The Interior
Washington, D.C.   Jun 19-1913

The within will approved pursuant to the provisions of the Act of June 25, 1910 (36 Stats. L., 855-6) as amended by Act of February 14, 1913 (Public 381).

              Signed   Lewis C. Laylin
                          Assistant Secretary

C O P Y

LAST WILL AND TESTAMENT OF DARWIN BEAR

IN THE NAME OF GOD, AMEN:

    I. **DARWIN BEAR**, aged 23 years, of Crow Creek Indian Reservation, Crow Creek, South Dakota, being of sound mind, memory and understanding, do hereby make and publish this my last will and testament, hereby revoking and annulling all wills heretofore made by me, and especially revoking and annulling the will made and executed by me on the 18th day of January, 1913, in manner and form following, that is to say:

NATIVE AMERICAN WILLS and PROBATE RECORDS, 1911 - 1921

FIRST. I give, devise and bequeath to Grace Bear, my sister, and to Dora Pratt, my sister, all of my allotment of land within the Crow Creek Indian Reservation, in South Dakota, and described as the South half of the Northwest quarter of section fourteen, Township one hundred eight, Range seventy-five, containing 80 acres, the same to be equally divided between my said two sisters named above.

SECOND. I give and bequeath to Smith Bear, my brother, the new wagon issued to me, and my said brother, Smith Bear, is to pay all my just debts and funeral expenses and the expenses of my last illness.

THIRD. I give and bequeath to John Bear, my brother, the plow and the harrow recently issued to me.

FOURTH. I give and bequeath to Mrs. Hannah Wizi, my grandmother, the hoe, axe, and pitch fork recently issued to me.

FIFTH. I give and bequeath to John Good Voice, my cousin, the set of harness which is to be issued to me, or to my account as Sioux Benefits.

AND LASTLY. I do hereby nominate, constitute and appoint Rev. Hachaliah Burt executor of this my last will and testament.

IN TESTIMONY WHEREOF, I have set my hand and seal to this, my last will and testament, at the home of Mrs. Hannah Wizi, near Crow Creek, South Dakota, this 20th day of January 1913, in the year of our Lord, One Thousand and Thirteen[sic].

Darwin Bear

SIGNED, SEALED, PUBLISHED AND DECLARED BY THE SAID DARWIN BEAR in our presence, as and for his last will and testament, and at his request and in his presence, and in the presence of each other, we have hereunto subscribed our names as attesting witnesses thereto.

Homer J. Bibb Residence, Crow Creek, S.D.
Hachaliah Burt Residence, Crow Creek, S.D.
Thomas W. Tuttle Residence, Crow Creek, S.D.

Department of The Interior,
Office of Indian Affairs
Washington, D.C.   Jul 31 1914

It is recommended that the within will be approved pursuant to the provisions of the act of June 25, 1910 (36 Stats. L., 855-6) as amended by the act of February 14, 1913 (37 Stat. L, 678).

Respectfully,
signed E. B. Meritt

NATIVE AMERICAN WILLS and PROBATE RECORDS, 1911 - 1921

                                                Assistant Commissioner
Department of The Interior
Washington, D.C.   August 13, 1914

The within will is hereby approved pursuant to the provisions of the act of June 25, 1910 (36 Stats. L., 855-6) as amended by act of February 14, 1913 (37 Stat. L., 678).

                                                signed Bo Sweeney
                                                Assistant Secretary

C O P Y

State of Wisconsin
Brown County

    I, **MOSES COOLONG**, of the twon[sic] of Hobart, County of Brown, and State of Wisconsin, being a widower of lawful age, do make this my last will and testament.

    I hereby confirm all the provisions of my former will dated May 25, 1911, and make this additional provision: To my daughter, Frances Coolong Johnson, in acknowledgement of her care and support during the past two years I give the northwest quarter of the southwest quarter of Sec. 1 T. 23 Range 19 E the 4th p.m. in Wisconsin, containing 40 acres.

    In witness whereof, I have signed, sealed, published and declared this instrument as my will, at Oneida, Wicsonsin, this 2nd day of December, 1912.

    Witness to mark,   Moses Coolong   His thumb mark.
       J.C. Hart
       Wickerson S. Asbury

    The said Moses Coolong, at Oneida, Wis. on the said 2nd day of December, 1912, signed and sealed this instrument and puvlished[sic] and declared the same as once for his last will in our presence, and we, at his request, and in his presence, and in the presence of each other, have hereunto written our names as subscribing witnesses.

                                                  J.C. Hart
                                                Wickerson S. Asbury

Office of Indian Affairs
    AUG 8 1914

The within will of Moses Coolong, is recommended for approval in accordance with the provisions of the Act of June 25, 1910 (36 Stats. L., 855-6) as amended by Act of February 14, 1913 (37 Stats. L., 678).

NATIVE AMERICAN WILLS and PROBATE RECORDS, 1911 - 1921

Department of The Interior
Office of The Secretary
AUG 8 1914

E.B. Meritt
Assistant Commissioner

The within will of Moses Coolong is approved in accordance with the Act of June 25, 1910 (36 Stats. L. 855-6) as amended by Act of February 14, 1913 (37 Stats. L. 678).

Bo Sweeney
Assistant Secretary

I, **WE-HAW-KO**, being of full age and of sound and disposing mind and memory do declare this to be my last will and testament.

FIRST. I direct that all my just debts be paid.

SECOND. I will and bequeath all my property of which may die seized as follows to-wit: Funds on deposit at the Toledo Savings Bank, Toledo, Iowa, the same being held under the supervision of the Superintendent Sac & Fox Sanitorium Toledo, Iowa, as individual Indian money.

To my husband, John McIntosh, 1/3 one third of the above fund, the remainder of the fund to be held in trust by the Superintendent of the Sac & Fox Reservation for my grand daughter We-pah-pe-nah-qua or Ora Ward.

I hereby nominate the Superintendent Sac & Fox Reservation to be my executor without bond of this my last will and testament.

In witness whereof I have hereunto set my hand and seal to this my last will and testament this 17 day of Feb. 1914.

We-haw-ko   Her thumb mark

Witness
 Glenn E. Judy
  Teacher at Fox Day Schoo., Tama, Iowa.
 Clifford M. Ellis

We hereby certify that on this 17 day of Feb. 1914, at the Sac & Fox Reservation in Indian Village Township Tama County, Iowa, We-haw-ko to us personally known did, in our presence, sign the foregoing instrumentand declare the same to be her last will and testament and we at her request and in her presence and in the presence of each other, do subscribe our names as witnesses thereto.

    Glenn E. Judy

NATIVE AMERICAN WILLS and PROBATE RECORDS, 1911 - 1921

Teacher at Fox Day Schoo., Tama, Iowa.
Clifford M. Ellis

Department of The Interior,
Office of Indian Affairs
Washington, D.C.   JUL 10-1914

It is recommended that the within will be approved pursuant to the provisions of the Act of June 25, 1910 (36 Stats. L., 855-6) as amended by the Act of February 14, 1913 (37 Stat. L, 678).

Respectfully,
signed C.F. HAUKE
Second Assistant Commissioner

Department of The Interior
Washington, D.C.   JUL 16-1914

The within will is hereby approved pursuant to the provisions of the Act of June 25, 1910 (36 Stats. L., 855-6) as amended by Act of February 14, 1913 (37 Stat. L., 678).

signed Bo Sweeney
Assistant Secretary

WILL

KNOW ALL MEN BY THESE GREETINGS: That I, **IRON HORN BULL**, allottee No. 443, of the Fort Peck Indian Reservation, being of sound mind, hereby make and declare this to be my last will and testament.

1st. I hereby direct and request that Mrs. Amelia Casper, of Homestead, Montana, be appointed executor of this will, and request that she be not required to give bond.

2nd I hereby direct that my executor, above names, pay all of my just debts and funeral expenses.

3rd. I hereby devise, give and bequeath to Mrs. Amelia Casper, of Homestead, Montana, my allotment on the Fort Peck Indian Reservation in Montana, as an appreciation for her many kindnesses she has show to me in the past.

4th. I make no provision for my wife, Red Road, as she has an allotment of her own, and make no provision for other near relations, as my near relations have not cared for me in times past when I was unable to support myself.

IN WITNESS WHEREOF, I have hereunto set my hand, this eighteenth day of May, in the year 1914.

Iron Horn Bull   His thumb mark

NATIVE AMERICAN WILLS and PROBATE RECORDS, 1911 - 1921

We, the undersigned, of legal age, hereby certify that we were present, and saw the above named Iron Horn Bull make his mark on this will, and we certify that he acknowledged to us that the same was his last will and testament, in witness whereof, we hereunto set our names, in the presence of one another and of the above named Iron Horn Bull, this 18th day of May A.D. 1914.

Joseph Culbertson
George G. Commons
J. George Kurtz
All residents of Poplar, State of Montana.

Department of The Interior,
Office of Indian Affairs
JUL 15-1914

It is recommended that the within will be approved pursuant to the provisions of the Act of June 25, 1910 (36 Stats. L., 855-6) as amended by the Act of February 14, 1913 (Public 381).

Respectfully,
signed E. B. Meritt
Assistant Commissioner

Department of The Interior
Washington, D.C.   JUL 15-1914

The within will is hereby approved pursuant to the provisions of the Act of June 25, 1910 (36 Stats. L., 855-6) as amended by Act of February 14, 1913 (Public 381).

signed Bo Sweeney
Assistant Secretary

LAST WILL AND TESTAMENT
OF
NO NAME

IN THE NAME OF GOD, AMEN:

I, **NO NAME**, of Crow Agency, Montana, being of sound mind, memory and understanding, do hereby make and publish this my last will and testament, hereby revoking and annulling all wills by me heretofor made, in manner and form following, that is to say:

FIRST. I direct that all my just debts and funeral expenses, and expenses of my last illness shall be paid by my executor hereinafter named as soon after my decease as shall be convenient;

NATIVE AMERICAN WILLS and PROBATE RECORDS, 1911 - 1921

SECOND. I give devise and bequeath to William Stewart, Joseph Stewart, Strong, and Red Hair, the SW1/4 of SE1/4 16 2s 33e and NE1/4 of SW1/4 23, and W½ of SE¼, 23, 2s, 32e Allotment No. 184.

THIRD. All the rest and residue of my estate, both real, personal and mixed, I give, devise, and bequeath to the above named parties in equal shares.

AND LASTLY, I do hereby nominate, constitute and appoint F.E. Miller, Hardin, Montana, executor of this my last will and testament.

IN TESTIMONY WHEREOF, I have set my hand and seal to this, my last will and testament, at Big Horn, Montana, this 8th day of February in the year of our Lord one thousand and eleven.

No Name   Her thumb mark
SIGNED, SEALED, PUBLISHED AND DECLARED

By the said No Name in our presence, as and for her last will and tesatment, and at her request and in her presence, and in the presence of each other, we have hereunto subscribed our names at attesting witnesses thereto.

> H.S. Hana, Sr.
> Residence, Crow Agency,M ontana.
> Mary Owl Above
> Big Horn, Crow Reservation

Department of The Interior,
Office of Indian Affairs
Washington, D.C.
JUL 17-1914

It is recommended that the within will be disapproved pursuant to the provisions of the Act of June 25, 1910 (36 Stats. L., 855-6) as amended by the Act of February 14, 1913 (Public 381).

> Respectfully,
> signed E. B. Meritt
> Assistant Commissioner

Department of The Interior
Washington, D.C.
JUL 28-1914

The within will is hereby disapproved pursuant to the provisions of the Act of June 25, 1910 (36 Stats. L., 855-6) as amended by Act of February 14, 1913 (Public 381).

> signed Bo Sweeney
> Assistant Secretary

<<<<<<<<>>>>>>>

NATIVE AMERICAN WILLS and PROBATE RECORDS, 1911 - 1921

IN THE NAME OF GOD, AMEN:

I, **STRIKES BOTH WAYS** (English Name) or **NOOPTUSH DICHIS**, (Indian Name), of Crow Agency, in the County of Rosebud, State of Montana, ninety-nine years of age and being of sound and disposing mind and memory and not acting under duress, menace, fraud of undue influence of any person whatsoever, do make and publish and declare this to be my last will and testament in the manner following, that is to say:

I hereby give and bequeath to my good friend (No Name) all my property, both real and personal, of which I may die possessed, and partifularly my allotment number 483 being the northwest quarter of the northeast quarter, Section Twenty, Township five south, range thirty-two east, and the northeast quarter of the southwest quarter and the north half of the southeast quarter, Section twenty-one, township eight south, range thirty-two east, containing one hundred and sixty acres, to have and to hold and receive possession and all benefits therefrom and finally to receive full and complete title thereto as fully as I might to.

I hereby direct that this my last will and testament shall be executed and carried into effect by theCommissioner of Indian Affairs through his official representatives and that no bond shall be required.

IN WITNESS WHEREOF, I have hereunto set my hand and seal this twenty-ninth day of October, A.D. 1910.

Strikes Both Ways Her thumb mark.

The foregoing instrument, consisting of page one, was at the date thereof, by the said Strikes Both Ways or Nooptush Dichis, signed sealed and published as and declared to be her last will and testament, in the presence of us, who, at her request and in her presence and in the presence of each other have subscribed our names as witnesses thereto.

A.A. Campbell, residing at Lodge Grass, Mt.
Ed. Schroeder, residing at Lodge Grass. Mt.

Department of The Interior,
Office of Indian Affairs
    JUL 10-1914

It is recommended that the within will be approved pursuant to the provisions of the Act of June 25, 1910 (36 Stats. L., 855-6) as amended by the Act of February 14, 1913 (Public 381).

Respectfully,
signed C.F. Hauke
Acting Assistant Commissioner

NATIVE AMERICAN WILLS and PROBATE RECORDS, 1911 - 1921

Department of The Interior
Washington, D.C.

The within will is hereby approved pursuant to the provisions of the Act of June 25, 1910 (36 Stats. L., 855-6) as amended by Act of February 14, 1913 (Public 381).

signed Bo Sweeney
Assistant Secretary

I, **CHARLES BRESETTE**, of Bayfield, Wisconsin, do hereby make and publish this as my last will and testament, hereby revoking all former wills by me made.

1st. I direct that all my just debts and funeral expenses be paid out of my estate.

2nd. After paying all my just debts and funeral expenses as above, I bequeath to my daughter, Mary Bresette Reil, all of my estate, real and personal, in form as it may appear to her sole and exclusive use forever.

IN WITNESS WHEREOF, I, Charles Bresette, have to this my last will and testament, consisting of one page of paper, subscribed my name and set my seal this 21st day of November, 1911.

I hereby appoint Mary Bresette Reil executor of this my las will and testament.   His thumb
Witnesses to mark   Charles Bresette   O (Seal)
                                                          mark
F.V. Holston,
    Bayfield, Wis.

SIGNED, SEALED AND DECLARED by the Charles Bresette, as and for his last will and testament, in the presence of us, both being present at the same time, who at his request, in his presence, and in the presence of each other have hereunto subscribed our names as witnesses, November 21st, 1911.

    F. Kern of Bayfield, Wisconsin.
    J.V. Holson of Bayfield, Wisconsin.

Office of Indian Affairs
August 21, 1914
I have the honor to recommend that the certified copy of the will of Charles Bresette be laid before the President for his approval.

(signed) E. B. Meritt
Assistant Commissioner

NATIVE AMERICAN WILLS and PROBATE RECORDS, 1911 - 1921

Department of The Interior
Washington, D.C.

August 22, 1914

I have the honor to recommend that the certified copy of the will of Charles Bresette be approved

(Signed) Franklin K. Lane.

THE WHITE HOUSE

Approved: August 24, 1914

(Signed) Woodrow Wilson

IN THE NAME OF GOD, AMEN.

    I, **MARY CRANE GRAVES,** formerly Mary Crane, a member of the Winnebago Tribe of Indians, and a resident of Thurston County, Nebraska, being of sound and disposing mind and memory and considering the uncertainties of human life to[sic] make and publish this my last will and testament hereby revoking all wills by me at any time heretofore made.

    FIRST. I direct that my funeral expenses and all my just debts be paid as early as convenient after my death.

    SECOND. The east one-half of the northwest quarter of Section thirty-four in township twenty-seven range nine east of the sixth P.M. in Thurston County, Nebraska, I will, devise, and bequeath to my beloved husband, William J. O. Graves, and to his heirs and assigns forever, above described land being my allotment.

    THIRD. All my interest in heirship lands I will devise and bequeath to my three brothers, and my two sisters, share and share alike.

    FOURTH. All the rest residue and remainder of my estate I will devise and bequeath to my said husband, William J.O. Graves.

    FIFTH. I appoint my husband William J.O. Graves, executor of this my last will and testament.

    IN WITNESS WHEREOF, I have hereunto subscribed my name this sixth day of November in year of our Lord, one thousand nine hundred and eleven.

NATIVE AMERICAN WILLS and PROBATE RECORDS, 1911 - 1921

Mary Crane Graves, Her thumb mark

Witnessed to mark:
   Tilden T. Harris
   Joseph Grayhair
   Cora Grayhair

We whose names are hereunto subscribed do hereby certify that Mary Crane Graves, the testatrix, subscribed her name to this instrument in our presence and in the presence of each of us on the sixth day of November, 1911, and declared at the same time in our presence and hearing that this instrument was her last will and testament and we at her request signed our names hereto in her presence as attesting witnesses.

        Tilden T. Harris   Winnebago, Nebr.
        Joseph Grayhair   Winnebago, Nebr.
        Cora Grayhair   Winnebago, Nebr.

Department of The Interior,
Office of Indian Affairs
Washington, D.C.
        JUL 1-1914

It is recommended that the within will, insofar as it devises the testator's original allotment, be approved pursuant to the provisions of the Act of June 25, 1910 (36 Stats. L., 855-6) as amended by the Act of February 14, 1913 (37 Stat. L., 678).

        Respectfully,
        signed E. B. Meritt
        Assistant Commissioner

Department of The Interior
Washington, D.C.   JUL 20-1914

The within will, insofar as it devises the testator's original allotment, is approved pursuant to the provisions of the Act of June 25, 1910 (36 Stats. L., 855-6) as amended by Act of February 14, 1913 (37 Stat. L., 678).

        signed Bo Sweeny
        Assistant Secretary

<<<<<<<>>>>>>
LAST WILL AND TESTAMENT

of

SARAH RED CLOUD

IN THE NAME OF GOD, AMEN.

NATIVE AMERICAN WILLS and PROBATE RECORDS, 1911 - 1921

I, **SARAH RED CLOUD**, of Cheyenne River Reservation, South Dakota, being of sound mind, memory and understanding, do hereby make and publish this my last Will and Testament, hereby revoking and annulling all wills by me heretofore made, in manner and form following, that is to say:

FIRST. I direct that all my just debts and funeral expenss, and expenses of my last illness shall be paid by my executor hereinafter named as soon after my decease as shall be convenient;

SECOND. I give, devise and bequeath to my beloved daughter, Agnes Red Buffalo, or Mrs. James White Horse, my allotment of land on the Cheyenne River Reservation, known as Allotment No. 298. The S/2 of section 22, township 15 north, range 29 east of Black Hills Meridian, South Dakota, containing 320 acres;

THIRD. All the rest and residue of my estate, both real, personal and mixed, I give, devise and bequeath to my beloved daughter, Agnes Red Buffalo, or Mrs. James White Horse;

FOURTH. I give, devise and bequeath nothng to my son Edward Roan Bear;

AND LASTLY. I do hereby nominate, constitute and appoint Truby Iron Moccasin, of Cheyenne River Reservation, South Dakota, executor of this my last Will and Testament.

IN TESTAMONY WHEREOF, I have set my hand and seal to this, my last Will and Testament, at Cheyenne River Agency, Cheyenne Agency, South Dakota, this eleventh day of May in the year of our Lord one thousand nine hundred and eleven.

Witnesses to Mark: Sarah Red Cloud Her thumb mark

Stephen Hunts the Enemy
W. M. Warnock

SIGNED, SEALED, PUBLISHED AND DECLARED

By the said Sarah Red Cloud in our presence, as and for her last Will and Testament, and at her request and in her presence, and in the presence of each other, we have hereunto subscribed our names as attesting witnesses thereto.

Nellie Clark
Residence, Cheyenne Agency, S.D.
John J. Backus
Residence, Cheyenne Agency, S.D.

NATIVE AMERICAN WILLS and PROBATE RECORDS, 1911 - 1921

Penn Garfield
Residence, Cheyenne Agency, S.D.

Department of The Interior,
Office of Indian Affairs
Washington, D.C.   Aug. 12, 1911

The Secretary:

I hereby recommend that the within will be approved so far as it relates to the original allotment of devisor, viz: S1/2 Sec. 22, T. 15 N. R. 29 E., B.H.M., South Dakota.

Respectfully,
F. H. Abbott
Acting Commissioner.

Will approved:

Samuel Adams
C.J.C.
First Assistant Secretary,
W.C.P.

<<<<<<<><>>>>>>>

I, **STEELE STANDS BLACK**, Ponca Allottee No. 763, of White Eagle, Oklahoma, do hereby make, publish and declare this my last Will and Testament, in manner and form following:--------------------------

First. I direct that all my just debts and funeral expenses be paid as soon fter my decease as conveniently can be done.

Second. I give and bequeath to my half-brother, Irving Stands Black, to my half-sister, Grace S.B. No Ear, to my niece, Lizzie Calls Him and to my nephew, Dewey Hairy Back, each the sum of one dollar; And in the event that any of such persons shall have died before me, leaving lawful issue, him or her surviving, then I give and bequeath the sum of one dollar to each of such lawful issue me surviving.

Third. I give, devise and bequeath to Nina Weak Bone, who raised and cared for me and who was one of the wives of my father, Stands Black, all the certain real estate in Kay County, Oklahoma, described as follows, to-wit:

My own allotment, same being the West half (W1/2) and the North-east quarter (NE1/4) of the North-east quarter (NE1/4) of Section eleven (11), Township 24, North, of Range 1, East of I.M.;

NATIVE AMERICAN WILLS and PROBATE RECORDS, 1911 - 1921

My two-ninths (2/9) interest in the allotment of my father, Stands Black, same being the South half (S1/2) of the Southeast quarter (SE1/4) of Setion three (3), Township twenty-five (25) North, of Range 2, East of the ndian Meridian;

My eleven twenty sevenths (11/27) interest in the allotment of my mother, Packs Wood, same being the East half (1/2) of the South-west quarter of Section thirteen (13), Township 24, North, of Range 1, East of I.M., and the North-east quarter (NE1/4) of the North-west quarter (NW1/4) of Section twenty-four (24), Township 24, North, of Range 1, East of I.M.;

My two-ninths (2/9) interest in the allotment of my sister, Violet Packs Wood, same being the East half (E1/2) of the North-east (NE1/4) and the North-east quarter (NE1/4) of the Southeast quarter (SE1/4) of Section twenty-three (23), Township 24, North, of Range 1, East of I.M.; and,

My two-ninths (2/9) interest in the allotment of my brother, Carl Packs Wood, same being the West half (W1/2) of the Northeast quarter, and the North-west quarter (NW1/4) of the Southeast quarter (SE1/4) of Section twenty-three (23), Township 24, North, of Range 1, East of I.M;

all of my said relatives, Stands Black, Packs Wood, Violet Packs Wood, and Carl Packs Wood, being now deceased.

I nominate, constitute and appoint George Primeaux, an educated Ponca Indian, and my personal friend, executor of this my last Will and Testament, I direct that he shall not be required to give any bond or security for the proper discharge of his duties as such executor.

In witness whereof, I have hereunto subscribed my name at the home of Weak Bone, near Ponca City, Oklahoma, this 25th day of June, A.D., 1914, in the presence of V.N. Souligny and L.A. Maris, whom I have asked to become attesting witnesses hereto.

(Signed) STEELE STANDS BLACK

The foregoing instrument was subscribed, published and declared by Steele Stands Black as and for his last Will and Testament, in our presence and, in the presence of each of us, and we, at the same time, at his request, in his presence and in the presence of each other, hereunto subscribe our names and residences as attesting witnesses this 25th day of June, 1914.

(Signed) VENETTE M. SOULIGNY Ponca City, Okla.
(Signed) L. A. MARIS, Ponca City, Okla.

NATIVE AMERICAN WILLS and PROBATE RECORDS, 1911 - 1921

WILL.

I, **GEORGE IRON TUSK**, non-competent allottee of the Standing Rock Indian reservation and at this time a resident of Morton County, North Dakota, being of sound and disposing mind and memory, do make, publish and declare this to be my last will and testament, hereby revoking all former wills by me made:

Item 1. I bequeath and devise to my half-sister, Mrs. Killing Thunder, of Poplar, Montana, in lieu of her right by law or otherwise in my estate, the following described property, both real and personal: The east 1/2 of section 32, T. 131 N., R. 81 W., in North Dakota containing 320 acres; one spring wagon, one bay horse and a one-fifth share in any moneys that I may inherit through the estate of my deceased son, Louis Iron Tusk.

Item 2. I bequeath and devise to my niece, Mrs. Joseph Culbertson, of Poplar, Montana, in lieu of her right by law or otherwise in my estate, the following described property both real and personal: The SE1/4, E1/2, of E1/2 of SW1/4, Lot 1 and E3/4 of lot 2, SE1/4 of NE1/4 and E3/4 of SW1/4 of NE1/4 of Section 4, T. 130 N., R. 81 W., in North Dakota, containing 319 acres; one lumber-wagon, one set of heavy harness, one grey mare with colt, one buckskin horse, one frame house partly furnished and a three-fifth share in any moneys that I may inherit through the estate of of[sic] my deceased son Louis Iron Tusk.

Item 3. I bequeath and devise to my niece, Mrs. David Manning, of Poplar, Montana, in lieu of her right by law or otherwise in my estate, the following described property both real and personal: The SE 1/4 of section 7, T. 129 N., R. 82 W., in North Dakota, containing 160 acres and a one-fifth in any moneys that I may inherit through the estate of my deceased son Louis Iron Jaw[sic].

WITNESS MY HAND AND SEAL THIS TWELFTH DAY OF JUNE, NINETEEN HUNDRED THIRTEEN AT FORT YATES, NORTH DAKOTA.
Witness:
                                His
                George Iron Tusk   thumb   SEAL
                                mark

E. C. Means
    P.O. Ft. Yates, N.D.
Asa Lindecrow, Interpreter
    P.O. Ft. Yates, N.D.

The foregoing instrument, signed, sealed and acknowledged by said testator, as and for his last will and testament, in our presence, who, at his request, in his presence, and in the presenc of each other, have subscribed our names as witnesses thereto this TWELFTH DAY OF JUNE, NINETEEN HUNDRED AND THIRTEEN

NATIVE AMERICAN WILLS and PROBATE RECORDS, 1911 - 1921

                                                  E. C. Means
                                                  P.O. Ft. Yates, N.D.
                                         Asa Lindecrow, Interpreter

Department of The Interior,
                                                   P.O. Ft. Yates, N.D.
Office of Indian Affairs
Washington, D.C.   October 7, 1914

I recommend that the within will be approved pursuant to the provisions of the Act of June 25, 1910 as amended by the Act of February 14, 1913.

                                                 Respectfully,
                                               E. B. Meritt
                                               Assistant Commissioner

Department of The Interior
Washington, D.C.   October 8, 1914

Within will approved pursuant to the provisions of the Act of June 25, 1910, as amended by Act of February 14, 1913.

                                                 Bo Sweeney
                                               Assistant Secretary

                        LAST WILL AND TESTAMENT OF ROOT.

IN THE NAME OF GOD, AMEN.

    I, **ROOT**, of Crow Creek Indian reservation, Crow Creek Agency, South Dakota, being of sound mind, memory and understanding, do hereby make and publish this my last Will and Testament, hereby revoking and annulling all will by me heretofore made, in manner and form following, that is to say:

    FIRST. I direct that all my just debts and funeral expenses, and expenses of my last illness shall be paid by my executor hereinafter named as soon after my decease as shall be convenient.

    SECOND. I give devise and bequeath to my step daughter, Mabel Lodge, all of my undivided one-half interest in and to the allotment of White Ghost, deceased, said allotment being described as the East half (E1/2) of the West half (W1/2) of section three (3) and the East half (E1/2) of the West half (W1/2) of section ten (10) all in Township one hundred six (106 north of Range seventy-one (71) West of the Fifth Principal Meridian in South Dakota, containing 319.92 acres according to the survey thereof.

    THIRD. All the rest and residue of my estate, both real, personal and mixed, including all funds remaining on deposit to my credit under the

NATIVE AMERICAN WILLS and PROBATE RECORDS, 1911 - 1921

supervision of any Indian Agent or Superintendent, at the time of my death, I give, devise and bequeath to my said step-daughter, Mabel Lodge.

I had only two children who grew up to manhood and womanhood; these are Yellow Hair, wife of Shoots Enemy, and Kin-yan-hi-ya-ya, my son, who died a few years ago. I give Yellow Hair nothing for the reason that she has never done anything for me, and for the further reason while my husband, White Ghost, was alive, we helped her with money and other things. White Ghost and I also gave several horses to my deceased son, Kin-yan-hi-ya-ya, therefore I give nothing to his children, for the reason that they have never done anything for me nor shown me any kindness in my old age. I do not know the names of the children of Kin-yan-hi-ya-ya.

AND LASTLY. I do hereby nominate, constitute and appoint Rev. H. Burt, executor of this my last Will and Testament.

IN TESTIMONY WHEREOF, I have set my hand and seal to this, my last Will and Testament, at Crow Creek Agency Office, Crow Creek, South Dakota, this 11th day of April, in the year of our Lord one thousand nine hundred and thirteen.

                                                    Her
                                   ROOT   thumb
                                                    mark

Signed, sealed, published and declared by the said Root, in our presence, as and for her last Will and Testament, and at her request and in her presence, and in the presence of each other, we have hereunto subscribed our names as attesting witnesses thereto.

                                    W.O. Kohumuig
                          Residence, Crow Creek, So. Dakota
                                    Homer J. Bibb
                          Residence, Crow Creek, So. Dakota
                                    Thomas W. Tuttle
                          Residence, Crow Creek, So. Dakota

Department of The Interior, Office of Indian Affairs
Washington, D.C.   November 6, 1913.

I recommend that the within will receive Departmental approval pursuant to the provisions of the Act of February 14, 1913 (37 Stat. L. 678).

                                    C.F. Hauke
                                    Second Assistant Commissioner

NATIVE AMERICAN WILLS and PROBATE RECORDS, 1911 - 1921

Department of The Interior
Washington, D.C.   November 8, 1913

The within will approved pursuant to the provisions of the Act of February 14, 1913 (37 Stat. L. 678).

Lewis C. Laylin
Assistant Secretary

Last WILL and TESTAMENT of NOAH.

I, **NOAH**, of Greenwood, South Dakota, County of Charles Mix, being of sound mind, memory and understanding, do hereby make, publish and declare this to be my last Will and Testament:

FIRST: I give and bequeath to my daughter, Eugenia Noah Brownthunder, the South-east quarter of the North-east quarter of Section Thirteen (13) Township Ninety-five (95) North of Range Sixty-five (65) containing 40 acres.

SECOND: I give and bequeath to my Grand-daughter, Lucy Brownthunder, Southwest quarter of the North west quarter Section eighteen (18) Township Ninety-five (95) North of Range Sixty-four (64), and the North west quarter of the South west quarter of Section eighteen (18) Township Ninety-five (95) North of Range Sixty-four (64), containing 83.98 acres, and all the buildings on the above described land.

THIRD: I give and bequeath to my Grand-daughter, Mercy Brownthunder, the North-east quarter of the South-west quarter of Section Eighteen (18) township Ninety-five (95) North of Range Sixty-four (64), and the South-west quarter of the South-west quarter of Section Eighteen (18) Township Ninety-five (95) North of Range Sixty-four (64), containing 81.95 acres.

FOURTH: From my Cash and personal property, I decree that after all my legal indebtedness is paid the sum of Four Hundred Dollars or as much thereof as is necessary be set aside for the defraying of my funeral expenses and the erection of a suitable stone for my grave and after the settlement of these expenses are made I bequeath out of the remainder of my personal property Fifty Dollars ($50.00) to my Grand-daughter, Lillian Ree, and to my Grand-son, Oscar Bernie.   I bequeath the sum of Ten Dollars (10.00) to my grand-daughter, Josephine Bernie. I bequeath the sum of Ten Dollars ($10.00) to my Grand-son Obee Bernie. I bequeath the sum of Ten Dollars ($10.00), and of the remainder of my personal property, including Cash, I bequeath in equal amounts to my daughter, Eugenia Noah Brownthunder, and her three daughters, Mercy

NATIVE AMERICAN WILLS and PROBATE RECORDS, 1911 - 1921

Brownthunder, Lucy Brownthunder and Angelic Brownthunder, share and share alike.

FIFTH: By this my last Will and testament I revoke any former Wills made and published by me. I hereby appoint Peter St. Pierre as administrator of this my last Will and testament.

IN WITNESS WHEREOF, I have this 14th day of July, Nineteen Hundred and thirteen set and[sic] hand and seal at Greenwood, South Dakota, Charles Mix County.

Interpreter: NOAH His thumb mark
Moses Archambeau,
     Interpreter.

SIGNED, SEALED and declared published by the said Noah as his last Will and testament, in presence of us who at his request, and in his presence, and in the presence of each other, have subscribed our names as witnesses hereto.

Dr. L.A. Collier   residing at Greenwood, South Dakota
W.B. McCown   residing at Greenwood, South Dakota

Department of The Interior, Office of Indian Affairs
Washington, D.C.   Sept. 30, 1914

It is recommended that the within will be approved pursuant to the provisions of the Act of June 25, 1910 (36 Stats. L., 855-6) as amended by the Act of February 14, 1913 (37 Stat. 678).

          E.B. Meritt
          Assistant Commissioner

Department of The Interior, Washington, D.C.
     October 3, 1914

The within will is approved pursuant to the provisions of the Act of June 25, 1910 (36 Stats. L., 855-6) as amended by Act of February 14, 1913 (37 Stat. 678).

          Bo Sweeney
          Assistant Secretary

<<<<<<<>>>>>>>

LAST WILL AND TESTAMENT OF

Pretty Bird or Mrs. Iron Blanket.

IN THE NAME OF GOD, AMEN.

NATIVE AMERICAN WILLS and PROBATE RECORDS, 1911 - 1921

I, **PRETTY BIRD**, or **MRS. IRON BLANKET**, of Crow Creek Reservation in South Dakota, being of sound mind, memory and understanding, do hereby make and publish this my last Will and Testament, hereby revoking and annulling all wills by me heretofore made, in manner and form following, that is to say:

FIRST. I direct that all my just debts and funeral espenses of my last illness shall be paid by my executor hereinafter named as soon after my decease as shall be convenient;

SECOND. I give devise and bequeath to Charles Briggs 7/16 of all my real estate; to Baptists Lambert 5/16 of all my real estate; Mrs. Agard 1/8 of all my real estate and to White Water Woman of Yankton agency 1/8 of all my real estate. I am possessed of the following lands: A 3/4 interest in the allotment of Iron Blanket, allottee No. 161, my deceased husband, described as the South-half (S1/2) of Section thirty-five (35) Township 107, R 71, containing 320 acres, situated within the Crow Creek Indian reservation within South Dakota; and I am also entitled to a 1/2 interest in the allotment of Gray Haired Bear, allottee No. 177, my deceased son, described as the West half (W1/2) of the South-west quarter (SW1/4) of section 29, and the East half (E1/2) of the South-east quarter (SE1/4) of section 30, in Township 106, range 70 within the Crow Creek Indian reservation, South Dakota.

THIRD. All the rest and residue of my estate, both real and personal, I give, devise and bequeath to the above mentioned devisees in the same proportion they are to take my real estate.

I have no father nor mother living and no child nor children; no grandchildren living; no husband; I have one brother living on the Fort Peck reservation in Montana, named Swift Wing, but I give him nothing for the reason that he has not come to visit me during my sickness. I have not seen him for over forty years. I have no other brothers or sisters nor any children of deceased brothers of sisters living.

AND LASTLY. I do hereby nominate, constitute and appoint Joseph Irving, executor of this my last Will and Testament.

IN TESTIMONY WHEREOF, I have set my hand and seal to this, my last Will and Testament, at my home, on the Crow Creek reservation in South Dakota, this 24th day of March, in the year of our Lord One thousand, nine hundred and thirteen.

Her
Pretty Bird or Mrs. Iron Blanket   thumb
mark

SIGNED, SEALED, PUBLISHED AND DECLARED by the said Pretty Bird or Mrs. Iron Blanket, in our presence, as and for her last Will and Testament,

NATIVE AMERICAN WILLS and PROBATE RECORDS, 1911 - 1921

and at her request and in our presence, and in the presence of each other, we have hereunto subscribed our names as attesting witnesses thereto.

  Ernest Allen, residence, Crow Creek, So. Dak.
  Wcswpunuipy, residence, Crow Creek, So. Dakota.
  Russell Harrison, residence, Crow Creek, So. Dak.

Department of The Interior, Office of Indian Affairs
Washington, D.C. Sept. 10, 1914

It is recommended that the within will be approved pursuant to the provisions of the Act of June 25, 1910 (36 Stats. L., 855-6) as amended by the Act of February 14, 1913 (37 Stat. 678).

        Respectfully,
        E.B. Meritt
        Assistant Commissioner

Department of The Interior, Office of the Secretary,
Washington, D.C. Sept. 17, 1914

The within will is hereby approved pursuant to the provisions of the Act of June 25, 1910 (36 Stats. L., 855-6) as amended by Act of February 14, 1913 (37 Stat. 678).

        Bo Sweeney
        Assistant Secretary

W I L L.

I, **NATHANIEL MANNINGTON**, of Pawnee, Pawnee County, Oklahoma, a member of the Pawnee Indian Tribe, being now of sound and disposing mind and sensible of the uncertainty of life and desiring to make disposition of my property and affairs while in health and strength, do hereby make, publish, and declare the following to be my last will and testament, hereby revoking and cancelling all other and former wills by me at any time made.

 I direct the payment of all my just debts and funeral expenses.

 I make this my last will and testament with the full knowledge that I have no children living.

 I give and devise to my wife Phoebe Mannington, the following described real estate: All of the North East Quarter (NE/4) of Section Thirty-three (33) in Township Twenty-three (23) North of Range Four (4) East of the Indian Meridian, situated in Pawnee County, Oklahoma, except a certain tract of said

NATIVE AMERICAN WILLS and PROBATE RECORDS, 1911 - 1921

land constituting the East portion of the said Quarter Section, which said tract of land is described as follows: Beginning at the Northeast Corner of the said Quarter Section heretofore described, thence running West along the North boundary line of the said Quarter Section, sixty (60) rods, thence South parallel to the East Boundary line of said Quarter Section one hundred and sixty (160) rods to the South boundary line of said Quarter Section, thence East along the South boundary line of said Quarter Section Sixty (60) rods, thence North along the East boundary line of said Quarter Section one hundred sixty (160) rods, to the point of beginning, containing sixty (60) acres more or less.

I give and devise to my only sister of full blood, Mary Osborn, the above described and last mentioned sixty (60) acre tract of land.

It is my intention and desire that my said wife and sister have the above described Quarter Section of land, my said wife to have One Hundred acres of the same and my said sister Sixty acres of the same, the said Sixty acres being described as above.

I give and bequeath all the rest, residue and remainder of my personal property and real estate to my beloved wife Phoebe Mannington.

I hereby appoint and designate James H. Hale, of Pawnee, Oklahoma, sole executor, with bond, of this my last will and testament.

In witness whereof, I, Nathaniel Mannington, have to this my last will and testament, consisting of two sheets of paper subscribed my name this twenty-fourth day of July 1913.

                                                                                                                   His
                          NATHANIEL MANNING[sic]   thumb
                                                                                                                       mark.

Subscribed by Nathaniel Mannington, in the presence of each of us the undersigned and at the same time declared by him to us to be his last will and testament and we thereupon at the request of Nathaniel Mannington, in his presence and in the presence of each other sign our names hereto as witnesses this the 24th day of July 1913, at Pawnee, Oklahoma.

                                                 George W. Nellis
                                               Victor E. Norton
                                                      Pawnee, Okla.
                                             who signed the name of
                                             Nathaniel Mannington to
                                             this his last will.

                                                             Sept. 5, 1914

The will of Nathaniel Mannington allottee No. 152 of the Pawnee Tribe is herewith recommended for approval pursuant to the provisions of the Act of June 25, 1910 (36 Stats. L., 855-6) as amended by the Act of February 14, 1913 (37 Stat. 678).

NATIVE AMERICAN WILLS and PROBATE RECORDS, 1911 - 1921

E.B. Meritt
Assistant Commissioner

Sept. 19, 1914

The will of Nathaniel Mannington, allottee No. 152 of the Pawnee Tribe is herewith approved pursuant to the provisions of the Act of June 25, 1910 (36 Stats. L., 855-6) as amended by Act of February 14, 1913 (37 Stat. 678).

Bo Sweeney
Assistant Secretary

<<<<<<<>>>>>>>

I, **MUD BAY CHARLIE**, an Indian, being upwards of the age of twenty-one years, and of sound and disposing mind and memory and not acting under duress, menace, fraud, or undue influence of any person whatever, do make, publish and declare this my last wil and testament in manner following, that is to say:

FIRST: I direct that upon my death my body be decently buried with proper regard to my station and condition in life, and the circumstances of my estate.

SECONDLY: I direct that my executor, hereinafter named, as soon as he has sufficient funds in hand, pay my funeral expenses and the expenses of my last sickness and the allowance made to my family.

THIRDLY: Should I die without having sold my land in Lots One and Two in Section 12, Township 18, North of Range 3 West of the W.M., I give and devise to John Smith, and[sic] Indian, residing upon the Chehalis Reservation, twenty (20) acres off of the North end of Lot one in section 12, Township 18 North of Range 3 West, said twenty acres to be bounded on the south by a straight line drawn due East and West a sufficient distance south from the northerly boundary of said Lot One to contain 20 acres.

Should, however, my land be legally sold prior to my death so that I no longer own said twenty acres above described. In that event I do give, devise and bequeath to John Smith, above described, one-half of the property that I then own, whether the same be realty or personal - it being my intention that all indebtedness and all expenses of administration whatsoever shall be paid out of my estate before division thereof between the said John Smith and my other legatee hereinafter mentioned in Paragraph 4 of this, My last will and testament.

FOURTHLY: Should I die prior to having legally disposed of my real estate, to-wit: Lots one and Two in Section 12, Township 18, North of Range 3 West, it is my desire and I do hereby give, devise, and bequeath to my step-son, Little Charlie, twenty acres off of the southerly end of Lot Two, Section 12, Township 18, North of Range 3 West, the said twenty acres to be bounded on its northerly side my a straight line running due east and west drawn a sufficient distance northerly from the south boundary line of Lot Two to contain twenty acres.

In the event of my having legally sold my real property above described prior to my death, I do give, devise and bequeath to my step-son, Little Charlie, the one-half portion of my net estate after the payment of all my indebtedness

NATIVE AMERICAN WILLS and PROBATE RECORDS, 1911 - 1921

together with all charges and expenses connected with the administration of my estate.

FIFTHLY: Should I die prior to the sale of my real estate, then and in that event in addition to the specific devises made above to John Smith and Little Charlie of twenty acres of land each, I do give, devise and bequeath all of the rest, residue and remainder of my estate both real and personal of whatever kind or nature owned by me at the time of my death, to said John Smith and Little Charlie share and share alike.

LASTLY: I hereby nominate and appoint Milton Giles, of Olympia, Washington, the executor of this, my last will and testament, and I hereby revoke all former wills by me made.

    IN WITNESS WHEREOF I have hereunto set my hand and seal this thirteenth day of May, A.D., 1913.
                                       his
                           Mud Bay Charlie   X   L.S.
                                        mark

    The above and foregoing instrument was at the date hereof, by the said Mud Bay Charlie, signed and sealed and published as and declared to be his last will and testament in the presence of us, who at his request and in his presence and in the presence of each other have subscribed our names as witnesses thereto.

                                 Milton Giles
                                 Residing at Olympia, Washington
                                 Mollie Peters
                                 Residing at Mud Bay, Washington

    I, Milton Giles, one of the attesting witnesses to the above will, do hereby further certify that I did, on the thirteenth day of May, 1913, at the request of Mud Bay Charlie, and in his presence, and in the presence of the other attesting witness, sign his name to the above will, he signing the same by his mark.
                                                 Milton Giles

STATE OF WASHINGTON   )
) SS.
        County of Thurston.)

    I, D.G. Parker, County Clerk of Thurston County and ex-officio Clerk of the Superior Court of the State of Washington, for Thurston County, holding session at Olympia, do hereby certify that the foregoing is a true and correct copy of the original will of Mud Bay Charlie   Cause No. 1765 as the same appears on file and of record in my office.
    IN WITNESS WHEREOF, I have hereunto set my hand and affixed the seal of said Court thie 4th day of Sept 1913.
                                        D.G. Parker
                         County Clerk and Clerk of the Superior Court
                            of Thurston County, State of Washington.

NATIVE AMERICAN WILLS and PROBATE RECORDS, 1911 - 1921

Department of The Interior,
Office of Indian Affairs
Washington, D.C.   OCT 13, 1914

It is recommended that the within will be approved pursuant to the provisions of the Act of June 25, 1910 (36 Stats. L., 855-6) as amended by the Act of February 14, 1913 (37 Stat. 678).

Respectfully,
E.B. Meritt
Assistant Commissioner

Department of The Interior,
Washington, D.C.   OCT 15, 1914

The within will is hereby approved pursuant to the provisions of the Act of June 25, 1910 (36 Stats. L., 855-6) as amended by Act of February 14, 1913 (37 Stat. 678).

Bo Sweeney
Assistant Secretary

In the name of God, Amen. I, **LAURA WE YAH LAH HOME**, an allottee of the Nez Perce Reservation, Idaho, over the age of 80 years, and being of sound mind and disposing memory and not acting under duress, menace, fraud, or undue influence, of any person whatsoever do make, publish and declare this my last will and Testament in the manner following, that is to say

First. I direct that my body be decently buried with proper regard for my station in life and the circumstances of my estate.

Secondly. I direct that Jennie Lott and Amelia Stevens shall pay all my funeral expenses and the expenses of my last sickness.

Thirdly. I give and devise to the said Jennie Lott and Amelia Stevens in equal shares, their heirs and assigns my own allotment No. 584 described as the East one-half (1/2) of the South West quarter (1/4) of Section 23, Township 36 N., Range 3 West Boise Meridian containing Eighty (80) acres and all of my interest in the allotment of my deceased husband Philip Heyume toe lote Nez Perce allottee No. 583 described as the North East quarter (1/4) of the North East quarter (1/4) and the South West quarter (1/4) of the South East quarter (1/4) of section 23 and the South East quarter (1/4) of the South East quarter (1/4) of section 14, all in Township 36 North Range 3 West, Boise Meridian containing one hundred twenty acres.

NATIVE AMERICAN WILLS and PROBATE RECORDS, 1911 - 1921

My reason for making this Will are that I wish my property to go to my daughter and my granddaughter and that there shall be no misunderstandings after I am gone.

In Witness Whereof I have set my hand and seal this 29 day of March in the year of our Lord, One Thousand Nine Hundred and Fourteen.

                                                                  her
Witnesses: Laura We-yah-lah-home thumb
                                                                  mark

    S. J. Maxwell
    Sam Morris Jr.

The foregoing instrument was at the date hereof by the said Laura We yah lah home, signed sealed and published and declared to be her last Will and Testament in the presence of us, who at her request, and in her presence and in the presence of each other have subscribed our names as witnesses hereto.

                                          S. J. Maxwell
                                          Sam Morris Jr.

Department of The Interior,
Office of Indian Affairs
Washington, D.C.   OCT 10, 1914

It is recommended that the within will be approved pursuant to the provisions of the Act of June 25, 1910 (36 Stats. L., 855-6) as amended by the Act of February 14, 1913 (37 Stat. 678).

                                          Respectfully,
                                          E.B. Meritt
                                          Assistant Commissioner

Department of The Interior,
Office of the Secretary
Washington, D.C.   OCT 14, 1914

The within will is hereby approved pursuant to the provisions of the Act of June 25, 1910 (36 Stats. L., 855-6) as amended by Act of February 14, 1913 (37 Stat. 678).

                                          Bo Sweeney
                                          Assistant Secretary

NATIVE AMERICAN WILLS and PROBATE RECORDS, 1911 - 1921

Last Will and Testament of Peter Wakasheya.

I, **PETER WAKASHEYA**, of Greenwood, South Dakota, County of Charles Mix, being of sound mind and memory, do hereby make, publish and declare this to be my last will and testament.

First: I give and bequeath to my beloved wife, Julia Wakasheya, all of my allotment number 20, described as follows: NE/4 of the SW/4, NW/4 of the SE/4, Lots 5 and 6, all in Section 33, Twp. 94, North of Range 62, West of the 5th P.M., containing 167.16 acres, to be held in trust by her and for her sole use so long as she lives, and upon her death to be divided equally among my surviving Grandchildren.

Second: I give and bequeath to my wife all of my personal property consisting of horses, farm mplements, wagons, and all property that I may have, with the exception of one gray mare which I bequeath to my son, Andrew Makeke.

Third: I hereby appoint C. M. Conger as executor of this Will.

IN TESTIMONY WHEREOF, I have set my hand and seal by thumb mark, written by W.F. McCown, Lease Clerk, at my home, 12 miles east of Greenwood, South Dakota, this 10th day of May, 1914.

                                                                His
                              Peter Wakasheya   thumb
                                                                  mark

Signed, Sealed, Published and Declared this 10th day of May, 1914, by the said Peter Wakasheya, in our presence, as and for his last will testament and at his request and in his presence and in the presence of each other we have subscribed our names as witnesses hereto.

<u>Homer Redlightning</u>, Greenwood, S.Dak.
      Interpreter.
   <u>John Selwyn</u> , Greenwood, S.Dak.

Department of The Interior,
Office of Indian Affairs
Washington, D.C.   SEP 23 1914
It is recommended that the within will be approved pursuant to the provisions of the Act of June 25, 1910 (36 Stats. L., 855-6) as amended by the Act of February 14, 1913 (37 Stat. 678).

                                      Respectfully,
                                      E.B. Meritt
                                      Assistant Commissioner

NATIVE AMERICAN WILLS and PROBATE RECORDS, 1911 - 1921

Department of The Interior,
Office of the Secretary
Washington, D.C.   SEPT 24 1914

The within will is hereby approved pursuant to the provisions of the Act of June 25, 1910 (36 Stats. L., 855-6) as amended by Act of February 14, 1913 (37 Stat. 678).

Bo Sweeney
Assistant Secretary

<<<<<<<<>>>>>>>>

LAST WILL AND TESTAMENT

of

BELORE CHINO

I, **BELORE CHINO**, Jicarilla Apache allottee number 110 on the Jicarilla Apache Indian Reservation, residing at Dulce, New Mexico, being in possession of a sound mind and entire judgment, of the age of eighty-three years, and in all respects qualified to execute a will under the laws of the Territory of New Mexico and Section 2 of the Act of Congress of June 25, 1910 (36 Stat., 855-858), desiring to recognize the devotion of my grand-daughter, Tonito Chino Vicenti, wife of Edward Ladd Vicenti, of Dulce, New Mexico, and to reward her for her painstaking, kind and generous care and treatment of me during my declining years, and especially for her constant care and support of me furing the past two years during which period I have been afflicted with blindness, do hereby give, devise and bequeath to my said grand-daughter, Tonito Chino Vincenti, daughter of my deceased son Lorenzo Chino, Sr., and wife of Edward Ladd Vincenti, of Dulce, New Mexico, all of my right, title and interest in and to the following described lands now held in trust for the period of twenty-five years by the United States Government, viz: The north half of Section fourteen and the southeast quarter of Section ten in Township twent-nine north of Range one west, and the northwest quarter of the southwest quarter of the northwest quarter of the northwest quarter of Section twenty-two in Township twenty-nine north of Range two west of the New Mexico Principal Meridian, New Mexico, containing four hundred, eighty-two and fifty-hundredths acres, more or less, the said Tonito Chino Vincenti, of Dulce, New Mexico, to become possessed of said premises at my death.

I hereby designate Edward Ladd Vincenti, of Dulce, New Mexico, as the executor of this, my will, to act without bond, and request that he shall acept the appointment and faithfully and punctually discharge the duties of the office and execute the aforementioned provisions of my will.

NATIVE AMERICAN WILLS and PROBATE RECORDS, 1911 - 1921

I request that the subscribing witnesses hereto shall sign my name hereto and in affixing my mark hereon I acknowledge that such execution has been made at my request and with my consent in my presence and in the presence of the subscribing witnesses.

Done at Dulce, New Mexico, this sixteenth day of February, 1911.
Signed & sealed in the presence of:

		her
Edward Ladd Vincenti	BELORE CHINO	(thumb)
Address Dulce, N.M.		mark

Emmet Wirt
Address Dulce, N.M.

Louis M. Salazar
Address Dulce, N.M.

Department of The Interior,
Office of Indian Affairs
Washington   Mar 6 1911

I hereby recommend that the inclosed[sic] will be approved so far as it relates to the original allotment of the devisor still remaining in trust.

(Signed) C.F. HAUKE
Acting Commissioner

Mar 7 1911

Approved as recommended:

(Signed) Frank Pierce
First Assistant Secretary

(COPY)

WILL

I, **COMES IN SIGHT** of Pine Ridge Agency, South Dakota, Allottee number 4922 do hereby make and declare this to be my last will and testament, in accordance with Section 2 of the Act of June 25, 1910, (36 Stat. 855-858) hereby revoking all former wills made by me:

1.   I heeby direct that, as soon as possible after my decease, that all my debts and funeral and testamentary expenses be paid out of my personal estate.

2.   I give and devise my allotment on the Pine Ridge Reservation, South Dakota, described as follows:

NATIVE AMERICAN WILLS and PROBATE RECORDS, 1911 - 1921

    S/2 of Sec. 10, T. 39, R 35 W of 6th P.M.
    S/2 of Sec. 9, T. 39, R 35 W of 6th P.M.

in the following manner:

    To Matilda Surrounded, nee Red Track, grand-daughter, SE/4 of Sec. 9, T 39, R 35 W of 6th P.M.
    To Jacob White Cow Killer, Step-son, SW/4 of Sec. 9, T 39, R 35 W of 6th P.M.
    To White Wolf, cousin and to Iron Bear, nephew (in equal shares) SW/4 of Sec. 10, T 39, R 35 W of 6th P.M.

3.   of my personal property of whatsoever and wheresoever situated unto

4.   All the rest of my property, real or personal, now possessed or hereafter acquired, or whatsoever nature and wheresoever situated, I hereby give, devise and bequeath unto

    To Matilda Surrounded, nee Red Track.

    In witness whereof I have hereunto set my hand this day 25th of October 1913.
                                                      her
                                     Comes In Sight thumb
                                                         mark

    The above statement was, this 25th day of October 1913, signed and published by Comes In Sight as her last will and testament, in the joint presence of the undersigned, the said Comes In Sight then being of sound and vigorous mind and free from any constraint or compulsion; whereupon we, being without any interest in the matter other than friendship, and being well acquainted with her, but not members of her family, immediately subscribed our names hereto in the presence of each other and of the said testator, for the purpose of attesting the said will, as she requested us to do, and that, I, H. E. Wright, at the request of the Testatrix, affixed her name in ink and she attached her thumb-mark.

                                                           Post-Office address
(Signed) H.E. Wright, Farmer, Pine Ridge Agency   South Dakota
    Thomas High Pine, Policeman, Pine Ridge Agency   South Dakota.

                                                      Pine Ridge, South Dakota.
                                                     June 1, 1914.

    I hereby certify that I have fully inquired into the mental competency of the Indian, signing the above will; the circumstances attending the execution of the will; the influence that may have induced its execution, and the names of those entitled to share in the estate under the law of descent in South Dakota; reasons for the disposition of the property proposed by the will, differing from disposition had the property descended.

NATIVE AMERICAN WILLS and PROBATE RECORDS, 1911 - 1921

I respectfully forward the will, above, with the recommendation that it be approved.

Signed: John R. Brennan.
Supt. & Spl. Disb. Agent

Department of The Interior,
Office of Indian Affairs
OCT. 20, 1914.

The within will of Comes in Sight is recommended for approval in accordance with the Act of June 25, 1910 (36 Stats. L., 855-6) as amended by the Act of February 14, 1913 (37 Stat. 678).

Signed: E.B. Meritt
Assistant Commissioner

Department of The Interior,
Office of the Secretary
OCT. 21, 1914.

The within will of Comes In Sight is approved in accordance with the Act of June 25, 1910 (36 Stats. L., 855-6) as amended by Act of February 14, 1913 (37 Stat. 678).

Signed: Bo Sweeney
Assistant Secretary

WILL

I, **AMBROS HERNANDEZ** of Pine Ridge Agency, South Dakota, Allottee number 1409 do hereby make and declare this to be my last will and testament, in accordance with Section 2 of the Act of June 25, 1910 (36 Stat. 855-858) hereby revoking all former wills made by me.

1. I hereby direct that, as soon as possible after my decease, that all my debts and funeral and testamentary expenses be paid out of my personal estate.

2. I give and devise my allotment on the Pine Ridge Reservation, South Dakota, described as follows:

W1/2 of Sec. 26 Twp. 39N of Range 42 W. of 6th P.M. So. Dak. containing 320 acres.

in the following manner: The N.W. 1/4 of Sec. 26 Twp. 39N of Range 42 W. of 6th P.M. So. Dak. to be given to my wife Sophia Hernandez. The N 1/2 of S.W. 1/4 of Sec. 26 Twp. 39N of Range 42 W. of 6th P.M. So. Dak. to be given to my son Joseph Hernandez. The S. 1/2 of the S.W. 1/4 of Sec. 26 Twp. 39N. of Range 42 W. of the 6th P.M. So. Dak. to be given to my daughter Cecelia Hernandez.

NATIVE AMERICAN WILLS and PROBATE RECORDS, 1911 - 1921

Ambrose Hernandez.

3. I give and bequeath all of my personal property of whatsoever nature and wheresoever situated unto
My daughter Cecelia to receive 4 cows two 2 yr. old heifers, three mares and one colt, this stock to be branded with C in front of the brand already on animals.
My son Joseph to feceive five head of cattle and one mare and colt, all to be branded with J in front of the brand already on these animals.

4. All the rest of my property, real or personal, now possessed or hereafter acquired, or[sic] whatsoever nature and wheresoever situated, I hereby give, devise and bequeath unto
My wife Sophia Hernandez.
Ambrose Hernandez.   Witness: John S. Lindley

In witness whereof I have hereunto set my hand this day 24th of June 1913.
Witness: <u>Judson Shook</u>
District Farmer.

The above statement was, this 24th day of June 1913, signed and published by Ambros Hernandez as his last will and testament, in the joint presence of the undersigned, the said Ambros Hernandez then being of sound and vigorous mind and free from any constraint or compulsion; whereupon we, being without any interest in the matter other than friendship, and being well acquainted with him, but not members of his family, immediately subscribed our names hereto in the presence of each other and of the said testator, for the purpose of attesting the said will, as he requested us to do.

Chas. Clifford, Sr.   Post Office address.
J. S. Lindley   Scenic, So. Dak.
                             "   "   "

Pine Ridge, South Dakota,
June 24th 1913.

I hereby certify that I have fully inquired into the mental competency of the Indian, signing the above will; the circumstances attending the execution of the will; the influence that may have induced its execution, and the names of those entitled to share in the estate under the law of descent in South Dakota; reasons for the disposition of the property proposed by the will, differing from disposition had the property descended.

I respectfully forward the will, above, with the recommendation that it be approved.

NATIVE AMERICAN WILLS and PROBATE RECORDS, 1911 - 1921

Approved:
John R. Brennan.
Superintendent.

Judson Shook
Farmer

May 26, 1914.

This is to certify that Jusson Shook, Farmer, acted in the above as my personal representative, and I hereby make his action my own.

John R. Brennan
Supt. & Spl. Disb. Agent

Office of Indian Affairs
OCT. 24 1914

The within will of Ambros Hernandez is recommended for approval in accordance with the provisions of the Act of June 25, 1910 (36 Stats. L., 855-6) as amended by the Act of February 14, 1913 (37 Stat. 678).

E.B. Meritt
Assistant Commissioner

Department of The Interior,
Office of the Secretary
OCT. 27 1914.

The within will of Ambros Hernandez is approved in accordance with the provisions of the Act of June 25, 1910 (36 Stats. L., 855-6) as amended by Act of February 14, 1913 (37 Stat. 678).

Bo Sweeney
Assistant Secretary

<<<<<<<>>>>>>>

WILL OF LOUIS BENOIST
GRANTING AND DEVISING HIS ALLOT-
MENT OF LAND ON THE CHEYENNE
RIVER INDIAN RESERVATION

I, **LOUIS BENOIST**, a resident of Dewey County, State of South Dakota, and residing upon the Cheyenne Indian Reservation and a member of the Cheyenne River Tribe of Sioux Indians, being of sound mind and disposing memory and being over twenty-one years of age, do hereby make, publish and declare this instrument as and for my last Will and Testament, so far as the same may apply to my allotment of land on the Cheyenne River Indian Reservation in said State of South Dakota, said allotment having been made under the provisions of the statutes of the United States, and said allotment being described as follows, to-wit:

Allotment numbered two, being the Northwest Quarter, the West

NATIVE AMERICAN WILLS and PROBATE RECORDS, 1911 - 1921

half of the Northeast Quarter, and the Lots One and Two of Section Twenty-eight in Township Sixteen North of Range Thirty-one East; and the East half of the Northwest Quarter, the South half of the Northeast Quarter, the North half of the Southeast Quarter, and the East half of the Northeast Quarter of the Southwest Quarter of Section Sixteen, and the Southwest Quarter of the Northwest Quarter and the Northwest Quarter of the Southwest Quarter of Section Fifteen in Township Sixteen North of Range Twenty-four East of the Black Hills Meridian, South Dakota, containing Six Hundred Forty-one and Eighty-eight Hundredths acres:

I

I hereby give, grant, devise and bequeath unto my beloved wife, Mary Agnes Benoist, should she survive me, that portion of my said allotment containing about Three Hundred One and Eighty-eight Hundredths acres, upon which I now reside, described as follows; to-wit:

The Northwest Quarter, the West Half of the Northeast Quarter, and the Lots One and Two of Section Twenty-eight in Township Sixteen North of Range Thirty-one East of the Black Hills Meridian, South Dakota.

II

I also give, devise, grant and bequeath unto my said wife, Mary Agnes Benoist, should she survive me, an undivided one-half interest in and to the balance of my said allotment, described as follows, to-wit:

The East Half of the Northwest Quarter, the South Half of the Northeast Quarter, the North half of the Southeast Quarter, and the East Half of the Northeast Quarter of the Southwest Quarter of Section Sixteen; and the Southwest Quarter of the Northwest Quarter and the Northwest Quarter of the Southwest Quarter of Section Fifteen in Township Sixteen, North of Range Twenty-four East of the Black Hills Meridian, South Dakota.

III

The rest, residue and remainder of my said allotment, being an undivided one-half interest in and to the following described real estate, to-wit:
The East Half of the Northwest Quarter, the South Half of the Northeast Quarter, the North Half of the Southeast Quarter, and the East Half of the Northeast Quarter of the Southwest Quarter of Section Sizteen; and the Southwest Quarter of the Northwest Quarter and the Northwest Quarter of the Southwest

NATIVE AMERICAN WILLS and PROBATE RECORDS, 1911 - 1921

Quarer of Section Fifteen in Township Sixteen North of Range Twenty-four East of the Black Hills Meridian, South Dakota.

I hereby give, grant, devise and bequeath to the children who may be living at the time of my death, of William Benoist, a deceased brother, Narcisse Benoist, a deceased brother, Katherine Traversie, a deceased sister, and Ambrose Benoist, brother, as follows, viz:

An undivided one-fourth interest therein to the children of said William Benoist; an undivided one-fourth interest therein to the children of Said Narcisse Benoist; an undivided one-fourth interest therein to the children of the said Katherine Traversie; and an undivided one-fourth interest therein to the children of the said Ambrose Benoist.

Should, at the time of my death, there be no children living of any one or more of my said brothers or sister, then the share, or shares, which would have gone to such children if living, shall be added to the interest to be divided among the living children of my other brothers or sister, by right of representation.

IV

Should there be no children living, at the time of my decease, of my said brothers and dister, then and in that event I hereby give, grant, devise and bequeath unto my said beloved wife, Mary Agnes Benoist, all of my said allotment of land.

V

Should my said wife, Mary Agnes Benoist, be dead at the time of my decease, and I leave no wife living, but there be children living of any or all of my said brothers and sister, then I hereby give, grant devise and bequeath all of my said allotment to the children of my said brothers and sister, by right of representation; but should I leave a wife living other than said Mary Agnes Benoist, then and in that event, I give, grant, devise and bequeath unto such living wife the portions of my said allotment which are herein given, granted, devised and bequeathed to the said Mary Agnes Benoist.

IV

Should I, at the time of my death, leave no wife, and all the children of my said brothers and sister be dead, then and in that event, I hereby give, grant, devise and bequeath all of my said allotment of land to my heirs.

IN TESTIMONY WHEREOF, I, Louis Benoist, do hereto subscribe my name in the presence of the attesting witnesses, Orson A. Leonard and George Thwing, of Timber Lake, South Dakota, and do hereby acknowledge and declare that the foregoing instrument, consisting of three and one-half pages of typewritten matter, containing one hundred fourteen lines, is my last Will and

NATIVE AMERICAN WILLS and PROBATE RECORDS, 1911 - 1921

Testament, in so far as relates to my said allotment of land, and I further declare that the two said witnesses attest my signature at my request and in my presence and in the presence of each other.

Dated, Timber Lake, South Dakota. November 22nd in the Year of our Lord One Thousand Nine Hundred Thirteen.

(Signed) LOUIS BENOIST (Seal)

The above instrument was, at the date thereof, subscribed by said Louis Benoist in the presence of us and each of us and he, at the time of making such subscription, acknowledged that he executed the same and declared said instrument, so subscribed by him, to be his last Will and Testament, so far as the same relates to his allotment of land, whereupon we then and there, at his request and in his presence and in the presence of each other, subscribed our names in witness thereof.

Name	Residence
Orson A. Leonard	Timber Lake, So. Dakota
George Thwing	Timber Lake, So. Dakota

Department of The Interior,
Office of Indian Affairs
    Oct 6 1914

The within will of Louis Benoist is recommended for approval in accordance with the Act of June 25, 1910 (36 Stats. L., 855-6) as amended by the Act of February 14, 1913 (37 Stat. 678).

(Signed) E.B. Meritt
Assistant Commissioner

Department of The Interior,
Office of the Secretary
    Oct 29 1914

The within will of Louis Benoist is approved in accordance with the Act of June 25, 1910 (36 Stats. L., 855-6) as amended by Act of February 14, 1913 (37 Stat. 678).

(Signed) Bo Sweeney
Assistant Secretary

(COPY)

LAST WILL AND TESTAMENT
of
WILLIAM RED THUNDER

IN THE NAME OF GOD, Amen.

I, **WILLIAM RED THUNDER**, of the Crow Creek reservation, South Dakota, being of sound mind, memory and understanding, do hereby make and

NATIVE AMERICAN WILLS and PROBATE RECORDS, 1911 - 1921

publish this my last will and testament, hereby revoking and annulling all wills by me heretofore made, in manner and form following, that is to say:

FIRST: I direct that all my just debts and funeral expenses, and the expenses of my last illness, shall be paid by my executor hereinafter named as soon after my decease as shall be convenient.

SECOND: I give, devise, and bequeath to my wife, Anna Red Thunder, the whole of my own allotment on the Crow Creek reservation, described as the West half of the Southwest quarter of Section 21 in Township 108 North of Range 71 West, containing 80 acres; I also give, devise and bequeath to my said wife Anna Red Thunder the whole of the South half of the Northeast quarter of Section 31 in Township 109 North of Rangew 74 West, containing 80 acres, the same being one-half of the land allotted to my daughter Rose Red Thunder now deceased; I also give and bequeath to my said wife Anna Red Thunder one of my mares and her colt and the wagon and the harness issued to me by the Government last August, and any and all moneys remaining on deposit to my credit under the supervision of the Superintendent of the Crow Creek Indian School.

THIRD: I give, devise, and bequeath to my sister, Agnes Red Thunder, the whole of the North half of the Northeast quarter of Sedtion 31 in Township 109 North of Range 74 West, containing 80 acres, the same being one-half of the land allotten to my daughter Rose Red Thunder now deceased; I also give and bequeath to my said sister Agnes Red Thunder one of my mares and her colt issued to my by the Government last August, and my said sister is to have her choice of the mares.

FOURTH: I give, devise and bequeath to my only living child, Celeste Red Thunder, the whole of my interest in the lands allotted to Alma How, my deceased wife, the said lands allotted to Alma How being described as the Northeast quarter of Section 36 in Township 106 North of Range 71 West, on the Crow Creek reservation. My said daughter, Celeste Red Thunder, has been legally adopted by Ellen How, a sister of my deceased wife Alma How, and is in her charge and care.

AND LASTLY: I do hereby nominate, constitute and appoint the Reverend H. Burt, of Crow Creek, South Dakota, executor of this my last will and testament.

IN TESTIMONY WHEREOF: I have hereunto set my hand and seal to this my last will and testament at my father's house on the Crow Creek reservation, South Dakota, this 31st day of March, A.D. 1913.

(Signed) WILLIAM RED THUNDER

NATIVE AMERICAN WILLS and PROBATE RECORDS, 1911 - 1921

SIGNED, SEALED, PUBLISHED AND DECLARED by the said William Red Thunder in our presence as and for his last will and testament, and at his request and in his presence and in the presence of each other, we have hereunto subscribed our names as attesting witnesses hereto.

(Signed) ERNEST J. ALLEY, Residence, Crow Creek, S.D.
(Signed) RUSSELL HARRISON, Residence, Crow Creek, S.D.
(Signed) HOMER J. BIBB, Residence, Crow Creek, S.D.

Department of The Interior,
Office of Indian Affairs
Washington, D.C.   OCT. 19, 1914.

It is recommended that the within will be approved pursuant to the provisions of the Act of June 25, 1910 (36 Stats. L., 855-6) as amended by the Act of February 14, 1913 (37 Stat. 678).

Respectfully,
(Signed) E.B. Meritt
Assistant Commissioner

Department of The Interior,
Office of the Secretary
Washington, D.C.   Oct. 22, 1914.

The within will is hereby approved pursuant to the provisions of the Act of June 25, 1910 (36 Stats. L., 855-6) as amended by Act of February 14, 1913 (37 Stat. 678).

(Signed) BO SWEENEY
Assistant Secretary

<<<<<<<>>>>>>
C O P Y.

LAST WILL AND TESTAMENT.

I, **LULU OLD PLUM**, a member of the Rosebud tribe of Indians, residing in Todd County, South Dakota, being of sound mind and memory, and being now in ill health, do hereby make, publish and declare this to be my last will and testament.

First. I am the daughter of Old Plum, deceased, and Gets Mad Old Plum, members of the Rosebud tribe of Indians, and am now about 23 years of age.

Second. I state and declare that I was married about September 1913 to Cleveland High Bull, a member of the Pine Ridge tribe of Indians; that the said High Bull did ill treaties of 1835-6-46 me while we lived together, and that about February 1914 he left me, taking some of my property away and that I have not

NATIVE AMERICAN WILLS and PROBATE RECORDS, 1911 - 1921

seen him or lived with him since then. I further state and declare that I have never been married other than as stated herein and that I have never had any children.

Third. I further state and declare that I am now the owner of Indian allotment No. 3670, SW/4 of Section 16, Township 37, Range 29, Todd County, S.D., containing 160 acres, and that I am part heir to my father's allotment, containing 320 acres, and through my father a part heir to the allotment of my deceased brother, John Old Plum, containing 160 acres.

Fourth. I further state and declare that I am now the owner of two mares and colts, two cows and calves, one buggy and one set of harness.

Fifth. I do hereby give and bequeath unto my husband, the said Cleveland High Bull, ten dollars ($10.00), to be paid him from any of the proceeds of my estate, which shall be his only and and sole share in any property or estate left by me.

Sixth. I do hereby give and bequeath unto my mother, the said Gets Mad Old Plum, all property, both real and personal, left by me after the ten dollars willed to my husband as set forth above has been paid, and to her heirs and assigns to have and to hold forever. This shall include any share in the estate of my father and my brother (both deceased) as set forth above.

In testimony whereof I have attached my signature by affixing my thumb-mark hereto, this the 19th day of August in the year of Our Lord, ninteen hundred and fourteen, near St. Francis, Todd County, South Dakota.   Her
                                                Lulu Old Plum (thumb)
                                                Mark

We, the undersigned, do hereby certify that we were present on the day of the date above written and witnesses the making and execution of the last will and testament of Lulu Old Plum, all as set forth above, and that such will was made at her request and in accordance with her wishes and that we have signed as witnesses hereto at her request. Correction "Plum" made before signing.

        (Signed) Charles L. Davis, of Rosebud, South Dakota.
        (Signed) William R. Bebout of Rosebud, South Dakota.
        (Signed) Clement W. Soldier of Rosebud, South Dakota.
                                                              Interpreter.

Department of The Interior,
Office of Indian Affairs
Washington, D.C.   OCT. 1, 1914.

It is recommended that the within will be approved pursuant to the provisions of the Act of June 25, 1910 (36 Stats. L., 855-6) as amended by the Act of February 14, 1913 (37 Stat. 678).

NATIVE AMERICAN WILLS and PROBATE RECORDS, 1911 - 1921

Department of The Interior,
Office of the Secretary
Washington, D.C.

Oct. 2, 1914.

Respectfully,
(Signed) E.B. MERITT
Assistant Commissioner

The within will is hereby approved pursuant to the provisions of the Act of June 25, 1910 (36 Stats. L., 855-6) as amended by Act of February 14, 1913 (37 Stat. 678).

(Signed) BO SWEENEY
Assistant Secretary

<<<<<<<<>>>>>>>

LAST WILL AND TESTAMENT
of
ZIWIN.

IN THE NAME OF GOD, AMEN.

I, **ZIWIN**, of Fort Totten, North Dakota, being of sound mind, memory and understanding, do hereby make and publish this my last Will and Testament, hereby revoking and annulling all wills by me heretofore made, in manner and form following, that is to say:

FIRST, I direct that all my just debts and funeral expenses and expenses of my last illness shall be paid by my executor hereinafter named as soon after my decease as shall be convenient;

Second, I give devise and bequeath to Theresa Little Ghost, or Tiyowakanhdiwin, my daughter, that part of my allotment of land situated on the Devils Lake Reservation, North Dakota described as the Southwest quarter of the Southwest quarter of Sec. 22, Twp. 151 N. R. 65 W. 5th P.M.

To Matthias Comingcloud, my adopted son, the southeast quarter of southwest, Sec. 23, Twp. 151, N.R. 65 and to Sunkahowaste, my husband, the South half of Southeast Quarter of Sec. 14, Twp. 151, N. Rg. 65, W. 5th Prin. Meridian.

THIRD, All the rest and residue of my estate, both real, personal and mixed, I give, devise, and bequeath to my legal heirs.

AND LASTLY, I do hereby nominate, constitute and appoint Sunkahowaste executor of this my last Will and Testament.

NATIVE AMERICAN WILLS and PROBATE RECORDS, 1911 - 1921

IN TESTIMONY WHEREOF, I have set my hand and seal to this, my last Will and Testament, at Fort Totten, North Dakota this 7th day of February, in the year of our Lord 1913.

                                                          Her
                                           Ziwin Thumb
                                                Mark.

Signed, Sealed, Published and Declared by the said Ziwin in our presence, as and for her last Will and Testament, and at her request and in her presence, and in the presence of each other, we have hereunto subscribed our names at attesting witnesses hereto.

(Signed) MARTIN STRAIT, INTERPRETER   (Signed) HARRY W. CAMP
Residence, Fort Totten, N. Dak.   Residence, Fort Totten, N. Dak.

(Signed) A. R. WARNER   (Signed) C. M. ZIEBACH
Residence, Fort Totten, N. Dak.   Residence, Fort Totten, N. Dak.

Department of The Interior,
Office of Indian Affairs   NOV. 7, 1914

It is respectfully recommended that the within will be approved in accordance with the provisions of the Act of June 25, 1910 (36 Stats. L., 855-6) as amended by the Act of February 14, 1913 (37 Stat. 678).

                                       Respectfully,
                                       (Signed) E.B. MERITT
                                       Assistant Commissioner

Department of The Interior,
Office of the Secretary   NOV. 10, 1914

The within will is hereby approved in accordance with the provisions of the Act of June 25, 1910 (36 Stats. L., 855-6) as amended by Act of February 14, 1913 (37 Stat. 678).

                                       (Signed) BO SWEENEY
                                       Assistant Secretary

I, **LONE WOLF**, of the Pine Ridge Reservation, South Dakota, do hereby make and declare this to be my last will and testament, in accordance with the provisions of "An Act to provide for determining the heirs of deceased Indians, etc. etc. approved June 25, 1910 (Public - 313), hereby revoking all former wills made by me:

I give and devise to James Wilde, of Interior, South Dakota, the south half of Section five, township 42 north, range 38 west of the sixth P.M. in South

NATIVE AMERICAN WILLS and PROBATE RECORDS, 1911 - 1921

Dakota, being a portion of my allotment No. 3773, which is held in trust for me by the United States;

    In witness where of I have hereunto set my hand this twenty-third day of August, 1910.
His
Lone Wolf thumb
mark

    The above instrument, was, this twenty-third day of August, A.D. 1910, signed, sealed and published, by Lone Wolf, as his last will and testament, in the joint presence of the undersigned, the said Lone Wolf then being of sound mind and free from any constraint or compulsion; whereupon we, being without interest in the matter other than friendship, and being well acquainted with him, but not members of his family, immediately subscribed our names hereto in the presence of each other and of the said testator, for the purpose of attesting the said will, as he requested us to do.

                                 John R. Brennen Pine Ridge, S.D.
                                 Wm. Bergen   Pine Ridge, S.D.

    I hereby certify that I have fully inquired into the mental competency of the Indian, signing the above will; the circumstances attending the execution of the will; the influence that may have induced its execution, and the names of those entitled to share in the estate under the law of descent in South Dakota; reasons for the disposition of the property proposed by the will, differing from disposition had the property descended.

    I respectfully forward the will, above, with the recommendation that it be _____ approved.

                                 John R. Brennan.
                                 Supt. & Spl. Disb. Agent

Department of The Interior,
Office of Indian Affairs   OCT. 24, 1914.

The within will of Lone Wolf is recommended for approval in accordance with the Act of June 25, 1910 (36 Stats. L., 855-6) as amended by the Act of February 14, 1913 (37 Stat. 678).

                               E.B. Meritt
                               Assistant Commissioner

Department of The Interior, NOV 14, 1914
Office of the Secretary

The within will of Lone Wolf is approved in accordance with the Act of June 25, 1910 (36 Stats. L., 855-6) as amended by Act of February 14, 1913 (37 Stat. 678).

                               Bo Sweeney
                               Assistant Secretary

NATIVE AMERICAN WILLS and PROBATE RECORDS, 1911 - 1921

<<<<<<<<>>>>>>>

WILL.

LAST WILL AND TESTAMENT OF
EAT NO MEAT, OR NOOK-TI-SHE-MAY, C-345.

IN THE NAME OF GOD, AMEN.

I, **EAT NO MEAT, or NOOK-TI-SHE-MAY** of the Umatilla reservation, Oregon, being of sound mind, memory and understanding, do hereby make and publish this my last will and testament, hereby revoking and annulling all wills by me heretofore made, in manner and form following, that is to say:

FIRST, I direct that all my just debts and funeral expenses, and expenses of my last illness shall be paid from funds held by the U.S. Government for me, and that this action shall be taken as soon after my death as shall be convenient;

SECOND, I give, devise, and bequeth[sic] to my wife, Tal-te-a-kown, my allotment, Cayuse 345, described as the South West quarter of Section 29, Township 3 N., Range 35, EWM., in the State of Oregon, containing 160 acres.

THIRD, I give to John Mathews of Nez Perce Reseration, my interest in the allotment of Elametnonmi, deceased Cayuse allottee No. 344., described as the South West quarter of the NW/4 and the SE/4 of NW/4 of Sec. 29, T. 3, N. R. 35, EWM- 80 acres.

IN TESTIMONY WHEREOF: I have set my hand and seal to this, my last will and testament, at my home on the Umatilla Indian reservation, this 21st day of August 1914.

His
Eat No Meat. (Thumb)
Mark.

Signed, sealed, published and declared by the said Eat No Meat in our presence, as and for his last will and testament, and at his request, and in his presence, and in the presence of each other, we have hereunto subscribed our names as attesting witnesses thereto.

Leo Sampson
E. K. Swartzlander
Carrie Bergeven

Department of The Interior,
Office of Indian Affairs   November 21, 1914

The within will of Eat No Meat or Nook-Ti-She-May, is recommended for approval in accordance with the Act of June 25, 1910 (36 Stats. L., 855-6) as amended by the Act of February 14, 1913 (37 Stat. 678).

NATIVE AMERICAN WILLS and PROBATE RECORDS, 1911 - 1921

E.B. Meritt
Assistant Commissioner

Department of The Interior,
Office of the Secretary

November 24, 1914

The within will of Eat No Meat or Nook-Ti-She-May, is approved in accordance with the Act of June 25, 1910 (36 Stats. L., 855-6) as amended by Act of February 14, 1913 (37 Stat. 678).

Bo Sweeney
Assistant Secretary

<<<<<<<<>>>>>>>

The Last Will and Testament of Nancy Zimmerman
of Santee. Neb.

I, **NANCY ZIMMERMAN**, of Santee, Nebraska, do hereby make, publish and declare this my last will and testament in words and figures following:

I give and devise unto my daughter, Lillian Mary, one-half of all funds coming to me as an heir in the estate of my deceased father, Ben Zimmerman, and one-half to Mrs. Ellis Campbell on account of her care for me and my child during my recent sickness and on account of future care which she has promised to give to my child Lillian Mary.

Dated this 26th day of February, 1914, at Santee, Nebraska.

WITNESSES: Nancy Zimmerman
   F.E. McIntyre
   Guy W. Holmes

We, whose names are hereunto subscribed do hereby certify that Nancy Zimmerman, the testator, subscribed her name to this instrument in our presence, and in the presence of each of us, and declared at the same time, in our presence and hearing, that this instrument was her last will and testament, and we, at her request, sign our names hereunto in her presence at[sic] witnesses.

F. E. McIntyre
Guy W. Holmes

Department of The Interior,
Office of Indian Affairs

It is respectfully recommended that the within will be approved in pursuance to the provisions of the Act of June 25, 1910 (36 Stats. L., 855-6) as amended by the Act of February 14, 1913 (37 Stat. 678).

NATIVE AMERICAN WILLS and PROBATE RECORDS, 1911 - 1921

E.B. Meritt
Assistant Commissioner

Department of The Interior,
Office of the Secretary

DEC -8 1914

The within will is hereby approved in pursuance to the provisions of the Act of June 25, 1910 (36 Stats. L., 855-6) as amended by Act of February 14, 1913 (37 Stat. 678).

Bo Sweeney
Assistant Secretary

I, **RED ELK No. 2**, of Pine Ridge Agency, South Dakota, Allottee number 1708 do hereby make and declare this to be my last will and testament, in accordance with Section 2 of the Act of June 25, 1910 (36 Stat. 855-858), and Act of February 14, 1913, (Public No. 381), hereby revoking all former wills made by me:

1. I hereby direct that, as soon as possible after my decease, that all my debts and funeral and testamentary expenses be paid out of my personal estate.

2. I give and devise my allotment on the Pine Ridge Reservation, South Dakota, described as follows:

    The E/2 of Sec. 24 in Twp. 40 N. of Range 40 west of the 6th
    Principal Meridian, South Dakota, containing 320 acres.

in the following manner:

    The NE/4 of Sec. 24 in T. 40, R. 40, to be distributed equally among my four children, Alex Yellow Wolf, Angeline Chief Eagle, Lucy Horse, and Mollie Old Horse.

    The SE/4 of Sec. 24 in T. 40, R. 40, which is now advertised for sale, if a buyer is found for same, I would like for it to be sold and the money used in caring for me while I live. If all of the money is not used, I give the money remaining after any funeral expenses are paid to my daughter, Lucy Horse. Should this land not sell, to my daughter, Lucy Horse.

3. I give and bequeath all of my personal property of whatsoever nature and wheresoever situated unto my four children, named above.

4. All the rest of my property, real or personal, now possessed or hereafter acquired, of whatsoever nature and wheresoever situated, I hereby give, devise and bequeath unto my four children.

NATIVE AMERICAN WILLS and PROBATE RECORDS, 1911 - 1921

In witness whereof I have hereunto set my hand this 17th day of March, 1914.
Witnesses:
    George A. Trotter   Red Elk No. 2 (her thumb mark)
    Peter Chief Eagle

    The above statement was, this 17th day of March, 1914, signed and published by Red Elk No. 2 as her last will and testament, in the joint presence of the undersigned, the said Red Elk No. 2 then being of sound and vigorous mind and free from any constraint or compulsion; whereupon we, being without any interest in the matter other than friendship, and being well acquainted with her but not members of her family, immediately subscribed our names hereto in the presence of each other and of the said testator, for the purpose of attesting the said will, as she requested us to do. Her name being signed by George A. Trotter, one of the witnesses, at her request.
    Witnesses: Post Office address.
        George A. Trotter   Kyle, S.D.
        Peter Chief Eagle   Kyle, S.D.

    I hereby certify that I have fully inquired into the mental competency of the Indian, signing the above will; the circumstances attending the execution of the will; the influence that may have induced its execution, and the names of those entitled to share in the estate under the law of descent in South Dakota; reasons for the disposition of the property proposed by the will, differing from disposition had the property descended.
    I respectfully forward the will with the recommendation that it be approved.
                               John R. Brennan.
                               Supt. & Spl. Disb. Agent

Department of The Interior,
Office of Indian Affairs   Dec 16 1914
Washington, D.C.

The above will is recommended for approval in accordance with the Act of June 25, 1910 (36 Stats. L., 855-6) as amended by the Act of February 14, 1913 (37 Stat. 678).
                             E.B. Meritt
                             Assistant Commissioner

Department of The Interior,   Dec 18 1914
Office of the Secretary
Washington, D.C.

The above will is hereby approved in accordance with the Act of June 25, 1910 (36 Stats. L., 855-6) as amended by Act of February 14, 1913 (37 Stat. 678).

NATIVE AMERICAN WILLS and PROBATE RECORDS, 1911 - 1921

Bo Sweeney
Assistant Secretary

<<<<<<<<>>>>>>>
(COPY)

Fort Yates, North Dakota.
June 13th, 1911.

I, **LOUIS EAGLEDOG** of the County of Morton, State of North Dakota, being of lawful age, and being aware of my rapidly declining health, but being of sound mind and memory, and being fully aware of the laws of Succession of the State of North Dakota, do make and declare this to be my last will and testament, in manner following, towit:

In consideration of the support, food and care given be by my half sister Mrs. Susan Frosted and her husband Thomas Frosted, for the past twenty seven years, I will and bequeath to the said Susan Frosted the SE1/4, Sec. 7, T. 130 N. R. 80 W. 5th P.M., to have and to hold and dispose of as her own. The balance of my land I desire to go to my lawful heirs as determined by existing law. All of my personal property, horses, cattle, implements, etc., I will and bequeath to my only living son, Philip Eagledog.

In witness whereof, I Louis Eagledog to this my last will and testament, have hereunto set my hand and seal this 13th day of June, in the year of our Lord, One Thousand Nine Hundred and Eleven;
His
(Signed) LouisThumb   Eagledog
Mark

Signed, sealed and declared by Louis Eagledog as and for his last will and testament, in the presence of him, who at his request and in his presence and in the presence of each other have hereunto subscribed our names as witnesses thereof.

(Signed) Philip Eagle dog   (Signed) Thomas Frosted
                                   (Signed) Annie Eagledog
                                   Witness to signature

Subscribed and sworn to before me this 13th day of June, 1911.
(Signed) J.Y. Hamilton
Superintendent

(Signed) Edward Afraid of Hawk
Interpreter and Witness to signature.

Department of The Interior,
Office of Indian Affairs
Washington, D.C.   DEC 18, 1914

NATIVE AMERICAN WILLS and PROBATE RECORDS, 1911 - 1921

It is respectfully recommended that the within will be approved according to the provisions of the Act of June 25, 1910 (36 Stats. L., 855-6) as amended by the Act of February 14, 1913 (37 Stat. 678) insofar as it applies to the SE1/4, Sec. 7, T. 130 N. of R. 80 W. of 5 P.M.

(Signed) E.B. MERITT
Assistant Commissioner

Department of The Interior,
Office of the Secretary
Washington, D.C.   DEC 19, 1914

The within will is hereby approved pursuant to the provisions of the Act of June 25, 1910 (36 Stats. L., 855-6) as amended by Act of February 14, 1913 (37 Stat. 678) insofar as it applies to the SE1/4, Sec. 7, T. 130 N. of R. 80 W. of 5 P.M.

(Signed) BO SWEENEY
Assistant Secretary

Colonial Beach, Virginia,
June 14, 1914

I, **WILLIAM GRANT**, this day June 14, 1914, will to my daughter, Jennie Longee five dollars: and I will five dollars to my daughter Maggie Grant. The balance of my personal estate and all of my real estate I will to my wife, Mary E. G. Grant.

Signed: I want Ignatius Court executor
Wm. Grant.   without bond.

Written by Beulah L. Blockiston,
Phar. D.

Witnesses:
    Mrs. Henderson
    Mrs. F. E. Gaither
    Beulah L. Blockiston, Phar. D.
        1331--8th St. N.W.
           Wash. D.C.

Department of The Interior,
Office of Indian Affairs
Washington, D.C.   Nov. 20, 1914

It is respectfully recommended that the within will be approved in so far as it relates to trust property over which this Department has jurisdiction in

NATIVE AMERICAN WILLS and PROBATE RECORDS, 1911 - 1921

accordance with the provisions of the Act of June 25, 1910 (36 Stats. L., 855-6) as amended by the Act of February 14, 1913 (37 Stat. 678).

(Signed) E.B. Meritt
Assistant Commissioner

Department of The Interior,
Office of the Secretary
Washington, D.C.

Dec. 28, 1914

The within will is hereby approved in so far as it relates to trust property over which this Department has jurisdiction in accordance with the provisions of the Act of June 25, 1910 (36 Stats. L., 855-6) as amended by Act of February 14, 1913 (37 Stat. 678).

(Signed) Bo Sweeney
Assistant Secretary

WILL

I, **FRANCES MILOT**, of Wanette, State of Oklahoma, being of sound mind and sensible of the uncertainties of life, and desiring to make this disposition of my property and affairs while in sound mind; do hereby publish and declare the following to be my last Will and testament, hereby revoking and cancelling all other or former wills by me at any time made:

I give and devise to my daughter, Louisa Weddle, the following described land towit: The Northwest 1/4 of the Southwest 1/4 of section 21, Township 6 North, Range 2 East Indian Meridian, Pottawatomie County, Oklahoma, containing 40 acres, more or less.

This gift and devise is made to my daughter, the said Louisa Weddle, in consideration of love and affections and that the said Louisa Weddle is to provide me a home and all the necessarys of life until my death, during which time Louisa Weddle is to have the use or rentals derived from above described land until my death, after which time, all my right, title and interest in the land is to pass to the said Louisa Weddle.

Should Louisa Weddle fail to provide me with a home and all the necessarys of life, the devise or gift would be void and revocable at the descretion of the Secretary of the Interior, when positive evidence of this fact was shown to him. It is also understood that this land is to be held in trust for the same length of time as specified in the trust patent.

NATIVE AMERICAN WILLS and PROBATE RECORDS, 1911 - 1921

In WITNESS WHEREOF, I have to this, my last will and testament, consisting of one sheet of paper for will and another on which names of witnesses are subscribed, subscribed my name this 8 day of January 1914.
(signed) Frances Milot.

Page Number Two.

Subscribed to in the presence of each of us undersigned and at the same time declared by her to us to be her Last Will and Testament; and we hereby at the request of Frances Milot and in her presence, and in the presence of each of us, sign our names hereto as witnesses this 8 day of January, 1914 (Nineteen fourteen) Wanette, Oklahoma.

(Signed) Emily Holloway, Wanette, Oklahoma
    Daughter of Frances Milot.
(Signed) Mary A. Vieux, Wanette, Oklahoma.
    Daughter of Frances Milot.
(signed) M.C. Coker, Wanette, Oklahoma.
(signed) W.M. Lambert, Wanette, Oklahoma.

------ooOoo------

I hereby certify that the above is a true copy of the Will and Testament made by Frances Milot under date of January 8, 1914.
(signed) John A. Buntin, Superintendent and Special Disbursing
    Agent, Shawnee Indian Agency, Shawnee, Oklahoma.

Department of The Interior,
Office of Indian Affairs
Washington, D.C.   Nov. 30, 1914

It is recommended that the within will be approved pursuant to the provisions of the Act of June 25, 1910 (36 Stats. L., 855-6) as amended by the Act of February 14, 1913 (37 Stat. 678).

    Respectfully,
    (Signed) E.B. Meritt
    Assistant Commissioner

Department of The Interior,
Office of the Secretary
Washington, D.C.

The within will is hereby approved pursuant to the provisions of the Act of June 25, 1910 (36 Stats. L., 855-6) as amended by Act of February 14, 1913 (37 Stat. 678).

    Assistant Secretary

<<<<<<<<>>>>>>>

NATIVE AMERICAN WILLS and PROBATE RECORDS, 1911 - 1921

C O P Y

LAST WILL AND TESTAMENT OF HIGH BEAR.

IN THE NAME OF GOD, AMEN.

I, **HIGH BEAR**, 74 years of age, an Indian of Crow Creek Indian Reservation, South Dakota, being of sound mind, memory, and understanding, do hereby make and publish this my last Will and Testament, hereby revoking and annulling all wills by me heretofore made, in manner and form following, that is to say:

FIRST: I direct that all my just debts and funeral expenses, and expenses of my last illness shall be paid as soon after my decease as shall be convenient.

SECOND: I give, devise, and bequeath my 320 acre allotment described as the E1/2 of W1/2 and W1/2 of E1/2 of section 28, T 106 N, R 70 W., 5th P.M. to the following persons each to take the share designated:

To Mrs. Walking Crane, of Cheyenne River Agency, South Dakota, my sister, the SE1/4 of the SW1/4 and the SW1/4 of the SE1/4 of section 28, T 106 N R 70 W. 5th p.M. containing 80 acres.

To Pretty Day (Mrs. Little Cloud) my sister, the SW1/4 of the NE1/4 of section 28, T 106 N., R 70 W. 5th P.M., containing 40 acres.

To Susan McBride, my half-sister, the NW1/4 of the SE1/4 of section 28, T 106 N., R. 70 W. 5th P.M. containing 40 acres.

To Edward Long Crow, Of Dixon, South Dakota, my cousin, the W1/2 of the NE1/4 of the SW1/4 of section 28, T 106 N., R 70 W., 5th P.M., containing 20 acres.

To Hok-si-na (brother to Edward Long Crow) my cousin, the E1/2 of the NE1/4 of the SW1/4 of section 18, T 106 N., R 70 W., 5th P.M., containing 20 acres.

To Van Philip High Bear, my nephew, the SE1/4 of the NW1/4 of section 28, T 106 N., R 70 W., 5th P.M., containing 40 acres.

To Jay Carpenter, my cousin, the NW1/4 of the NE1/4 of section 28, T 106 N., R 70 W., 5th P.M. containing 40 acres.

To Rosa Day, my second cousin, the NE1/4 of the NW1/4 of section 28, T106 N., R 70 W., 5th P.M. containing 40 acres.

I desire that the jouse, barn and all fences on my entire allotment shall go to Rosa Day and in case a survey should show that such house, barn, and all fences are not on that part of my allotment I have heretofore designated as her share, then I direct that such house, barn, and fences shall be moved to that part of my allotment I have given to said Rosa Day as her share, the same to become her property in the event of my death.

NATIVE AMERICAN WILLS and PROBATE RECORDS, 1911 - 1921

THIRD: I give, devise and bequeath unto Elsie Carpenter, my second cousin, any and everything in my dwelling house, belonging to me, that she may desire to take. To Rosa Day, I give devise and bequeath, all of my farming implements, one cow and two heifers, one black mare, and all of my household articles not taken by Elsie Carpenter as heretofore provided. And it is my wish that no one shall molest the said Rosa Day in the peaceful possession of such property. To Pretty Day, my sister, I give, devise and bequeath my one bay mare.

All the rest and residue of my personal property not hereinbefore specifically mentioned I give, devise and bequeath unto Rosa Day.

My father and mother are both dead; I have no wife, no children and no grand-children; I have only two sisters living and I have mentioned them herein; I have only one nephew living, heretofore mentioned, and no nieces. Van Philip High Bear is the son of my deceased brother Isaac High Bear.

AND LASTLY: I am satisfied that the officers of the Department of the Interior of rhw United States will make proper provision for carrying into effect this my last Will and Testament, and therefore, I have not appointed as[sic] executor to administer my estate.

IN TESTIMONY WHEREOF, I have set my hand and seal to this my last will and Testament at my home on the Crow Creek Indian Reservation, South Dakota, this 12th day of April, in the year of our Lord one thousand nine hundred and fourteen.

(Signed) HIGH BEAR

Signed, sealed, published and declared by the said High bear in our presence as and for his last Will and Testament, and at his request and in his presence and in the presence of each other we have hereunto subscribed our names as attesting witnesses thereto.

(Signed) CHARLES BRIGGS, Residence Crow Creek Reservation, S.D.
Post Office, Grosse, So. Dakota.
(Signed) EDWARD ASHLEY, Residence Crow Creek Reservation, S.D.
Post Office, Grosse, So. Dakota.
(Signed) JAY CARPENTER, Residence Crow Creek Reservation, S.D.
Post Office, Crow Creek, S. Dakota.

Department of The Interior,
Office of Indian Affairs
Washington, D.C.   Dec 19, 1914

It is recommended that the within will be approved pursuant to the provisions of the Act of June 25, 1910 (36 Stats. L., 855-6) as amended by the Act of February 14, 1913 (37 Stat. 678).

Respectfully,

NATIVE AMERICAN WILLS and PROBATE RECORDS, 1911 - 1921

Department of The Interior,
Office of the Secretary
Washington, D.C.

(Signed) E.B. MERITT
Assistant Commissioner

Dec 30, 1914

The within will is hereby approved pursuant to the provisions of the Act of June 25, 1910 (36 Stats. L., 855-6) as amended by Act of February 14, 1913 (37 Stat. 678).

(Signed) BO SWEENEY
Assistant Secretary

COPY

LAST WILL AND TESTAMENT OF CYRUS BLACKBIRD OR LITTLE VILLAGE MAKER.

I, **CYRUS BLACKBIRD** or **LITTLE VILLAGE MAKER**, being of sound mind and desposing memory, but realizing the uncertainties of life do hereby make, publish and declare this my last will and testament as follows:

First. To my son, Alfred Blackbird, I give devise and bequeath that portion of my allotment on the Omaha Reservation in Nebraska described as the northwest quarter of the southwest quarter of section twenty-three, township twenty-five north, range nine east of the six principal meridian in Nebraska and containing according to the Government survey forty acres.

Second: To my son, John Blackbird, I give, devise and bequeath that portion of my allotment on the Omaha Reservation in Nebraska described as the northeast quarter of the southwest quarter of section twenty-three, township twenty-five north, range nine east of the sixth principal meridian in Nebraska and containing according to the Government survey forty acres.

Third: To my daughter, Mary Lydia Blackbird, I give devise and bequeath that portion of my allotment on the Omaha Reservation in Nebraska described as the southwest quarter of the southwest quarter of section twenty-three, township twenty-five north, range nine east of the sixth principal Meridian in Nebraska and containing according to the Government survey forty acres.

Fourth: To my dughter, Poncasa Robinson, I give devise and bequeath that portion of my allotment described as the southeast quarter of the southwest quarter of section twenty-three, township twenty-five north, range nine east of the sixth principal meridian in Nebraska and containing according to the Government survey forth acres.

This will is drawn under the provisions of the Act of Congress of June 25, 1910, and subject to the condition that no sale or conveyance of the land described by the devisees, their heirs, administrators or legal representatives prior

NATIVE AMERICAN WILLS and PROBATE RECORDS, 1911 - 1921

to the eleventh day of July 1919, shall be valid unless approved by the Secretary of the Interior.

                Cyrus Blackbird   )
                        or   ) His (Thumb)
                Little Village Maker) Mark

     The said testator at this time signed his name to the above and foregoing instrument and in the presence of the undersigned and at the same time declared it to be his last will and testament, and we at his request and in his presence, and in the presence of each other do hereby sign our names as witnesses.

Signed	Signed	Signed
Albert H. Kneale.	Roger C. Mackenstady.	Alfred Blackbird.

Department of The Interior,
Office of Indian Affairs
                        Nov. 23, 1914

The within will of Cyrus Blackbird or Little Village Maker is recommended for approval under the provisions of the Act of June 25, 1910 (36 Stats. L., 855-6) as amended by the Act of February 14, 1913 (37 Stat. 678).
                        (Signed) E.B. MERITT
                        Assistant Commissioner

Department of The Interior,
Office of the Secretary
                        Jan. 16, 1915.

The within will of Cyrus Blackbird or Little Village Maker is approved under the provisions of the Act of June 25, 1910 (36 Stats. L., 855-6) as amended by Act of February 14, 1913 (37 Stat. 678).
                        (Signed) BO SWEENEY
                        Assistant Secretary

<<<<<<<◇>>>>>>>
                        (COPY)
KNOW ALL MEN BY THESE PRESENTS:

     That I, **SHEH-TAHS**, a resident of Jackson County, Kansas, being of sound mind and memory, do hereby make, publish and declare this to be my last will and testament, hereby revoking all other and former wills by me at any time made.

        ITEM I.   I desire and direct that the executor of this will shall, as soon as convenient after my death, pay all my just debts, including my funeral expenses and the expenses of my last sickness, out of the personal property owned by me at the time of my death.

        ITEM II.   I give, devise and bequeath to my daughter, <u>Lucy M. Daugherty</u>, all my right, title and interest in and to allotment No. 404, and which is described as the South one-half of the

NATIVE AMERICAN WILLS and PROBATE RECORDS, 1911 - 1921

Southeast quarter of section eleven (11), township eight (8), range fourteen (14), East of the 6th P.M., in Jackson County, Kansas, to be hers for her use and benefit so long as she may live and, at her death, I desire that said land shall become and be the property of her lawful heirs.

It is understood, however, that my right to dispose of said property is not absolute, but is restricted by certain laws, rules and regulations imposed upon me by the Government of the United States, which restrictions will be removed at the end of a period of time fixed by the U.S. Government.

ITEM III. I give, devise and bequeath to my daughter, Gertie M-joe-tah (Now-kum-go-quah), allotment No. 403, which land I inherited from Witch-e-wah, my late husband, and which is described as the Northwest quarter of the Northwest quarter of section thirteen (13), township eight (8), range fourteen (14), and the Southwest quarter of the Southwest quarter of section twelve (12), township eight (8), range fourteen (14), all East of the 6th P.M., in Jackson County, Kansas, to be hers for her use and benefit so long as she may live and, at her death, said property I desire to be and become the property of her lawful heirs and it is understood, however, that my right to dispose of said property is not absolute, but is restricted by certain laws, rules and regulations imposed upon me by the Government of the United States, which restrictions will be removed at the end of a period of time fixed by the United States Government.

ITEM IV. I will, devise and bequeath to my son, Harry Witch-e-way, all my right, title and interest in and to allotment No. 637, which allotment I inherited from Kaw-batche, a deceased child of mine, said allotment being described as the South one-half of the Northeast quarter of section fifteen (15), township eight (8), range fourteen (14), East of the 6th P.M., in Jackson County, Kansas, to be his for his use and benefit so long as he may live and, at his death, said property is to be and become the property of his lawful heirs.

It is understood, however, that my right to dispose of said property is not absolute, but is restricted by certain laws, rules and regulations imposed upon me by the Government of the United States, which restrictions will be removed at the end of a certain period of time fixed by the United States Government.

ITEM V. It is my desire that my son, Harry Witch-e-way, shall have the two horses and the harness which I now own, which shall be subject, however, to the payment of my debts and funeral expenses as provided for in Item I, provided there is not

NATIVE AMERICAN WILLS and PROBATE RECORDS, 1911 - 1921

sufficient money on hand or in the hands of the Government of the United States or its agents to pay the said debts, funeral expenses and expenses of last sickness, and if there is sufficient funds with which to pay said debts, funeral expenses and expenses of last sickness, then I desire that the personal property above enumerated shall pass to my son, Harry, to be his absolutely.

ITEM VI. I will and bequeath to my granddaughter, Ethel M-joe-tah, the Jersey cow which I now own.

ITEM VII. It is my wish and will that the parties to whom I have bequeathed the above described land, and each and every one of them, shall be restricted in this that they shall not have the right to sell, mortgage or otherwise incumber said land during their lifetime, but that same shall pass, at their death, to their legal heirs unincumbered.

IN WITNESS WHEREOF, I have hereunto set my hand this 20th day of October, 1914.

    A. R. Snyder   Her
    Mayetta, Kans.   Sheh-tahs   thumb
                                          mark

We, and each of us, do hereby certify that we saw Sheh-tahs sign her name to the foregoing will and heard her declare that it was her last will and testament and we, in her presence, and in the presence of each other, and at her request, sign the same as witnesses thereto.

IN WITNESS WHEREOF, we have hereunto set our hands this 20th day of October, 1914.

                                 A.R. Snyder
                        P.O.   Mayetta, Kans.
                             Richard Rice
                        P.O.   Mayetta, Kans.

Department of The Interior,
Office of Indian Affairs
Washington, D.C.   JAN 16, 1915

The within will if[sic] recommended for approval pursuant to the provisions of the Act of June 25, 1910 (36 Stats. L., 855-6) as amended by the Act of February 14, 1913 (37 Stat. 678).

                         Respectfully,
                         E.B. Meritt
                         Assistant Commissioner

NATIVE AMERICAN WILLS and PROBATE RECORDS, 1911 - 1921

Department of The Interior,
Office of the Secretary
Washington, D.C.   JAN 20, 1915

The within will is hereby approved pursuant to the provisions of the Act of June 25, 1910 (36 Stats. L., 855-6) as amended by Act of February 14, 1913 (37 Stat. 678).

Bo Sweeney
Assistant Secretary

<<<<<<<>>>>>>>

LAST WILL AND TESTAMENT OF TALL

IN THE NAME OF GOD, amen.

I, **TALL**, of Canadian County, State of Oklahoma, an Arapaho Indian, being now in fair health, strength, clear in mind, and sensible of the uncertainty of life, and the certainty of death, and desiring to make disposition of my property and affairs while in health and strength, do hereby make public and declare the following to be my LAST WILL AND TESTAMENT:

I hereby give, devise, and bequethe[sic], and also desire, that my allotment #1559, of the Cheyenne and rapaho Agency, Oklahoma, the North-east quarter of Sec. 11, twp. 11 north, Range 9 west, Indian meridian, in Canadian County, Oklahoma, containing 160 acres, should go to my direct heirs and relatives who survive me according to law:

I hereby give, devise, and bequeathe[sic] whatever undivided interest or fixed interest that I may possess at my death to my direct heirs and relatives who survive me according to the laws of descent.

I hereby give, devise and bequeathe[sic] two horses color black, now in my possession, and the harness pertaining thereto, also all the farm machinery and tools now in use at my home and consisting mainly of 1 mower, 1 wheat drill, 1 riding cultivator, 1 riding lister, 1 disc harrow, 1 double go-devil, 1 riding two gang plow, 1 stalk cutter, 1 horse hay rake, 1 harrow, to Cut Nose, my brother, to him and his heirs forever.

I hereby direct the payment of all my just debts, and necessary funeral expense by the executor of this my last will.

I hereby appoint and constitute my said brother, Cut Nose, to act as sole executor, without bond, of this my last will and testament.

NATIVE AMERICAN WILLS and PROBATE RECORDS, 1911 - 1921

IN WITNESS WHEREOF I, Tall, have to this, my last will and testament, consisting of two sheets of paper, subscribed my name this second day of April, A.D., 1914.

Witness:
    Dewitt C. Hayes   (Signed)   Tall   His Thumb Mark
    Richard J. Barnes

Subscribed by Tall above named in presence of us, the undersigned and in the presence of each other and declared by him to be his last will and testament, and the provisions of said will having been interpreted to him by a member of the Arapaho Tribe, and he fully understands all the provisions contained therein.

Witness our hands this second day of April, 1914
(Signed)   _Dewitt C. Hayes_
(Signed)   _Richard J. Barnes_
(Signed)   _Clarence Powderface_, Interpreter

Department of The Interior,
Office of Indian Affairs
                    January 15, 1915

The within will of Tall, allottee #1559 of the Cheyenne and Arapaho tribe is recommended for approval under the Act of June 25, 1910 (36 Stats. L., 855-6) as amended by the Act of February 14, 1913 (37 Stat. 678).

                    (Signed) E.B. Meritt
                    Assistant Commissioner

Department of The Interior,
Office of the Secretary
                    January 25, 1915

The within will of Tall allottee #1559 of the Cheyenne and Arapaho tribe is hereby approved under the Act of June 25, 1910 (36 Stats. L., 855-6) as amended by Act of February 14, 1913 (37 Stat. 678).

                    (Signed) Bo Sweeney
                    Assistant Secretary

LAST WILL AND TESTAMENT
OF
POHA

IN THE NAME OF GOD, AMEN,

    I, **POHA**, of Fort Totten, North Dakota, Devils Lake Sioux allottee No. 737, being of sound mind, memory and understanding, do hereby make and

NATIVE AMERICAN WILLS and PROBATE RECORDS, 1911 - 1921

publish this my last Will and Testament, hereby revoking and annulling all wills by me heretofore made, in manner and form following, that is to say:

FIRST, I direct that all my just debts and funeral expenses, and expenses of my last illness shall be paid by my executrix hereinafter named as soon after my decease as shall be convenient;

SECOND, I give devise and bequeath to Winona Mazawanapeya, the daughter of my cousin, who has cared for me for a long time, and is the only one who has looked out for my welfare since I am old, all of my allotment of land situated on the Devils Lake Reservation in North Dakota, described as the S1/2 of SE1/4 and NE1/4 of SE1/4 Sec 23, Twp. 152 N. R. 66, and the SE1/4 of NE1/4 of Sec 7, Twp. 151 N. R. 66, containing 160 acres.

THIRD, All the rest and residue of my estate, both real, personal and mixed, I give, devise, and bequeath to Winona Mazawanapeya, above-named.

AND LASTLY, I do hereby nominate, constitute and appoint Winona Mazawanapeya executrix of this my last Will and Testament.

IN TESTIMONY WHEREOF, I have set my hand and seal to this my last Will and Testament, at Fort Totten, North Dakota, this 24th day of April in the year of our Lord one thousand nine hundred and fourteen.

Her
POHA Thumb
Mark

SIGNED, SEALED, PUBLISHED AND DECLARED

By the said Poha in our presence, as and for her last Will and Testament, and at her request and in her presence, and in the presence of each other, we have hereunto subscribed our names as attesting witnesses thereto.

Harry W. Camp
Fort Totten, N. Dak.

Martin Strait
Fort Totten, N. Dak.

C. M. Ziebach
Fort Totten, N. Dak.

Department of The Interior,
Office of Indian Affairs   Jan. 21, 1915
Washington, D.C.

NATIVE AMERICAN WILLS and PROBATE RECORDS, 1911 - 1921

The within will is hereby recommended for approval in accordance with the provisions of the Act of June 25, 1910 (36 Stats. L., 855-6) as amended by the Act of February 14, 1913 (37 Stat. 678).

(Signed) E.B. Meritt
Assistant Commissioner

Office of the Secretary   *Jan. 16, 1915*

The within will is hereby approved in accordance with the provisions of the Act of June 25, 1910 (36 Stats. L., 855-6) as amended by Act of February 14, 1913 (37 Stat. 678).

(Signed) Bo Sweeney
Assistant Secretary

<<<<<<<O>>>>>>>

LAST WILL AND TESTAMENT
OF
HORN DOG

IN THE NAME OF GOD, AMEN:

I, **HORN DOG**, of Crow Creek Indian Reservation, Crow Creek, Buffalo County, South Dakota, being of sound mind, memory and understanding, do hereby make and publish this my last will and testament, hereby revoking and annulling all wills by me heretofore made, in manner and form following, that is to say:

FIRST, I direct that all my just debts and funeral expenses and the expenses of my last illness shall be paid by my executor herein after named as soon after my decease as shall be convenient.

SECOND, I give, devise and bequeath all of my own allotment of land located within the Crow Creek Indian Reservation in Buffalo County, South Dakota, described as the South East Quarter (SE1/4) of Section seven (7) and the South West Quarter (SW1/4) of Section eight (8) in Township one-hundred seven (107) North, Range Seventy-one (71) West 5th P.M., to my son John Horn Dog, and to my wife Red Wood Woman (Can-du-ta-win). I give the South East quarter (SE1/4) of Section seven (7), Township one hundred seven (107) N., Range seventy-one (71) W., 5th P.M., to my son, John Horn Dog, and the South West quarter (SW1/4) of Section eight (8) township one hundred seven (107), range seventy-one (71) W. 5th P.M. to my wife Red Wood Woman (Can-du-ta-win).

THIRD, I give and bequeath to my son, John Horn Dog, my two mowers, hay rake, riding plow, cultivator, wagon and harness, saddle, one bay gelding, one spring wagon and light set of harness, one roan gelding pony and one colt.

NATIVE AMERICAN WILLS and PROBATE RECORDS, 1911 - 1921

To my wife I give and bequeath one sorrel mare and all my household goods and tent. All money due me from any source whatsoever, I give and bequeath in equal shares to my wife Red Wood Woman and to my son John Horn Dog.

FOURTH, In case of the death of my wife Red Wood Woman and John Horn Dog, my son, should any of the property, either real or personal, mentioned in this my last will and testament, remain in their possession, then I direct that such property shall be given to Shoots Enemy, a relative to my said wife, Red Wood Woman, and a friend to me. Provided that said property shall not pass to Shoots Enemy until both my said wife, Red Wood Woman and my son John Horn Dog shall have died. In case my Son John Horn Dog, shall die first and he is possessed of any property, either real or personal, herein devised or bequeath, then such property shall pass to my wife, Red Wood Woman, and after her death if any such property remain in her possession it shall pass to Shoots Enemy. In case my Wife Red Wood Woman shall die before my son John Horn Dog, all the property herein bequeath or devised to her, shall pass to my son, John Horn Dog and in case any of said property is still in his possession at the time of his death, then it shall pass to Shoots Enemy.

AND LASTLY, I do hereby nominate, constitute and appoint Shoots Enemy, of Crow Creek, South Dakota, executor of this my last will and testament.

IN TESTIMONY WHEREOF, I have hereunto set my hand and seal to this my last will and Testament at my home on the Crow Creek Reservation, Crow Creek, South Dakota, this 25th day of July, 1913.

HORN DOG, His thumb mark.

Signed, sealed, published and declared by the said Horn Dog in our presence as and for his last will and testament, and at his request and in our presence and in the presence of each other, we have hereunto subscribed our names as attesting witnesses thereto.

W. C. Kohlenberg Residence, Crow Creek, S.D.
P. J. Pibb Residence, Crow Creek, S.D.
Russell Harrison Residence, Crow Creek, S.D.

Office of Indian Affairs Aug. 24, 1914.
Washington, D.C.

It is recommended that the within will be approved pursuant to the provisions of the Act of June 25, 1910 (36 Stats. L., 855-6) as amended by the Act of February 14, 1913 (37 Stat. 678).

Respectfully,
E.B. MERITT

NATIVE AMERICAN WILLS and PROBATE RECORDS, 1911 - 1921

Department of The Interior,
Office of the Secretary
Washington, D.C.

Assistant Commissioner
Aug. 25, 1914

The within will is hereby approved pursuant to the provisions of the Act of June 25, 1910 (36 Stats. L., 855-6) as amended by Act of February 14, 1913 (37 Stat. 678).

Bo Sweeney
Assistant Secretary

<<<<<<<<>>>>>>>

IN THE NAME OF GOD, AMEN. I, **ANTOINE MORAIS**, of the City of Polson, County of Flathead, State of Montana, of the age of sixty years, and being of sound and disposing mind and memory, and not acting under duress, menace, fraud, or undue influence of any person whatever, do make, publish, and declare this my last Will and Testament, in the manner following, that is to say:

First: I direct that my body be decently buried with proper regard to my station and condition in life and the circumstances of my estate.

Secondly: I direct that my executor hereinafter named, as soon as he has sufficient funds in his hand, pay my funeral expenses and the expenses of my last sickness, and the allowance made to my family.

Thirdly: I give and bequeath to my wife, Mary Ann Morais, and to my minor child, Annie Pearl Morais, to be divided equally between them, share and share alike, all my real and personal property of every kind, character, and description owned by me and of which I am possessed at the time of my death.

Lastly. I hereby nominate and appoint Frank L. Gray, of said City of Polson, County of Flathead, the executor of this, my last Will and Testament, and hereby revoke all former will by me made.

IN WITNESS WHEREOF, I have hereunto set my hand and seal this 19th day of September, in the year of our Lord one thousand nine hundred and twelve.

Antoine Morais, (SEAL)

The foregoing instrument consisting of one page was, at the date hereof, by the said Antoine Morais, signed and sealed and published as, and declared to be, his last Will and Testament, in presence of us, who at his request, and in his presence, and in the presence of each other, have subscribed our names as witnesses thereto.

W. A. Myhre
Residing at Polson, Montana.

NATIVE AMERICAN WILLS and PROBATE RECORDS, 1911 - 1921

C. H. Larson
Residing at Polson, Montana.

STATE OF MONTANA, ELEVENTH JUDICIAL DISTRICT,)
      COUNTY OF FLATHEAD,   ) SS

I HEREBY CERTIFY the foregoing to be a full, true and correct copy of the original:

WILL OF ANTOINE MORAIS,
In the Matter of the Estate of
Antoine Morais,
      Deceased,
          Now on file in my office.

IN WITNESS WHEREOF, I have hereunto set my hand and affixed the seal of said Court, this <u>19th</u> day of <u>April A.D. 1913</u>.

      Sam D. McNeely, Clerk.
(SEAL)   By R. N. Eaton, Deputy Clerk.

Department of The Interior, Office of Indian
Affairs   Washington.
      Jan. 9, 1915.
The within will of Antoine Morais, deceased Flathead allottee No. 1378, is hereby recommended for approval in so far as it relates to the part of the original allotment still held in trust, pursuant to the provisions of the Act of Congress of June 25, 1910 (36 Stats. L., 855-6) as amended by the Act of February 14, 1913 (37 Stat. 678 -- Public 381).

      E.B. Meritt
      Assistant Commissioner

Department of The Interior, Office of the
Secretary   Washington.
      Feb. 6, 1915
The within will is hereby approved in so far as it relates to the part of the original allotment of Antoine Morais, deceased Flathead allottee No. 1378, still held in trust, pursuant to the provisions of the Act of Congress of June 25, 1910 (36 Stats. L., 855-6) as amended by Act of February 14, 1913 (37 Stat. 678 -- Public 381).

      (Signed) Bo Sweeney
      Assistant Secretary

<<<<<<<>>>>>>>

NATIVE AMERICAN WILLS and PROBATE RECORDS, 1911 - 1921

(COPY)

State of South Dakota
              ss
County of Bennett

March 14, 1914.

By the Grace of God, Amen:

Be it known that I **MARY HALL** of Bennett Co. So. Dakota, knowing the uncertainty of this mortal life, and being of sound mind do hereby make and publish and declare this as my last will and testament. Now be it known that I direct that after my death I bequeath to my husband Albert E. Hall the following described real estate to-wit West 1/2 half SW 1/4 Sec. 5 W 1/1 of rhw NQ 1/4 of Sec. 8 and NE 1/4 Sec. 7 of Tp 35 Rg 34 all other property that I may own at the time of my death shall be equally divided between my children share and share alike.

                                              Mary Hall

We the undersigned hereby certify that we was[sic] present at the time that Mary Hall did sign the above her last will and testament and that in her presence in the presence of each other and at her request we have affixed our signatures as witnesses to same this 14th day of March, 1914.
Philip F. Nelson of Cody, Nebr.,
Thos Bowman, Cody, Nebr.

Department of The Interior,
Office of Indian Affairs   Jan. 31, 1915.
Washington, D.C.

The within will of Mary Hall is respectfully recommended for approval insofar as it relates to trust property under government control, pursuant to the provisions of the Act of June 25, 1910 (36 Stats. L., 855-6) as amended by the Act of February 14, 1913 (37 Stat. 678).

                              Respectfully,
                              (Signed) E.B. Meritt
                              Assistant Commissioner

Department of The Interior,
Office of the Secretary
Washington, D.C.   Feb. 13, 1915,

The within will of Mary Hall is hereby approved insofar as it relates to trust property under government control, pursuant to the provisions of Act of June 25, 1910 (36 Stats. L., 855-6) as amended by Act of February 14, 1913 (37 Stat. 678).

                              (Signed) Bo Sweeney
                              Assistant Secretary

<<<<<<<>>>>>>

NATIVE AMERICAN WILLS and PROBATE RECORDS, 1911 - 1921

LAST WILL AND TESTAMENT
Of
MEGRETAE BLACKBIRD.

-0-

I, **MEGRETAE BLACKBIRD**, of the Omaha Reservation, Thurston County, Nebraska, being of sound and disposing mind and memory, do hereby and by these presents make, publish, and declare this instrument to be my last Will and Testament in manner and form following:

FIRST

I am an Indian and a member of the Omaha Indians in Thruston County, Nebraska, and I am at present possessed of an allotment of land on the Omaha reservation described as the West half of the Southweat quarter of section sixteen (16) in township twenty-four (24) North of Range eight (8) East of the 6th P.M., Nebraska.

SECOND

I give, devise and bequeath unto my daughter Watawe Blackbird Burt the Southwest quarter of the Southwest quarter of section sixteen (16) in township twenty-four (24) North of Range eight (8) East of the 6th P.M., Nebraska.

THIRD

I give, devise and bequeath unto my grandaughters, Maggie Webster Grant, Dora Webster Wolf and Julia Webster Knows The Country each an undivided one third interest in the Northwest quarter of the Southwest quarter of section sixteen (16) in township twenty-four (24) North of Range eight (8) East of the 6th P.M., Nebraska.

FOURTH.

I hereby revoke any former will I may have made.

IN WITNESS WHEREOF, I have hereunto subscribed my name this 5th day of November 1914.

                                                          Her

                             Me gr tae Blackbird   Thumb

In the presence of: Mark

Alfred Blackbird

Louis Dick

The foregoing instrument was subscribed, published and declared by Me-gre-tae Blackbird to be her last will and testament in our presence and in the presence of

NATIVE AMERICAN WILLS and PROBATE RECORDS, 1911 - 1921

each of us and we at the same time at her request and in the presence of her and in the presence of each other hereunto subscribed our names as attesting witnesses this 5th day of November, 1914.

Alfred Blackbird
Louis Dick

Department of The Interior, Office of Indian Affairs
Nov. 21. 1914

The within will of Megretae Blackbird is recommended for approval under the provisions of the Act of June 25, 1910 (36 Stats. L., 855-6) as amended by the Act of February 14, 1913 (37 Stat. 678).

E.B. MERITT
Assistant Commissioner

Department of The Interior, Jan. 21, 1915

The within will of Megretae Blackbird is hereby approved under the provisions of the Act of June 25, 1910 (36 Stats. L., 855-6) as amended by Act of February 14, 1913 (37 Stat. 678).

Bo Sweeney
Assistant Secretary

<<<<<<<◇>>>>>>>
(COPY)

LAST WILL AND TESTAMENT OF JAMES A. TATIYOPA.

IN THE NAME OF GOD, AMEN:

I, **JAMES A. TATIYOPA**, 21 years of age, an Indian of Crow Creek Indian Reservation, South Dakota, being of sound mind, memory, and understanding, do hereby make and publish this my last Will and Testament, hereby revoking and annulling all wills by me heretofore made, in manner and form following, that is to say:

FIRST, I direct that all my just debts and funeral expenses, and expenses of my last illness shall be paid as soon after my decease as shall be convenient.

SECOND, I give, devise, and bequeath to Joseph Irving, my half-brother all of my allotment of land #1065, described as the North-east quarter (NE/4) of section twenty-three (23), Township one-hundred-seven (107) North of Range seventy (70), W. Fifth (5th) principal meridian in South Dakotak, containing one hundred sixty - (160) acres.

THIRD, I give and bequeath all monty I may have in bank under the supervision of the Crow Creek Indian Agency, to my sister, Mary Santee.

FOURTH, All the rest and residue of my estate, both real and personal and mixed, I give, devise and bequeath to my sister, Mary Santee.

AND LASTLY, I am satisfied that the officers of the Department of the Interior of the United States will make proper provision for carrying into effect this my last Will and Testament, and, therefore, I have not appointed an executor to administer my estate.

IN TESTIMONY WHEREOF, I have set my hand and seal to this my last Will and Testament at the home of Mary Santee on the Crow Creek Indian Reservation, Buffalo County, South Dakota, this 12th day of July, A.D. 1914.

JAMES A. TATIYOPA.

Signed, sealed, published and declared by the said James A. Tatiyopa, in our presence, as and for his last Will and Testament, and at his request and in his presence and in the presence of each other, we have hereunto subscribed our names as attesting witnesses, thereto.

(Signed) Esther Sprague, Crow Creek, South Dakota.
(Signed) Mae Wheelock, Crow Creek, South Dakota.
(Signed) W.C. Kohlenberg, Crow Creek, South Dakota.

Department of The Interior,
Office of Indian Affairs   Jan. 6, 1915

The within will of James A. Tatiyopa is recommended for approval in accordance with the provisions of the Act of June 25, 1910 (36 Stats. L., 855-6) as amended by the Act of February 14, 1913 (37 Stat. 678).

(Signed) E.B. Meritt
Assistant Commissioner

Department of The Interior
Office of the Secretary   Feb. 13, 1915

The within will of James A. Tatiyopa is approved in accordance with the provisions of the Act of June 25, 1910 (36 Stats. L., 855-6) as amended by Act of February 14, 1913 (37 Stat. 678).

(Signed) Bo Sweeney
Assistant Secretary

WILL OF JOSEPH YELLOW EAGLE (JOSEPH BULTZ)

IN THE NAME OF GOD, AMEN,

I, **JOSEPH YELLOW EAGLE (JOSEPH BULTZ)** of Chicago, in the County of Cook and State of Illinois, being of sound mind and memory, and considering the uncertainty of this frail and transitory life, do therefore make, ordain, publish and declare this to be my last Will and Testament:

First, I order and direct that my Execut___ hereinafter named pay all my just debts and funeral expenses as soon after my death as conveniently may be.

NATIVE AMERICAN WILLS and PROBATE RECORDS, 1911 - 1921

Second, After the payment of such funeral expenses and debts, I give, devise and bequeath 1st to Margaret Culbertson The North 100 acres of Joseph Yellow Eagle's Allotment No. 1080 on Fort Peck Reservation Montana (320 Acres). 2nd To Frank Hong and Lillie Hong, the remainder of Joseph Yellow Eagles Allotment No. 1080 on Fort Peck Reservation, Montana containing 320 acres. Grazing land W 1/2 of Sec 36 Twp 31. N. R. 50 E containing 320 acres and Timber land E 1/2 of S.E. 1/4 of SW 1/4 of Sec. 24 Twp. 27 N, R 50 E containing 20 acres. Irrigable land. N.E. 1/4 of N.W. 1/4 of Sec. 12 Twp. 30, N. R. 50 E containing 40 acres all in township North and ranges East of the Montana Meridian Montana.

Lastly I make constitute and appoint C. B. Lohmiller of Poplar Montana to be executor of this my Last Will and Testament, hereby rrevoking all former wills by me made.

In Witness Whereof, I have hereto subscribed my name and affixed my seal, the 16th day of November in the year of our Lord one thousand nine hundred and thirteen.

                            Joseph Yellow Eagle Seal
                                                His
                            Joseph   X Bultz
                                      Mark

This instrument was on the day of the date thereof signed, published and declared by the said testator Joseph Yellow Eagle (Joseph Bultz) to be his last Will and Testament, in the presence of us who at his request have subscribed our names thereto as witnesses, in his presence, and in the presence of each other.

                                                              His
                            Joseph Yellow Eagle   X
                                    His   Mark
                                Joseph X Bultz
                                   Mark

                              Mrs. Bessie Goodrich
                              Peramelia Slaughter

Department of The Interior,
Office of Indian Affairs   Jan. 21, 1915
Washington, D.C.

It is recommended that the within will be disapproved pursuant to the provisions of the Act of June 25, 1910 (36 Stats. L., 855-6) as amended by the Act of February 14, 1913 (37 Stat. 678).

                          Respectfully,
                          E.B. Meritt
                          Assistant Commissioner

NATIVE AMERICAN WILLS and PROBATE RECORDS, 1911 - 1921

Department of The Interior
Office of the Secretary   Feb. 13, 1915
Washington, D.C.

The within will is hereby disapproved pursuant to the provisions of the Act of June 25, 1910 (36 Stats. L., 855-6) as amended by Act of February 14, 1913 (37 Stat. 678).

Bo Sweeney
Assistant Secretary

(COPY)

STIPULATION.

THIS AGREEMENT, made and entered into this 12th day of May, 1914, by and between Margaret Culbertson, of Poplar, Montana, party of the first part, and Frank Hong and Lillie Hong, of Chicago, Illinois, parties of the second part; WITNESSETH:

WHEREAS, Joseph Yellow Eagle, allottee No. 1080 of the Fort Peck Indian Reservation died on or about the 29th day of November, 1913, leaving as his natural heir Margaret Culbertson, the party of the first part, and,

WHEREAS, the said Joseph Yellow Eagle did, on or about the 26th day of November 1913, execute a will, bequeathing certain portions of his allotment to the said Margaret Culbertson, and portions to Frank Hong and Lillie Hong, now,

THEREFORE, it is hereby agreed by and between the party of the first part and the parties of the second part, that the allotment of Joseph Yellow Eagle shall be divided and apportioned as follows:

To Margaret Culbertson, party of the first part: The E/2 of the SE/4 of the SW/4 of Sec. 24, Twp. 27 N. R. 50 E., and the NE/4 of the NW/4 of Sec. 12, Twp 30 N. R. 50 E., and the N/2 of the NW/4 of Sec. 36, Twp. 31 N. R. 50 E., Montana Meridian, Montana, containing 140 acres.

To Frank Hong and Lillie Hong, parties of the second part: the S/2 of the NW/4 & the SW/4 of Sec. 36, Twp. 31 N. R. 50 E., Montana Meridian, Montana, containing 240 acres.

IT IS EXPRESSLY UNDERSTOOD AND AGREED that this stipulation is and shall be binding only upon approval thereof by the Secretary of the Interior.

NATIVE AMERICAN WILLS and PROBATE RECORDS, 1911 - 1921

It is further understood and agreed that this stipulation is entered into only for the purpose of effecting a settlement of the estate of Joseph Yellow Eagle, without involving litigation.

IN WITNESS WHEREOF, the parties hereto have hereunto set their hands this 12th day of May 1914.

(Signed) Margaret Culbertson
In the presence of: (Signed) Frank Hong
G. G. Commons, (Signed) Lillie Hong
Witnesses to the signature
of Frank Hong and Lillie Hong.
Soren Mathison,
Henry W. Chalmer

Department of The Interior,
Office of Indian Affairs   Jan. 21, 1915
Washington, D.C.

It is recommended that the within agreement be approved pursuant to the provisions of the Act of June 25, 1910 (36 Stats. L., 855) and the regulations of the Department.

Respectfully
(Signed) E.B. Meritt
Assistant Commissioner

Department of The Interior
Office of the Secretary   Feb. 13, 1915

The within agreement is hereby approved pursuant to the provisions of the Act of June 25, 1910 (36 Stats. L., 855) and the regulations of the Department.

(Signed) Bo Sweeney
Assistant Secretary

(COPY)

IN THE NAME OF GOD, AMEN.

I, **JACOB SWIFTBEAR** of Charles Mix County, State of South Dakota, being of sound mind and memory do make and publish this my last will and testament:

FIRST: I give and bequeath to my beloved cousin Louisa Hope, the north-east quarter of the south-west quarter (NE/4 SW/4) of Section three (3) also West one half of the south west quarter of the south-east quarter of said section three (3) in Township ninety-three (93) north of range sixty-three (63) containing in all sixty (60) acres, according to the Government Survey.

NATIVE AMERICAN WILLS and PROBATE RECORDS, 1911 - 1921

SECOND: I give and bequeath to my beloved cousin Sophia La Claire the north-west quarter of the south-west quarter of section three (3) also the east one-half of the south west quarter of the south east quarter of said section three (3) in township ninety-three (93) north of range sixty three (63) all in Charles Mix County, South Dakota, containing sixty acres.

THIRD: I devise and bequeath unto my legal heirs all the residue of my property, both real and personal, after my just debts are paid for my last sickness, death and burial.

FOURTH: I nominate Guy W. Williamson of Greenwood, South Dakota, to be the sole executor of this my last will and testament.

IN TESTIMONY WHEREOF, I hereunto set my hand and seal and publish this to be my last will and testament in the presence of the witnesses named below this 17th day of August A.D. 1912.

        (Signed) Jacob Swiftbear his
                        thumb
                        mark

Signed, sealed and declared by the said Jacob Swiftbear as for his last will and testament in presence of us who at his request and in his presence and in the presence of each other have subscribed our names as witnesses hereto.
(Signed) W. C. Grant, Residing at Greenwood, S.D.
Louie Shrink, Residing at Greenwood, S.D.

Department of The Interior,
Office of Indian Affairs Feb. 20, 1915

It is respectfully recommended that the within will be approved in accordance with the provisions of the Act of June 25, 1910 (36 Stats. L., 855-6) as amended by the Act of February 14, 1913 (37 Stat. 678) in so far as it relates to the original allotment of the testator.

        (Signed) E.B. Meritt
        Assistant Commissioner

Department of The Interior

        Feb. 23, 1915

The within will is hereby approved in accordance with the provisions of the Act of June 25, 1910 (36 Stats. L., 855-6) as amended by Act of February 14, 1913 (37 Stat. 678) in so far as it relates to the original allotment of the testator.

        (Signed) Bo Sweeney
        Assistant Secretary

NATIVE AMERICAN WILLS and PROBATE RECORDS, 1911 - 1921

WILL

I, **STRIKES PLENTY** of Pine Ridge Agency, South Dakota, allottee Number 1405, do hereby make and declare this to be my last will and testament, in accordance with Section 2 of the Act of June 25, 1910, (36 Stat. 855-856), and Act of February 14, 1913 (Public No. 381), hereby revoking all former wills made by me:

1. I hereby direct that, as soon as possible after my decease, that all my debts and funeral and testamentary expenses be paid out of my personal estate.

2. I give and devise my allotment on the Pine Ridge Reservation, South Dakota, described as follows: The north half of Section 12 in Twp. 39N. of Range 42 West of the 6th Principal Meridian in South Dakota, containing 320 acres, in the following manner:

> To Jeff Strikes Plenty, my son, the NE/4 of Section 12 in T.39, Range 42 west of the 6th P.M.
> To Swollen Face, my wife, the NW/4 of Sec. 12 in Twp. 39 N. of Range 42 West of the 6th P.M.

3. I give and bequeath all of my personal property of whatsoever nature and wheresoever situated in the following manner:

> To Sallie Strikes Plenty, my grand-daughter, one issue mare.
> To Swollen Face, my wife, the remainder of my personal property.

4. All the rest of my property, real, now possessed or hereafter acquired, of whatsoever nature and wheresoever situated, I hereby give, devise and bequeath unto my grand-children in equal shares, named as follows: Sallie, Ollie, Nancy and Lillie Strikes Plenty, Samuel and Howard Kills in Water.

In witness whereof I have hereunto set my hand this 27th day of March, 1914.

Witnesses:		His
(SGD) GEORGE A TROTTER	STRIKES PLENTY	Thumb
(Sgd) Peter Chief Eagle		Mark

The above statement was, this 27th day of March, 1914, signed and published by Strikes Plenty as his list[sic] will and testament, in the joint presence of the undersigned, the said Strikes Plenty, then being of sound and vigorous mind and free from any constraint or compulsion; whereupon we, being without any interest in the matter other than friendship, and being well

NATIVE AMERICAN WILLS and PROBATE RECORDS, 1911 - 1921

acquainted with him, but not members of his family, immediately subscribed our names hereto in the presence of each other and of the said testator, for the purpose of attesting the said will, as he requested us to do, and that I, George A. Trotter, at the request of the testatrix[sic], wrote his name in ink and he affixed his thumb-mark.

              Post Office address:
  (Sgd) GEORGE A. TROTTER Kyle, South Dakota
  (Sgn) PETER CHIEF EAGLE Kyle, South Dakota

              Pine Ridge, South Dakoa[sic]
                March 27, 1914.

  I hereby certify that I have fully inquired into the mental competency of the Indian, signing the above will; the circumstances attending the execution of the will; the influence that may have induced its execution, and the names of those entitled to share in the estate under the law of descent in South Dakota; reasons for the disposition of the property proposed by the will, differing from disposition had the property descended by operation of law.

  I respectfully forward this will with the recommendation that it be approved.

  Approved:
  (Sgd) JOHN R. BRENNAN.   (SGD) JUDSON SMOOK
    Suptintendent.   Farmer.

Department of The Interior,
Office of Indian Affairs FEB. 6, 1915
Washington, D.C.

The within will of Strikes Plenty is recommended for approval in accordance with the provisions of the Act of June 25, 1910 (36 Stats. L., 855-6) as amended by the Act of February 14, 1913 (37 Stat. 678).

            Respectfully,
            (Sgd) E.B. MERITT
            Assistant Commissioner

Department of The Interior
Office of the Secretary Feb. 16, 1915
Washington, D.C.

The within will of Strikes Plenty is approved in accordance with the provisions of the Act of June 25, 1910 (36 Stats. L., 855-6) as amended by Act of February 14, 1913 (37 Stat. 678).

            (Sgd) BO SWEENEY
            Assistant Secretary

NATIVE AMERICAN WILLS and PROBATE RECORDS, 1911 - 1921

THE LAST WILL AND TESTAMENT

IN THE NAME OF GOD, AMEN, I,

EUGENE KENNEDY, Allottee No. 155, of the Colorado River Indian Reservation, Parker, Arizona, County of Yuma, being of sound and disposing mind and memory, do make this my last WILL AND TESTAMENT, hereby revoking and making null and void all other last Wills and Testaments by me made heretofore.

FIRST- My Will is that all my just debts and all other expenses shall be paid out of my Estate, as soon after my decease as possible.

SECOND- I give, devise and bequeath to, Jennie Y. Honadick, my mother the followind described by Trust Patent No. 391182:

> The West half (W/2) of the West half (W/2) of the Northwest quarter (NW/4) of the Northwest quarter (NW/4), of Section 13, in Township 9, North of Range 20, west of the Gila and Salt River Meridian, Arizona, containing

ten acres more or less according to Government survey.

My reasons for making the above will are that my mother has always cared for me from babyhood and even in my days of sickness, and feeling that I owe my existence to her I wish to leave the above property that she may be taken care of during the rest of her life. For the above reason also I hereby cut off all my legal heirs whomever they might be. I knowing that I will die of tuberculosis in a very short time make this will with the wish that it will be carried out, that my mother may benefit from my land.

IN TESTIMONY WHEREOF, I have set my hand to this, my Last Will and Testament, at Parker, Arizona, this 2nd day of December, 1914, in

Signed in the presence of: EUGENE KENNEDY (His thumb mark)

ANNIE DRENNAN
FRANK SAHOTCAROW

Subscribed and sworn to before me this 2nd day of December, 1914.

OMAR L. BABCOCK.
Supt. & S.D. Agent.

Department of The Interior,
Office of Indian Affairs   February 24, 1915

NATIVE AMERICAN WILLS and PROBATE RECORDS, 1911 - 1921

It is respectfully recommended that the within will be approved in accordance with the provisions of the Act of June 25, 1910 (36 Stats. L., 855-6) as amended by the Act of February 14, 1913 (37 Stat. 678).

E.B. MERITT
Assistant Commissioner

Department of The Interior
Office of the Secretary   February 25, 1915

The within will is hereby approved in pursuance to the provisions of the Act of June 25, 1910 (36 Stats. L., 855-6) as amended by Act of February 14, 1913 (37 Stat. 678).

BO SWEENEY
Assistant Secretary

LAST WILL AND TESTAMENT OF

Sophia Dyer.

IN THE NAME OF GOD, AMEN:

I, **SOPHIA DYER**, of Mission, Todd County, South Dakota, being of sound mind and memory, and considering the uncertainty of this frail and transitory life, and desiring at this time, while in possession of my mental faculties, to make a proper disposition of my worldly estate, do therefore make, ordain, publish and declare this to be my Last Will and Testament.

First: I order and direct that my executrixes hereinafter named, pay all my just debts and funeral expenses as soon after my decease as conveniently may be.

Second: After the payment of all my funeral expenses, the expenses of my last sickness and the expense of administering my estate and paying all my debts, I give and bequeath to my beloved daughter, Fanny Dyer, the Northeast Quarter (NE1/4), Section Nine (9), Township Thirty-nine (39), North, Range Twenty-eight (28), Todd County, South Dakota; to my beloved daughter, Eliza Dyer, I give and bequeath the Northwest Quarter (NW1/4), of Section Ten (10), Township Thirty-nine (39), North, Range Twenty-eight (28), Todd County, South Dakota; and to my beloved son, Oliver Dion, I give and bequeath the sum of One Hundred Dollars ($100.00).

Third: To each and all of my grand-children who may be living at the time of my death, I give and bequeath, One Dollar ($1.00), each.

NATIVE AMERICAN WILLS and PROBATE RECORDS, 1911 - 1921

Fourth: To my husband, Robert Dyer, I give and bequeath, One Dollar $1.00, which sum shall not be paid in case he has obtained from me a valid divorce.

Fifth: To my son, William Gay, in the event he shall yet be living, and this fact should become known before the settlement of my estate, I give and bequeath One Dollar ($1.00).

Sixth: To my beloved daughters, Fanny Dyer and Eliza Dyer, I give and bequeath the remainder and residue of my estate, either real or personal, of which may die possessed and which shall remain after the payment of all my just debts, funeral expenses, and expenses of my last sickness, administrating my estate, etc.

Seventh: I make the foregoing bequests and the disposition of my property and estate, believing it only just and right that my beloved daughters, who have shared with me all the hardships, privations, unhappiness and sorrows of the closing years of my life, and who have bestowed upon me years of patient care, love and affection should receive the greater portion of my estate. My beloved son, Oliver Dion, has lived separate and apart from me since his childhood, and while I still bear for him all the love and affection of a mother towards her son, I feel that is is my bounden duty to leave the bulk of my estate to my daughters who are alone and unprotected.

Eighth: I make, constitute and appoint my beloved daughters, Fanny Dyer and Eliza Dyer, to be the executrixes of this my Last Will and Testament, for all property not held in trust by the government, and I hereby revoke all former wills by me mde and particularly the will made by me on the 7th day of August, 1914. It is my wish and desire that no bond be required of my executrixes except their personal obligation.

IN TESTIMONY WHEREOF I have hereunto subscribed my name this 26th day of August, in the year of our Lord One Thousand Nine Hundred and Fourteen. (Her)
Sophia Dyer (thumb)
J. P. Schweigman (mark)
R. B. LaFlesche

This instrument was, on the day of the date thereof, signed, published and declared by the said testator, Sophia Dyer, to be her Last Will and Testament, in our presence, who, at her request, have subscribed our names hereto as witnesses, in her presence, and in the presence of each other.

Chas. L. Davis
of Rosebud, South Dakota.
J. P. Schweigman
of Rosebud, South Dakota.

NATIVE AMERICAN WILLS and PROBATE RECORDS, 1911 - 1921

R. B. LaFlesche
of Rosebud, South Dakota.

Department of The Interior,
Office of Indian Affairs   Mar 13 1915

The within will of Sophia Dyer is recommended for approval in so far as it applies to property under the jurisdiction of the Department, in accordance with the provisions of the Act of June 25, 1910 (36 Stats. L., 855-6) as amended by the Act of February 14, 1913 (37 Stat. 678).

(Signed) E.B. Meritt
Assistant Commissioner

Department of The Interior
Office of the Secretary   Mar 20, 1915

The within will of Sophia Dyer, in so far as it applies to property under the jurisdiction of the Department, is approved in accordance with the Act of June 25, 1910 (36 Stats. L., 855-6) as amended by Act of February 14, 1913 (37 Stat. 678).

(Signed) Bo Sweeney
Assistant Secretary

<<<<<<<<>>>>>>>

LAST WILL AND TESTAMENT
OF
JEANETTE IRON WING, CHEYENNE RIVER ALLOTTEE NO. 1946.

I, **JEANETTE IRON WING**, a resident of Dewey County, State of South Dakota, and residing upon the Cheyenne River Indian Reservation and a member of the Cheyenne River Tribe of Sioux Indians, being of sound mind and disposing memory and being over twenty-one years of age, do hereby make, publish and declare this instrument as and for my last will and testament, so far as the same may apply to my allotment of land on the Cheyenne River Indian Reservation in said State of South Dakota, said allotment having been made under the provisions of the statutes of the United States, and said allotment being described as follows, to-wit:

> Allotment No. 1946, being the Southwest Quarter (SW/4) of Section Eleven (11) and the Northwest Quarter (NW/4) of Section Fourteen (14) in Township Sixteen (16) North, Range Twenty-five (25) East of Black Hills Meridian in South Dakota, containing Three Hundred and Twenty (320) acres.

NATIVE AMERICAN WILLS and PROBATE RECORDS, 1911 - 1921

FIRST, I give, devise and bequeath that part of my allotment described as the Southwest Quarter (SW/4) of Section 11, Township Sixteen (16) North, Range Twenty-five (25) East of Black Hills Meridian in South Dakota, containing 160 acres, to my beloved daughter, Phoebe Iron Wing.

SECOND, I give, devise and bequeath that part of my allotment described as the Northwest Quarter (NW/4) of Section Fourteen (14), Township Sixteen (16) North, Range Twenty-five (25) East of Black Hills Meridian in South Dakota, containing 160 acres, to my beloved daughter, Cordelia Iron Wing.

THIRD, to my beloved husband, George Iron Wing, I give no part of the foregoing described allotment, for the reason that he has an allotment of his own of 640 acres and has interests in other inherited lands.

AND LASTLY, I do hereby nominate, constitute and appoint Truby Iron Moccasin, of La Plant South Dakota, executor of this my last will and testament.

IN TESTIMONY WHEREOF, I have set my hand and seal to this, my last will and testament, at La Plant, South Dakoga, this Twenty-third day of January, in the year of our Lord, One Thousand, Nine Hundred and Fourteen.

JEANETTE IRON WING

SIGNED, SEALED, PUBLISHED AND DECLARED

By the said Jeanette Iron Wing, in our presence, as and for her last will and testament, and at her request and in her presence, and in the presence of each other, we have hereunto subscribed our names as attesting witnesses thereto.

DORA BOWKER
Residence La Plant, South Dakota.

RICHARD BOWKER
Residence, La Plant, South Dakota.

Department of The Interior,
Office of Indian Affairs   March 19, 1915
The within will is recommended for approval in accordance with the provisions of the Act of June 25, 1910 (36 Stats. L., 855-6) as amended by the Act of February 14, 1913 (37 Stat. 678).

E.B. MERITT
Assistant Commissioner

Department of The Interior
Office of the Secretary   March 22, 1915

NATIVE AMERICAN WILLS and PROBATE RECORDS, 1911 - 1921

The within will is hereby approved in accordance with the provisions of the Act of June 25, 1910 (36 Stats. L., 855-6) as amended by Act of February 14, 1913 (37 Stat. 678).

BO SWEENEY
Assistant Secretary

LAST WILL AND TESTAMENT OF MRS. SITTING DOWN

IN THE NAME OF GOD, AMEN.

Know all men by these presents, that I, **MRS. SITTING DOWN**, an Arapaho Indian 73 years of age, of Calumet, Canadian County and State of Oklahoma, being now in fair health strength and clear in mind, but sensible of the uncertainty of life and the certainty of death and desiring to make disposition of my property and affairs while in health and strength, do hereby make publish and declare the following to be my last Will and Testament:

1st. I direct the payment from my estate of all my just debts and expenses of my funeral.

2nd. I give, devise and bequeath unto Singing After, wife of Charles Campbell, my granddaughter, the West half or Eighty (80) Acres of my allotment No. 3232 of the Cheyenne and Arapaho Reservation, Oklahoma, described as the W/2 of the NE/4 of Section 13, Township 13 N. of R. 10 W., I.M. to her and her heirs forever.

3rd. I give, devise and bequeath to Dan Wheeler, my nephew, by reason of his kindness to me, the East half of my said allotment No. 3232, described as the E/2 of the NE/4 of Section 13, Township 13 N., of R. 10 W., I.M., Eighty (80) acres, to him and his heirs forever.

In Witness Whereof, I, Mrs. Sitting Down, have to this my Last Will and Testament, subscribed my name this 28th day of May, A.D. 1914, clearly understanding all of its provisions as interpreted to me by Lewis Miller, a member of my own Arapaho tribe, hereby revoking any and all former wills made by me.

IN PRESENCE OF: Mrs. SITTING DOWN Her Thumb Mark.
DeWitt C. Hayes
Louis Miller

WITNESSES.

NATIVE AMERICAN WILLS and PROBATE RECORDS, 1911 - 1921

Subscribed by Mrs. Sitting Down in presence of us the undersidned and declared by her to be her last Will and Testament, and at the request of Mrs. Sitting Down in her presence and in the presence of each other, sign our names hereto as witnesses this 28th day of May, A.D. 1914.

                                     DeWitt C. Hayes
                                     Louis Miller
                                     Lida W. Barnes

Examined Oct. 16, 1914

Department of The Interior, Office of Indian Affairs Mar. 15, 1915
The within will is recommended for approval in accordance with the Act of June 25, 1910 (36 Stats. L., 855-6) as amended by the Act of February 14, 1913 (37 Stat. 678).
                             E.B. Meritt Assistant Commissioner

Department of The Interior. Office of the Secretary Mar. 24, 1915
The within will is hereby approved in accordance with the Act of June 25, 1910 (36 Stats. L., 855-6) as amended by Act of February 14, 1913 (37 Stat. 678).
                             Bo Sweeney Assistant Secretary

                             Missoula, Mont.

                             Jan. 24, 1914.

I will everything to my husband, Charles Landgreen.

                             (Signed) **Emily Landgreen**.
                             Witness J. T. Walford.
J. T. Walford
    Asst. Engr., N.P. Ry.
    Livingston, Montana.

Department of The Interior,
Office of Indian Affairs   Mar. 19, 1915.

The within will is recommended for disapproval so far as it relates to property over which the United States has jurisdiction, under the Act of June 25, 1910 (36 Stats. L., 855-6) as amended by the Act of February 14, 1913 (37 Stat. 678).
                         (Signed) E.B. Meritt
                         Assistant Commissioner
Department of The Interior
Office of the Secretary   Mar. 19, 1915.

NATIVE AMERICAN WILLS and PROBATE RECORDS, 1911 - 1921

The within will so far as it relates to property over which the United States has jurisdiction is hereby disapproved under the Act of June 25, 1910 (36 Stats. L., 855-6) as amended by Act of February 14, 1913 (37 Stat. 678).

(Signed) Bo Sweeney
Assistant Secretary

The above disapproved will was returned to the Superintendent upon his request for the reason that it bequeathed property over which the United States has no jurisdiction.

WILL.

In the name of God, Amen. I, **ANNIE BEAR**, an allottee of the Nez Perce Reservation, Idaho, over the age of 76 years and being of sound mind and disposing memory and not acting under duress, menace, fraud or undue influence, of any person whatsoever, do make, publish, and declare, this my last WILL and testament in the manner following, that is to say.

FIRST. I direct that my body be decently buried, with proper regard for my station in life, and the circumstances of my estate.

SECONDLY. I direct that Martha Yellow Bear shall pay all of my funeral expenses, and expenses of my last sickness.

THIRDLY. I give and devise to the said Martha Yellow Bear 1/2 interest of that certain lot, piece, or parcel of land, situated, lying, and being in the county of Idaho, State of Idaho, bounded and described as follows, to wit:

W1/2 NE; NW1/4 SE1/4, NE1/4,	Sec. 8	
E1/2 NW1/4 NE1/4	Sec. 8	
S1/2 SW1/4 SE1/4	Sec. 5	Twp. 32, R. 4 E.
Lot 7 & 8	Sec. 15,	32, R 2 E.

Reason for giving my interest in this land to my sister, Martha Yellow Bear, is that she has been kind to me and cared for me when I needed help during my declining years, and during my last illness.

In witness whereof I have set my hand and seal this 3rd day of September in the year of our Lord One thousand Nine hundred and Fourteen.

Witnesses   SIGNED Annie Bear, her thumb mark
John J. Guyer
Osias Lawrence.

NATIVE AMERICAN WILLS and PROBATE RECORDS, 1911 - 1921

The foregone instrument was at the date hereof, by the said Annie Bear, signed, sealed and published and declared to be her last WILL and testament in the presence of us, who at her request, and in the presence of each other, have subscribed our names as witnesses hereto.

                               James Stuart
                                  Interpreter.
                               Osias Lawrence.

Department of The Interior,
Office of Indian Affairs   MAR 11 1915

It is respectfully recommended that the within will be approved in pursuance to the provisions of the Act of June 25, 1910 (36 Stats. L., 855-6) as amended by the Act of February 14, 1913 (37 Stat. 678).

                               E.B. Meritt
                               Assistant Commissioner

Department of The Interior
Office of the Secretary   MAR 23 1915

The within will is approved under the provisions of the Act of June 25, 1910 (36 Stats. L., 855-6) as amended by Act of February 14, 1913 (37 Stat. 678).

                               Bo Sweeney
                               Assistant Secretary

(COPY)

WILL

I, **PRETTY HORSE** of Pine Ridge Agency, South Dakota, Allottee number 6646 do hereby make and declare this to be my last will and testament, in accordance with Section 2 of the Act of June 25, 1910, (36 Stat. 855-858), and Act of February 14, 1913, (Public No. 381), hereby revoking all former wills made by me.

1. I hereby direct that, as soon as possible after my decease, that all my debts and funeral and testamentary expenses be paid out of my personal estate.

2. I give and devise my allotment on the Pine Ridge Reservation, South Dakota, described as follows:

         S/2 of S/2 of NW/4 of Sec. 13, T. 38 N., R. 44 W., S/2 of NE/4
         of Sec. 17, NE/4 of NE/4 of Sec. 17, and SE/4 of Sec. 17, all in
         T. 40 N., R. 45 W. of the 6th P.M. in S.D. containing 320 acres

in the following manner:

         All of my allotment to Henry Horse, my nephew

NATIVE AMERICAN WILLS and PROBATE RECORDS, 1911 - 1921

3. I give and bequeath all of my personal property of whatsoever nature and wheresoever situated unto Henry Horse, consisting of 40 head of horses, three head of cows with calves, a wagon and harness.

4. All the rest of my property, real or personal, hereafter acquired, of whatsoever nature and wheresoever situated, I hereby give, devise and bequeath unto my nephew, Henry Horse

In witness whereof I have hereunto set my hand this 28th day of October 1914.

                                 Pretty Horse   her thumb mark

        The above statement was, this 28th day of October 1914, signed and published by Pretty Horse as her last will and testament, in the joint presence of the undersigned, the said Pretty Horse then being of sound and vigorous mind and free from any constraint or compulsion; whereupon we, being without and interest in the matter other than friendship, and being well acquainted with her, but not members of her family, immediately subscribed our names hereto in the presence of each other and of the said testator, for the purpose of attesting the said will, as requested us to do and that I, Robert H. Stelzner, at the testatrix's request signed her name and she affixed her thumb mark hereto.

                                           Post Office address.
                    Robert H. Stelzner   Pine Ridge, S.D.
                    Frank C. Goings   Pine Ridge, S.D.

                                          Pine Ridge, South Dakota.
                                          February 8, 1915.

I hereby certify that I have fully inquired into the mental competency of the Indian, signing the above will; the circumstances attending the execution of the will; the influence that may have induced its execution, and the names of those entitled to share in the estate under the law of descent in South Dakota; reasons for the disposition of the property proposed by the will, differing from disposition had the property descended by operation of law.

        I respectfully forward this will with the recommendation that it be approved.

                                     John R. Brennan
                                     Supt. & Spl. Disb. Agent.

Department of The Interior,
Office of Indian Affairs   MAR 17 1915
Washington, D.C.

It is recommended that the within will be approved pursuant to the provisions of the Act of June 25, 1910 (36 Stats. L., 855-6) as amended by the Act of February 14, 1913 (37 Stat. 678).

NATIVE AMERICAN WILLS and PROBATE RECORDS, 1911 - 1921

E.B. Meritt
Assistant Commissioner

Department of The Interior
Office of the Secretary   MAR 25 1915
Washington, D.C.

The within will is hereby approved pursuant to the provisions of the Act of June 25, 1910 (36 Stats. L., 855-6) as amended by Act of February 14, 1913 (37 Stat. 678).

Bo Sweeney
Assistant Secretary

<<<<<<<<>>>>>>>
(COPY)

LAST WILL AND TESTAMENT

Banks #1559

IN THE NAME OF GOD, AMEN.

I, **BANKS**, of Crow Agency Mont. being of sound mind, memory and understanding, do hereby make and publish this my last will and testament, hereby revoking and annulling all wills by me heretofore made, in manner and form following, that is to say:

First: I direct that all my just debts and funeral expenses, and expenses of my last illness shall be paid by my executor hereinafter named as soon after my decease as convenient;

Second: I give, devise and bequeath to my brother Smart Enemy or Charges Madly on the Enemy, part of my allotment #1559, described as Lots 1 & 2, Sec. 30, Tp 5 S. R 37 E. (79.88).

Third: I give devise & bequeath to my niece Mary Hill or Young Cat-tail the NE 1/4 of N e 1/4 Sec 25, Tp 5 S. R. 36 E. forty acres;

Fourth: I give, devise & bequeath the balance of my allotment #1559, to my beloved wife, Pretty Feather Woman, and Howard Shane, my adopted son, to be divided equally between them.

All the rest and residue of my estate, both real, personal and mixed, I give, devise, and bequeath to my heirs as determined by the Secretary of the Interior.

NATIVE AMERICAN WILLS and PROBATE RECORDS, 1911 - 1921

And Lastly: I do hereby nominate, constitute and appoint The Superintendent of Crow Reservation Montana executor of this my last Will and Testament.

In Testimony Whereof, I have set my hand and seal to this, my last Will and Testament, at Crow Agency Montana, Montana, this 30th day of October, in the year of our Lord, One thousand and nine hundred and thirteen.

Banks.   his thumb mark.

Signed, sealed, published and declared by said Banks, in our presence, as and for his last Will and Testament, and at his request and in our presence, and in the presence of each other, we have hereunto subscribed our names as attesting witnesses hereto.

        Walter P. Squires   of Crow Agency, Mont.
        James B. Kirch   of Crow Agency, Mont.
        Sidney J. Shisk   of Crow Agency, Mont.
        Edward Lieurance   Crow Agency, Mont.

Department of The Interior,
Office of Indian Affairs   Mar 5 1915
Washington, D.C.

It is recommended that the within will be approved, pursuant to the provisions of the Act of June 25, 1910 (36 Stats. L., 855-6) as amended by the Act of February 14, 1913 (Public 381), so far as it relates to the property over which the United States has jurisdiction.

                        E.B. Meritt
                        Assistant Commissioner

Department of The Interior   MAR 23, 1915
Washington, D.C.

The within will is hereby approved, pursuant to the provisions of the Act of June 25, 1910 (36 Stats. L., 855-6) as amended by Act of February 14, 1913 (Public 381), so far as it relates to property over which the United States has jurisdiction.

                        Bo Sweeney
                        Assistant Secretary

<<<<<<<<>>>>>>>>
(Will)

I, **EYES-OPEN**, being of sound and disposing mind, hereby make and declare this my last will and testament.

I give to Bear goes to the other ground all the property, both real and personal, of which I may die possessed and especially I give to him the land

NATIVE AMERICAN WILLS and PROBATE RECORDS, 1911 - 1921

embraced in my allotment, and described as follows. The south-west quarter of the South-east quarter of Section 21, Tp 4, S., Range 35, E-the South-east quarter of Northwest quarter and Lots 3 and 4, Section 3, Tp. 5, South, Range 37 E. containing 157 and 16/100 acres.

And to this I have this day subscribed my name in the presence of the witnesses hereon appearing this 19th day of March 1911.

Witnessed by   Eyes-Open   her X mark.
   Mary Johnson
   Frank Shane
   W.W. Scott.

Department of The Interior,
Office of Indian Affairs   MAR 26 1915
Washington, D.C.

It is recommended that the within will be approved in so far as it relates to the original allotment of the devisor, pursuant to the provisions of the Act of June 25, 1910 (36 Stats. L., 855-6) as amended by the Act of February 14, 1913 (37 Stat. 678).

                          Respectfully,
                          E.B. Meritt
                          Assistant Commissioner

Department of The Interior
Office of the Secretary   MAR 31 1915
Washington, D.C.

The within will is hereby approved in so far as it relates to the original allotment of the devisor, pursuant to the provisions of the Act of June 25, 1910 (36 Stats. L., 855-6) as amended by Act of February 14, 1913 (37 Stat. 678).

                          Bo Sweeney
                          Assistant Secretary

W I L L.

IN THE NAME OF GOD, AMEN:

    I, **GEORGE SICKMAN**, an Indian of the Quiniault Reserve Chehalis County, in the State of Washington, of the age of about sixty (60) years and married, being of sound and disposing mind and memory and not acting under duress, menace, fraud or undue influence of any person or persons whatsoever, do

NATIVE AMERICAN WILLS and PROBATE RECORDS, 1911 - 1921

make, publish and declare this my LAST WILL AND TESTAMENT in manner following, hereby revoking any and all wills made heretofore by me.

I direct that all my just debts and obligations be paid first and to that end I nominate and appoint ALICE JACKSON, an Indian woman, as Executrix of this my LAST WILL AND TESTAMENT and I direct that in case of my death she be and is hereby empowered to take, hold and be seized and possessed of, and vested with the title of my estate for the purpose of carrying into effect this will, and without the further intervention of any Court or of the issuance of any letters Testamentary or of Administration except to admit this will to Probate and to cause a true inventory of the property of the estate to be filed and notice be published to creditors, all subject to the will of the Indian Department of the United States Government.

I hereby expressly provide that no Bond be given for security and so far as in any case may be the said Executrix, Alice Jackson, be and she is hereby relieved from the supervision of all Courts.

I hereby direct in order that all my just debts be paid and in the settlement of my said estate the said Executrix be and she is empowered to make any and all contracts, sales and other instruments necessary to carry out the provision of my Will.

After the payment of all of my just debts and obligations I give and devise and bequeath all of my property of every kind, name and description, of all kinds both real and personal and especially my Fishing Rights given to me by the United States Government on the Quiniault River, to my wife MARY SICKMAN. I have no children and all my property shall go to my wife.

I further direct that the said ALICE JACKSON care for and provide for my said wife, and that she be paid a reasonable compensation for so doing, and that she continue to handle said estate until such time as she thinks best to close the same with the approval of the proper authority of the United States Government.

IN WITNESS WHEREOF, I have hereunto set my hand and seal this Second day of february, A.D. 1915.

George Sickman His right thumb mark.

The foregoing instrument consisting of one page and a quarter is the LAST WILL AND TESTAMENT OF GEORGE SICKMAN, and was on the day and year above written, signed, sealed, published and declared to be his Last Will and Testament by the said George Sickman in the presence of us, who, at his request and in his presence, and in the presence of each other, have subscribed our names as witnesses thereto, and we do hereby solemnly certify that the said George Sickman was not acting under duress or restraint and was of sound and disposing mind and memory.

NATIVE AMERICAN WILLS and PROBATE RECORDS, 1911 - 1921

       L. H. Brewer
       Occupation, Lawyer
       Residing at Hoquaim, Chehalis Co. Wash.
       L. W. Taft
       Occupation Bookkeeper,
       Residing at Hoquiam, Chehalis Co. Wash.
       H. W. Bale
       Occupation Lumberman
       Residing at Hoquiam, Chehalis Co. Wash.

Department of The Interior,
Office of Indian Affairs APR 1 1915

The within will of George Sickman, Quinaielt[sic] allottee No. 71 is hereby recommended for approval. pursuant to the provisions of the Act of February 14, 1913 (37 Stat. 678).

       Respectfully,
       E.B. Meritt
       Assistant Commissioner

Department of The Interior
Office of the Secretary MAR 25 1915

The within will of George Sickman, Quinaielt[sic] allottee No. 71, is hereby approved pursuant to the provisions of the Act of February 14, 1913 (37 Stat. 678).

       Bo Sweeney
       Assistant Secretary

(COPY)

In the name of God, Amen:-

Be it remembered that I **ELEANOR GARDIPE**, Flathead allottee No. 1870, now a resident of the Flathead Indian Reservation in the County of Flathead and State of Montana, of the age of 37 years, being of sound and disposing mind and memory, and not acting under duress, fraud, or under influence of of[sic] any person whom so ever, do make, publish and declare this, my last will and testament, in the following manner, that is to say:-

  I leave, will and devise to my beloved Children, Jennie Cardipe, Victoria Gardipe, Joseph Gardipe, George Wilford Gardipe, Charlie Gardipe, Margarite Gardipe, Bertha Gardipe, Matilda Gardipe and Bernard Gardipe an equal share of my allotment consisting of the W 1/2 of the N W 1/4 Sec.12 Twp 22 N. R. 20 W. Montana Meridian containng 80 acres of land. To my beloved son Bernard Gardipe I leave will and devise the 10 acres more or less on which my residence is situated, and being the 10 acres reserved by me of my Dec'd. husbands allotment and in Sec. 1 Twp. 22 N. R. 20 W. M. M.

NATIVE AMERICAN WILLS and PROBATE RECORDS, 1911 - 1921

I hereby nominate and appoint Martin A. Myhre the executor of this, my last will and testament. And I hereby revoke all former wills by me made.

In Witness Whereof, I have hereunto set my hand and seal this the 28th day of January in the year of our Lord, one thousand nine hundred and thirteen.

       Eleanor Gardipe (Seal)

The foregoing instrument, consisting of these two pages, was, at the date thereof, by said Eleanor Gardipe, signed, sealed and published as, and declared to be, her last will and testament, in the presence of us, who, at her request, and in her presence and in the presence of each other, have subscribed our names as witnesses thereto.

  Name. George K. Light   Address, Polson, Mont.
  Name, Jas. D. Hoskinson,   Address, Polson, Mont.

Department of The Interior,
Office of Indian Affairs MAR -6 1915

The within will of ELEANOR GARDIPE is recommended for disapproval in accordance with the Act of June 25, 1910 (36 Stats. L., 855-6) as amended by the Act of February 14, 1913 (37 Stat. 678).

       E.B. Meritt
       Assistant Commissioner

Department of The Interior
Office of the Secretary MAR 25 1915

The within will of ELEANOR GARDIPE is disapproved in accordance with the Act of June 25, 1910 (36 Stats. L., 855-6) as amended by Act of February 14, 1913 (37 Stat. 678).

       Bo Sweeney
       Assistant Secretary

<<<<<<<>>>>>>

(COPY)

WILL

I, **TALL-WOMAN**, of Pine Ridge Agency, South Dakota, Allottee number 847 do hereby make and declare this to be my last will and testament, in accordance with Section 2 of the Act of June 25, 1910, (36 Stat. 855-858), and Act of February 14, 1913, (Public 381), hereby revoking all former wills made by me:

NATIVE AMERICAN WILLS and PROBATE RECORDS, 1911 - 1921

1. I hereby direct that, as soon as possible after my decease, that all my debts and funeral and testamentary expenses be paid out of my personal estate.

2. I give and devise my allotment on the Pine Ridge Reservation, South Dakota, described as follows:

> The south 1/2 of the south west 1/4 and the south east 1/4 of section 11, township 39 N, range 43 W, 6th P.M. S.D.

in the following manner: south 1/2 of south west 1/4 and south east 1/4 of section 11, township 39 N, range 43 W, of 6th P.M. S.D. and all improvements upon the land, To my Grand-daughter, Rosie Eagle-fox, One wagon 1 set harness, Mares, and all cattle branded S-S.

3. I give and bequeath all of my personal property of whatsoever nature and wheresoever situated unto the above describe[sic] land to my Grand-daughter Rosie Eagle-fox.

4. All the rest of my property, real or personal, now possessed or hereafter acquired, of whatsoever nature and wheresoever situated, I hereby give, devise and bequeath unto My Grand-daughter Rosie Eagle-fox.

In witness whereof I have hereunto set my hand this 2nd day of April 1914.

            Tall-Woman, her thumb mark

Witness to Signature by mark:
 Chas. D. Parkhurst, Farmer
Witness to Signature by mark:
 John Rock, Laborer.

The above statement was, this 2nd day of April 1914, signed and published by Tall-woman as her last will and testament, in the joint presence of the undersigned, the said Tall-woman then being of a sound and vigorous mind and free from any constraint or compulsion; whereupon we, being without any interest in the matter other than friendship, and being well acquainted with her, but not members of her family, immediately subscribed our names herebo in the presence of each other and of the said testator, for the purpose of attesting the said will, as she requested us to do.

            Post Office address.
Charles D. Parkhurst.   Porcupine, S.D.
John Rock   Porcupine, S.D.

            Pine Ridge, South Dakota.
            July 28, 1914.

NATIVE AMERICAN WILLS and PROBATE RECORDS, 1911 - 1921

I hereby certify that I have fully inquired into the mental competency of the Indian, signing the above will; the circumstances attending the execution of the will; the influence that may have induced its execution, and the names of those entitled to share in the estate under the law of descent in South Dakota; reasons for the disposition of the property proposed by the will, differing from disposition had the property descended by operation of law.

I respectfully forward this will with the recommendation that it be approved.

John R. Brennan
Supt. & Spl. Disb. Agent.

Department of The Interior,
Office of Indian Affairs   MAR -6 1915

The within will of Tall Woman is recommended for approval in accordance with the Act of June 25, 1910 (36 Stats. L., 855-6) as amended by the Act of February 14, 1913 (37 Stat. 678).

E.B. Meritt
Assistant Commissioner

Department of The Interior
Office of the Secretary   MAR 17 1915

The within will of Tall Woman is approved in accordance with the Act of June 25, 1910 (36 Stats. L., 855-6) as amended by Act of February 14, 1913 (37 Stat. 678).

Bo Sweeney
Assistant Secretary

W I L L.

I, **HENRY DU MARCE**, of Sisseton R. F. 5 in the County of Roberts, and State of South Dakota, being of sound mind and memory, and considering the uncertainty of this frail and transitory life, do therefore make, ordain, publish and declare this to be my LAST WILL AND TESTAMENT.

First. I order and direct that the executor, hereinafter named, pay all my just debts and funeral expenses as soon after my decease as conveniently may be.

Second. After the payment of such funeral expenses and debts I give, devise and bequeath unto Mathilda A. Du Marce, my daughter and nearest of kin, all my property including land and such other property as I may leave and my interest in any land or money accruing to me.

NATIVE AMERICAN WILLS and PROBATE RECORDS, 1911 - 1921

Lastly, I make, constitute and appoint Hazen A. Du Marce to be Executor of my last Will and Testament, hereby revoking all former Wills by me made.

IN TESTIMONY WHEREOF, I have hereunto subscribed my name and affixed my seal the 25 day of February in the year of our Lord One Thousand Nine Hundred and fourteen 1914.

<u>Henry A. Du Marce (his X mark.</u> (Seal)

This Instrument was on the day of the date thereof signed, published and declared by the said testator, Henry A. Du Marce to be his Last Will and Testament in our presence, who, at his request, have subscribed our names thereto as witnesses in his presence and in the presence of each other.

Chas Oneroad, Henry Achen
Residing at Sisseton R. F 5
Moses Bear
Residing at Sisseton R. F 5
Don Marks Luffman

Department of The Interior,
Office of Indian Affairs   MAR - 1 1915

It is recommended that the within will be approved pursuant to the provisions of the Act of June 25, 1910 (36 Stats. L., 855-6) as amended by the Act of February 14, 1913 (37 Stat. 678).

E.B. Meritt
Assistant Commissioner

Department of The Interior
Office of the Secretary   MAR 15 1915

The within will is hereby approved pursuant to the provisions of the Act of June 25, 1910 (36 Stats. L., 855-6) as amended by Act of February 14, 1913 (37 Stat. 678).

Bo Sweeney
Assistant Secretary

<<<<<<<>>>>>>>

Last will and testament
of Goes First.

IN THE NAME OF GOD AMEN:

NATIVE AMERICAN WILLS and PROBATE RECORDS, 1911 - 1921

I, **GOES FIRST** of Crow Agency, Montana, being of sound mind, memory and understanding, do hereby publish this my last will and testament, hereby revoking and annulling all wills by me heretofore made, in manner and form following, that is to say:

First, I direct that all my just debts and funeral expenses, and expenses of my last illness shall be paid by my executor hereinafter named as soon after my decease as convenient;

Second: I give, devise and bequeath to my beloved husband, Lots of Stars, that part of my allotment No. 87, described as Lot two, section 25, range 33 east, 48.44 acres, and to Clarence Old Horn, who has lived with me and helped care for me, I give that part of my allotment described as Lot 8 and SW/4 of NW/4, section 6, township 2 south, range 34 east, 77.48 acres.

Third: All the rest and residue of my estate, both real, and personal and mixed, I give, devise and bequeath to my lawful heirs as determined after my decease.

And lastly: I do hereby nominate, constitute and appoint the Superintendent of Crow Reservation, Montana, executor of this my last will and testament.

In testimony whereof, I have set my hand and seal to this, my last will and testament, at Crow Agency, Montana, this 10th day of April in the year of our Lord one thousand nine hundred and fourteen.

Signed, sealed, published and declared by said Goes First in our presence, as and for her last will and testament, and at her request and in our presence, and in the presence of each other, we have hereunto subscribed our names as attesting witnesses thereto.

(Signed) W.P. Squires of Crow Agency, Montana.
(Signed) Josephine Laforge of Crow Agency, Montana.
(Signed) Paul Harry Wolf of Crow Agency, Montana.

Department of The Interior,
Office of Indian Affairs   MAR 11 1915

The within will of Goes First is recommended for approval in accordance with the provisions of the Act of June 25, 1910 (36 Stats. L., 855-6) as amended by the Act of February 14, 1913 (37 Stat. 678).

(Signed) E.B. Meritt
Assistant Commissioner

Department of The Interior
Office of the Secretary   MAR 27 1915

NATIVE AMERICAN WILLS and PROBATE RECORDS, 1911 - 1921

The within will of Goes First is hereby approved in accordance with the provisions of the Act of June 25, 1910 (36 Stats. L., 855-6) as amended by Act of February 14, 1913 (37 Stat. 678).

(Signed) Bo Sweeney
Assistant Secretary

WILL

I, **PIUS QUAPAW**, Quapaw allottee, No. 167-2nd of Ottawa County, State of Oklahoma, being now in good health, strength of body and of mind, but sensible of the uncertainty of life, and desiring to make disposition of the part of my property herein described while in health and in strength, do hereby make, publish, and declare the following to be my last will and testament.

I give and devise to my granddaughter, Elnora Quapaw, now seven years of age, the following described real estate which is a portion of my allotment.

> The South-east Quarter of the North-west Quarter of Section Five (5) in Township Twenty-eight (28) North and Range Twenty-four (24) Eat of the Indian Meridian, Oklahoma, containing forty (40) acres, more or less.

In witness Whereof, I, Pius Quapaw have to this my last will and testament, consisting of one sheet of paper, subscribed my name by thumb mark, this the 1st day of April, 1914.

The name of Pius Quapaw was written by me at his request and in his presence, and mark made by him in my presence.	His thumb mark Pius Quapaw.
Ira C. Deaver, Supt. Witness to mark:	

Attest: Newakis Quapaw.

Subscribed by Pius Quapaw in the presence of each of us, the undersigned, and at the same time declared by him to us to be his last will and testament, and we, thereupon at the request of Pius Quapaw in his presence and in the presence of each other sign our names hereto as witnesses, this 1st day of April, 1914, at Wyandotte, Oklahoma.

C. O. Lemon, Wyandotte, Okla.   B. N. O. Walker, Wyandotte, Okla.
                                            Ida A. Deaver, Wyandotte, Okla.

NATIVE AMERICAN WILLS and PROBATE RECORDS, 1911 - 1921

Department of The Interior,
Office of Indian Affairs
Washington, D.C.   Mar. 29, 1915

It is recommended that the within will be approved pursuant to the provisions of the Act of June 25, 1910 (36 Stats. L., 855-6) as amended by the Act of February 14, 1913 (37 Stat. 678).

Respectfully,
E.B. Meritt
Assistant Commissioner

Department of The Interior
Office of the Secretary   Apr. 7, 1915
Washington, D.C.

The within will is hereby approved pursuant to the provisions of the Act of June 25, 1910 (36 Stats. L., 855-6) as amended by Act of February 14, 1913 (37 Stat. 678).

Bo Sweeney
Assistant Secretary

<<<<<<<<>>>>>>>>

STATE OF OKLAHOMA,)
) S. S.
COUNTY OF BLAINE   )

WILL

I, **WHITE RABBIT**, of State of Oklahoma, being now in poor health, and knowing that I may die before long, and desiring to make disposition of my property and affairs while conscious, do hereby make, publish, and declare the following to be my last will and testament, hereby revoking all other or former wills by me at any time made.

FIRST. I direct the payment of all my just debts and funeral expenses.

SECOND. I give and devise all of my allotment Numbered 2354 for the Southwest Quarter (SW1/4) of Northwest (NW1/4), and Lots 3, 10, 11 and 12 of Section 2, Township 17 North, Range 13 West, of Indian Meridian, Oklahoma, containing 149 and 29/100 acres, to my wife, Bug; to my son, Jay Gould; and to my two nieces, Cut Nose and Red Mouth, to be divided equally among them.

THIRD. I hereby appoint and designate my wife, Bug, sole executrix without bond of this, my last will and testament.

NATIVE AMERICAN WILLS and PROBATE RECORDS, 1911 - 1921

In witness whereof, I, White Rabbit, have to this my last will and testament consisting of one sheet of paper, subscribed my name this 12th day of August, 1914.

His
White Rabbit. (thumb)
mark.

Subscribed by White Rabbit, in the presence of each of us, the undersigned, and at the time declared by him to us to be his last will and testament, and we, thereupon at the request of White Rabbit, in his presence and in the presence of each other, sign our names heretoo as witnesses this 12th day of August, 1914, at near Carlton, Oklahoma.

	Chase Harrington
	Dan Tucker
Frank Harrington,	Dave Bighead
Interpreter.	Ira Saulay
	Sam B. Lincoln
	U.S. Indian Farmer

Office of Indian Affairs
    Mar. 29, 1915

The within will is hereby recommended for approval in accordance with the Act of June 25, 1910 (36 Stats. L., 855-6) as amended by the Act of February 14, 1913 (37 Stat. 678).

E.B. Meritt
Assistant Commissioner

Department of The Interior
Office of the Secretary
    Apr. 6, 1915

The within will is hereby approved in accordance with the Act of June 25, 1910 (36 Stats. L., 855-6) as amended by Act of February 14, 1913 (37 Stat. 678).

Bo Sweeney
Assistant Secretary

W I L L.

I, **ELLA LITTLE SOLDIER**, Ponca Allottee No. 476, of Whiteagle, Oklahoma, do hereby make, publish and declare, this my last will and testament, in manner and form following:

<u>First</u>: I direct that all my just debts and funeral expenses be paid as soon after my decease as can conveniently be done.

NATIVE AMERICAN WILLS and PROBATE RECORDS, 1911 - 1921

Second: I give, devise and bequeath to my husband Little Soldier and my sister Henrietta First Moon, certain real esate situate in May and Noble Counties, in the State of Oklahoma, described as follows, towit: The North half (N/2) of the southwest quarter (SW/4) of Section nine (9) in township twenty-five (25) North of range one (1) East of the Indian Meridian and Lot one (1) in Section twenty three (23) in township twentyfour (24) North of range three (3) East of the Indian Meridian and all the rest, residue and remainder of my estate, real, personal and mixed, wheresoever situate, of which I may die seized or possessed, or to which I may be entitled at the time of my decease, in equal portions, share and share alike; this division, however, to be subject to the condition that my husband Little Soldier live with and care for his other wife who is my sister Henrietta First Moon, during her life time, or until his death. Should my husband Little Soldier, after my decease marry to other than my sisterHenrietta First Moon during her life time, then I give, devise and bequeath all of my estate, real and personal and mixed, wheresoever situate, of which I may die seized or possessed, or to which I may be entitled at the time of my decease, to my sister Henrietta First Moon.

IN WITNESS WHEREOF, by my direction, I being unable to write, Mike Roy has hereunto subscribed my name and I have affixed my mark hereto by an impression of my right thumb, this 28th day of July, 1914, in the presence of Mike Roy, Grover Story Teller and May LeClair, whom I have asked to become attesting witnesses.

                                                       Her
                                    Ella Little Soldier Thumb
                                                            print.

The foregoing instrument was subscribed, published and declared by Ella Little Soldier, as her last will and testament, in our presence and in the presence of each of us, and we, at the same time, at her request, in her presence and in the presence of each other, hereunto subscribe our names and residences as attesting witnesses this 28th day of July 1914. We carefully explained the provisions of the above and foregoing instrument to Ella Little Soldier and interpreted it in the Ponca Indian language in so explaining it to her, so that she fully understood its contents and provisions immediately prior to the time she signed the same. Then by her direction the undersigned Mike Roy wrote her name hereto above.

                              Mike Roy, Whiteagle, Okla.
                              Grover Story Teller, Whiteagle, Okla.
                              May LeClair, Whiteagle, Okla.

Department of The Interior,
Office of Indian Affairs
                                    Mar. 29, 1915

The within will is hereby recommended for approval in accordance with the Act of June 25, 1910 (36 Stats. L., 855-6) as amended by the Act of February 14, 1913 (37 Stat. 678); and it is further adjudged that inasmuch as the condition set out by the testatrix for the inheritance of any share in this estate by her husband,

NATIVE AMERICAN WILLS and PROBATE RECORDS, 1911 - 1921

Little Soldier, has been broken, this entire estate, both real and personal, passes in accordance with the terms of the will to Henrietta First Moon, sister of the testatrix.

                                        Respectfully,
                                        E.B. Meritt
                                        Assistant Commissioner

Department of The Interior
Office of the Secretary   Apr. 6, 1915
Washington, D.C.

The within will is hereby approved in accordance with the Act of June 25, 1910 (36 Stats. L., 855-6) as amended by Act of February 14, 1913 (37 Stat. 678); and it is further adjudged that inasmuch as the condition set out by the testatrix for the inheritance of any share in this estate by her husband, Little Soldier, has been broken this entire estate, both real and personal, passes in accordance with the terms of the will to Henrietta First Moon, sister of the testatrix.

                                        Bo Sweeney
                                        Assistant Secretary

County of Canadian   Calumet, Okla. Nov. 21, 1914.

                        The last will and testament of
                                Lean Bear.

I **LEAN BEAR** of Calumet, Oklahoma, being now in good health, strength of body and mind, but sensible of the uncertainty of life, and desiring to make disposition of my property and affairs while in strength and health do hereby make, publish, and declare the following to be my last will and testament, hereby revoking and cancelling all other or former wills by me at any time made.

      1. I direct the payment of all my just debts and funeral expenses.

      2. I give and devise to my three great grand children, vix. Nellie Matches Wicks, Morgan Matches Wicks and Walter Matches Wicks, each to share alike, the following property, all of real estate which consists of the North West (NW) one fourth (1/4) of Sec. Seventeen (17) Township thirteen (13) Range nine (9) West I.M. together with all improvements on said land.

      3. I give to my same three great grand children, each to share alike, any money that may be to my credit at the time of my demise.

NATIVE AMERICAN WILLS and PROBATE RECORDS, 1911 - 1921

4. I hereby appoint the Supt. of the Cheyenne & Arapaho Agency at Darlington, Oklahoma to be sole executor, without bond, of this my last will and testament.

In witness whereof, I Lean Bear, have to this my last will and testament, consisting of this sheet of paper, subscribed my name this 21st day of November 1914.

Witness   her
                     Lean Bear (thumb)
                             mark

Herbert Walker
Mina A. Tardy
Tom Cloud Chief

Subscribed by Lean Bear in the presence of each of us, the undersigned, and at the same time declared by her to us to be her last will and testament and we, thereupon at the request of Lean Bear in her presence and in the presence of each other, sign our names hereto as witnesses this 21st day of November 1914.

Herbert Walker,
       Calumet, Okla.
Eugene M. Tardy
       Calumet, Okla.
Mina A. Tardy
       Calumet, Okla.

Department of The Interior,
Office of Indian Affairs
Washington, D.C.   Jan. 28, 1915

It is recommended that the within will be approved pursuant to the provisions of the Act of June 25, 1910 (36 Stats. L., 855-6) as amended by the Act of February 14, 1913 (37 Stat. 678) and the Regulations of the Department.

                             Respectfully,
                             E.B. Meritt
                             Assistant Commissioner

Department of The Interior
Office of the Secretary   Feb. 24, 1915

The within will is hereby approved pursuant to the provisions of the Act of June 25, 1910 (36 Stats. L., 855-6) as amended by Act of February 14, 1913 (37 Stat. 678) and the Regulations of the Department.

                             Bo Sweeney
                             Assistant Secretary

NATIVE AMERICAN WILLS and PROBATE RECORDS, 1911 - 1921

Last Will and Testament of Wa win tin nokt or Annie Bear.

I, **WA WIN TIN NOKT** or **ANNIE BEAR**, of the town of Kamiah, in the County of Lewis and State of Idaho, do hereby make this my lat will and testament:

    1st. I direct the payment of all my just debts and funeral expenses.

    2nd. Unto Minnie Amera, I give devise and bequeath Lots numbered one and two of Section Fifteen and the lots numbered six, seven, and eight of Section Fourteen in Township Thirty two North of Range two east of Boise Meridian, containing one hundred acres more or less according to the Government survey thereof, the above tract known as Allotment No. 1642 -- to be hers absolutely.

    3rd. I hereby nominate and appoint the Superintendent of the Fort Lapwai Schools Executor of this my last will and testament and should he not be in position to act as such executor the court in which this will is probated shall make such appointment.

    In witness whereof, I have to this my last will and testament subscribed my name this 28th day of June, 1911.

                            Wa win tin nokt or Annie Bear
Witnesses to mark.   Her Thumb Mark.
Samuel J. Sanidon
    Act. Ind. Sub-Agent
    Kamiah, Idaho.

We hereby certify that on this 28th day of June A.D. 1911 at Kamiah in the County of Lewis and State of Idaho, Wa win tin nokt or Annie Bear to us personally know, did, in our presence, sign the foregoing instrument and declare the same to be her last will and testament and we, at her request, and in her presence, and in the presence of each other, do hereby subscribe our names as witnesses thereto.

                            Samuel J. Sanidon, Act Ind-Sub-Agent.
                            Sam W. Frank interpreter.
                            Geo. H. Waterman.

Department of The Interior,
Office of Indian Affairs
Washington, D.C.   Feb. 9, 1914.

It is recommended that the within will be approved pursuant to the provisions of the Act of June 25, 1910 (36 Stats. L., 855-6) as amended by the Act of February 14, 1913 (37 Stat. 678).

                            Respectfully,
                            (signed) E.B. Meritt
                            Assistant Commissioner

NATIVE AMERICAN WILLS and PROBATE RECORDS, 1911 - 1921

Department of The Interior
Washington, D.C. Feb. 9, 1914.

The within will is hereby approved pursuant to the provisions of the Act of June 25, 1910 (36 Stats. L., 855-6) as amended by Act of February 14, 1913 (37 Stat. 678).

          (signed) Lewis C. Laylin
          Assistant Secretary

IN THE NAME OF GOD, AMEN:-

  BE IT REMEMBERED THAT I, **JUDGE LOUISON**, Flathead allottee No. 1626, now a resident of the Flathead Indian Reservation in the County of Missoula, and State of Montana, of the age of seventy-five years, being of sound and disposing mind and memory, and not acting under duress, fraud or under influence of any person whomsoever, do make, publish and declare this, my last will and testament, in the following manner, that is to say:

  I leave, will and devise to my beloved wife, Christine Louison, Flathead allottee No. 1627, and to Louie Topsseh, Flathead allottee No. 1647, who in the last few years has been the only one of my relatives to look after and care for me, all of my allotment No. 1626, consisting of the Lot 3 of section 2, and NW1/4 of SE1/4, N1/2 of SW1/4 of SE1/4, and NE1/2 of SE1/4 of SW1/4 of section 16, T. 16 N., R. 19 W., M. M., containing 109.84 acres; and all stock belonging to me, both cattle and horses, said Christine Louison and Louis Topsseh to share equally in the property hereby devised.

  I hereby nominate and appoint Christine Louison the executor of this, my last will and testament. And I hereby revoke all former wills by me made.

  IN WITNESS WHEREOF, I have hereunto set my hand and seal this the 5th day of February, in the year of our Lord, one thousand nine hundred and twelve.

                His
         Judge Louison thumb
Witness to mark: Mark
John Finley.

  The foregoing instrument, consisting of this one page, was, at the date thereof, by said Judge Louison, signed, sealed and published as, and declared to be, his last will and testament, in the presence of us, who, at his request, and in his presence and in the presence of each other, have subscribed our names as witnesses thereto.

NATIVE AMERICAN WILLS and PROBATE RECORDS, 1911 - 1921

H.S. Allen   Fred C. Morgan

Department of The Interior,
Office of Indian Affairs
April 3, 1915.
It is recommended that the within will be approved, insofar as it relates to the original allotment of the devisor, pursuant to the provisions of the Act of June 25, 1910 (36 Stats. L., 855-6) as amended by the Act of February 14, 1913 (37 Stat. 678).

(signed) E.B. Meritt
Assistant Commissioner

Department of The Interior
Washington, D.C.   April 8, 1915

The within will is hereby approved, insofar as it relates to the original allotment of the devisor, pursuant to the provisions of the Act of June 25, 1910 (36 Stats. L., 855-6) as amended by Act of February 14, 1913 (37 Stat. 678).

(Signed) Bo Sweeney
Assistant Secretary

LAST WILL AND TESTAMENT OF DANIEL FIRE CLOUD.

IN THE NAME OF GOD, AMEN.

I, **DANIEL FIRE CLOUD**, sixty-two years of age, an Indian of Crow Creek Indian Reservation, South Dakota, being of sound mind, memory, and understanding, do hereby make and publish this my last Will and Testament, hereby revoking and annulling all wills by me heretofore made, especially the will made by me on January 5, 1915, in manner and form following, that is to say:

FIRST: I direct that all my just debts and funeral expenses and expenses of my last illness shall be paid as soon after my decease as shall be convenient.

SECOND: I am possessed of an allotment of land within the Crow Creek reservation, South Dakota, described as the South half (S1/2) of Section Thirty-two (32) Township One hundred eight (108) North, of Range Seventy-three (73) West of the fifth principal meridian in South Dakota. I give, devise and bequeath my said allotment of land to the following named persons, to-wit:

To Anna Fire Cloud, or Pretty Woman, my wife, I give, devise and bequeath the West half (W1/2) of the South-west quarter (SW1/4) of said section 32, Township 108 N., Range 73 W., 5th P.M. containing 80 acres.

NATIVE AMERICAN WILLS and PROBATE RECORDS, 1911 - 1921

To Rebecca Fire Cloud, my daughter, I give devise and bequeath the North-east quarter (NE1/4) of the South-west quarter (SW1/4) of said section 32, Township 108 N., Range 73 W., 5th P.M. containing 40 acres.

To Ada Fire Cloud, my daughter, I give, devise and bequeath the Southeast quarter (SE1/4) of the Soputhwest quarer (SW1/4) of said section 32, Township 108 N., Range 73 W., 5th P.M. containing 40 acres.

To James Fire Cloud, my son, I give, devise and bequeath the East half (E1/2) of the Southeast quarter (SE1/4) of said section 32, township 108 N., Range 73 W., 5th P.M. containing 79.40 acres.

To Thomas Fire Cloud, my son, I give, devise, and bequeath, the West half (W1/2) of the South-east quarter (SE1/4) of said section 32, Township 108 N., Range 73 W. 5th P.M., containing 80 acres.

THIRD: I have an interest in the allotment of Rebecca Red Woman, described as Lots 1, 2, 3 and 4 of section 5, T. 107 N., R. 73 W. and the W1/2 of Section 33, T. 108 N., R. 73 W. 5th P.M., containing 321.20 acres. I give devise, and bequeath all my interest in said allotment of Rebecca Red Woman, to my niece, Lucy Sazue, and to my niece, Mabel Lodge, the same to be divided between them equally.

FOURTH: I am the sole heir of Abel Fire Cloud, deceased, to whom was allotted the Northeast quarter (NE1/4) of Section 31, Township 108 N., Range 73 W. 5th P.M., in South Dakota.

I give, devise and bequeath to Anna Fire Cloud, or Pretty Woman, my wife, the SW1/4 of the NE1/4 of said section 31, T. 108 N., R. 73 W., containing 40 acres.

I give, devise, and bequeath to Charles Briggs, the SE1/4 of the NE1/4 of section 31, T. 108 N., R. 73 W., 5th P.M. containing 40 acres.

I give, devise and bequeath to James Fire Cloud, my son, to Thomas Fire Cloud, my son, to Rebecca Fire Cloud, my daughter, and to Ada Fire Cloud, my daughter, the N1/2 of the NE1/4 of section 31, T. 108 N., R. 73 W., 5th P.M. containing 80 acres, the same to be divided among them equally, each to share alike.

FIFTH: All the personal property and all funds I may have at the time of my death, I direct shall be divided and distributed among my wife and living children, after my death, by the Superintendent in charge of the Crow Creek Agency, South Dakota, according to his judgment.

AND LASTLY: I am satisfied the Officers of the Department of the Interior of the United States will make proper provision for carrying into effect of this my

NATIVE AMERICAN WILLS and PROBATE RECORDS, 1911 - 1921

last will and testament, and therefore, I have not appointed an excutor[sic] to administer my estate.

I have only the four children living for whom I have made provision herein, and no children of any deceased children.

IN TESTIMONY WHEREOF, I have set my hand and seal to this my last will and testament at the Crow Creek Indian Agency Office, Crow Creek, South Dakota, this 8th day of January 1915.

        (signed) Daniel Fire Cloud.

Signed, sealed, published and declared by the said Daniel Fire Cloud, in our presence, as and for his last Will and Testament, and at his request and in his presence and in the presence of each other we have hereunto subscribed our names as attesting witnesses thereto.

  Peter W. Lightfoot, Residence, Crow Creek, South Dakota.
  Russell Harrison, Residence, Crow Creek, South Dakota.
  Alex. Suzu, Residence, Crow Creek, South Dakota.

Department of The Interior,
Office of Indian Affairs
  Mar. 9, 1915

It is recommended that the within will be approved pursuant to the provisions of the Act of June 25, 1910 (36 Stats. L., 855-6) as amended by the Act of February 14, 1913 (37 Stat. 678).

      (signed) E.B. Meritt
      Assistant Commissioner

Department of The Interior
Office of the Secretary Mar. 22, 1915

The within will is hereby approved pursuant to the provisions of the Act of June 25, 1910 (36 Stats. L., 855-6) as amended by Act of February 14, 1913 (37 Stat. 678).

      (signed) Bo Sweeney
      Assistant Secretary

Index

ABBOTT, F H 214,228
ACHEN, Henry 307
ADAMS
    Alithea 40
    John 150,151
    Samuel 228
AFRAID OF HAWK, Edward 262
AFRAID OF HORSES, Lucy 11
AFRAID OF THE LODGE ... 215,216
AGARD, Mrs 235
AGNES, Mrs 105
AH-LOU-WAH-TSON-MY 85
ALBERT 42
ALEXANDER, Celia 113
ALLEN
    Ernest 236
    H S 317
    John J 45
ALLEY, Ernest J 253
AMERA, Minnie 315
AMOUX, James M 108
ANDERS
    Millie 157,158,159,161,162
    Mrs Millie 154,155,156,160
ANDERSON, Jas 69
ANDY, Elizabeth 98,99
ANN-PO-HE 130
ANT, Walter 14
ANTELOPE, Trenton 167
ANTELOPE NOSE, Mrs 65
ANTONE, Mary 39
ARCHAMBEAU, Moses 234
ARCHDALE, Henry, Jr 182
ARCHIBALD, F M 88
ARMSTRONG, Lucy 185
ARPAN, Angiluque 165
ASBURY
    C H 98
    Wickerson S 218
ASHFORD, John 87
ASHLEY
    Edward 267
    Wallace 9
AUN-PAU-HOM 130
AXELBERG, H P 51,52,53
AXELBERT, H P 54
BABCOCK, Omar L 289
BACKUS, John J 227

BAD BOY, David 82
BAID, Charles M 30
BAKER, F A 191
BALE, H W 303
BANKS 299,300
BARBOUR, Alvin 2
BARNES
    Lida W 295
    Richard J 273
BARROW, A M 95
BARTCH, Frank 169
BEAR
    Annie 296,297,315
    Darwin 217
    Grace 217
    John 217
    Moses 307
    Smith 217
BEAR CHILD 131,132
BEAR GOES TO THE OTHER
    GROUND 300
BEAR GRAND, Otto 138
BEARSKIN, Edward 121
BEAVER, Frank 207
BEAVERTAIL 194
BEBOUT, William R 254
BECKER
    Abraham J 193
    A J 111,192
    M 111
    Magdalena 111,192,193
BEGS HIS OWN 194
BENEDICT, Birdie 35
BENOIST
    Ambrose 250
    Louis 248,250,251
    Mary Agnes 249,250
    Narcisse 250
    William 250
BENSELL, Arthur 151
BENT
    George, Jr 208,209
    Julia 208
    Neal 208
    Nellie 209
BERGEN, Wm 257
BERGEVEN, Carrie 258
BERKEUPAS, Anna G 19

Index

BERNIE
    Josephine 233
    Obee 233
    Oscar 233
BIBB, Homer J 217,232,253
BICHEA 146,147
    Mrs 147
BIG FOOT 92
BIG HAT 137,138,139
BIG HAWK 46,47
    Luella 46
BIG HORN, Maurice 194
BIG LAKE, Thomas 97
BIG SHIELD, Pins [Illegible] 92
BIG SUSIE 15
BIGHEAD, Dave 311
BILL, Amy 39
BINGHAM, Ettie 202
BIRD HORSE
    Hobart 24
    Leo 23
    Robert 23
    Willie 23
BLACK, S F 26
BLACK BEAR
    Eliza 67
    Nancy 22
BLACK CLOUD, Mrs Jane 115
BLACK HAIR
    Frank 173,174
    Mary 173
    Percy 173
    Sidney 173
    Wilbur 173
BLACK PINE, Mrs Mary 6,7
BLACKBIRD
    Alfred 268,269,280,281
    Cyrus 268,269
    John 268
    Mary Lydia 268
    Me gr tae 280
    Me-gre-tae 280
    Megretae 280,281
BLACKCLOUD, Jane 115,116
BLACKDEER
    Bruce 19
    Connokaw 19
BLACKHAWK, Eli 138

BLOCKISTON, Beulah L 263
BLUEDOG, Cecelia 25
BLUESTONE
    Mrs Adam 30
    Rebecca 28
BOGGESS, O M 15
BOMMIN, J S 46
BONGA
    Francis 7,8
    Jack 8
    John 8
    Pete 8
BONNIN, Peidine 209,210
BORDEAUX
    Alex 70
    Arthur, Jr 69
    Levi 69
BOUNT, Isaac 182
BOURISSAU, James 177
BOURISSEAU, James 178
BOWED HEAD 9
BOWKER
    Dora 293
    Richard 293
BOWMAN, Thos 279
BOY, Sam 9
BRAVE BIRD
    Edward 43
    Rosa 43
BRAZZILL, Wm F 107
BREED, Jacob 190
BRENNAN, John R 196,198,199,
201,246,248,257,261,288,298,306
BRENT, Jacob 96
BRESETTE, Charles 224,225
BRETSCHNEIDER
    H 130
    H E 124,131
BREWER, L H 303
BRIGGS, Charles 235,267,318
BRIGHT WOMAN NO MOTHER
    135,136
BRISETTE, Mary 51
BROCK, Leta E 185
BROKEN KNIFE 5,6,7
BROKEN PIPE, Samuel 41
BRONCHE
    Josphine 85

Index

Louie 85
BRONCHEAN, Matilda 143
BROOKS
   Charles 90,142,187
   Chas 90,188
BROWN
   Charley 37,38
   Kate 37
   Perry F 85,86
   Victor E 122
BROWN EAGLE, Grace D 115
BROWN TURTLE, Victor E 116
BROWNING
   Fannie 91
   Mrs Otto 91
BROWNTHUNDER
   Angelic 234
   Eugenia Noah 233
   Lucy 233,234
   Mercy 233,234
BRUCE, Harold E 101
BRYANT, W W 167
BUCKLEY, Abraham 5,7
BUG 62,63,310
BULL BEAR, Jock 146,147
BULTZ, Joseph 282,283
BUNTIN, John A 265
BURBER
   Chuck 53
   Orulf 18
BURN, Rev Hachaliah 217
BURNETTE, Mrs Susan 50
BURNS
   Nellie 209
   Nellie Bent 208
   Robert 209
BURT
   Hachaliah 217
   Rev H 232
   Reverend H 252
   Watawe Blackbird 280
BURTON
   Burt 117
   U A 89
BUTLER, Ben 205
BUTTERFIELD, Alex 51,52
CALLS HIM, Lizzie 228
CAMP, Harry W 256,274

CAMPBELL
   A A 223
   Charles 294
   Mrs Ellis 259
CAN-DU-TA-WIN 275
CANTOW, Louis C 76
CANWAPA 33
CARMICHAEL
   Charles 150
   Mollie 150
CARPENTER
   Elsie 267
   Jay 266,267
CARR, Don 99
CARRUTH, Leo 123
CARUFEL, Wm 55,56
CASPER, Mrs Amelia 220
CASSEL, R J 125,126
CAT
   Albert 20
   Fred 20
   Lizzie 20
   Susie 20,21
   Winston 20
CENTER WOMAN 66,67
CHA-BE-SA 62,63
CHADRON, Mary 215,216
CHAH-YE-A-TO 103,104
CHALMER, Henry W 285
CHARCOAL 146,147
   Mrs 147
CHARGES MADLY ON THE ENEMY
   299
CHASING HAWK 170,171
CHIEF EAGLE
   Angeline 260
   Peter 261,287,288
   Susie 11
CHIEF GHOST 100
CHIEFGHOST 100
   Bedoza 100
CHINO
   Belore 243
   Lorenzo, Sr 243
CHRISTIAN, Julia 135
CHRISTY, Frank 164
CHURCH, Al 119
CIJAN, Michael 163,164

Index

CIMAMINO, Josette 8
CIQUWICAKTE 23,24
CIRCLING EAGLE 36
CLAIRMONT, John 76
CLARK
   Nellie 227
   Ransom R 99
CLAYMORE
   Ines Henry 44
   James 43
CLIFFORD, Chas, Sr 247
CLOUD CHIEF, Tom 314
COBURN, John W 58
COCKRELL
   Cora E 93,94,95
   Pearl Annie 93,94
   Samuel McKee 93
   W G 93
   Wheeler Gordon 93
   Woodrow Wilson 93
COKER, M C 265
COLBURN, Margaret 79
COLBURNE
   Mahgeet 80,81
   Margaret 80,81
COLHOFF
   Frederick 56
   George, Jr 56
   John R 56
   Louis 56
   Mary 56,57
   William 56
COLLIER, Dr L A 234
COMES IN SIGHT 244,245,246
COMINGCLOUD, Matthias 255
COMMONS, George G 221
CONGER, C M 242
CONHEPE, Charlie 126,127
CONWAY
   Clara 203
   Willie 204
COOK
   Annie 83
   Elmyra 83
   Geo M 40,41
   John M 83
   Joseph 83
   Joseph H 177

   Joseph T 81
COOLONG, Moses 218,219
CORBETT
   Billy 96
   Felix 96
   Nancy 96
   Paul 96
   Paul, Sr 96
   Pierre 96
   Susan Holmes 96
   Susie Moody 114
COTTONWOOD, Jerome 154
COUNTER, Reuben 100
COVINGTON, Robt H 172,173
COZAD
   Julia 103
   Louis 104
CRAIGE, R C 214
CRANE, Mary 225
CRAWFORD, Mary Agnes 2
CROSH, G W 80
CROSS, Jasper 18
CROSS KILLER 62
CROW FEATHER, Moses 3,4
CROWFEATHER, Moses 4
CULBERTSON
   Joseph 91,133,135,172,173,
   186,221
   Margaret 283,284,285
   Mrs Joseph 230
CUT EAR 137,138,139,140
CUT NOSE 272,310
DANSON, Robert W 69
DAUGHERTY
   Lucy 26
   Lucy M 174,269
DAVIS
   Charles L 254
   Chas L 291
   Nellie 19
   Susan 19
DAWSON, John 121
DAY
   Minnie 116
   Rosa 266,267
DAY COMES OUT 197
DEAVER
   Ira A 309

Index

Ira C 309
DECORAH
  Carrie 77
  David 115
DEER, Sam V 46
DEFORE
  John F 71
  Katie 71
DENNIS
  C E 80
  Mrs Lizzie Sheff 55
DEVENS, Elizabeth 89
DICK
  Eddie 99
  John 98,99
  Lena 99
  Louis 280,281
  Waters 98,99
DICKENS
  Emma 63,64
  Mamie 63,64
  May 64
  Willard 64
DICKSON
  Clayton 189
  Freda 189
  Susie McConville 189,190
DIDDOCK, Marguerite La F 72
DION, Oliver 290,291
DIRT KETTLE 200,201
  Julia 200
  Mary 200
DIVES BACK WARDS, Rufus 60
DOG HORN
  Betseu 184
  Betsey 183
DOG LISTENS 92,93
  Holy Woman 92
DOG SKIN
  Samuel 152
  William 151,152
DOGSKIN, William 152,153
DOSHINKA, Grover 74
DOSS
  Hon W A 160,162
  William A 162,163
DOUGHERTY
  Albert 13

Louise 13
DOUGLAS, Stephen 154
DOWNS, Col 121
DRENNAN, Annie 289
DU MARCE
  Hazen A 307
  Henry 306
  Henry A 307
  Mathilda A 306
DUBE
  John 79,80
  Margaret 79,80,81
DUCHENEAUX
  Baryney 165
  Camille 165
  Douglass 165
  Fred 165
  Henry 165
  Lille 165
  Mabel 165
  Mamie 165
  Moses 165
  Napoleon 165,166
  Patrick 165
  Victor 165
  Willie 165
DUCK, Thomas 116
DUNN, W E 1
DYER
  Eliza 290,291
  Fanny 290,291
  Robert 291
  Sophia 290,291,292
EAGLE
  Eunice 25
  James 65
  James Y 64
  Stella 64
  Thomas 24,25
EAGLE HEAD 30,31
EAGLE WOMAN 200
EAGLEDOG
  Annie 262
  Louis 262
  Philip 262
EAGLE-FOX, Rosie 305
EAT NO MEAT 258,259
EATON, R N 278

Index

EDDY, Elmo 81
EDIGAR, J B 167
EGNA, Louis 214
EHY, Harry W 147
ELAMETNONMI 258
ELLARD, Chas B 20,21
ELLIS, Clifford M 219,220
ENNO
    Alex 213
    Antoine 212
    Antoine Louis 212
    Antoine, Sr 212
    Catherine 212
    Louis 212
    Sarah 212
ENOS, Henry 96
ENSIGN, Charles F, MD 25
E-PA-LEE-LOT-WE-YAH-LA-SON-MY 85
ESTES, J F 107
ETHEL 144
EYAPAHA, John 90,187
EYES-OPEN 300,301
FARRELL, F E 92,100,144,194
FARRENSBY
    John 125
    Kate 124,125,126
FARUOR, US I D 92
FAST HORSE, Bessie 38
FAY, Harvey 155,159,160,161, 162,163
FEW TAILS, Samuel 196
FIELDER, Allen 216
FIELDS, George 206
FINLEY
    Anne 109,110
    John 316
FINNEGAN, Fannie 202
FINNEY, E B 18,45,54
FIRE CLOUD
    Abel 318
    Ada 318
    Anna 317,318
    Daniel 317,319
    James 318
    Rebecca 318
    Thomas 318
FIRKE, Charles W 161,162

FIRST, Leslie 63
FIRST MOON, Henrietta 312,313
FISHER
    J J 51
    John J 52
FLEURY, Dorothy 13,14
FODDER, Albert M 1
FOOL BEAR, Darks 154
FOX
    Mrs Louisa 23
    Smile 142
FRANK, Sam W 315
FRASS, George 210,211
FREDERICK
    Agnes 128
    Eunice 83
    Isabelle 83
    Peter 83
    Sophia 83
FREEMONT, Henrietta 72,73
FRENCH
    Lizzie 89
    Mary W 31
    Mrs Carlo 31,32
FRIDAY, Moses L 31
FROSTED
    Mrs Susan 262
    Thomas 262
GABE, George 24
GAITHER, Mrs F E 263
GALE, Edward R 161,162
GARDIPE
    Bernard 303
    Bertha 303
    Charlie 303
    Eleanor 303,304
    George Wilford 303
    Jennie 303
    Joseph 303
    Margariet 303
    Matilda 303
    Victoria 303
GARDNER
    Glora A 44
    W L 44
GARFIELD, Penn 4,214,216,228
GARNER, Garrett J 146
GARREAU, John 214

Index

GARRETT, Lloyd..........................94
GARTER
   Joseph 101
   Nancy 101
GAY, William...............................291
GENERATION, Louisa................129
GEORGE, Samuel 39
GILES, Milton 239
GODFREY, F 170
GOES FIRST 307,308,309
GOINGS, Frank C 298
GOOD BEAR, Mrs John...............153
GOOD GOES AHEAD.................139
GOOD TAIL WOMAN DUMB 92
GOOD TAIL WOMN DUMB 92
GOOD VILLAGE
   David......................................75,76
   William 75
GOOD VOICE, John 217
GOODELL, J L......................150,151
GOODRICH, Mrs Bessie..............283
GOODWIN, F M 1,5,6,8,10,11,12,14,
   15,16,21,23,24,25,27,28,30,31,32,33,34,
   37,38,39,40,42,43,44,47,48,49,50,58,
   59,82
GOULD, Jay 310
GRACE..42
GRANT
   Hanika.......................................206
   Hattie Wells 206
   Maggie 206,263
   Maggie Webster.......................280
   Mary E G 263
   Mercy..206
   Nattie Wells 206
   W C..286
   William 263
   Wm 263
GRAVES
   Mary Crane 225,226
   William J O 225
GRAY, Frank L 277
GRAY BEAR
   Gerald 153,154
   Mrs Gerald 153
GRAY HAIRED BEAR................235
GRAY SPOTTED HORSE....179,180
   Mrs......................................178,179

GRAYHAIR
   Cora...226
   Joseph.......................................226
   Nellie 19
GREENCROW
   Charles..61
   Mrs 61,62
GROVES, Pearl...... 154,155,156,157,
   158,159,160,161,162
GUEER, Daniel 19
GUYER, John J 296
GWYN, John J...............................96
HA HAI TA, Mary 68
HAAG, Mack 211
HACKETT, J F..............................49
HAIL, Mathew 62
HAIR FACE 136,137
HAIRY BACK, Dewey 228
HAKE..141
HALE
   Adelia 144
   James H 237
HALL
   Albert E 279
   Mary 279
   Sophie...45
HAMILTON
   J Y..262
   Rose..58
HAMINE, Monroe G.....................45
HAMMACK, Dave 125,126
HANA, H S, Sr.............................222
HANTEMAZAWIN.....................164
HAPA, Mrs John 181
HARDING, Warren G...................54
HARDY, Lee C 148,149
HARE, DeWitt 13
HARGRAVE, John F 121
HARNEY, Joe................................43
HARRINGTON
   Chase..311
   Frank...311
HARRIS
   Jennie Tavoots.................. 204,205
   Tilden T....................................226
HARRISON, Russell 236,253,276,319
HARRY..26
HART, J C....................................218

HARVEY, Weep 205
HAS A TAIL 9
HAUKE, C F 204,210,216,220, 223,232,244
HAVARD, R 181
HAWLEY, D 109
HAYES
    DeWitt C 294,295
    Dewitt C 209,211,273
HAZEN, Amy M 2
HEAD
    Belva 30
    John 30
    Winnie I 30
HEADBIRD, Lizzie 70,71
HEADERICH, G M 132
HEAP-OF-BIRDS
    Alfred 167
    Esther 167
    Ruth 167
HELEN 42
HENAULT
    Carrie 58
    Mary 58
    Mose 58
    Nelson 58,59
    Steve 58
HENDERSON, Mrs 263
HER BLANKET COMES OUT,
    Elizabeth 3
HERNANDEZ
    Ambros 246,247,248
    Ambrose 247
    Cecelia 246,247
    Joseph 246,247
    Sophia 246,247
HEYUME TOE LOTE, Philip 240
HE-YUME-WA-KE-MA-LITS . 84,85
HIGH BEAR 266,267
    Isaac 267
    Van Philip 266,267
HIGH BULL
    Albert 195
    Chas 195
    Cleveland 195,253,254
    Susie 195
HIGH CRANE 90,91,92
    Mrs 91

HIGH PINE, Thomas 245
HILL
    Fred 165
    Henry 165
    Mary 299
HILLS IN HOUSE 140
HINKANKOYAKEWIN 181
HITIKIA, Mary B 83
HODGKISS, Jesse 215
HOK-SI-NA 266
HOLCOMB
    P D 17
    Phineas D 17
HOLDEN, E J 17
HOLDIMAN, Charles W 188
HOLLOWAY, Emily 265
HOLLOWBREAST, Hubert 14
HOLMES, Guy W 259
HOLSON, J V 224
HOLSTEIN
    Allen L 40
    A L 40
HOLSTON, F V 224
HOLY ROCK
    Jonas 66,67
    Polly 67
    Victoria 67
    Zona 67
HOLY WOMAN DOG LISTENS .. 92
HONADICK, Jennie Y 289
HONG
    Frank 283,284,285
    Lillie 283,284,285
HOO-IYE-DAY-AS-SUN-A-SIS-SUS
    123
HOPE, Louisa 286
HOPKINS
    S G 60,61,62,63,64,66,68, 69,70,71,73,75,76,77,78,81,83,84,86, 88,87,90,92,93,95,97,98,99,101, 103,104,106,107,109,110,111,112, 113,114,116,117,118,119,121,122, 123,124,126,127,129,130,132,133, 134,136,137,138,140,141,142,144, 145,146,148,150,151,153,154,163, 164,166,168,169,171,173,174,178, 179,182,183,184,185,187,188,189, 190,192,193,195

Index

W C ... 31
HOPSIN ... 2
HORN, Lucy ... 142,143,144
HORN DOG ... 275,276
  John ... 275,276
HORSE
  Henry ... 297,298
  Lucy ... 260
HOSKINSON, Jas D ... 304
HOUK, C O ... 155
HOULE
  Frank, Jr ... 79
  Julia ... 79
  Lizzie ... 79,80
  Nancy ... 79,80
HOW
  Alma ... 252
  Ellen ... 252
HOWLING ELK, Harry ... 46,47
HOW-WY-HOW-WY ... 96
HUNTER
  F G ... 32,33
  Hugh ... 61,62
HUNTS THE ENEMY, Stephen ... 227
HUTO ... 136
HUWLEY, Isaac ... 76
ILLEGIBLE
  Albert ... 46
  Simon ... 182
IRON BEAR ... 245
IRON BLANKET ... 235
  Mrs ... 234,235
IRON HORN ... 180
  Mack ... 179
  Sophie ... 179
IRON HORN BULL ... 220,221
IRON JAW, Louis ... 230
IRON MOCCASIN, Truby ... 227,293
IRON TUSK
  George ... 230
  Louis ... 230
IRON WING
  Cordelia ... 293
  George ... 293
  Jeanette ... 292,293
  Phoebe ... 293
IRON-CEDAR ... 22
IRVING
  Joe ... 10
  Joseph ... 281
ITEOKAHI, David ... 136,137
ITOPAKTENA ... 33
IYATOYIK ... 1,2
IYOSANAJINWIN ... 102
JACK
  Alex ... 120
  Lizzie ... 99
  Maggie ... 113
  Mary Ann ... 120,121
  Stuck ... 120
JACKSON
  Alice ... 302
  Charles ... 121,122
JACOBS, D E ... 54,55
JANDRON
  Albert ... 177
  Amelia ... 177
  Asa ... 177,178
  Esau ... 176,177,178
  Felix ... 176,177
  Frank, Sr ... 177
  Katie ... 177
  Louis ... 177
JENNIE ... 42
JEWETT ... 180
  Frank ... 179
  Magie ... 179
JIMMIE, Jennie Baker ... 148
JOHNS
  Joseph ... 90
  Mary Sampson ... 127
JOHNSON
  Chas ... 49,50
  Frances Coolong ... 218
  Frank ... 77,78,79,115
  Jim ... 50
  Joseph ... 187
  Marie ... 49
  Mary ... 301
  Narguerite L ... 32
JONAS, Hannah ... 84,85,86
JONES ... 213,214
  Jim ... 75
  Paul ... 16
JOSEPHINE ... 96
JOURDAN, Lucy ... 188,189

Index

JUDY, Glenn E 219
KA-LU-LA-SON-MY 84,85
KAW-BATCHE.....................175,270
KAY-KAT 44
KE-AH-PAUM 103
KEEFE, Harry L 72
KEEL, A J 31
KEEPS BONE 66,67,68
KELL, C E 70
KELLER
   Henry 186
   Oscar H 127
KENNEDY, Eugene 289
KENTUCK, Moses 96
KERN, F 224
KESSLER
   Mrs W H 165
   W H 165
KETCH, Jas B 24
KEZENA, Freddie 128
KIDNEY, Mrs 65,66
KILLER, J K 196,197,199,201
KILLING THUNDER, Mrs 230
KILLS IN WATER
   Howard 287
   Samuel 287
KILLS IN WINTER
   Benjamin 22
   Thomas 22,23
KILLS THE CHIEF 97
KIMIMIKOYAKEWIN...............89,187
KINCAID, G P 40
KINGMAN, Agnes 101
KINGSLEY, Emma 210
KIN-YAN-HI-YA-YA 232
KIOWA LITTLE BEAR 210
KIOWA WOMAN 208,209,210
KIRCH, James B 300
KIT-CHI-KWE 44
KITT, James B 178,180,181
KNEALE, Albert H...............207,269
KNOWS THE COUNTRY, Julia
   Webster 280
KOHLENBERG, W C 276,282
KOHUMUIG, W O 232
KOOD-LAW-KOY 130,131
KOPLOTS, Susie 15,16
KOPLOTSILPILP 15,16

KOWS-PA-AH-LOO 85
KUNSPEE, Mary 76,77
KURTZ, J George 221
LA CLAIRE, Sophia 286
LADIANY, Sam 43
LADINEY, Sam 67
LAFLESCHE, R B 291,292
LAFORGE, Josephine 308
LAMBERT
   Baptists 235
   W M 265
LAMPSON, Lee 2
LAMUE, Charles 75
LAND, Paul 146
LANDGREEN
   Charles 295
   Emily 295
LANDMAN, Adrian M 203
LANE, Franklin K 225
LANGIE, Frances 141,142
LANGLOIS, Ben 117
LANTZ, Chas 13
LARONGE, Joe 18
LARRABEE
   David 3,4
   George 6
   Nellie 6,7
LARSON, C H 278
LAST HORSE, Mrs Mattie 170
LAW
   Grace P 104
   John A 104
LAWRENCE, Osias 296,297
LAWYER, Corbett B 185
LAYLIN, Lewis C 196,198,200,
201,203,204,205,207,208,213,215,216,
233,316
LEAF, Charles 33
LEAN, Mr 92
LEAN BEAR 313,314
LEBEAU
   Alex 215
   Felix 215
   Henry 216
   John B 216
   Jose 165
LECLAIR, May 312
LECLAIRE

Index

Antoine 148,149,150
Herbert 148,149
Hubert 148
LeRoy 148,149
LEFTBEAR, Bessie 164
LEMON, C O 309
LEONARD, Orson A 250,251
LESTER
   Mrs William 35,36
   William 134
LIEURANCE, Edward 300
LIGHT, George K 304
LIGHTFOOT, Peter W 10,30,152,319
LIKE HIM, Mrs Mary 29
LINCOLN
   Eva 87,145
   Henry 62,63
   Sam B 311
LINDECROW, Asa 230,231
LINDLEY
   J S 247
   John S 247
LITTLE, John 147
LITTLE CHARLIE 238,239
LITTLE CLOUD, Mrs 266
LITTLE COYOTE 166,167
LITTLE GHOST, Theresa 255
LITTLE HOOP, Chas 171
LITTLE KILLER 23,24
LITTLE OX
   Frances 31
   Mary 31
LITTLE SOLDIER 312,313
   Ella 311,312
   Henry 183
LITTLE VILLAGE MAKER . 268,269
LITTLE WOMAN 136,167
LITTLEBEAR
   Adam 77
   Amos 77
   Dan 77
   Thomas 77
LITTLECROW, Asa 153,154
LIVINGSTON, Annie 55
LIZZARD 147
LOBEHAN, Annie 120
LOCKE, Frank L 173,174
LODGE

Josephine 9
Mabel 231,232,318
LOHMILLER, C B 283
LONE FIRST BORN 9
LONE WOLF 256,257
   Mary 202,203
LONEWOLF, Dr 202
LONG BEAT, Howard 41
LONG CAT 38,39
   Ellen 38
   Elsie 38
LONG CROW, Edward 266
LONGTAIL
   Joseph 32
   Mrs Joseph 31
LOOKING BACK, Kate 23
LOOP, Mrs H E 125,126
LOTS OF STARS 82,83
LOTT, Jennie 240
LOUDER, Mrs Eliza 119
LOUISON
   Christine 316
   Judge 316
LOVES WAR, Harry 24
LOWE, Julia 129
LUFFMAN, Don Marks 307
LYMAN, Max 81
MA MA 70
MACKENSTADY, Roger C 269
MADISON
   Cornelia 88,105
   George 105
   Josephine 105
   William 105
MAGMUSSON, Hennan V 37
MAGPIE, Paul W 184
MAG-QUAT, Gertie 26
MAHPIICASNA 102,103
MAHPIICICASNA 103
MAHPIYAICICASNAWIN 103
MAJOR, Mary 168
MAKEKE, Andrew 242
MAKES GOOD, Joseph 171
MALLETTE, Susan 129,130
MALLORY, Grover 19
MANN, Oliver D 156,157,158,161
MANNING
   Mrs David 230

Index

Nathaniel 237
MANNINGTON
   Nathaniel 236,237,238
   Phoebe 236,237
MANY WOMEN 65,66
MARGARET 144
MARIS, L A 229
MARKS, Virgil L 112
MARPELIS, Frances 99
MARSHALL, Charles 179
MART, Fred 205
MARTIN, Jewell D 205
MATCHES WICKS
   Morgan 313
   Nellie 313
   Walter 313
MATHER, S G 40
MATHEWS, John 258
MATHISON, Soren 285
MATT, James 32,33
MAXWELL, S J 241
MAYLE, Emma 129
MAY-MAUSH-KOW-UN-AH-MO-QU
AY 105
MAY-ZHUCK-E-GE-SHIG .. 104,105
MAZAWANAPEYA, Winona 274
MCBRIDE
   Charles 10,152
   Susan 266
MCCLELLAND, John M 188,189
MCCOMBE, W W 169
MCCOWN
   W B 234
   W F 242
MCDONALD
   Jas 181
   M 181
MCINTOSH, John 219
MCINTYRE, F E 259
MCKENZIE, Clara 203
MCNEELY, Sam D 278
MCNEILLY, E E 128
MCPHERSON, W G 155
MEAD, Mary Celina 89
MEAN, Mary Celina 187
MEAN BEAR SMITH, Grace ... 47,48
MEANS, E C 230,231
MEDICINE, James 92

MEDICINE BEAR, Mrs 91
MEDICINE BULL 167
MEDICINE HORSE, David 133
MEEGAN, Emma 46
MEES, Alphonse 162
MEET-ME-TAH-MA-NIN-MY 96
MEIS, Alphonse 157,158,162
MERITT
   E B 1,2,3,4,5,8,10,11,12,13,15,
   16,17,19,21,22,24,25,27,28,30,31,33,
   34,36,37,39,40,42,43,44,45,46,48,
   49,50,57,59,60,61,62,63,64,66,68,69,
   70,71,73,75,76,77,78,81,82,83,84,
   86,87,88,90,91,93,95,97,98,99,100,
   101,103,104,106,107,108,111,112,
   113,114,115,117,118,119,121,122,
   123,124,126,127,129,130,131,132,
   133,134,135,137,138,139,141,142,
   143,145,146,147,150,151,152,154,
   163,164,166,168,169,171,173,174,
   176,177,179,181,182,184,185,186,
   188,189,190,191,193,194,196,198,
   200,201,203,205,207,211,213,217,
   219,221,222,224,226,231,234,236,
   238,240,241,242,246,248,251,253,
   255,256,257,259,260,261,263,264,
   265,268,269,271,273,275,276,278,
   279,281,282,283,285,286,288,290,
   292,293,295,297,299,300,301,303,
   304,306,307,308,310,311,313,314,
   315,317,319
   E G 110
MILES
   Chas C 113
   James 86
MILLER
   Edgar H 74
   Eliza 143
   F E 222
   Geo L 47,48
   Lewis 294
   Louis 294,295
MILLS, Mrs John 190
MILOT, Frances 264,265
MIN-DA-MIN 44
MINTHORN, Annie 85
MITCHELL, Daniel 140,141
M-JOE-TAH

Index

Ethel 175,271
Gertie 175,270
MOCCASIN
   Charles 27,28
   Eugene 27
   Isaac 27
   Mrs Nellie 27
MONROE
   Elizabeth Ann 108
   Joseph 108
MONTGOMERY, C E 102
MOODY
   Andrew 143
   Charles 114
   George 143
   James 113,114
   Lydia 114
MORAIS
   Annie Pearl 277
   Antoine 277,278
   Mary Ann 277
MORGAN
   F M 83
   Fred C 317
MORRIS
   Alex 120
   Harry 71
   Jesse 71,72
   John 71,72
   Ma-zae-pa-we 71,72
   Mazapawe 72,73
   Sam, Jr 241
MORRISON, Elizabeth M 56
MORTSOLF, Jesse B 3
MOSSMAN, E D 91,133,134,
140,172,182,186
MUD BAY CHARLIE 238,239
MUNROE, Joseph 108
MURPHY, D E 66
MYHRE
   Martin A 304
   W A 277
NAKISKINWIN 164
NAKS-TSA-A-LO 85
NEIL, M A O 58
NELLIS, George W 237
NELSON, Philip F 279
NEWMAN, Samuel 66

NEWTON, John C 47,48
NIGHT WALKER 146,147
NO EAR, Grace S B 228
NO NAME 60,221,222,223
NOAH 233,234
NOEL, John Ieska 141,142
NOOK-TI-SHE-MAY 258,259
NOOPTUSH DICHIS 223
NORTON
   Charles E 47
   Victor E 237
NOW-KUM-GE-QUAH 175
NOW-KUM-GO-QUAH 270
NUM-KUM-GO-QUAH 26
NUNNE, Grant A 50
OBESHAW
   Anna 118
   Eliza 119
   Frank 119
   Julia 118
   Robert 118,119
OBIE, Albert 3
O-CUAY GUN 44
OJIBWAY, John B 80
OKRA 205
OLD BEAR, Ned 139
OLD HAIR
   Alfred 199
   Belle 199
   Josie 199
   Stephen 198,199
   Thomas 199
OLD HORN, Clarence 82,308
OLD HORSE, Mollie 260
OLD MARY 16,17
OLD PLUM 253
   Gets Mad 253,254
   John 254
   Lulu 253,254
OLDBEAR, Vincent 59,60
ONE FEATHER 4
   Alfred 4
   Elizabeth 3,4
   Ida 3
   James 3,4
   Joseph 3,4
   Moses 3,4
ONE TOOTH 8,9,10

Index

ONE WHO FLIES 152
ONEFEATHER, Moses 4
ONEROAD, Chas 307
ONIHA, Elizabeth........................106
ONONHAL[?], Miss Isabel 108
OOKIYE, Joseph 137
ORTON, Bensell............................188
OSBORN, Mary............................237
OWENS, Alan L 34
OWL ABOVE, Mary 222
O-YE-BI..20
    Freeman 20
    Thomas 20
OYEMAZANA......................89,187
PABLO, Lawrence........................109
PACKINEAU
    Joseph 65,66
    Mrs Joseph 66
PACKS WOOD 229
    Carl 229
    Violet 229
PAHAKADOKISENI, Geo............181
PALMER, Lucy C 75
PANASO, Lucy 16
PANE, Jesse.................................143
PANKASKEWIN 178
PARISIEN, Louis 213
PARKER
    D G..239
    Kelsey 110
PARKHURST
    Charles D 305
    Chas D 305
    Eugene 8,9,10
    Joseph Purcell 9
    Josephine....................................9
    Samuel Emerson 9
PAU-KO-YA 130
PAU-KO-YE.................................130
PAUL
    Charles 1
    Thomas 68,69
PENDLETON, Carrie 167
PERKINS, N J 82
PETE, Joe.....................................127
PETERS
    Mollie.....................................239
    Susin C 20,21

PETERSON
    Adelia.....................................144
    Adelia Hale 145
    Charles....................................144
    Jeanette.....................................32
PETRY, Austin.............................155
PHILBRICK
    Adah Irene 29
    Annie 29
    Charley 29
    Edith 29
    Elvirah 29
    Ernest..29
    Rebecca 28,29,30
    Robert E....................................29
    Robert G 29
PIBB, P J 276
PICARD, Chas 102
PIERCE, Frank.............................244
PILLOW SHOOTER............. 122,123
PINCKNEY
    G H 14
    H 14
PINK, Mrs 89
PIT-YOU-STUNS NEY 113
POCHA, Mrs Jane Mary 108
POFFENBERGER, Carroll R...........1
POHA 273,274
POLKEY, John...............................32
POND, Elias 143
POOLAW, Edward.........................21
POPOPA..181
POUNDS THE IRON...............97,98
POWAUKEE
    Amos H 114
    Louie A...................................114
POWDERFACE, Clarence............273
PRATT
    Dora..217
    J J..74
PRENTISS, Julia 208,211
PRESTON, Mary............................46
PRETTY BIRD 234,235
PRETTY DAY 266,267
PRETTY EAGLE, Loretta..............97
PRETTY FACE.....................213,214
PRETTY FEATHER WOMAN ...299
PRETTY HORSE.... 137,139,297,298

Index

PRETTY SHIELD 139
PRETTY WOMAN 317,318
PRIMEAUX, George 229
PROCTOR
    Eliza S 172
    Eliza Smith 173
    Ethel 172
    Mrs Eliza S 172
    Peter 172
PRUNTY, William Eagle 44
QUAPAW
    Elnora 309
    Pius 309
QUETON, Oscar 130,131
RADCLIFF, Perrin C 204
RAIN WALKING WOMAN 77,78,79
RANDOLPH, W C 27,28,204
RATTLING HOUSE WOMAN 41
RATTLING LEAF SHOOTS TIGER
.... 116,117
RATTLING THUNDER, Lucy 35
RAWHIDE, Gus 23
RAY, Frank 105
RAYMOND 42
REABIGSKINNY, Homer 118
READ, J L 147
REAUSSIN, Eustache 212
REAY, L S 149
RED
    Daisy 186
    Dorothy 186
    George 186
    Iron Wing 186
    Minnie 186
RED BOY, Eugene 134
RED BUFFALO, Agnes 227
RED CLOUD
    Alfred 11
    Charles 11
    Jack 10,11
    James, Jr 11
    James, Sr 11
    John 11
    Joseph 11
    Nancy 11
    Sarah 226,227
RED DRESS 100
RED EAGLE, Harold 92,132,194

RED ELK
    Herman 91
    Mrs 85
RED ELK NO. 2 260,261
RED HAIR 222
RED HAWK, Sophie 23
RED MOUTH 310
RED PHEASANT
    Sam 178,180,181
    Samuel 179
RED PHESANT, Sam 180
RED ROAD 220
RED THUNDER 60,61
    Anna 252
    Celeste 252
    Rose 252
    William 251,252,253
RED TRACK, Matilda 245
RED WOMAN, Rebecca 318
RED WOOD WOMAN 275,276
REDLIGHTNING, Homer 242
REDSTONE, Richard 36
REE
    David 118
    Lillian 233
REED
    J H 8
    O A 8
REEL, Frowin 170
REIL, Mary Bresette 224
RENCOUNTRE
    Dinah 29
    Mrs James 29
REVARRE, Anthony 154,155,156,
157,158,159,160,161,162,163
REYNOLDS, Chas A 120
RICE
    Dan 207
    Richard 176,271
RICHARDS
    P 75
    R A 48
RIDES BEHIND THE OTHER WAY
.... 139
RILEY, James 60,61
ROAN BEAR, Edward 227
ROBINSON
    Henry 112

Index

Poncasa 268
ROCK, John 305
RODGERS, John H 114
ROE, Edith 46
ROMSA, Jesse 58
ROOT 231,232
ROSEBERRY
    Annie 191
    Jack 191
ROSS
    Charles 122
    O C 57,197
ROTH, Burton F 35,36,134,135, 140,141
ROUILLARD
    Antoine 112
    Gabriel 112
    Theodore 112
ROW STANDING 166,167
ROY
    Lizzie 12
    Mike 312
RUCKMAN, C W 209
RUNNING HORSE, Russel 43
RUNS ABOVE 196,197
    George 197
    Peter 197
RUNS AGAINST, Jacob 67
RUSLER, Wm 45
RUSSELL, John 59
SABINE, Pierre 76
SAGE WOMAN 167
SAHOTCAROW, Frank 289
SAINTE BAPTISTE 44
SALAZAR, Louis M 244
SALLEE, L T 94,95
SAMPSON, Leo 258
SANIDON, Samuel J 315
SANTEE, Mary 281,282
SATE-PE-AH-TAW 130
SAUL, Thomas 4
SAULEY, Ira 311
SAUMTY, Emma 103
SAUN-KE-AH, Jasper 131
SAUNKEAH, Jasper 131
SAUNTY, Emma 104
SAWYER
    Chett B 86

Corbett B 32,33
SAZUE, Lucy 318
SCHNEIDER, John C 8
SCHNIEDER, H C 83
SCHROEDER, Ed 223
SCHWEIGMAN, J P 291
SCOTT
    Jennie 16,17
    Job 73,74,75
    W W 301
SCRIBNER, J S 8
SEABAY, William 34
SECKES, William N 185
SEE-AH-VAH 192
SELWYN, John 242
SENECA, Rosa 210
SETTER
    Angeline 18
    Frank 18
    Mamie 18
SEVENSON, S W 24
SHANE
    Frank 301
    Howard 299
SHARP, Mrs James 77,78
SHE-BI-AS-I-NO-KWE 44
SHEFF
    John 55
    Vincent 55,56
SHEFF-GOKEY, Mrs Mary 55
SHEH-TAHS 25,26,27,174,176, 269,271
SHELL 178
SHERMAN
    Annie 128
    Clorina 128
    Edgar 128
    Fannie 128
    Henry 128
    Marcella 128
    Rosalie 128
    Stella 128
    Susan 127,128,129
SHICK, S J 98,139
SHIELD, Silas 200
SHIPMAN, R H 138
SHISK, Sidney J 300
SHOOD, Judson 247

Index

SHOOK
    Judson 22,67,248
    Jusson 248
SHOOTS ENEMY 232,276
SHOOTS TIGER 116
SHRINK, Louie 286
SHULTIS, C A 214
SICKMAN
    George 301,302,303
    Mary 302
SIMMONS, David 130
SINGING AFTER 294
SITTING DOWN, Mrs 294,295
SKINNER
    Cecelia 23
    Genevieve 23
    Mrs Wm 23
SKUNK, L 137
SLAUGHTER, Peramelia 283
SLICKPOO
    Mrs James 85
    Sam 85
SLOW EAGLE, Mary 69,70
SMART ENEMY 299
SMITH
    Alice Blackduck 140
    Cecelia 172
    Charles M 203
    Frank 140,141
    George 47,48
    Grace M B 47,48
    Irene 47
    Jennie 140
    John 238,239
    John, Jr 164
    Julian 172
    L L 183,184
    S M 165
    Vina 172
SMOOK, Judson 288
SNYDER, A R 176,271
SOCE, Bill 39,40,41
SOLDIER, Clement W 254
SOULIGNY
    V N 229
    Venette M 229
SPEARS, A H 209
SPENCER

Annert 168
    Eliza Major 168,169
SPOTTED CALF 210
    Mary 210
    Mrs 210,211
SPOTTED OWL, Joshua 67
SPOTTED WOLF 167
SPRAGUE, Esther 282
SPURLING, Fannie S 13
SQUASH 65
SQUIRES
    W P 308
    Walter 300
ST PIERRE
    Gilbert 130
    Peter 234
STABLER, DeLodge 12
STANDING
    Barnard 121
    Patty 121
STANDING BEAR, Oliver Wellard
.... 41
STANDING BUFFALO 78
STANDINGBULL
    Agnes 129
    Moses 129
STANDS BLACK 228,229
    Irving 228
    Steele 228,229
STANDSINTIMBER, John 15
STAR
    Jennie 1
    Louis 1
STARR
    Ellen 2
    Harry 2
    Red 2
    Richard 2,3
STEAD
    Charles 43,44
    James 43
STEALS BEAR, William 65
STECKLEY, L A 117
STEELE, William 65
STELZNER, Robert H 39,57,197,298
STEVENS, Amelia 240
STEWARD, Geneva 108
STEWART 108

Index

E S 39,57,68
  Edward S 41
  Joseph 222
  William 222
STILLS, George 43
STONECOAL
  Ella 190,191,192
  Sampson 191
STOOPS TO CHARGE 82
STORY TELLER, Grover 312
STPIERRE
  Louis 106,107
  Lydia 107
  Nancy 106
  Samuel 107
STRAIT, Martin 90,142,164, 187,256,274
STRIKES BOTH WAYS 223
STRIKES PLENTY 287,288
  Jeff 287
  Lillie 287
  Nancy 287
  Ollie 287
  Sallie 287
STRONG 222
STUART, James 297
STUCKI, Jacob 115
SUNKAHOWASTE 255
SUN-TOSE 123
SURROUNDED, Matilda 245
SUZU, Alex 319
SWAN, William 6,7
SWARTZLANDER, E K 258
SWEENEY, Bo 2,3,17,19,131, 176,212,218,219,220,221,222,224,226, 231,234,236,238,240,241,243,246,248, 251,253,255,256,257,259,260,262,263, 264,268,269,272,273,275,276,278,279, 281,282,284,285,286,288,290,292,294, 295,296,297,299,300,301,303,304,306, 309,310,311,313,314,317,319
SWEENEY BO 307
SWENSON, John K 46,54,56
SWIFT, Frank 123
SWIFT EAGLE, Mrs Eli 153
SWIFTBEAR, Jacob 286
SWOLLEN FACE 287
TAFT, L W 303

TAH-LAH-TO-TI 103,104
TAKE THE SHIELD, Joseph 179
TAKES THE BOW, Abraham 7
TAKES THE HORSE ON THE PRARIE 82
TAKES THE SHIELD 180
  James 169,170
  Joseph 170,179,180
  Joseph, Sr 170
  Mrs Joseph 178
  Robert 169,170
  Thrissie 170
TAKES THEM, Charles 193,194
TALL 272,273
TALL WOMAN 306
TALL-WOMAN 304,305
TAL-TE-A-KOWN 258
TARDY
  Eugene M 314
  Mina A 314
TASAGYEGYEGIWIN 136
TASINAHINAPEWIN 3
TATANKAGINA 164
TATANKANPA 164
TATIYOPA, James A 281,282
TAWOHOLAKONZEWIN 181
THOMAS
  Albert 86,87,145,146
  Joseph 203,204
  Joseph Duff 99
  O G 60,61
THOMPAON, Mary 185
THOMPSON
  C C 211
  Lizzie 22
  Mary 184
  Titus 185
THOMSON, Minnie Sibbits 116
THREE STARR, Clarence 171
THUNDER, Tom 78
THUNDER CLOUD, Sarah 49
THWING, George 6,7,250,251
TIBBETS, James E 190
TIDWELL, H M 12,22,39, 41,43,57,68,171,184
TILDEN, Sam 190
TIMS, Mary 73,74
TINE-GOO AH 20

Index

TINE-GOO-AH 20,21
TIPPETT, J C 160
TIYOWAKANHDIWIN 255
TOBACCO SACK
    Agnes 213,214
    Nancy 213,214
TOLURTILLOTT, J H 25
TOM, Brookie 182,183
TO-PAY 110
    Kelsey 110
TOPSSEH, Louie 316
TO-WA-KO-NIE (JIM) 123,124
TO-WIS-CHY, Elsie 110
TOWNSEND, W H 94
TOWTI 32
TRAVERSIE, Katherine 250
TROTTER, George A 261,287,288
TROTTOCHAND, Peter G 88,105
TSOU LICK, Kentuck 96
TSOU-LICK, Kentuck 95
TUCKER, Dan 311
TUNKAAHEWIN 1
TURLEY
    C Myrtle 162
    Myrtle 159
TUTTLE
    John 70
    Thomas W 217,232
TWO ELK, Robert 41
TWO HEARTS, Luke 179
TWO WOMAN 122
VALLEE
    Baptiste 68
    David 68
VAN HORN
    Anna 209,210
    Mrs Anna 209
VANDALL, L L 84
VANDEVENTER
    Andrew Jackson 50,51
    Benjamin 51
    Charles 51
    Edward 51
    George 51
    A J 51,52,53,54
    Joseph 51,52
    Mike 51,52,53
VIEUX, Mary A 265

VINA 42
VINCENT, C M 78
VINCENTI
    Edward Ladd 243,244
    Tonito Chino 243
WA JASHK, SR 45
WA WIN TIN NOKT 315
WAHACANKAWANJINA 89,90, 187
WAH-BUN-UN-UNG-OKE 105
WAHSISE, Harry 16
WAH-WOON-AH-YETCHY 110,111
WA-JASAHK, SR 44
WA-JASHK, SR 45
WAJASHK, SR 45
WAK WAK, Elizabeth 15
WAKASHEYA
    Julia 242
    Peter 242
WAKINYANHUTE 60,61
WALFORD, J T 295
WALKER
    B N O 309
    Cherry 44
    Douglas 44
    Herbert 211,314
    Jannis 44
    Lucy 44
    Morris 44
    Stephen 44
WALKING BIRD 147
WALKING CRANE, Mrs 266
WALKING PRIEST 61,62
WALKING RED 193,194,195
WALKINGBIRD 147
WALKS FAST, Lizzie 22
WANCAKUTE 102
WANJINA, Sarah 106
WARD, Ora 219
WARNER
    A R 256
    Susie 15
WARNOCK
    W M 227
    William 214
    Wm 216
WARPEZEWIN 33,34
WASHINGTON, Isaac 188,189

Index

WASTEINAPEWIN 153
WATCHES LODGE 92
WATERMAN, Geo H................... 315
WATKINS, R J 94
WAWENOTWAY 15
WAY-SHAY-WASH-KO-GI-JIG .. 44
WCSWPUNUIPY 236
WE YAH LAH HOME, Laura...... 240
WEAK BONE............................... 229
    Nina....................................... 228
WEBB, Amy J 113
WEDDLE, Louisa......................... 264
WE-HAW-KO 219
WELLS
    Eliza...................................... 206
    Peter...................................... 206
    Pollock 206
WE-PAH-PE-NAH-QUA 219
WER-WICK-AH................... 192,193
WEST, Mrs G O 131,132
WESTON, Louisa......................... 106
WETTLIN, Phillip 144
WE-YAH-LAH-HOME, Laura..... 241
WHEELER, Dan........................... 294
WHEELOCK, Mae 282
WHIRLWIND
    Dick.. 59
    Mrs Thomas 59
    Thomas 59
WHIRLWIND HORSE................. 171
WHITE
    Charles 102
    John.. 75
    Robert 121
    Sarah 25
    Wm H..................................... 82
WHITE BEAR, Wm 39
WHITE COW KILLER, Jacob 245
WHITE EYES, Jacob..................... 22
WHITE FEATHER
    George 35
    Joshua 35
    Lucy 35
WHITE GHOST 231
WHITE HORSE, Mrs James......... 227
WHITE MAGPIE, Paul 183,184
WHITE RABBIT.................. 310,311
    Lute 49

WHITE WATER WOMAN 235
WHITE WHIRLWIND, Alice...... 195
WHITE WOLF 245
WHITEAGLE, Joseph.................. 100
WHITEFEATHER 34,35,36,37
    George 34,36
    Joshua 34,36
    Lucy 34,36
    Red 35
WHITESPIRIT, Bobby 86
WHITRIGHT
    Jennie Irondoor..................... 133
    Robert 133
WICANHPIDUTA 141,142
WILBUR
    Charles A.............................. 125
    Dave 125
WILDE, James 256
WILKINSON
    David...................................... 31
    Mrs David.............................. 31
    Wehunkaw......................... 31,32
WILLIAM 178
WILLIAMS
    Barney 202
    Blanche................................ 202
    Cleopatra 202
    Maggie M 202
    R H 94
WILLIAMSON, Guy W 286
WILNEETH, Warner L 124
WILSON
    Chas...................................... 139
    Emma..................................... 37
    J Ivan 166
    Woodrow.............................. 225
WIND
    Christopher 88,89
    Edgar 89
    Elizabeth................................ 89
    Lillian N 89
    Lizzie 89
    Minnie 89
    Thomas 89
WIND BLOW
    Anna 49
    Annie 49
    Nellie 49

Index

Sam 48,49
WINDBLOW, Sam 49
WIRT, Emmet 244
WITCH-E-WAH 175
   Harry 26
   Maggie 27
   Mary 26
WITCH-E-WAY, Harry 175,270, 271
WIZI, Mrs Hannah 217
WOLF
   Dora Webster 280
   Fannie 206
   John, Jr 123
   Paul Harry 308
WOMANS DRESS, Lizzie 38
WOODBURN
   E D 26
   Lillian 26
WOODBURY
   John 17
   Orrie 17
WOODS, Harry F C 27,28
WRAPPEDHAIR 14,15
WRIGHT
   H E 12,197,199,201,245
   Pete 8
   S G 45
YAH-HAT-KOO-TAH-TE-MOON 85
YANKTON, Creighton 42
YANNER
   Charles 150
   Jane 150,151
   Mary 150
YELLOW BEAR, Martha 296
YELLOW EAGLE, Joseph ... 282,283, 284,285
YELLOW HAIR 232
YELLOW HEAD 139
YELLOW WOLF, Alex 260
YELLOWFOX, William 14
YELLOWHAIR, Daniel 128
YELLOWROBE, William 59
YOUNG
   E M 191
   S A M 90,142,164,187,188
YOUNG CAT-TAIL 299

YUME-YEN-YEKT 96
ZHUCK GE SHIG, May 87,88
ZIEBACH, C M 256,274
ZIMMERMAN
   Ben 259
   Ellen 136
   Lillian Mary 259
   Nancy 259
ZIWIN 255,256

www.ingramcontent.com/pod-product-compliance
Lightning Source LLC
Chambersburg PA
CBHW020243030426
42336CB00010B/598